FOUNDATIONS OF COUNSELING AND HUMAN SERVICES

FOUNDATIONS OF COUNSELING AND HUMAN SERVICES

George M. Gazda
University of Georgia

William C. Childers
University of Georgia

David K. Brooks, Jr.
Syracuse University

McGRAW-HILL BOOK COMPANY
New York   St. Louis   San Francisco   Auckland   Bogotá
Hamburg   Johannesburg   London   Madrid   Mexico   Milan   Montreal   New Delhi
Panama   Paris   São Paulo   Singapore   Sydney   Tokyo   Toronto

This book was set in Helvetica by Publication Services.
The editor was Bettina Anderson;
the designer was Amy Becker;
the production supervisors were
Diane Renda and Friederich Schulte.
Project supervision was done by Publication Services.
R.R. Donnelley & Sons Company was printer and binder.

**FOUNDATIONS OF COUNSELING AND HUMAN
SERVICES**

1 2 3 4 5 6 7 8 9 0   DOCDOC   8 9 4 3 2 1 0 9 8 7

ISBN 0-07-022992-9

Library of Congress Cataloging-in-Publication Data

Gazda, George Michael, (date)./
    Foundations of counseling and human services.

    Bibliography: p.
    1. Counseling.   I. Childers, William C.,
(date).   II. Brooks, David K.   III. Title.
BF637.C6G358   1987   158'.3   86–27637
ISBN 0–07–022992–9

To Our Families

ABOUT THE AUTHORS

George M. Gazda, Ed.D., received his doctorate from the University of Illinois with a major in counseling. He served as assistant and research assistant professor at the University of Illinois from 1959 to 1962 and as assistant professor at the University of Missouri-Columbia from 1962 to 1963. Since 1963 he has been associate professor, professor, and research professor in the Department of Counseling and Human Development Services, University of Georgia. Since 1967 he has concurrently held the positions of consulting and now clinical professor in the Department of Psychiatry, Medical College of Georgia. In addition he is associate dean for Research, College of Education, University of Georgia, and director of the APA Accredited Counseling Psychology Program, University of Georgia.

Dr. Gazda has held several national offices including president of the following associations: Associations of Counselor Education and Supervision, Association for Specialists in Group Work (which he cofounded), American Personnel and Guidance Association (now Association for Counseling and Development), and Division 17 (Counseling Psychology) of the American Psychological Association. Dr. Gazda is a fellow of the American Psychological Association and the American Society of Group Psychotherapy and Psychodrama. He is a certified trainer of psychodrama and a licensed psychologist in Georgia.

Dr. Gazda has authored, coauthored, or edited 13 books and 12 revisions. In addition he has had published over 100 chapters, manuals, articles, and monographs in the professional literature. Major areas of emphasis of his publications include general counseling, group counseling, interpersonal communications, and life skills training. He has consulted with numerous organizations and universities both nationally and internationally, and has received several awards for research and service. Dr. Gazda's wide range of professional experiences and associations make him eminently qualified to be the senior author of a text focusing on counseling and human services.

William C. Childers, Ph.D., is senior public service associate at the University of Georgia Center for Continuing Education, where he develops and conducts life skill programs both on campus and around the country. His guest relations program for hospitals, A Step Ahead in Caring, has gained wide acceptance as an effective interpersonal skills development program for health care staff.

Dr. Childers' four books on interpersonal effectiveness reflect his strong interest in developing materials and programs that assist others in affecting the interpersonal environment in a positive way.

David K. Brooks, Jr., is assistant professor of counseling and guidance at Syracuse University. He received his Ph.D. in counseling and student personnel services from the University of Georgia in 1984. A former secondary school counselor, his research interests include life-skills training and the impact of statutory regulation on professional practice.

Long active in professional associations, Dr. Brooks has served as president of the American Mental Health Counselors Association and as a member of the Governing Council and the Executive Committee of the American Association for Counseling and Development (AACD). He is a past president of the North Carolina Association for Counseling and Development and former chair of the AACD Licensure Committee. Dr. Brooks holds professional certification from both the National Board of Certified Counselors and the National Academy of Certified Clinical Mental Health Counselors.

CONTENTS

PREFAC

Graduate programs in counseling and guidance are presently in a state of transition and instability. Until recently the focus of most programs at the master's level was to train counselors for positions in elementary and secondary schools. Now well over one-half of the master's graduates each year are taking positions in non-school settings, principally in mental health and other community-based human service agencies. Transition is also reflected in professional identification. The term "guidance" was once used to describe the entire field of counseling and related services. But the current increasing emphasis on counseling and skill development is reflected in the name change of the national professional organization, from the American Personnel and Guidance Association (APGA) to the American Association for Counseling and Development (AACD).

The traditional 30-hour master's program designed to train school counselors is being supplanted by programs of from 45 to 60 semester hours in many institutions. More than two dozen counselor education programs have been accredited in the past three years by the Council for Accreditation of Counseling and Related Education Program (CACREP), a new independent accrediting body initiated by AACD. These programs are all at least 45 semester hours in length and several are 60 semester hours. However, the AACD Board of Directors has encouraged counselor education programs to move to 60 semester hours as a standard. The result will be that more courses will be added to programs nationwide, courses for which in many cases there are no texts at present.

Because of the change in the length of programs, the nature of the introductory course (commonly called "Principles of Guidance") is changing dramatically as well. Most graduates are entering positions in other than school settings, and so the introductory course must now cover a broader range of settings and issues than was heretofore the case. There are at present no introductory texts that deal with counseling and human development services in the wide variety of agency settings, let alone ones that deal with counselors as members of interdisciplinary human services teams. This text accommodates both of these needs. It provides a unique two-prong thrust: a broad overview of human services *and* a model for training and treatment that is applicable to a number of disciplines. It should therefore be appropriate for consideration for several of the new courses that are being developed.

The economics of delivering human services increasingly demands patterns of differentiated staffing and interdisciplinary cooperation. These objectives are fostered in part by an emphasis in graduate training programs on broad-based awareness of the human services. The lines that have traditionally divided the various disciplines are becoming less defined in practice. It follows naturally that a more interdisciplinary focus in training will better prepare future practitioners for the realities of the professional world. Present texts focus narrowly on such separate human services disciplines as counseling and guidance, counseling psychology, social work, psychiatric nursing, clinical psychology, and the like with no attempt to compare and contrast these areas in terms of origins, philosophical bases, treatment modalities, and interdisciplinary commonalities.

The basic purpose of this text is to fill the void in currently available material with a text that provides the human services with an introductory overview. Its emphasis on common themes along the various disciplines should make it attractive to instructors in such areas as social work, psychiatric nursing, and clinical psychology, in addition to counseling and guidance and counseling psychology.

In Chapter 1 of this text, we provide an overview of eight human services disciplines. Then each of the first seven chapters deals with topics that are both common to the various disciplines as well as, when apropros, with the facets that make each unique. The reader will rapidly compare, for example, the position of his or her discipline on a given ethical issue with the position of the other seven disciplines. Similar comparisons can be made on training and credentialing requirements, approaches to preventive and remedial interventions, assessment, and the common ground of utilization of community resources.

Chapters 8 to 12 present an implementation model, Life-Skills Training, appropriate for both the preventive and the remedial roles of the eight disciplines, regardless of professional identity. Chapter 8 begins with a comparison of the several skills training model currently employed and provides a rationale for the Life-Skills Training Model. As part of this model, there are four generic life-skills areas that were identified through a national Delphi survey. One chapter is devoted to each of these areas. Each of those chapters explores a comprehensive application of the generic skill area to prevention and remediation in the human services professions in the settings of home, school, work, and community. Sample training exercises and the life-skills descriptors obtained through the Delphi survey are included, thus providing readers with a universe of skill objectives so they can write their own training programs. The Life-Skills Training model is presented because the authors believe strongly in the need to demonstrate some follow-through or application of a theoretical model to the human services in order to complete the gestalt.

ACKNOWLEDGEMENTS

With the production of most textbooks there are many people who contribute in addition to the author(s). This one was no exception. Numerous individuals made contributions and we would like to recognize them here. In addition to the authors, the person who made the greatest contributions to this text through her comprehensive editing and contributions to Chapters 10 and 11 was Carole Pistole. Others made special contributions to specific chapters. Dr. James Barclay developed Chapter 3. Robert Hooper contributed to Chapter 4 and assisted in editing and checking references. R. Ernest Taylor, J.D., made very significant contributions to Chapters 6 and 7. Dr. Jane Jones and Dr. Harry DuVall were instrumental in the development of Chapter 11. Jill Hollifield made significant editorial contributions to Appendix A. Inese Wheeler assisted with references. Ellen Klein contributed significantly to Appendix B. Finally, without the typing assistance of Barbara Gazda, Carole Pistole, Jean Nash-Pullian, Cynthia Pool, and Jane Rhames this text could not have been completed. We would like to thank the following reviewers for their useful comments and suggestions: Jack Duncan, Virginia Commonwealth University; Richard E. Pearson, Syracuse University; T. R. Renick, St. Lawrence University; and James Wigtil, Ohio State University.

There were others who also assisted with the development of the book. Christian Mediate, our first McGraw-Hill editor, was instrumental in selecting the authors to produce this book. Stephanie Happer followed as the next editor. She handled the development of the first and second drafts and reviews. Bettina anderson was our third editor, who formally put the book into production. For the assistance of all of the above-named individuals, we are very grateful.

George M. Gazda
William C. Childers
David K. Brooks, Jr.

FOUNDATIONS OF COUNSELING AND HUMAN SERVICES

CHAPTER 1

OVERVIEW OF THE HUMAN SERVICES PROFESSIONS

It is impossible to fix a date on which the human services professions "began," and it is almost as difficult to describe the development of these professions in more than the most cursory detail. Likewise, to advocate a point of view, an approach to service delivery, that purports to be relevant to all human services is a consummately ambitious undertaking. This is, however, the purpose of this text.

The spectrum of professional activity falling under the general rubric of human services or mental health services is so vast and so varied that merely to account for it, let alone understand it, is a task of formidable proportions. In the broadest possible definition of human services, they encompass any service rendered by one person to another for the second party's benefit. Such a definition would include retail sales, banking, landscape maintenance, and a host of other occupations that are obviously beyond our concern. For the purposes of this text, human services are synonymous with *mental* health services, in a rather broad sense. We will exclude such fields as education, physical medicine, and recreation *as professions* from our consideration, although these fields and others are certainly important adjuncts to the practice of the professions we will include. In focusing on helping professions that are *primarily* mental health, we will be concerned with counseling and guidance, counseling psychology, clinical psychology, school psychology, industrial organizational (I/O) psychology, clinical social work, psychiatric nursing, and psychiatry.

The argument will doubtless be made that this list is too limited. Why do we not include, for example, marital and family therapy, pastoral counseling, or human resource development? While we do not intend to slight these or similar professional groups, our position is that these and other human services emphases are contained within the eight professions that we will discuss in this chapter. We will therefore limit our attention to these eight as the dominant human services disciplines.

OVERVIEW

We believe that all the human services disciplines stand on a common ground and that they are more alike than they are different. In taking a broad view, we see that there are themes or threads uniting the disciplines, despite their differences. As we will demonstrate in this book, their histories are closely intertwined, and they are all involved to varying degrees in both preventive and remedial activities. Further, all of the professions utilize community resources, including each other; all of them are increasingly concerned with being able to measure the effectiveness of what they do; and all of them adhere to standards for ethical practice, disciplining those in their ranks whose activities violate the standards. In addition, the movement toward "training" as a preferred therapeutic modality has had at least some impact on all of the professions and will, we predict, become increasingly influential during the next two decades.

These unifying threads are, in our view, the same ones that tend to cross the artificial boundaries of the disciplines. While these threads may become frayed or even disappear in the heat of occasional battles for turf or status, they are, for the present, the real community property of the human services. As such they form the framework of this text. Accordingly, in each of the first seven chapters, we will focus on one of the themes. In this first chapter, we will emphasize the historical background, work settings, and claimed competencies of the human services professions. Our focus for Chapter 2 will be theories of counseling and psychotherapy, for Chapter 3 assessment, and for Chapter 4 remediation and prevention. The common themes we emphasize in the remaining three of this set of chapters are community resources, ethical standards, and legal issues in chapters 5, 6, and 7, respectively. Throughout the remainder of the book, we will present a model for service delivery that we believe stands on these common themes and also is relevant to each of the human services disciplines, despite their differential emphases. Therefore, in Chapters 8 through 12, we will develop the Life-Skills Training model (LST) as a practical vision for the future of the human services. The LST model is a developmentally based approach to prevention and remediation that we believe can lead to a new common ground upon which mental health services can be delivered by all practitioners, regardless of their discipline of origin.

HISTORICAL BACKGROUND

We have argued that the histories of the human services professions are closely intertwined and that they share a number of other common elements as well. Specifically, there are four movements that influenced the human services disciplines: (1) the humanitarian tradition, (2) the development of psychotherapies, (3) testing and assessment, and (4) the impact of legislation. In this section, we will briefly sketch these developments. For more specific information, a historical time line for each of the eight professions is presented in Appendix A.

The Humanitarian Tradition

With the exception of psychiatry, the human services disciplines originated within the twentieth century. They are founded, however, on a tradition of humanitarian treatment that has its roots in the late eighteenth century. Prior to that time, mental illness was viewed as a consequence of sinful acts. The medieval horror of witches lingered long in Europe, and while burning at the stake declined after the seventeenth century, negative attitudes persisted toward persons exhibiting abnormal behavior. These unfortunates either existed as itinerant paupers, driven from town to town, or were confined in asylums such as Bethlehem Hospital, London's infamous Bedlam, where they endured conditions of incredible filth, overcrowding, physical restraint, flogging, malnutrition, and public display for the amusement of the populace.

In the early 1790s, at the height of the French Revolution, Philippe Pinel was appointed as director of the two largest asylums in Paris, the Bicetre and the Salpetriere, an institution for women. Bringing his egalitarian principles with him, Pinel freed the inmates from their chains. He introduced what came to be called "moral" treatment, which was based on the idea that if patients were treated humanely, they would respond appropriately and their symptoms would disappear. Contrary to the prevailing medical opinion, moral treatment worked. Inmates were released back into the larger society, and while recidivism statistics of the time are unreliable, the institutionalized population of France declined.

One would think that so simple an approach that yielded such dramatic results would become widely adopted. However, although Pinel's methods were well publicized, they were not well received by the psychiatric establishment, with the exception of a few enlightened centers in other European countries.

On this side of the Atlantic, psychiatry was emerging but without the emphasis on humanitarian treatment. The first public mental hospital had been established in Williamsburg, Virginia, in 1773, but its treatment methods and those of its successors were primarily custodial. Even with the actual beginning of American psychiatry, usually dated as 1783 when Benjamin Rush joined the staff of the Pennsylvania Hospital in Philadelphia, the approach fared no better. Although he has been accorded generally high esteem by medical historians, Rush believed in such primitive approaches as corporal punishment and "spinning therapy" (Murray, 1983). In the latter, patients were strapped into a swivel chair and spun at high speeds.

In the United States, the humanitarian tradition received its real push almost entirely through the efforts of Dorothea Dix. A retired Boston school teacher, Dix spent the last half of her life in a tireless crusade for humane treatment of the mentally ill. Beginning about 1840, she traveled, spoke to state legislatures, and wrote thousands of letters appealing to the consciences of public officials. She was the driving force behind the establishment of numerous state hospitals which, while far from ideal treatment settings, were nonetheless improvements over county jails and poorhouses in which many of the mentally ill of the time had been housed. She was successful in persuading both houses of Congress to pass a law granting several million acres of public land for the support of treatment facilities. Had the law not been vetoed by President Pierce on the ground that it violated states' rights, it would have been the forerunner of present federal mental health legislation and support (Joint Commission, 1961).

The work of Clifford W. Beers is also a part of the humanitarian attitude. During much of his early adulthood, Beers was a patient in several state mental hospitals. Upon his release, he determined to spend his life trying to improve the treatment of the mentally ill in this country. In 1908 he published *A Mind That Found Itself*, an autobiographical account of his hospital experiences. The book caused such a stir that in 1909 he found a receptive climate for the formation of the National Committee for Mental Hygiene, the forerunner of the present National Association for Mental Health.

The mental health movement in the United States is a legitimate descendant of Pinel, Dix, and other early humanitarians whose efforts, until recently, had few lasting effects. Although the sustained efforts of American mental health advocates in this century have created the atmosphere which has enabled the present level of development of the human services professions, the task is far from finished. New efforts to promote positive mental health struggle for public acceptance and adequate funding.

The Development of Psychotherapies

In addition to the humanitarian tradition, human service providers are united by a common psychotherapeutic background. Our modern American psychotherapies originated in and evolved from a European influence, beginning with the work of Sigmund Freud.

Freud is usually credited with being the father of modern psychotherapy. After graduating from the University of Vienna, he opened his practice in that city in 1882, specializing in neurology and psychiatry. Freud was a prolific theory builder, a gifted writer, and an always active practitioner. His impact on American human service providers dates from 1909 when he presented his theory of psychoanalysis (see Chapter 2 for a brief overview) to the American psychiatric community in his famous lectures at Clark University.

In addition to providing the first systematic theory of psychotherapy, Freud made an impact on the development of psychotherapies in another way. From the time that his ideas began circulating in the early 1890s until his death in London in 1939, Freud was the center of controversy. It is safe to say that the majority of the psychotherapeutic approaches of the first half of the twentieth century were developed in response to Freud. Alfred Adler, the founder of individual psychology, and Carl Jung, who introduced analytic psychology, were both disciples of Freud who broke with him over key tenets of psychoanalysis and developed their own approaches. Eventual opponents did not come only from within Freud's circle, nor was he without large numbers of "true believers," many of whom still decry any deviation from psychoanalytic orthodoxy. Those reactions—revisionism, outside opposition, and slavish adherence to dogma—are not uncommon responses to revolutionary ideas, and Freud's were revolutionary.

The professional community in the United States was not simply the passive recipient of European ideas during the early 1900s but provided its own contributions to psychotherapy. About the time of Freud's lectures at Clark University, Adolph Meyer introduced psychobiology, another dynamic psychological system. Morton Prince founded the Harvard Psychological Clinic and, working with co-conscious phenomena, added considerably to the understanding and treatment of hysteria, multiple personality, and hallucinations. Rudolph Dreikurs, a disciple of Adler, brought his mentor's ideas to the United States and began working with whole families in therapy, an idea that would not come into its own for several decades.

American professionals were also active in pioneering group therapy. Joseph Pratt introduced the group approach in Boston in 1905, but it was not until later with the work of Jacob Moreno and Samuel R. Slavson that group therapy became a generally accepted treatment modality. Moreno introduced the psychodrama approach, while Slavson and his colleagues modified psychoanalytic approaches for use in the group medium. In the late 1940s, work in applied social psychology, done by Kurt Lewin and his colleagues at the National Training Laboratory, led to another American innovation, the T-group. The T-group was not designed for psychotherapeutic ends but was intended to improve the functioning of management teams. Nonetheless, many of the research findings from T-group experimentation led to new procedures and new understanding in group therapy.

Carl Rogers originated the first truly American therapy, which he now calls the person-centered approach. Beginning with *Counseling and Psychotherapy* (Rogers, 1942), Rogers has produced four decades of work emphasizing that the conditions of the relationship between client and counselor are the primary vehicle for behavior change. During this time frame, Rogers has extended the scope of his interest to include group work and marital counseling. Like Freud, Rogers has generated a host of detractors, revisionists, and true believers.

During the first half of the twentieth century, American psychologists had developed a substantial body of knowledge related to learning and conditioning. Their work was gradually applied in the mental health domain as behavior therapy. B. F. Skinner's operant conditioning and Joseph Wolpe's systematic desensitization were major contributions to this approach. More recent innovators in the area of behavior therapy have included Albert Bandura, John Krumboltz, and Marvin Goldfried.

The humanistic-existentialistic school of psychotherapy has also been very influential among American human services professionals. While Rogers is sometimes included in this group, the major figures are Fritz Perls, who popularized gestalt therapy; Viktor Frankl, who developed logotherapy; and Abraham Maslow, who emphasized positive self-actualization and developed the well-known hierarchy of needs. All of these theorists stress human potential and the search for meaning in life.

The last twenty years have produced a variety of "new" therapies. Among these are transactional analysis, popularized by Eric Berne; reality therapy, developed by William Glasser; and the various approaches to sex therapy pioneered by William Masters and Virginia Johnson. Family therapy has received tremendous attention, influenced largely by such writers and practitioners as Virginia Satir, Jay Haley, and Salvador Minuchin. Aaron Beck, Albert Ellis, and Donald Meichenbaum are among the leaders in cognitive-behavioral therapy, an approach that combines new knowledge about the impact of cognitive processes with the somewhat more traditional behavioral interventions. Hypnosis as a psychotherapeutic technique has been practiced since well before Freud's time, but the writings of Milton Erickson have been instrumental in creating substantial new interest in the field. An adaptation of Erickson's work, known as neuro-linguistic programming, has been developed by Richard Bandler and John Grinder and is one of the newest psychotherapies.

Psychological skills training, another new therapy, was initially developed by Robert Carkhuff and his colleagues in the late 1960s. Taking Rogers's work in identifying the core conditions necessary for behavior change as a starting point, skills training advocates have developed a number of systematic approaches to training clients as well as practitioners in the acquisition of these skills (see Chapter 8). The approach has proven effective with psychiatric patients, public school students, and a variety of lay populations. It, therefore, seems useful for all human service providers.

Testing and Assessment

The third unifying theme of the human services disciplines is testing and assessment (see Chapter 3 for a detailed treatment of this area). Activity that began just before the turn of the twentieth century has during the last eighty years become an influence that touches every aspect of life.

Prior to the collaboration of Alfred Binet and Theodore Simon in France in the early 1900s, Francis Galton and others had estimated mental ability according to a speculated connection between intelligence and heredity. Binet and Simon were interested in detecting measurable differences in ability between normal and retarded children so that the latter could be placed into special education programs, and they developed, by trial and error, a series of standardized tasks that could be performed by children of different mental ages. Their use of the difference between mental age and chronological age as an index of retardation was later converted to the now-familiar concept of intelligence quotient ($IQ = MA/CA \cdot 100$). Lewis Terman of Stanford University adapted and expanded the Binet-Simon scales into what is now known as the Stanford-Binet Intelligence Scale, first published in 1916 and revised in 1937, 1960, 1973, and 1985.

Whereas the Binet scales were originally designed to measure mental ability in children and were later normed for use with adults, David Wechsler was initially concerned with adult intelligence. What is now the Wechsler Adult Intelligence Scale–Revised (WAIS-R, 1981) was first published in 1939. Wechsler later developed tests for children (Wechsler Intelligence Scale for Children (WISC), 1950; Wechsler Intelligence Scale for Children–Revised (WISC-R), 1974) and preschoolers (Wechsler Preschool and Primary Scale of Intelligence (WPPSI), 1967), extending the basic structure of his approach downward in the life span. The Wechsler scales yield subtest scores for various verbal and performance abilities, unlike the Binet scales which produce only one score.

The Wechsler and Binet scales are individual measures of intelligence, requiring in some cases nearly three hours to administer plus additional time for scoring and interpretation. Group intelligence testing was initially developed in response to the demand for military screening devices, created by the entry of the United States into World War I. Army psychologists, working under the leadership of Robert M. Yerkes, developed the Army Alpha, which required reading and writing ability, and the Army Beta, which did not, for the purpose of determining fitness for officer training as well as for other assignments. Later, in 1918, Army psychologists developed trait and aptitude tests.

Group intelligence testing was extended in 1918 when Arthur Otis published the first battery of group intelligence tests for use in educational settings. Norms were developed for students from fourth grade through college. Group intelligence tests are now administered in conjunction with batteries of achievement tests in schools to determine expected versus actual performance.

Concurrent with the development of measures of general mental ability, a variety of tests aimed at determining specific aptitudes were developed. Among the first of these were the tests for the selection of streetcar motormen and telephone operators developed in 1912 by Hugo Munsterberg of Harvard University. Terman published tests for prospective telegraphers, office clerks, and engineering students. The first test of general mechanical aptitude was developed by John Stenquist in 1923. Currently, there are tests that purport to measure specific abilities in a wide range of job tasks, from clerical speed to music and art.

Another area in which substantial work has been done is vocational interest measurement. E. K. Strong published the Strong Vocational Interest Blank for men in 1927 and for women in 1933. The two forms were merged in the 1970s under the direction of David Campbell, yielding the Strong-Campbell Interest Inventory. G. Frederic Kuder was another pioneer in interest testing, publishing the Kuder Preference Record-Vocational in 1934. In addition, John Holland has developed a six dimensional model of vocational interests which is measured by the Vocational Preference Inventory and the Self-Directed Search. The most recent innovation in this area has been the development of computer-assisted programs that merge interest inventory data with career information and provide the user with an interactive format through which to explore various career possibilities. Examples of such programs are Discover (marketed by American College Testing Program) and the System for Interactive Guidance and Information (SIGI) (marketed by Educational Testing Service).

Personality assessment is yet another field in which American human services professionals have been active. Edward Elliott in 1910 developed what was probably the first objective personality test. The most widely used and most extensively researched personality instrument is the Minnesota Multiphasic Personality Inventory (MMPI), first published by Starke Hathaway and J. Charnley McKinley in 1940. Two projective instruments in general use for clinical diagnosis are the Rorschach inkblot test, first published in 1921, and the Thematic Apperception Test, developed by Henry A. Murray in 1938.

Providing accurate information based on tests and measurement devices in a form that can be easily understood and that can serve as the basis for policy decisions is a continuing challenge for the human services professions. For instance, at the present time there is considerable public debate over the state of the nation's schools. Critics frequently point to the decline in performance on the Scholastic Aptitude Test (SAT) over the last two decades (although there is now evidence of slight increases) as proof that public education is failing in its mission of producing graduates who are well equipped for democratic citizenship and the challenges of a technological future. The challenge for knowledgeable human services professionals is to gain the attention of decision makers and help to clarify what the various kinds of standardized tests do and do not measure.

The Impact of Legislation

That there are human services professions at all is largely a consequence of political decisions. To be sure, human services would be provided in some form even if the supportive legislation of the last seventy-five years had not been passed, but it is safe to say that the disciplines would have developed very differently and that some of them would probably not have developed at all.

The National Committee for Mental Hygiene (NCMH) was instrumental in improving mental hygiene education and patient treatment in the period prior to and immediately following World War I. The successor to the NCMH, the National Association for Mental Health, as well as a variety of professional organizations representing the various disciplines have been forceful advocates of mental health legislation in the period since World War II. In 1946, the national Mental Health Act was passed, authorizing the establishment of the National Institute of Mental Health (NIMH). This body has in turn supported the training of such human services providers as clinical and counseling psychologists and psychiatric nurses.

The National Mental Health Study Act of 1955 established the Joint Commission on Mental Illness. Based on its recommendations, Congress passed the Community Mental Health Centers Act of 1963. This legislation appropriated federal funds for states to plan, construct, and staff community mental health centers and to develop multidisciplinary treatment teams of professionals. For the first time resources were available on a large scale to effect what mental health advocates and human services professionals had been urging for years: the shifting of emphasis in mental health treatment away from the large state institutions to a more community-based approach. After a 1965 funding extension, additional services were mandated by legislation in 1970 that provided for programs for adolescents and children, for drug and alcohol abuse, and for mental health consultation. A 1975 amendment reemphasized the goals of the 1963 legislation and added seven additional mental health services: follow-up care, transitional living arrangements, child and adolescent treatment and follow-up, screening, and additional programs in alcohol and drug abuse.

The 1978 report of the President's Commission on Mental Health addressed the problems and inadequacies of the mental health services system and emphasized the need for community-based services that would include long- and short-term care, access to continuity of care, changes to meet the needs of special populations, and adequate financing. The report also recognized the tension among mental health professionals. This report led to the Mental Health Systems Act of 1980, which focused on services for children, youth, the elderly, minority populations, and the chronically mentally ill. The act was repealed in 1981 as part of severe federal budget cuts for mental health services.

The legislation discussed so far has had a far-reaching generalized effect on the human services disciplines, while being particularly relevant for clinical psychology, psychiatric nursing, clinical social work, psychiatry, and, to a more limited extent, counseling psychology. There is other legislation which had an impact on particular disciplines. Although this body of legislation is related to specific professional differences, we include it in the common themes because we feel it has had an impact on the mental health field in a generalized fashion.

A series of legislative acts is relevant to the development of the discipline of counseling and guidance. This profession received its initial funding boost with the passage of the Smith-Hughes Act in 1917, which, among other priorities, provided support for vocational guidance. Vocational guidance was supported by at least three other vocational education acts before the outbreak of World War II. Following the war, acts providing for veterans' educational benefits included funds for vocational guidance services, a benefit later extended to veterans of the Korean conflict.

The National Defense Education Act (NDEA) of 1958 provided the next major funding impetus for counseling and guidance. Passed in part as a reaction to the launching of the Sputnik satellite by the Soviet Union, the NDEA provided funds to help the United States "catch up," especially in mathematics and the physical sciences. One thrust of the NDEA was a testing program to identify students with math and science ability who were then "counseled" to go into these career fields. Other titles provided support for secondary school guidance programs and for a crash program to train secondary school counselors in massive numbers.

Amendments to the NDEA in 1964 provided for funding for counseling and guidance programs in elementary schools and community colleges.

The Elementary and Secondary Education Act (ESEA) of 1965 designated additional monies for school counseling and guidance. The Emergency School Assistance Act (ESAA) of 1971 provided for funding of school counselors to aid in the desegregation process. In addition to support for school guidance programs, the Education Amendments of 1976 authorized an administrative unit for guidance and counseling within the U.S. Office of Education. Concurrently, there was a short-lived federal initiative on career education in the late 1960s and early 1970s that provided temporary federal support for school counseling and guidance.

The Education for All Handicapped Children Act (P.L. 94-142) and its extensions have had some impact on school counseling, but school psychology has been most affected by it. The act introduced the concept of special education in the "least restrictive environment," and "mainstreaming" became the order of the day. School psychologists in particular were called upon to consult with school officials in the design of individual education plans for each handicapped child. Periodic assessments of children in special education programs to determine the advisability of their continued placement were mandated by the act.

Legislation particular to industrial/organizational interests began with the Civil Rights Act of 1964, which guaranteed, among other provisions, that equal employment opportunities were to be extended to all workers. The Equal Employment Opportunity Commission (EEOC) was established in 1966. The EEOC subsequently issued its *Guidelines on Employee Selection Procedures*, which had a major impact on industrial/organizational psychology. A nonlegislative action that had an even more dramatic effect was the 1971 Griggs decision in which the Supreme Court ruled that when a test has a disproportionate impact on minorities in hiring practices, the burden of proof is on the employer to demonstrate that test performance is related to job performance.

In sum, the human service disciplines have all, to varying extents, been formed and shaped by the humanitarian tradition, by the development of psychotherapies, by testing and assessment, and by legislation. Some of the differential impact of legislation was emphasized in this last section. Other examples of specific discipline variations can be noted within the other themes. For instance, in testing, projective tests are used most often in clinical psychology and psychiatry; vocational interest inventories are used most frequently in counseling psychology and counseling and guidance. In addition, the various psychotherapies are relatively influential across the particular professions. For example, the activities of industrial/organizational and of school psychologists tend not to focus on counseling and psychotherapy as primary services. Even where therapy is the primary professional activity, the differential impact of theories is difficult to assess within and between disciplines. Smith (1982) reported that among clinical and counseling psychologists an eclectic approach was by far the most prevalent, followed by psychoanalytic, cognitive-behavioral, and person-centered approaches. Looking across disciplines, we suspect that psychoanalysis would be endorsed more frequently by clinical social workers, psychiatrists, and psychiatric nurses, with eclecticism and family systems both having sizable numbers of adherents. Within counseling and guidance, person-centered and eclecticism would probably be the preferred orientations. Although it is important to recognize that differences exist for the professions within the common themes, a clearer way to distinguish profession-specific differences is to look at their development.

DEVELOPMENT OF THE HUMAN SERVICES DISCIPLINES

Recall that we said the common themes unite the human services professions in the sense that each of these themes, though emphasized differentially within each discipline, has impacted on all the disciplines. In keeping with our belief that professional expertise in the modern delivery of services is enhanced by a working knowledge of the other helping disciplines, we want to present a brief overview focusing on the different emphases of the eight professions. In doing this, we will present some additional history and discuss roles and work settings as well as the training and credentialing of the respective fields.

Counseling and Guidance

Counseling and guidance traces its roots to the founding of the Vocational Bureau by Frank Parsons in Boston in 1908. This was a social service agency, typical of many established during the Progressive Era, but with a specific focus on the problems of youth unemployment. Parsons coined the term "vocational guidance" and described his procedures in *Choosing a Vocation*, published posthumously in 1909.

Concern with assisting youth in making vocational decisions was not limited to New England. Advocates of such programs gathered from several states in Grand Rapids, Michigan, and founded the National Vocational Guidance Association (NVGA) in 1913. Vocational guidance drew supporters from education, psychology, and business as it gathered strength. As mentioned in the previous section, funding to support vocational guidance programs in the schools was provided by the Smith-Hughes Act of 1917 and by several subsequent pieces of vocational education legislation.

In 1951 the NVGA and three other counseling organizations combined to form the American Personnel and Guidance Association (APGA). Beginning with the formation of the American School Counselor Association

(ASCA) in 1952, the APGA gradually added divisions over the next twenty-five years until its affiliated bodies encompassed counselors in rehabilitation, employment, religious education, corrections, mental health, and military settings in addition to its founding divisions' ties to public and higher education. To reflect the shift in emphasis from vocational guidance to counseling the whole person, the association changed its name to the American Association for Counseling and Development (AACD) in 1983. Following this lead, the NVGA changed its name to the National Career Development Association (NCDA) in 1985.

Roles and Work Settings   Counseling and guidance professionals work in elementary and secondary schools, higher education, mental health centers, employment services, rehabilitation agencies, correctional institutions, community service agencies, family counseling centers, business and industry, and private practice. Depending upon the requirements of the setting, they may provide individual and group counseling, career information and planning, assessment, placement, research, referral, and consultation with teachers, parents, administrators, employers, and community groups. Obviously not all counselors do all these tasks all of the time, but the listing gives an indication of the variety and breadth of counselors' responsibilities and services. Professional counselors work primarily with children, youth, and adults in the normal range of adjustment, although mental health counselors frequently provide psychotherapy to more seriously disturbed individuals.

Training and Credentialing   Following the explosive growth of counseling and guidance resulting from the NDEA and other federal legislation, most professional counselors were employed in elementary and secondary schools. The ultimate authorities that determined training criteria were thus the departments of education of the fifty states. While there was initially tremendous variability from state to state, there has been a gradual trend since the early 1960s to require that persons certified as school counselors possess a master's degree in counseling and guidance from a regionally accredited university. Some states will still certify as school counselors persons with master's degrees in other fields who have a prescribed minimum of course work in counseling, but these are in the minority.

The growth toward more uniform training standards has been fostered by the professional organizations for nearly twenty years. Standards for training elementary and secondary school counselors and college student personnel workers were adopted in the 1960s. The Council for Accreditation of Counseling and Related Educational Programs (CACREP) was established by the AACD in 1981 to accredit counselor training programs according to combined standards first adopted in 1973. These standards specify that course work be included in the areas of human growth and development, social and cultural foundations, the helping relationship, group work, lifestyle and career development, appraisal, research and evaluation, and professional orientation, in addition to environmental and specialized studies. To date nearly three dozen counselor education programs have been accredited by the CACREP at the master's degree level and some at the doctoral level. The minimum length program acceptable for accreditation is a two-year master's degree.

During the last fifteen years, counselors have been accepting positions in a wide variety of settings other than elementary and secondary schools, and the school counselor certificate is no longer the passport to employability that it once was. By 1985, school counselors no longer constituted the largest division of AACD, that distinction having been claimed by the American Mental Health Counselors Association (AMHCA). The National Board for Certified Counselors (NBCC) was initiated by the AACD in 1982 to set up a national generic certification procedure for counselors regardless of setting. By 1985, the NBCC had screened, examined, and certified nearly 15,000 professionals as National Certified Counselors (NCC). Earlier, two of the AACD's divisions, the American Rehabilitation Counseling Association and the AMHCA, had been instrumental in the establishment of specialty certification boards for the credentialing of rehabilitation counselors and mental health counselors, respectively.

Prior to the 1970s, counselors trained at the doctoral level had been considered eligible for licensure as psychologists in most states. As psychology licensing boards increasingly restricted credentialing to individuals holding doctorates in psychology, the counseling profession began to work toward the passage of legislation that would license counselors for private practice. The first such law was passed in Virginia in 1976. By 1985, twelve more states had passed counselor licensure laws, and concerted efforts were underway to achieve such legislation in at least two dozen others.

Counseling Psychology

Like counseling and guidance, counseling psychology traces its origins to the vocational guidance movement. In fact, there has always been a substantial overlapping membership between Division 17 of the American Psychological Association (APA) and several divisions of the AACD, most notably the NCDA, the American College Personnel Association (ACPA), and the Association for Counselor Education and Supervision (ACES). Counseling psychology differs from counseling and guidance in that its practitioners *must* hold the doctorate and that they consider themselves psychologists rather than educators (although most counselors no longer consider themselves educators, either). The paths of the two disciplines began to diverge after World War II when the APA established its divisional structure. Division 17 was initially established as the Division of Counseling and Guidance, later changing its name in 1953 to the Division of Counseling Psychology.

Roles and Work Settings   A literature review by Pallone (1980) revealed at least three distinct roles of counseling psychologists. They serve in a variety of administrative positions such as academic department head or service coordinator; they work as counseling practitioners, either full or part time, institutional or private practice; and they serve as teachers, usually at the university level. Their counseling practice usually consists of the following responsibilities, in order of frequency: vocational counseling, assessment, educational counseling, personal adjustment counseling, student personnel work, counseling theory (teaching), psychotherapy, and rehabilitation (Manning and Cates, 1972). Pallone (1980) concludes that counseling psychologists are usually employed in higher education, that they engage in counseling and teaching more than any other activities, and that their specific competencies focus on the educational, vocational, and personal adjustment problems of their clients.

Training and Credentialing   Training in counseling psychology is based on the scientist-practitioner model. The scientific dimension of training provides the student with research methods and skills culminating in a Ph.D. or Ed.D. dissertation. The practitioner dimension is represented in supervised practice and a 1-year predoctoral supervised internship. In addition, a basic core of foundation psychology courses is included as well as professional counseling courses. The psychology core includes history and systems, social psychology, individual differences, learning, personality, and physiological psychology. Professional courses include at least individual and group counseling theory, vocational development theory, and psychological assessment. Counseling psychology training was formulated by the Northwestern Conference of 1951 and revised by the Greystone Conference of 1964, both of which were national gatherings of leaders convened for the specific purpose of reaching a consensus about appropriate training methodology. Counseling psychology training programs are accredited by the APA after an extensive review process. By December, 1985, forty-four such programs met the APA standards.

Graduates of counseling psychology programs are eligible for state licensure as psychologists, pending passage of written and oral examinations. After meeting additional requirements, they may apply for the Diploma in Counseling Psychology awarded by the American Board of Professional Psychology. State-licensed counseling psychologists are also eligible in most cases for inclusion in the National Register of Health Service Providers in Psychology.

Clinical Psychology

The beginning of clinical psychology as a professional discipline can be traced to the psychology clinic established by Lightner Witmer at the University of Pennsylvania in 1896. Witmer, in fact, coined the term "clinical psychology" to describe the services his clinic provided. In 1919, the APA established a clinical section, which developed standards for training and practice in 1935. After World War II, the clinical section was reorganized as Division 12 of the APA.

Roles and Work Settings According to Garfield and Kurtz (1976), clinical psychologists, on the average, spend 31 percent of their work time in therapy and behavior modification, 21.5 percent in teaching and supervision, 13 percent in administration, 10 percent in research, 10 percent in psychological testing, and 5 percent in consultation, 4 percent scholarly writing, and other, 5.5 percent. Clinical psychologists work in a wide variety of settings, "including community mental health centers, state, county, or Veterans Administration hospitals, independent outpatient clinics or private practice, general medical hospitals, residential treatment programs, and government and industry" (Kendall and Norton-Ford, 1982, p. 18). Super (1955) describes the difference between clinical and counseling psychologists as one of orientation; the clinical psychologist will look for abnormalities even in normal persons, and the counseling psychologist will look for normal characteristics even in persons exhibiting symptoms of extreme psychopathology.

Training and Credentialing Clinical psychology training, like that in counseling psychology, follows the APA scientist-practitioner model. The core curriculum of clinical psychology training usually includes "courses concerning the psychology of learning and motivation, and relationship of brain physiology to behavior, the psychology of human development, theories of personality, and the application of statistics and research design to clinical questions" (Kendall and Norton-Ford, 1982, p. 48). The core curriculum is designed to ensure that the student is well grounded in basic psychological science. The training reflects the position that clinical psychologists are psychologists first, with a speciality in the clinical area.

The typical program for the Ph.D. degree in clinical psychology consists of five years of graduate work. Four of these years are spent in completing academic, research, and practicum requirements; the fifth is a supervised internship in a clinical setting. Some programs offer the doctor of psychology degree (Psy. D.), in which the research component of the Ph.D. program is deemphasized in favor of a greater concentration on clinical training and supervision. The Psy.D. is in most cases issued by professional schools of psychology, which may be either freestanding institutions or affiliated with a university department of psychology. Accreditation by the APA is available for clinical training programs leading to both degrees.

Graduates of clinical psychology training programs are usually licensed by state psychology licensing boards and are eligible for inclusion in the National Register of Health Service Providers in Psychology. The American Board of Professional Psychology offers a Diploma in Clinical Psychology.

School Psychology

Like clinical psychology, school psychology traces its roots to the psychology clinic established by Witmer at the University of Pennsylvania. Concurrently, the Child Study Center of the Chicago Public Schools was established. It was not until after World War II, however, that the Division of School Psychology (Division 16) was formed within the APA. In 1969, the APA's insistence on the doctorate as the basic standard for training and practice led to the formation of a new organization, the National Association of School Psychologists (NASP).

Roles and Work Settings   As their name implies, school psychologists work almost entirely in schools and school systems, although increasing numbers are becoming involved in outside consultation and private practice. According to Cates (1970), doctoral level school psychologists reported that they spent 56 percent of their time administering psychological tests, 14 percent in general administrative tasks, 8 percent teaching, 6 percent counseling, 6 percent in clinical practice, and 10 percent miscellaneous.

Training and Credentialing   Training in school psychology presents a rather confused picture. The organization of the NASP in 1969 led to training standards at the master's and specialist's level. In contrast, the APA recognizes and accredits training programs at the doctoral level only. In addition, state departments of education have separate and different sets of training standards. For doctoral level training, standards set by the 1954 Thayer conference and recognized by the APA require a curriculum based on the scientist-practitioner model, an organized sequence of courses providing a basic knowledge in psychology, and extensive supervised experience in assessment and appraisal procedures.

School psychologists trained at the doctoral level are usually eligible for state licensure as psychologists. With additional experience they many also apply for the Diploma in School Psychology issued by the American Board of Professional Psychology.

Industrial/Organizational Psychology

Walter Dill Scott and Hugo Munsterberg are generally considered to be the founders of the discipline of industrial/organizational (I/O) psychology in the United States. Scott demonstrated the application of psychological principles to advertising and selling, while Munsterberg developed scientific aptitude tests and published the influential text *Psychology and Industrial Efficiency* in 1913. The first school of industrial psychology was established in 1915 at the Carnegie Institute of Technology (now the Carnegie-Mellon University) by Walter V. Bingham. The American Association of Applied Psychology was founded in 1937 as the official organization for I/O psychology, being reorganized as Division 14 of the APA following World War I.

Roles and Work Settings   According to Landy and Trumbo (1980), the principal roles of I/O psychologists are management, applied research, teaching, basic research and test development, training, implementing personnel programs, and engineering/human factors design. The major work settings are universities, industry, consulting firms, government and military, individual consulting, and research organizations.

Training and Credentialing   Division 14 of the APA has developed training standards for I/O psychologists, but there is at present no accreditation process for I/O as there is for counseling, clinical, and school psychology. Doctoral programs in I/O psychology are similar in core content to the other applied areas but tend to offer specific electives and cognate or minor studies in such outside departments as management. Most states consider I/O psychologists eligible for licensure and the American Board of Professional Psychology offers a diploma in the area.

Clinical Social Work

No single date or person can be cited for founding the social work profession. However, social work education was initiated in 1898 by the New York Charity Organization Society when it established its Summer School of Philanthropy. Medical social service was introduced at Massachusetts General Hospital in 1905, and in 1918 the American Association of Hospital Social Workers was founded. Also in 1918 Smith College established a training school for psychiatric social workers.

Professionalization of social work came with the organization of the Association of Training Schools for Professional Social Work in 1919 and the American Association of Social Workers (AASW) in 1921. By 1932 the AASW had adopted a minimum curriculum for the first graduate year of professional education. The AASW and other specialized social work organizations merged to form the National Association of Social Workers (NASW) in 1955. The Council on Social Work Education (CSWE) was founded in 1956 to accredit social work education.

Roles and Work Settings   With the possible exception of counseling and guidance, no other human services discipline performs as many roles in as many settings as social work does. The central task of social workers, according to Morales and Sheafor (1983) is "to help persons resolve existing or potential problems in social functioning which may involve changing either the individual or the environment or both" (p. 16). Most social workers are employed in public or private agencies, including schools, hospitals, residential treatment settings, family and children's services, and community service organizations.

Training and Credentialing   The NASW has established four levels of social work practice: basic professional, specialized professional (requires master's degree in social work (MSW) from a program accredited by the CSWE), independent professional (requires MSW plus two years post-master's supervised experience), and advanced professional (usually requiring doctoral degree). The independent and advanced professional levels are eligible for certification by the Academy of Certified Social Workers (ACSW), which was established in 1960. Over half the states regulate the independent practice of social work through statutory certification or licensure.

Psychiatric Nursing

A precise date for the initiation of psychiatric nursing is not discernible, but Linda Richards, who graduated in 1873 from the New England Hospital for Women and Children, has been called the first American psychiatric nurse. She obtained this distinction because of her pioneering work in developing nursing care in psychiatric hospitals and because of her work in organizing educational programs in Illinois's state hospitals.

Roles and Work Settings   The roles performed by psychiatric nurses are generally dependent upon the setting in which they are employed. In conventional health care institutions, the psychiatric nurse tends to be in a dependent role, but in less conventional settings, she or he may assume a variety of roles, including many traditionally performed by psychiatrists (excluding the prescribing of medication) and social workers. Leach (1982) cites the following subroles: "mother," technician, teacher, socializing agent, counselor, and manager. Psychiatric nurses work in both general and psychiatric hospitals, community mental health clinics, public health departments, college mental health centers, and private independent group practice.

Training and Credentialing   The first fully developed course in psychiatric nursing was offered at Johns Hopkins University in 1913. By 1950, the National League for Nursing required nursing schools to provide an experience in psychiatric nursing in order to be accredited. In 1982, the Council of Specialists in Psychiatric and Mental Health Nursing published the revised *Standards of Psychiatric and Mental Health Nursing*. The baccalaureate degree in nursing with a specialization in psychiatric nursing constitutes the basic academic preparation for entry into the field. Licensure by a state board is required for independent practice, and specialty certification is available through the American Nurses Association.

Psychiatry

Psychiatry is both the oldest and the most prestigious of the human services professions. American psychiatry is dated from 1783 when Benjamin Rush joined the staff at the Pennsylvania Hospital. The forerunner of the American Psychiatric Association was founded in 1844 as the Association of Medical Superintendents of American Institutions.

Roles and Work Settings   Psychiatrists are physicians who specialize in treating mental disorders. They are frequently members of and consultants to interdisciplinary treatment teams. Most maintain at least a part-time private practice, with the remainder of their time spent working in community mental health centers, community agencies, general hospitals, and academic institutions. Psychiatrists are the only human services professionals who can prescribe medication for the treatment of mental disorders. They are frequently consulted by other disciplines when medication appears to be warranted in the course of treatment.

Training and Credentialing   Psychiatrists must first of all be medical doctors and must then complete a four-year residency program in psychiatry. Such programs generally give them a broad range of supervised experiences, including rotations in state hospitals, psychiatric wards of general or teaching hospitals, and community mental health clinics, among others. Residencies typically combine directed study with direct service to a broad range of clients. Psychiatrists must be licensed by the state to practice medicine and be certified by the American Board of Psychiatry and Neurology to use the title of psychiatrist ethically.

SUMMARY

The human services disciplines appear on the surface to be very different, but they have much in common in their histories, training, skills, and practice. Four themes that tend to characterize their similarities are the humanitarian tradition that began in the eighteenth century and has continued to the present time, with occasional fits and starts; the development of psychotherapies that tend to cross disciplinary lines; testing and assessment to measure human development and to provide indices for dysfunction as well as for performance; and legislation that has established national mental health priorities at various points in American history. The most salient commonality, however, is that all eight disciplines address effective individual functioning in an environmental context. They are thus concerned with assessment of both the individual and the environment; with promoting a person-environment fit, whether the means chosen are preventive, remedial, or a combination of the two; and with practicing their respective arts on a defensible theoretical base and in an ethical and responsible manner. All of these aspects of professional practice are true of both the psychiatrist and the industrial/organizational psychologist, whose disciplines appear to have the least in common.

In the chapters that follow, we will consider theoretical foundations, assessment, remediation and prevention, community resources, and ethical and legal implications in greater depth. We will then present Life-Skills Training as an overarching intervention strategy with potential to further connect the human services disciplines and to enhance their effectiveness with a variety of populations and settings. We turn now to a discussion of the theoretical foundations of counseling and psychotherapy.

REFERENCES

Beers, C. W. (1908). *A mind that found itself*. New York: Doubleday.

Cates, J. A. (1970). Psychology's manpower: Report on the 1968 National Register of Scientific and Technical Personnel. *American Psychologist, 25*, 254–263.

Council of Specialists in Psychiatric and Mental Health Nursing (1982). *Standards of Psychiatric and Mental Health Nursing*. Washington, D. C.: Author.

Garfield, S. L., & Kurtz, R. (1976). Clinical psychologists in the 1970s. *American Psychologist, 31*, 1–9.

Joint Commission on Mental Health/Illness (1961). *Action for Mental Health*. New York: Basic Books.

Kendall, P. C., & Norton-Ford, J. D. (1982). *Clinical psychology: Scientific and professional dimensions*. New York: Wiley.

Landy, F. J., & Trumbo, D. A. (1980). *Psychology of work behavior*. Homewood, Il: Dorsey Press.

Leach, A. M. (1982). Context of care. In J. Haber, A. M. Leach, S. M. Schudy, & B. F. Sideleau (Eds.), *Comprehensive psychiatric nursing* (2d ed.) (pp. 275–301). New York: McGraw-Hill.

Manning, T. T., & Cates, J. A. (1972). Specialization within psychology. *American Psychologist, 27*, 462–467.

Morales, A., & Sheafor, B. W. (1983). *Social work: A profession of many faces* (3d ed.). Boston: Allyn & Bacon.

Munsterberg, H. (1913). *Psychology and industrial efficiency*. Boston: Houghton Mifflin.

Murray, D. J. (1983). *A history of Western psychology*. Englewood Cliffs, NJ: Prentice-Hall.

Pallone, N. J. (1980). Counseling psychology: Toward an empirical definition. In J. M. Whitely & B. R. Fretz (Eds.), *The present and future of counseling psychology* (pp. 39–49). Monterey, CA: Brooks/Cole.

Parsons, F. (1909). *Choosing a vocation*. Boston: Houghton Mifflin.

Rogers, C. R. (1942). *Counseling and psychotherapy*. Boston: Houghton Mifflin.

Smith, D. (1982). Trends in counseling and psychotherapy. *American Psychologist, 37*, 802–809.

Super, D. E. (1955). Transition: From vocational guidance to counseling psychology. *Journal of Counseling Psychology, 2*, 3–9.

CHAPTER 2

THEORIES OF COUNSELING AND PSYCHOTHERAPY

"There's nothing quite as practical as a good theory." This professional dictum, attributed to Kurt Lewin, the great social psychologist, is sometimes greeted with skepticism by both students and practitioners. The most frequent response to such statements goes something like this: "I don't have a theory; I just use what works." Or "I'm an eclectic; I think there's some good in all theories."

The position taken here is that effective counseling and psychotherapy cannot take place without some theoretical base. In any situation in which one person is providing help to another, the helper is operating from some set of beliefs, however unconscious, inarticulate, or inelegant, about human nature and about behavior change. Obviously some of these belief systems are more coherent, consistent, empirically validated, and therapeutically effective than others. But the fact remains that even the clumsiest attempts at helping spring from some rudimentary belief system that may be loosely labeled as theory. We hope that this chapter will enable the reader to understand the truth behind Lewin's assertion.

THEORETICAL CONSIDERATIONS

Antitheoretical statements such as the skeptical remarks in the first paragraph of this chapter reflect a basic misunderstanding of what theory is. Theory is far more than a statement of abstract ideas with no apparent practical application. Rather a theory is an organized parsimonious system of ideas that meets the following characteristics:

1 *Theory is derived from systematic observation.* In the physical or behavioral sciences, theoretical formulations always begin with direct, systematic observation of phenomena.

2 *Theory attempts to explain why and how.* If observation alone were sufficient to explain all phenomena, there would be no need for theory. This is especially true in counseling and psychotherapy where aspects of behavior are not susceptible to observation, at least not always at a given moment. Theory therefore serves as a bridge to explain phenomena that are not directly observable or that may be confounding to the observer.

3 *Theory is logically consistent.* In theory building we must be concerned with internal coherence; the theory must "hang together." This is one of the bases by which we assess the difference between good theory and bad.

4 *Theory generates testable hypotheses.* Regardless of how elegantly it may be stated, a theory is useless if it does not lend itself to the development of a scientific hypothetical statement that can be tested under experimental conditions.

5 *Theory is never proven or disproven.* This is perhaps the most difficult aspect of theory for students to grasp. It is the *hypotheses* that are tested, *not* the theory itself. Depending upon the outcome of experimentation, the hypothesis is said to support or not support the theory. A series of successful hypothetical tests leads a theory to be held in high regard and leads to further experimentation. An unsuccessful research history can lead to a theory being disregarded as a source of further hypotheses, but the theory is never disproven.

6 *Theory generates reasonable predictions about related phenomena.* To be truly useful, theory must enable those who employ it to "branch out" to study related phenomena.

7 *A theory is often linked with other theories.* An adequate theory rarely stands alone. It is frequently combined with other theories in an attempt to explain broader phenomena.

In addition to meeting these characteristics, theories of psychotherapy that are useful in a counseling relationship provide or describe specific kinds of information. In this sense, the theory must contain several elements. These elements must be present to some degree whether practitioners adhere unswervingly to one of the major "schools" or whether their theoretical base is the result of combining aspects of several theories, commonly called an eclectic approach.

First of all, a theory of psychotherapy must provide the practitioner with a comprehensive description of human nature. It must address, although not necessarily resolve, such issues as free will versus determinism, nature versus nurture, and the relative importance of intrapsychic processes as opposed to social or group influence. It should account for human growth and development and should present a picture of the healthy individual's characteristics in terms of the developmental framework.

As a corollary to its description of healthy, normal development and behavior, counseling theory must also account for the development of dysfunctional behavior. Such an account should include etiology, symptomatology, and some guidelines for predicting future developments.

In addition, an adequate theory of counseling or psychotherapy must outline the nature of the relationship between practitioner and client. The kinds of issues to be addressed here include the personality of the counselor; the extent to which the counselor should inject his or her personality into the relationship; the climate of the relationship (i.e., level of activity, directiveness); and finally, the degree to which the relationship itself is a vehicle for behavior. Relatedly, psychotherapy theory should provide the practitioner with technical guidelines. That is, the theory must be able to be translated into specific intervention strategies that can be used by the therapist.

Finally, the theory should account for the process of behavior change and should give the practitioner some means for evaluating client progress. If a theory does not provide this element, counseling and psychotherapy become rather meaningless activities.

OVERVIEWS OF SELECTED THEORIES

As the reader will recall from Chapter 1, the scientific study of human behavior is a very young science. The application of psychological knowledge to the alleviation of human problems is an even newer undertaking, with Sigmund Freud's introduction of psychoanalysis in the closing decade of the nineteenth century being the generally accepted starting point. Parloff (1979) has stated that there are at present more than 130 different approaches to counseling and psychotherapy. Even though we are dealing with a very young science, counseling and psychotherapy have experienced an overwhelming burst of activity in theory building, research studies, and claims of efficacy.

Even if counseling theory were the primary focus of this text, and it is not, it would be difficult to describe in respectable detail more than 130 different theories. The authors contend, moreover, that students in counseling and human services programs do not need to be exposed to the entire array of therapeutic approaches before choosing one that is "right" for them. What we feel is appropriate in a text such as this one is a comparative overview of several major theoretical approaches.

In selecting the theories to be included in such an overview, we have necessarily made some arbitrary decisions as to which approaches to include and which ones to leave out. We believe that our selections are representative of the current state of the art. Smith (1982) reported that the six approaches to be discussed in this chapter were utilized by 42.2 percent of a national sample of counseling and clinical psychologists. Another 41.2 percent described themselves as eclectic in their approach, while of the remainder the largest group described itself as "other." It should be pointed out that Smith's study is not descriptive of human services providers as a whole, since it does not include master's level practitioners such as mental health counselors, school counselors, or clinical social workers. So, we have had to rely on our own professional judgment in making the final determination as to which theories to include.

The six theories to be discussed are psychoanalytic psychotherapy, Adlerian counseling and psychotherapy, the person-centered approach, behavior therapy, rational-emotive therapy, and reality therapy. Each of these will be presented in light of the elements outlined previously, namely, human nature and normal development, dysfunctional behavior, the counseling relationship, intervention strategies, and evaluation of behavior change.

Before proceeding further a word of clarification is in order about our use of the terms "counseling" and "psychotherapy." Traditionally counseling and psychotherapy have been used as ranges on a continuum of helping relationships. The counseling range has been characterized as dealing with individuals more or less in the normal dimensions of psychological functioning whose presenting concerns are short-term, situational, and developmental. Psychotherapy, on the other hand, has referred to helping relationships with persons who are experiencing more serious, dysfunctional problems, ameliorations of which require long-term intervention involving some personality reconstruction. More recently these two terms have tended to be used more or less interchangeably. We believe that good counseling is therapeutic and that good psychotherapy is based on a sound counseling relationship. We will therefore use the terms in this and succeeding chapters relatively interchangeably, the major consideration being modal preference expressed in primary sources. In other words, when psychoanalysis is presented, psychotherapy will be used more frequently than counseling; when we are discussing the person-centered approach, we will use counseling more often than psychotherapy. In general discussion one term will be used about as frequently as the other.

Psychoanalytic Psychotherapy

Sigmund Freud (1856–1939) was the founder and remains the central figure of psychoanalytic psychotherapy. Psychoanalysis is a world view, a comprehensive theory of personality, a therapeutic treatment modality, and an approach to scientific inquiry. Its influence on current theory and practice is demonstrated by the fact that virtually every major system is to some degree a reaction to psychoanalysis. Freud was a prolific writer throughout his career, and one of the difficulties in acquiring a thorough understanding of psychoanalysis is that as he developed new premises, Freud rarely discarded the old. The result is a collage of rich speculations from which various groups of his followers selectively draw, each claiming to be in possession of Freud's central truth.

Freud began his career as a young medical graduate of the University of Vienna. Rather than going immediately into practice, he worked for eight years in a neurology laboratory, then followed this with a stint in France studying with the influential hypnotherapist, Jean Charcot. Although Freud toyed with hypnosis after his return to Vienna, he was principally interested in what he had learned about the unconscious mind, which he proceeded to explore further using his own approaches.

Freud was exceptionally well grounded in nineteenth century science, especially the thermodynamic physics of his day. The orientation, which was really a refinement of Newtonian principles, stressed the exchange of energy, the release of tension caused by increase in mass, and the movement generated by trains of gears and cogs. Freud's postulations about human behavior show all of these influences.

Human Nature and Normal Development   Freud's view of human nature is a dynamic one based on unconscious conflicts occurring within the personality as individuals attempt to cope with life tasks (Freud, 1923/1961a). The basic structure of the personality consists of the id, which is unconscious; the ego which, though formed from the id, operates mostly in the conscious realm acting as a mediator between the id and the world of external reality; and the superego, which is formed from the ego and acts as the individual's conscience.

For Freud, the human personality is an energy system. The id, which is the seat of instinctual drives, is the source of the energy that drives the machine. (See Freud, 1940/1969.) The energy itself is described as sexual energy and is labeled by Freud as *libido*. Freud's definition of sexual energy is extremely broad, however, encompassing all pleasurable objects and experiences. Thus, the id is said to operate on the pleasure principle. Tension builds repeatedly in the id, the result of not having its desire for pleasures immediately gratified. The ego is the executive of the personality. Its function is to "ride herd" on the unconscious and primitive id and to deal with external reality. The ego is rational and responsible. Its general health is a primary concern of Freudian therapists, since it performs most of the work in personality functioning. The moral element of personality is the superego. Formed from the ego in early childhood, the superego tends to "nag" the ego about doing the right thing, thus putting the ego in a two-way bind. The ego must find a way to gratify the id in a way that pleases the superego.

Among his other revolutionary contributions, Freud was the first to postulate a stage-specific view of human development (Freud, 1923/1961b). His theory of psychosexual development paralleled physiological stages of growth. The oral stage corresponds to the first year of life. The human infant's needs during its first year center primarily on the mouth and on obtaining sufficient nourishment. From ages one to three, the primary focus shifts to control of bodily functions, specifically to becoming toilet trained. Freud called this period the anal stage, theorizing that issues of control and autonomy were paramount in psychological development at this time. The phallic stage occurs from ages three to five, approximately. During this time the young child discovers the pleasure of his or her genitals. This is a time of exploration and tentative attempts at establishing one's identity for the first time. This is also the time when the controversial Oedipal conflict arises and is hopefully resolved. From age five or so until the onset of puberty, Freud postulated that the individual is in a state of latency as far as psychosexual development is concerned. This is a time of much cognitive and social growth, coinciding with one's early experiences in school. Finally, accompanying the tremendous physical changes associated with puberty, the individual enters the genital stage. He or she is now capable of mature sexual identity and expression. The nature of social relationships changes as persons begin to seek partners, both as friends and as lovers, with whom more permanent relationships are possible.

Dysfunctional Behavior   The process of psychosexual development is by no means as smooth as the preceding paragraphs might indicate. Freud believed that there are intrapsychic conflicts associated with each stage which, if not satisfactorily resolved, can lead to adult neuroses. Dysfunctional behavior is thus the failure to accommodate unconscious conflicts associated with an earlier stage of development.

The Therapeutic Relationship   Freud was the first theorist to emphasize the importance of the therapeutic relationship. The psychoanalytically oriented therapist appears to be a relatively neutral figure in his or her relationship to the client. After initial history taking on a face-to-face basis, the client is usually encouraged to spend sessions on the famous couch, with the therapist sitting at the head so as not to disturb the process of free association. The therapist does not verbally intrude except to offer an occasional interpretation. The formation of a transference relationship is essential to the success of psychoanalysis; that is, the client projects the identity of a person from his or her past, usually a parent, onto the therapist. The client relates to the therapist as if he or she were the person from the past. "Working through" the transference, or settling the developmental issue in which the absent third party was a key figure, is perhaps the most important part of the therapeutic process.

Intervention Strategies   There are five primary therapeutic techniques in psychoanalysis (Freud, 1917/1963). The first and most central is free association. The client is encouraged to talk about whatever comes to mind, no matter how trivial or unrelated. This process is viewed as a key to the unconscious mind, which is the source of the conflicts the person is experiencing. The therapist offers occasional interpretations but basically assumes a rather passive stance. Interpretation, the second technique, is intended to move the therapeutic process forward. The third technique is dream analysis, which is also viewed as a window on the unconscious.

The last two techniques are analysis and interpretation of resistances and of the transference itself. Resistance is to be expected. The unconscious conflict arose in trauma, and so its resolution is likely to be somewhat painful as well. The final technique is analyzing and interpreting the transference. Once this is accomplished, the client achieves insight into his or her behavior and past issues. Insight is the basis upon which new adaptations to life and relationships can be made.

Evaluation of Behavior Change   Psychoanalysis often takes two to five years of three or four sessions per week in order to accomplish the desired results. It is not a process that lends itself well to experimental designs. Behavior change is evaluated by the acquisition of insight and the disappearance of symptoms. This determination is jointly decided by the therapist and client.

Adlerian Counseling and Psychotherapy

Alfred Adler (1870–1937) was a Viennese psychiatrist who early in his career was a colleague of Freud. Adler's disagreement with some of Freud's tenets led to their celebrated schism, following which Adler developed his own circle of adherents. Adler was a prolific writer and social activist whose common sense approaches won him a large following in Europe prior to the rise of Hitler. Escaping his native land in advance of the Nazi occupation, he eventually settled in New York. By the time of his death, his ideas and influence were gaining acceptance in many areas of the United States.

Human Nature and Normal Development   To Adler and his followers, human nature is socially based (Adler, 1927/1969). To be human is to live in community with others. The first community within which one interacts and learns is the family. In infancy and early childhood the individual feels inferior because of his or her small size. To counteract this, most individuals develop what Adler called a striving for superiority, which one might compare with Rogers's (see the following section) actualizing tendency as a life-force. Adler viewed the human personality holistically, contrary to Freud, who focused on the symptoms of the parts. Each individual is unique, according to Adler, and each develops a unique lifestyle which is his or her own way of viewing the self in the world. Human beings achieve purpose in life through their own efforts, as they attempt to implement their lifestyles. The hallmark of the healthy individual is what Adler called social interest. For Adler this is more than a superficial interest in other people. Since human beings are innately social, a commitment to the betterment of society and a willingness to incorporate into one's lifestyle a deep abiding concern for others expressed through one's choices and actions are the natural consequences of normal development.

Dysfunctional Behavior   As is the case with a number of counseling theories, Adlerians believe that the roots of dysfunctional behavior lie in childhood. All children experience feelings of inferiority to some degree, but in a supportive, encouraging family environment, most children compensate for these feelings so that they do not become neurotic. Adlerians devote much attention to the family constellation, the set of relationships within families that leads to children developing fairly predictable behavior patterns according to birth order. If the family atmosphere is not sufficiently encouraging to enable children to overcome their feelings of inferiority and to develop social interest, the seeds of dysfunctional behavior may develop.

The Adlerian system is basically a cognitive one. Thus, feelings of inferiority, whether in childhood or later in life, are really errors in thinking. Failure to develop social interest, which is the Adlerian definition of psychopathology, is at its root a cognitive failure. A seriously disordered individual is one whose thinking is distorted. The target of Adlerian therapeutic interventions is therefore the dysfunctional individual's cognitive processes.

The Counseling Relationship   Adler believed that the relationship between counselor and client is of primary importance in effecting behavior change. Although the Adlerian counselor has a broad range of techniques at his or her disposal, it is who he or she *is* that is crucial to effective therapy. The Adlerian practitioner is warm, friendly, nonjudgmental, open to self-disclosure when appropriate, and tends to take an active role in interactions with clients.

Intervention Strategies   According to Mosak (1979), the essence of Adlerian therapy is that it is an educative process. The counselor thus has a broad range of techniques from which to choose. Adlerians are shameless borrowers, but they have developed unique techniques of their own. Among these is the lifestyle analysis, a form of history taking that reveals through a person's family constellation and early recollections both their basic mistakes in thinking and their behavioral assets. In addition

Adlerians are credited with multiple therapy, in which more than one therapist works with a client at the same time, and with the first systematic approach to family counseling. Adlerians are also renowned for their preventive educational efforts through child study groups.

Evaluation of Behavior Change   The goals of psychotherapy are accomplished when the client achieves a restoration of social interest and when the cognitive distortions are brought more into line with social reality. The evaluative criteria for termination rest largely with the counselor's clinical judgment, but the client's views carry substantial weight as well.

The Person-Centered Approach

Carl Rogers is the founder of what is now known as the person-centered approach to counseling and psychotherapy. A clinical psychologist by training, Rogers has been a practitioner in a child guidance clinic, a university professor, a counseling center director, and throughout his career, a dedicated researcher. He is presently a senior fellow at the Center for Studies of the Person in La Jolla, California. His approach has evolved over the last four decades as a result of his clinical experience and his continuing research into the process of effective psychotherapy. Originally known as nondirective counseling and later as client-centered therapy, Rogers's theory was renamed the person-centered approach (PCA) in 1974.

Human Nature and Normal Development   The view of human nature expressed by Rogers and his colleagues (Meador and Rogers, 1979; Rogers, 1942; 1951; 1961; 1970; 1977) is optimistic, nondeterministic, and nonmechanistic. Rogers cites support from the philosophy of science that just as all matter is growing, developing, and moving toward greater perfection, so are human beings. For Rogers, the fundamental fact of human nature is the actualizing tendency. Given growth-inducing conditions, the human organism naturally strives toward self-actualization. Under these conditions, there is an openness to experiencing, trust in the organism, an internal locus of evaluation, and a willingness to be a process, rather than a product. Rogers maintains that these elements are present in the human infant prior to the onset of the socialization process. So long as the developing person experiences warmth, love, and support—what Rogers calls unconditional positive regard—in the immediate environment and in relationships with significant others, self-regard is congruent with experiencing. The actualizing tendency moves the person through life experiences in a state of congruence.

Dysfunctional Behavior   Upon experiencing negative regard (from parents and significant others), the developing person introjects "conditions of worth" that are incongruent with experiencing. An external locus of evaluation comes into play, undermining trust in the organism and denying to awareness the messages of experiencing. The result is a state of incongruence, which varies in degree. Most persons experience incongruence between their experiencing and the behavioral expectations that emanate from society's negative or conditional regard. The actualizing tendency or "flow" remains, but it is largely denied to awareness when individuals' self-concepts are so shaped by external conditions of worth. Extreme cases of this conditionality constitute a Rogerian definition of dysfunctional behavior. Most persons in the normal range of functioning experience some incongruence, but not to a dysfunctional extent.

The Counseling Relationship   In individual counseling or therapy, the counselor, through his or her unconditional positive regard for the client and an empathetic understanding of the client's feelings, enters the client's phenomenological world to the fullest extent possible. The counselor is a genuine, congruent person, open to his or her own experiencing as well as that of the client. The relationship itself is the vehicle for therapeutic change. The client experiences acceptance and freedom. The counselor's unconditional positive regard releases the client from conditions of worth and restores an internal locus of evaluation. The client becomes more and more open to experiencing. The actualizing tendency gains greater access to awareness, and self-concept is nurtured by its new, unobstructed, congruent experiencing. The client thus becomes a more fully functioning person.

Intervention Strategies   In the person-centered approach, intervention strategies are almost a contradiction in terms. The counselor eschews the notion of therapeutic technique almost entirely. Behaviors most prevalent among person-centered practitioners are active listening, reflection of content and feeling of client statements, limited self-disclosure, avoidance of advice and prescription, and a nonjudgmental attitude. Many of the therapist competencies necessary in the person-centered approach are personal characteristics that are by no means innate but that result from deeply held beliefs about human nature and from clinical and life experiences that tend to validate the tenets of the approach. A person-centered counselor is effective not because of what he or she *does* in a diagnostic or prescriptive sense, but because of who the counselor *is* as an experiencing, congruent, genuine, self-actualizing person; the counselor's ability to communicate his or her experiencing self to another in an empathetic, unconditional relationship; and the client's resulting experiencing.

Evaluation of Behavior Change   The person-centered approach holds that all persons, regardless of the degree of incongruence, can experience growth and a renewal of their openness of experiencing in an atmosphere or relationship characterized by unconditional positive regard, empathy, and genuineness. According to Rogers (1957), these are the necessary and sufficient conditions for behavior change. As one would expect, the person-centered approach trusts an internal locus of evaluation in determining effectiveness of the approach. When openness to experiencing is restored, the actualizing tendency operates once again at the level of awareness, and the client is no longer in need of the counselor's services. As Rogers would say, "Trust the organism."

Behavior Therapy

Unlike the other theories discussed in this chapter, behavior therapy has not evolved primarily from the work of a single individual. Indeed, one of the exciting aspects of behavior therapy is that a large number of human services professionals have made significant contributions to its development through their research and clinical efforts. It is true that all of the theories presented are in a state of ongoing development to some extent, but behavior therapy in particular seems to be characterized by a continuous stream of new therapeutic approaches and new research findings.

Human Nature and Human Development   Advocates for behavior therapy have not concerned themselves with elegant theoretical statements of human development. The approach is based almost exclusively on learning theory (for instance, see Bandura, 1969; Lazarus, 1981). Behavior therapists contend that all behavior is learned. If what is learned is maladaptive for an individual, it can be unlearned and replaced by more adaptive response modalities.

Dysfunctional Behavior   For behavior therapists, dysfunctional behavior is defined by the individual who is experiencing it. Behaviorists tend to avoid clinical labeling. The client is experiencing problems in living, and the therapeutic enterprise is a matter of defining the problems precisely and then implementing specific and measurable interventions.

The Therapeutic Relationship   Behaviorists place more emphasis on relationship dimensions than one would initially expect. Client and therapist are partners in the process of behavior change. The process of treatment is fully discussed with the client at every step. The client must be agreeable and willing to cooperate, or therapy cannot proceed. The climate of the relationship is generally warm, open, supportive, and nonjudgmental.

Intervention Strategies   Virtually all of the intervention strategies employed by behavior therapists are based on learning theory. Elements that tend to be common to a number of strategies are modeling, role playing, homework, behavioral rehearsal, and most important, reinforcement. In addition, there are several more complex interventions.

Systematic desensitization is an approach to anxiety reduction developed initially by Joseph Wolpe (1958, 1969). Clients are first trained in systematic muscle relaxation. Once they become skilled at this and can relax themselves completely in a relatively short time, they are asked by the therapist to imagine a pleasant, relaxing scene. The imaging process continues with the therapist presenting a series of progressively more anxiety-provoking scenes based on the client's previous descriptions of fearful situations. These anxiety-provoking images are interspersed with directions to reimagine the pleasant, relaxing scene. This process permits the client to reduce the anxiety he or she normally experiences because the fearful situations (even though imagined) are experienced without their dreaded consequences, thus breaking the previous stimulus-response bond.

Assertiveness training (Alberti and Emmons, 1970) is one of the most widely used behavioral interventions. It is a relatively simple approach designed to help people become more assertive in interpersonal relationships. Assertiveness training may be accomplished on an individual basis or in training groups. The training most frequently includes modeling, role playing, in vivo practice, feedback, and reinforcement.

Flooding is another approach to anxiety reduction. In this intervention, stimuli that are anxiety or fear provoking are presented either imaginarily or in vivo. As the client reports a subsiding of anxiety, the therapist adds new cues that increase the level of anxiety. The idea behind the treatment is that if a person can experience fear, even stark terror, in a safe environment over an extended period of time, his or her anxiety response will be reduced as a result of learning that no dreadful consequences will ensue.

Evaluation of Behavior Change   In terms of solid research studies to support its claims of efficacy, behavior therapy is probably the best documented of the approaches presented here. The goal of therapy is mutually agreed on with each client in very specific terms prior to the beginning of the treatment process. When the client achieves this goal according to the specified criteria and there are no other presenting problems to be addressed, therapy is terminated.

Rational-Emotive Therapy:
A Cognitive-Behavioral Approach

Cognitive-behavioral therapies (CBT) are among the most recent developments in the ongoing search for more effective approaches to counseling and psychotherapy. Whereas the behavior therapies tend to base their formulations on a strict stimulus-response (S-R) bond as the basis of learning and change, cognitive-behaviorists insist on the inclusion of the mind (or organism) as an intervening variable between stimulus and response. This cognitive mediation and its potential as a vehicle for intervention has attracted substantial interest in recent years from researchers and clinicians alike. Among the earliest of the cognitive-behavioral approaches is rational-emotive therapy (RET).

Albert Ellis is the progenitor of RET and a tireless and frequently controversial advocate of its principles. He was trained in classical psycho-analysis but early in his career abandoned the Freudian model. Ellis's numerous books and frequent speaking engagements have made him a popular figure among practitioners. He has made several films of therapy sessions that have given him broad exposure to students in a variety of human services disciplines. His often outrageous style marks him as a theorist whose approach is very different from the others included in this chapter. He is presently executive director of the Institute for Advanced Study in Rational Psychotherapy in New York City.

Human Nature and Normal Development Ellis (1973, 1979) maintains that human beings have the capacity to be both rational and irrational, to act in their own best interests as well as to be self-destructive. Individuals tend to think, feel, and act simultaneously. An intervention directed at one of these behavioral elements therefore affects the other two. He maintains that persons do not feel without thinking and do not act without both thinking and feeling. A normal individual who thinks logically therefore does not experience distressing feelings.

Dysfunctional Behavior According to Ellis (1979), dysfunctional behavior is the result of irrational thinking. He presents what has come to be called the A-B-C theory of psychotherapy. A person's emotional consequences (C) spring not from external activating events (A), but rather from the belief system (B) that the individual brings to bear in interpreting the activating event. Ellis is fond of quoting one of Shakespeare's lines: "Nothing is either good or bad, but thinking makes it so." Ellis's ideas therefore fit squarely into the same cognitive tradition as Adler's.

The Therapeutic Relationship It is in this dimension that Ellis departs radically from Adler, as well as from most of the other major theorists. Ellis maintains that the kind of warm, empathic relationship between counselor and client that Rogers and Adler advocate is not necessary. He goes even further and says that it is not even necessary for the therapist to like the client. Ellis believes that the therapist's role is to teach the client how to challenge his or her irrational beliefs. For him, the "counseling relationship" is just so much extra baggage.

Intervention Strategies   Rational-emotive therapy completes the A-B-C model by adding a "D" and an "E." The therapist's primary goal is to teach the client to dispute (D) his or her irrational beliefs (B), leading to a satisfactory effect (E). This is accomplished by very actively challenging anything the client says that contains even the germ of irrationality and pointing out to him or her why the statement is irrational. The therapist is never satisfied until the client understands the irrationality behind the statements and gradually begins to express his or her concerns using logical, rational language. The RET therapist frequently assigns homework to clients designed to enable them to act in a more rational manner and to help them to acquire the discipline necessary for rational living.

Evaluation of Behavior Change   It is not surprising that client behavior change is evaluated by RET practitioners in terms of the elimination of irrational thought. For Ellis, it is a foregone conclusion that rational thinking leads to the eradication of emotional distress and to wiser courses of action and more productive living.

Reality Therapy

Reality therapy is a very straightforward approach to counseling and psychotherapy developed by William Glasser in the late 1950s. Glasser has presented his ideas in systematic form in a book of the same name (1965) and in hundreds of training seminars for mental health professionals around the world. Glasser is a psychiatrist who eschews the medical model in favor of a simple set of principles for which he and his followers claim great success in therapy and in education.

Human Nature and Normal Development   For Glasser, the central fact of human nature is identity. Each individual person's identity is unique and makes him or her separate and distinct from all other persons on earth. The personal meaning one attaches to one's identity is the determinant of mental health. An individual with a success identity is mentally healthy, morally responsible for his or her actions, socially contributory, and personally fulfilled. While environment and life experiences play a role in determining whether one has a success identity, it is the personal responsibility one takes for oneself that is the crucial factor.

Dysfunctional Behavior   Glasser does not believe in mental illness in the traditional sense of the term. He does believe that there are persons with failure identities. There are many reasons that may be advanced for the development of a failure identity, but the only one Glasser will accept is that such a person does not take responsibility for his or her actions. Once the person begins to do so, the development of a success identity will be the result.

The Counseling Relationship   In his instructions to those who would become reality therapists, Glasser has only a few things to say: Be personal, accept no excuses, do not punish. The counselor is warm, friendly, and genuinely interested in the client, but he or she is a tough taskmaster in that the client is never allowed "off the hook" for any reason. The client is finally left with no choice but to accept personal responsibility.

Intervention Strategies   In intervening, the reality therapist adheres strictly to the principles of reality therapy, several of which were just stated. With somewhat more elaboration, these principles are as follows:

1 *Be personal.* The client should be aware that the counselor is personally involved and deeply interested in him or her. A success identity cannot develop unless a person feels accepted and nurtured by others.

2 *Focus on current behavior.* Reality therapists may listen briefly to tales of woe, but their primary concern is a client's present behavior. The most frequent counselor verbalization is "What are you doing?" not "How are you feeling?"

3 *Evaluation of behavior.* The therapist continually confronts the client with challenges to evaluate his or her behavior. This is something the counselor refuses to do because it is the client's responsibility. Evaluation is elicited not in terms of good or bad but rather in terms of questions such as "How is that helpful?" or "Does that contribute to your goals?"

4 *Planning alternatives.* This principle often involves the most intense work on the parts of both counselor and client. Once the client has expressed dissatisfaction with his or her present behavior, alternative patterns of response are jointly developed. The client must be sure that the alternative chosen represents something desirable, and the counselor tries to ensure that the task is one in which the client can experience success.

5 *Commitment.* The client must be committed to following through on the alternative plans developed. In this step he or she experiences the reality of responsibility for one's actions.

6 *No excuses.* The counselor accepts no excuses for the client's failure to follow through. This does not mean that the client is faced with a samurai alternative. Rather, counselor and client return to planning alternatives and formulate a new plan. The counselor never gives up unless the client simply withdraws from the relationship.

7 *No punishment.* In sharp contrast to some practitioners of other persuasions, the reality therapist never employs punishment. Punishment, according to Glasser, is counterproductive since it only reinforces the failure identity, and the reality therapist is directing all of his or her efforts to eliminating the failure identity.

Evaluation of Behavior Change   The criterion for therapeutic success is the achievement of a success identity. This is observable in the client's new behavior and in self-reports of greater happiness and satisfaction. Where reality therapy has been employed in psychiatric or penal institutions, Glasser cites increased release rates and reduced rates of recidivism following introduction of his approaches.

SYNTHESIS

We have briefly sketched six theoretical approaches to counseling and psychotherapy. While there are a number of differences between them, there are also many common themes. We believe that these areas of commonality are the hallmarks of any effective helping intervention.

As noted in Chapter 1, a recent national survey (Smith, 1982) indicated that 41.2 percent of counseling and clinical psychologists considered themselves to be eclectic in their approach. We suspect that this figure would be even higher if other human services professionals such as mental health counselors and clinical social workers had been included. Furthermore, since all effective practitioners, regardless of their professed allegiance to a particular school, modify their approaches based on their own clinical experience, eclecticism is more widespread than such studies would lead one to believe. With the exception of the "founders" (such as Rogers, Ellis, and Glasser), there are relatively few "pure" practitioners, regardless of their professed primary orientation. We believe that this eclecticism reflects the common themes crossing theoretical lines.

We present these themes in the belief that they incorporate the essential elements of all effective counseling and psychotherapy:

1 *Counseling is a learning process.* All of the theories subscribe to this principle, with the apparent exception of the person-centered approach. The case could be made, however, that the client in a Rogerian relationship *learns* to trust the counselor, *learns* that experiencing does not have to be anxiety provoking, and *learns* to apply his or her rediscovered awareness to situations outside the counseling room.

2 *The counseling relationship is the primary vehicle for behavior change.* Ellis would be the only apparent dissenter to this premise, but even he admits that he has no data to support his contention (Ellis, 1979, p. 194).

3 *The client has primary responsibility for the course of treatment and its outcomes.* Put another way, the lazy or unmotivated client does not get better.

4 *The counselor or therapist is highly active during counseling sessions.* Again, Rogers and his followers would be apparent exceptions, but again, not so. Practitioners of the person-centered approach are probably less verbally active, but they are no less involved. As any Rogerian will attest, maintaining the necessary levels of empathy, warmth, and genuineness such that the client perceives them accurately can be exhausting work!

5 *It is important to separate the personhood of the client from his or her ineffective behavior.* Perhaps the most common and disabling neurotic symptom is the client's belief that "I'm a bad person...." The therapist must constantly challenge such behaviors.

6 *The counselor or therapist is limited in what can be accomplished in the treatment session.* Human behavior being what it is, there is no way that the efficacy of a particular intervention can be assessed at the time it is applied. Every effective therapist knows that reinforcers or punishers occurring between sessions that are beyond the therapist's control can and do have a powerful impact, for good or ill, on the course of therapy. To extend the benefits of the therapy hour, many theorists specifically call for homework assignments.

7 *Effective approaches avoid diagnostic labels.* Psychoanalysis would be the apparent exception to this element if it were not for the fact that diagnoses are not shared with clients directly. The potential for behavior change is enhanced when clients are viewed holistically as individuals with strengths and weaknesses not as patients who are sick and who must be the passive recipients of treatment.

SUMMARY

The purpose of this chapter was to provide the reader with a basic introduction to theories of counseling and psychotherapy and the role that theory plays in helping relationships. We presented some general considerations about theory from a global perspective, including several misconceptions about the nature of theory and theory building, and also discussed what type of information is relevant to a theory of counseling and psychotherapy.

We then sketched six theories of counseling and psychotherapy: psychoanalysis, Adlerian counseling and psychotherapy, the person-centered approach, behavior therapy, rational-emotive therapy (as an example of cognitive-behavioral approaches), and reality therapy. In looking at each theory, we considered and also discussed what type of information is relevant including (1) the view of human nature and normal development,

(2) dysfunctional behavior, (3) the counseling relationship, (4) intervention strategies, and (5) evaluation of behavior change. At the end of the chapter, we synthesized several common themes that represent the similarities among the therapeutic approaches.

SUGGESTED READINGS

Alberti, R. E., & Emmons, M. A. (1970). *Your perfect right: A guide to assertive behavior.* San Luis Obispo, CA: Impact Press.

Ansbacher, H. L., & Ansbacher, R. (Eds.). (1956). *The individual psychology of Alfred Adler.* New York: Basic Books.

Bandura, A. (1969). *Principles of behavior modification.* New York: Holt, Rinehart & Winston.

Corey, G. (1982). *Theory and practice of counseling and psychotherapy* (3d ed.). Monterey, CA: Brooks/Cole.

Corsini, R. J. (Ed.). (1979). *Current psychotherapies* (2d ed.). Itasca, IL: F. E. Peacock.

Ellis, A. (1962). *Reason and emotion in psychotherapy.* New York: Lyle Ctuart.

Ellis, A., & Harper, R. A. (1975). *A new guide to rational living.* Englewood Cliffs, NJ: Prentice-Hall.

Glasser, W. (1965). *Reality therapy.* New York: Harper & Row.

Goldfried, M. R., & Davison, G. C. (1976). *Clinical behavior therapy.* New York: Holt, Rinehart & Winston.

Kaltenbach, R. F., & Glasser, W. (1982). Reality therapy in groups. In G. M. Gazda (Ed.), *Basic approaches to group psychotherapy and group counseling* (pp. 276–318). Springfield, IL: Charles C Thomas.

Rogers, C. R. (1961). *On becoming a person.* Boston: Houghton Mifflin.

Rogers, C. R. (1970). *Carl Rogers on encounter groups.* New York: Harper & Row.

Rogers, C. R. (1977). *Carl Rogers on personal power.* New York: Delacorte.

Wolpe, J. (1973). *The practice of behavior therapy.* New York: Pergamon.

REFERENCES

Adler, A. (1969). *Understanding human nature* (W. B. Wolfe, Trans.). New York: Fawcett Premier Books. (Original work published 1927).

Alberti, R. E., & Emmons, M. A. (1970). *Your perfect right: A guide to assertive behavior.* San Luis Obispo, CA: Impact Press.

Bandura, A. (1969). *Principles of behavior modification.* New York: Holt, Rinehart & Winston.

Ellis, A. (1973). *Humanistic psychotherapy.* New York: McGraw-Hill.

Ellis, A. (1979). Rational-emotive therapy. In R. J. Corsini (Ed.), *Current psychotherapies* (2d ed.) (pp. 185–239). Itasca, IL: F. E. Peacock.

Freud, S. (1958). The dynamics of transference. In J. Strachey (Ed.), *The standard edition of the complete psychological works of Sigmund Freud* (Vol. 12, pp. 97–109). London: Hogarth Press. (Original work published 1912).

Freud, S. (1961a). The ego and the id. In J. Strachey (Ed.), *The standard edition of the complete psychological works of Sigmund Freud* (Vol. 19, pp. 3–66). London: Hogarth Press. (Original work published 1923).

Freud, S. (1961b). The infantile genital organization: An interpretation into the theory of sexuality. In J. Strachey (Ed.), *The standard edition of the complete psychological works of Sigmund Freud* (Vol. 19, pp. 141–149). London: Hogarth Press. (Original work published 1923).

Freud, S. (1963). Introductory lectures on psycho-analysis. In J. Strachey (Ed.), *The standard edition of the complete psychological works of Sigmund Freud* (Vols. 15 and 16). London: Hogarth Press. (Original work published 1917).

Freud, S. (1969). *An outline of psychoanalysis.* J. Strachey (Ed. and Trans.). New York: W. W. Norton. (Original work published 1940).

Glasser, W. (1965). *Reality therapy.* New York: Harper & Row.

Lazarus, A. A. (1981). *The practice of multimodal therapy.* New York: McGraw-Hill.

Meador, B. D., & Rogers, C. R. (1979). Person-centered therapy. In R. J. Corsini (Ed.), *Current psychotherapies* (2d ed.) (pp. 131–184). Itasca, IL: F. E. Peacock.

Mosak, H. H. (1979). Adlerian psychotherapy. In R. J. Corsini (Ed.), *Current psychotherapies* (2d ed.) (pp. 44–94). Itasca, IL: F. E. Peacock.

Parloff, M. B. (1979). Can psychotherapy research guide the policymaker: A little knowledge may be a dangerous thing. *American Psychologist, 34,* 296–306.

Rogers, C. R. (1942). *Counseling and psychotherapy.* Boston: Houghton Mifflin.

Rogers, C. R. (1951). *Client-centered therapy.* Boston: Houghton Mifflin.

Rogers, C. R. (1957). The necessary and sufficient conditions of therapeutic personality change. *Journal of Consulting Psychology, 21,* 95–103.

Rogers, C. R. (1961). *On becoming a person.* Boston: Houghton Mifflin.

Rogers, C. R. (1970). *Carl Rogers on encounter groups.* New York: Harper & Row.

Rogers, C. R. (1977). *Carl Rogers on personal power.* New York: Delacorte.

Smith, D. (1982). Trends in counseling and psychotherapy. *American Psychologist, 37,* 802–809.

Wolpe, J. (1958). *Psychotherapy by reciprocal inhibition.* Stanford, CA: Stanford University Press.

Wolpe, J. (1969). *The practice of behavior therapy.* New York: Pergamon.

CHAPTER 3

ASSESSMENT IN HUMAN SKILL DEVELOPMENT

James R. Barclay, Ph.D.
University of Kentucky

Assessment is a ubiquitous activity. As a conceptual tool, assessment is utilized by professionals in the delivery of services, but it is also typically used by persons in their daily living. Consider the commonness of the following examples.

Ms. Marvin was leaving the school later than usual. As she walked out of the door, she saw Ricky Smith hurl a stone through a basement window. She knew Ricky because she had been doing some tutoring with Andrew, his older brother. Apprehending Ricky, she said to him, "Why did you do that?" At first Ricky did not answer. She continued talking to him—not in anger—but about what such vandalism cost the school. When she asked again for reason Ricky pointed to a group of three other boys who were watching the scene and said, "Because they won't let me play with them."

Carmen and Vera closed the door and started down the walk toward their car. "It's too bad about how Becky behaves," said Carmen. "It sure is," said Vera shaking her head. "You know it all started with the day of the tornadoes," continued Vera. "And that has been three years." "Well, that surely had something to do with it," rejoined Carmen, "but remember that it was just after the tornado that Sam died." Carmen and Vera were talking about Becky who had been head librarian at the public library for over twenty-five years and had retired when her husband also retired. They had many plans, but Sam died within a year of retirement. A month before his sudden death, the entire region had been raked by devastating tornadoes.

One had passed within a mile of Becky and Sam's home. After Sam's funeral, Becky became very concerned about the weather. She would look out in every direction whenever any kind of rainstorm came up. Later she would not leave the house if the weather was not perfect. In recent months, she had taken to drawing the shades and not leaving the house at all. She sent for her groceries and even was afraid to walk to the mailbox by the road.

These vignettes illustrate the importance of assessment in understanding human behavior. Ms. Marvin had a response from Ricky, but that response reflected a basic frustration and anger with the other boys. In order to assess what ought to be done with Ricky, it might be important to determine how often Ricky behaved this way, to examine his achievement record and class performance, to evaluate his peer relations, and to consider this behavior in the context of the family situation. The case of Becky shows that even untrained observers use assessment techniques and relate events to others as causes and effects. Though assessment is, thus, a common human activity, for the human services professional, assessment is a less casual, more complex matter. To better understand assessment in all its dimensions, in this chapter we will consider the nature of assessment; the history and development of assessment; the process of assessment including targets, criteria, and methods; and particular instruments and techniques of assessment.

THE NATURE OF ASSESSMENT

Assessment is a human survival skill. All individuals depend on making assessments of others. One of the earliest developmental tasks of the infant is to develop the ability to distinguish between objects, persons, and feelings and to classify objects as, for example, edible and inedible; persons as mama, papa, and others; and feelings as likable or dislikable. The ability to interpret the behavior of others and to make the accommodations in one's own behavior that are required in differing circumstances are important skills. Functionally, assessment requires adequate decoding of both verbal and nonverbal behaviors in others, the classification of those behaviors into various categories, and the ability to discriminate between categories. Basically, assessment is the functional ability to make valid inferences about the nature of the behavior of others.

More specifically, assessment is a professional skill of the human services professional. According to Sundberg (1977), assessment was first used in 1948 as a psychological term in the book *Assessment of Men* by the U.S. Office of Strategic Services. It is, therefore, a comparatively recent construct in psychology. Sundberg defines assessment in terms of personality characteristics thus: "The set of processes used by a person or persons for developing impressions and images, making decisions and checking hypotheses about another person's pattern of characteristics which determine his or her behavior in interaction with the environment" (Sundberg, 1977, p. 22). Further, the assessment process serves the three major goals of image making, decision making, and theory building. More concisely, assessment is "the procedures and processes employed in collecting information about evidence of human behavior" (Shertzer and Linden, 1979, p. 13).

For the individual and for the professional, assessment has as its general purpose the improvement of decision making. Sound decision making is the mark of intelligent behavior. In addition to this overall, general purpose, professional assessment is concerned with each of the following: (1) individual characteristics, needs, and problems; (2) group characteristics, needs, and problems; and (3) environmental characteristics. In this regard, assessment is both descriptive and actuarial. It is descriptive in terms of the evaluation of individual, group, and environmental conditions. In the actuarial sense, assessment attempts to match the descriptively defined characteristics (either positive or negative) with a set of alternative treatments (learning, counseling, management, etc.) which through research appear to be best for improving the development of the individual, group, or environment. In short, assessment seeks the answers to how human skills can be developed best. With assessment, we seek to understand how human characteristics are related to problems and needs and what resources can be used to effect progress in positive human development (Barclay, 1987).

HISTORY AND DEVELOPMENT

Every mature discipline attempts to understand something about its origins. Though the word assessment may be relatively new in usage, the history of assessment goes back to the beginning of humanity. Assessment, in the sense that appraisal of others was used, was a basic survival skill. Those who were more adept at such appraisal survived. Those who learned how to influence others through their assessment achieved positions of prominence. So, it is necessary to view the professional genealogy of assessment experts as extending from the roles of witch doctor, priest, physician, and astrologer to scientist and psychologist practitioner.

Development of the Scientific Paradigm

The development of professional assessment can be traced through three paradigms or culturally accepted world views. Being rooted in the beliefs about human nature of the time period, originally, assessment was used to placate the gods. In this, the ancient and primitive paradigm, many rituals were developed to ward off evil through the use of amulets, ceremonies, the watching of birds, and other such procedures.

Gradually, this "magical" paradigm was supplanted by a rational one that had its origins with the Greeks and Romans. This second paradigm still used some of the characteristics of the earlier one but depended heavily on reason and the explanation of natural causes through logical analysis. The third paradigm was based on scientific reasoning and empirical-experimental findings. Beginning in the fifteenth century with the development of astronomy and new findings about the nature of the earth in relationship to the sun, Copernicus, Galileo, Kepler, and Newton developed the basic tenets of modern science. Fueled by the discovery of printing and the proliferation of books, medical knowledge and freedom of scientific inquiry expanded. Then, late in the nineteenth century, the principles of science were coupled with the ideas of evolution and with the development of statistics, thereby forming a new branch of science for measuring individual differences through testing. This hybrid became known as psychometry.

Through the influence of psychometry, testing became the objective way to evaluate individual differences. Although most scientists believed that there was an interaction between heredity and environment, human differences were viewed as fixed by heredity and environment and thus not very susceptible to change. Therefore, during the first decades of this century, testing became associated with placement as a form of control.

Development of Testing and Current Assessment Practices

The richness of the testing field can be appreciated by taking a brief excursion through the numerous people whose work contributed relevant elements to current knowledge of assessing persons through testing. By looking at time periods, progress and movement as well as the technical complexity of testing can be noted. We have included more information than the reader can be expected to retain; however, it is important to convey the scope of contributions leading to present day delivery of service.

During the last decades of the nineteenth century (1870–1900), Francis Galton explored the role of heredity in the development of genius, Wilhelm Wundt initiated reaction time experiments in Leipzig, and James McKeen Cattell established the first testing laboratory in the United States at the University of Pennsylvania. Also, during this period, Cattell published the first definitive article on the nature of mental tests and their measurement (see Appendix A).

From this base, other major contributions expanded the testing movement from 1900 to 1920. For example, Karl Pearson enunciated the formula for correlation. In addition, Theodore Simon and Alfred Binet developed the first calibrated individual intelligence test, used for screening mentally retarded children in Paris; and Goddard and Terman popularized the use of the Stanford-Binet test in the United States. Edward Lee Thorndike published the first book dealing with mental and educational measurements, Clifford W. Stone published the first arithmetic achievement test, psychologists developed the Army Alpha and Beta tests for the evaluation of Army recruits, and over 220 cities established testing centers and classes for special education.

The period from 1921 to 1940 showed an even greater development of testing. Hermann Rorschach published his *Psychodiagnostics* describing the use of inkblot analysis for personality assessment. Group achievement and personality test batteries proliferated, the Psychological Corporation was established by J. M. Cattell, and E. K. Strong published the first test for evaluating vocational interests. In addition, Jacob Moreno developed the technique of sociometry for evaluating social interactions, David Wechsler developed the first individual intelligence test based on statistical inferences, Henry Murray and others developed the Thematic Apperception Test for the assessment of needs, and Lauretta Bender introduced the Bender Visual Motor Gestalt Test for assessing maturation, brain damage, and personality. Important statistical contributions were made by Louis Thurstone who developed and demonstrated the first factor analysis and by R. A. Fisher who developed the technique of analysis of variance.

After World War II until 1960, more sophisticated contributions were made to assessment, and the positivistic paradigm of classify and control began to be challenged. Paul Meehl and Lee J. Cronbach proposed the concept of construct validity and the multimethod, multitrait systems of data analysis; J. P. Guilford proposed a three-dimensional structure of the intellect; H. J. Eysenck provided evidence of the existence of broad temperament groupings of introversion and extroversion based on both physiological and psychometric studies; and Starke Hathaway and J. Charnley McKinley developed the Minnesota Multiphasic Personality Inventory. During this time, Cronbach suggested that tests should be used for decision making and not just for classification and control; and professional organizations developed standards for assessment.

Beginning in 1961, there has been increasing evidence that the nineteenth century determinist paradigm of placement and control is being replaced with another more humanistic and nondeterministic one. Much of this change resulted from a widespread and grass-roots opposition to bias in testing and school placements. Numerous federal court decisions restricted the use of testing. In response to this, behavioral assessment and performance assessment methods were developed, and evaluation became a separate discipline. With criterion-referenced tests (looking at an individual's ability to exhibit particular skills) developed as an alternative to norm-referenced ones (looking at an individual's performance in comparison with the average of age-related persons' performances), the development of skills became a viable target for assessment. This was augmented by the work of Herbert Walberg, Alexander Astin, and J. R. Barclay who added the dimension of evaluating classroom and learning environments. But above all, use of computers has enabled an expansion of technology in assessment that can be compared only to the invention of printing.

These changes suggest that a fourth paradigm is emerging. In current thinking, assessment is used to help human services professionals determine what kinds of changes might be made to help individuals realize their goals. The focus is on change and human skills development. Assessment is not used chiefly for the prediction and control of behavior but rather as a means to make more accurate estimates of what individuals need in order to develop their own skills. It is this paradigm of assessment which will be reflected throughout this book.

PROCESS OF ASSESSMENT

Before proceeding further, we wish to emphasize that determining where people are and what they need in order to develop their skills is a process. In the assessment process, we are concerned with targets, criteria, and methods of assessment. In addition, within each of these areas, as we will discuss, there are multiple dimensions of input. As mentioned previously, assessment is a conceptual tool. With multiple inputs, we are able to obtain a more comprehensive picture of the person and his or her level of skill development.

Targets of Assessment

When we talk about the targets of assessment, we are talking about whatever it is that we want to understand about the person. In this sense, the target of assessment is what we measure. The problem is more specifically reflected by the question: "What are we looking for?" As with any kind of a search, it is important to provide some clues. If, for example, you tell a person to go into a room and bring something back to you, just about anything satisfies those conditions. If you tell the person to look for a box, this narrows the focus—unless the room is full of boxes. In that case, you might ask the person to find a red box. The search then becomes very specific in target.

Though there is no consensus on which are the most important clues or how they should be used, human services specialists have access to several targets or units of assessment. In trying to understand a person, professionals make decisions about what to assess and whether to use multiple or single inputs. Frequently, the targets of assessment are personal constructs, and information from these may be synthesized with other targets such as process data and information about the environmental "press."

With regard to personal constructs, assessment targets are arranged hierarchically (see Figure 3-1). This statement is in accord with cognitive theorists' views that all forms of behavior represent indirect manifestations of brain functioning, which in turn are related to structural capacity (genetic inheritance) interacting with environmental influences through the course of development. We can specify six levels of constructs for assessment: (1) *response,* the basic unit of assessment, e.g., raising a hand; (2) *skill,* a set of learned experiences chained together, e.g., writing; (3) *trait,*

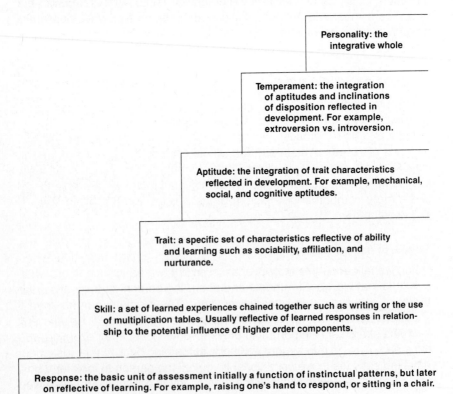

Personality: the integrative whole

Temperament: the integration of aptitudes and inclinations of disposition reflected in development. For example, extroversion vs. introversion.

Aptitude: the integration of trait characteristics reflected in development. For example, mechanical, social, and cognitive aptitudes.

Trait: a specific set of characteristics reflective of ability and learning such as sociability, affiliation, and nurturance.

Skill: a set of learned experiences chained together such as writing or the use of multiplication tables. Usually reflective of learned responses in relationship to the potential influence of higher order components.

Response: the basic unit of assessment initially a function of instinctual patterns, but later on reflective of learning. For example, raising one's hand to respond, or sitting in a chair.

Figure 3-1
Hierarchy of Assessment Constructs (Reproduced from J.R. Barclay, *Conceptual Foundations of Assessment Theory,* Praeger, 1987).

responses and skills chained together in a relatively enduring set of characteristics that reflect both learning and ability (e.g., sociability); (4) *aptitude,* cognitive reflection of functional characteristics, (e.g., mechanical ability); (5) *temperament,* motivational characteristics, (e.g., introversion, extroversion); and (6) *personality,* the overall integration of all the other levels, specifically related to the way the others interact with the environment.

In addition to these personal constructs, there are other components such as process data obtained from interviewing or verbal outputs; historical data, including information about socioeconomic conditions; and autobiographical information. This information must often be synthesized in relation to the person's past as a means of understanding both the present and the future.

Efforts have also been made to evaluate environmental conditions and the relationship of the environmental "press" (such as the expectations that employers or an organization may hold for performance in a given situation). In trying to understand the person, it is important to consider the impact of the environment. Interactions between people, whether in the family or in work situations, call for an analysis of environmental conditions. The need for environmental analysis has been addressed in several ways. Astin (1965) evaluated the learning climates of universities throughout the United States by characterizing them in terms of certain kinds of emphases. Occupations also reflect different thrusts with the kinds of skills needed to be a good artist or sculptor differing radically from those needed to be an accountant. Holland's classification system for vocational interests often provides information into the nature of an environmental press by cumulating the vocational interest profiles of people in that setting (Holland, 1966). In addition, Walberg (1974) has described a variety of techniques that can assist professionals in evaluating the environmental press characteristics of climates in schools; and Barclay (1972; 1983) has devised a multimethod, multitrait approach of estimating individual differences in the elementary and junior high school setting.

Of all the possible targets of assessment, one that is of particular interest to counselors and therapists is the target of skills analysis. Since a skill is a functional and observable response to environmental stimulation that reflects learning, it is a target of assessment that can be used to demonstrate performance and competency. In addition, skills often reflect aptitude and temperament. For instance, social skills relate to the ability to meet another person and to engage in reciprocal verbal and nonverbal behaviors that are characterized by attending and responding in a complementary manner. From an assessment point of view, a person's social skills reflect aptitude, in particular social intelligence, and temperament characteristics such as introversion or extroversion. Since skills reflect more complex dimensions, determining the nature of the skill through multiple inputs is important.

In addition, skills provide counselors with a useful assessment target because there are a variety of clusters of skills, and skills can be analyzed developmentally in relation to these clusters. Three major groups of skills that can be identified are sensory-motor, social-affective, and cognitive skills. Conveniently, researchers have developed taxonomies of skills in these three areas. Harrow (1972) has identified a taxonomy of motor skills that extends developmentally from reflex movements through basic locomotor and manipulative movements to perceptual, compound, discursive, and communicative movements. Krathwohl, Bloom, and Masia (1956) have classified affective skills as: (1) attending or receiving skills that include awareness and willingness to receive; (2) responding skills that include acquiescence in responding, willingness to respond, and satisfaction in response; (3) valuing that includes acceptance of a value, preference for a value, and commitment; (4) organization; and (5) the constitution of a value complex. Since cognitive skills are built upon the foundations of motor and affective skills, the cognitive taxonomy (Bloom et al., 1956) is stated as cognitive domain skills and tasks. The skill objectives are classified under six major groupings: (1) knowledge of specifics and universals; (2) comprehension, including translation, interpretation, and extrapolation; (3) application; (4) analysis in terms of elements, relationships, and organizational principles; (5) synthesis; and (6) evaluation.

In summary then, the targets of assessment can be focused on skill development. Skills are viewed as functional units within larger groupings of aptitude and temperament dimensions. They can be empirically observed, behaviorally measured, and psychometrically defined. Thus they become a highly viable target for human services professionals in their use of assessment.

Criteria of Assessment

With criteria, we are concerned with the standard we use in making judgments based on the information we have obtained. The criteria of assessment relate to what constitutes effective human behavior. This is an important consideration because it is from our criteria of adequate and inadequate human performance that we make inferences about whether a given response, skill, or trait is of negative or positive value. The judgments we make are clearly related to the question of values or what is good and what is bad relative to personal and social fulfillment. There are five sources for such criteria: (1) subjectivity, (2) normative standards, (3) statistical conclusions, (4) cultural norms, and (5) heuristic performance standards.

Subjectivity   Ultimately, the individual forms the basis of adequacy of behavior subjectively. Whether one takes a hedonistic position that all behavior is fundamentally related to animal characteristics or an altruistic position that all human beings should be treated as ends rather than means, a subjective judgment is involved that provides the individual frame of reference for behavior. Responsibility for behavior is, in the final analysis, a personal matter.

Normative Standards   In this context, normative means exemplar based. For the most part, we refer here to religious authorities and models. The Christian religion with its direct reference to the person of Christ is an explicit example of this approach. The values exemplified by moral leaders such as Jesus, Moses, Mohammed, Buddha, and Confucius have provided organizers for what constitutes effective human behavior for many millions of people. While this has had many positive implications in human life, some tenets of various religions may become obstacles to personal development in other areas.

Statistical Conclusions   Scientists approach behavior with statistics. Basically, this consists of determining what is the most frequent or usual human behavior in given circumstances or at particular developmental periods. The use of statistical methods such as mean, standard deviation, or range are helpful in determining what are the characteristics of given populations. When the accounting of such characteristics is extended over a time line, actuarial predictions can be made. Moreover, these predictions can be modified in terms of mediating variables. For example, the probable life span of individuals can be predicted actuarially in terms of variables such as stress, smoking, excessive drinking, weight, family history, and other determinants. But the obtaining of such statistical trends and data needs to be evaluated against other criteria of behavior. For example, the studies of Kinsey and his colleagues have indicated patterns of sexual behavior that are common to large portions of the population. This statistical fact (suggesting that everyone does it) does not alter the subjective feelings of individuals who believe in a religious model for their behavior.

Cultural Norms   Cultural norms refer to the sum total of environmental and behavioral patterns that influence individual human behavior. To a large extent, the construction of tests reflects cultural values, and items are often directed toward tapping socially approved (or disapproved) values. Regardless of whether an individual thinks a given behavior is good or bad, society often frames behavior within culturally approved or disapproved criteria.

For instance, cultural norms are often manifested in explicit or implicit expectations. Parents are expected to behave in certain ways toward their children, males are expected to behave toward other males and females in certain ways, and females are expected to behave differently than males. Expectations relate to thinking, behaving, performing, aspiring, and valuing. What constitutes effective human behavior in downtown Wall Street in New York City is not necessarily the same as what that effective behavior may be in a black ghetto or in a remote hollow of Appalachia.

Heuristic Performance Standards   In recent years, the emergence of a body of literature relating to criterion-related testing, performance objectives, and management by objectives has focused attention on the need to provide practical and interim goals and guidelines for behavior. This approach to criterion determination has been termed heuristic. The measurement possibilities from these developments have been considerable in that most often performance criteria of behavior provide some explicit suggestions for improvement or for meeting of such criteria through training. It is important to recognize that these more modern developments are only formal efforts to operationalize the expectations and presses of a specific environment.

Methods of Assessment

When operationalizing the targets and criteria of assessment, we are employing some kind of methodology. Most typically, there are two major methods utilized to gather data—empirical methods and psychometric methods.

Empirical Methods   Empirical methods refer to those that utilize direct person-to-person observation. There are three types of empirical observations. The first is unstructured, the second is behavioral, and the third is clinical.

Unstructured empirical observation is what happens in ordinary social interaction. It also occurs in the counseling or therapy interview. The keynote feature of this kind of observation is that it is informal. Although we are continuously making observations and judgments about our interactions with others, we are often more astute in our judgments if we have training in interviewing and assessment.

Structured empirical observations are often called behavioral observations. They are delimited or focused according to a specific set of assumptions about the nature or interpretation of observational phenomena. This is the approach generally taught by those who use the behavioral framework or some form of social learning theory. With this method, antecedent stimuli or events are analyzed in relationship to the responses of the organism and then in relationship to the consequences that the organism experiences. The intent of restricting empirical observation to a deliberate focus is to derive from the client the specific nature of the problem. Behavioral approaches focus on questions such as *where? when? how often?* and *with whom?* The question *why?* is avoided because why is often the consequence of the effects found in answer to the other questions.

Even as the behavioral focus tends to restrict empirical observations to very defined behaviors, so clinical insights derived from phenomenological thinking and Freudian theory expand the range of observations. *Clinical observations are those that are related to a specific set of constructs about learning and behavior which are psychodynamic in nature.* (Note that "clinical" here does not refer to clinical psychologists but rather to a set of inferences based on extensive training and adequate theoretical constructs.) In this broad clinical approach, all behaviors are purposeful, meaningful, and goal oriented (even though individuals may not know what the purpose is, and the meaningfulness sometimes needs to be interpreted in terms of unconscious dynamics). In interpreting the purposefulness of behavior with the clinical assessment process, we use several principles. For instance,

1 *Every culture is of paramount importance to the individual living in it.* Because this is true, it is valuable for human services professionals to know what experiences individuals have had. Socioeconomic status, years of education, illnesses, problems of an interpersonal or intrapersonal nature all are reflected in the developmental sequence of living. It is therefore important to understand where an individual "comes from" and where that individual "wants to go."

2 *Body movements reflect a correspondence between mental states and physiological responses.* According to Wolff (1943), expressive movements such as gestures, facial expressions, and gait are of an automatic nature. Basically, these movements, gestures, or facial expressions represent the thought process of the sender. For example, a client speaks of an episode in his or her life. While speaking, the client's expressive movements encode (transmit) the inner emotional experience. Thus trembling, breaks in voice transmission, downcast eyes, and efforts to wipe away tears all encode to the observer the message of grief and/or emotional reaction. The process on the assessor's end involves decoding and forming a set of interpretations or inferences.

3 *Emotional experiences condition and mediate the nature of cognitive experiences.* As documented from early Freudian analyses of behavior through the phenomenologists, cognition, in the sense that it involves aptitude skills, is very closely mediated by emotional conditions. Current research provides very strong evidence that physiological gradients of arousal and inhibition reveal themselves through perception. Therefore, what may be threatening or stress inducing to an introvert may be laughed at by an extrovert (Powell, 1979). In general, anxiety, stress, and "driven" behavior have an effect on cognitive development, and so a child or adult who is living in a threatening situation cannot develop adequate cognitive skills.

In summary, empirical assessment includes common, untrained evaluation of interpersonal behavior, professional training in behavioral methods, and further professional training in clinical assessment methods. The latter two represent the focus of most training programs in empirical assessment.

Psychometric Methods The psychometric method is an objective approach to the measurement of mental or physical characteristics that is based on the use of mathematics to infer characteristics. During the last decades of the nineteenth century, statistics became the tool for the development of a new approach to the measurement of individual differences. The responses that individuals made to an inventory or to questions could be standardized and evaluated along criteria determined by statistics. Psychometrics, "testing," then became a "scientific" method of evaluating individual differences through responses; and from the beginning of the twentieth century on, tests of all kinds were developed.

Underlying the use of any test are some basic assumptions common to all tests. For instance, in testing, we assume that (1) whatever exists in some quantity can be measured (attributed to E. L. Thorndike); (2) characteristics of individuals are distributed in a normal curve (that is, certain percentages of people obtain scores that fall within predictable areas; see Figure 3-2); (3) the accumulation of these characteristics can provide inferences about the nature of an individual expressed in units of standard deviation from the mean of the population; and (4) there is a correspondence between what individuals report in their response to a test item stimulus and what is characteristic of their thinking and behaving.

Though this last assumption holds generally, it is important to recognize that the validity of making inferences about test results clearly relates to a host of factors including the reasoning processes that led the test constructor to develop the item, the reliability of the item in relationship to the scale, the personal variables of the mood of the testee and circumstances of testing, and above all the various sources of error of measurement. Under optimum conditions when the test is both reliable (measures repeatedly the same outcomes and/or manifests internal consistency) and valid (measures what it says it measures), then the correspondence as-

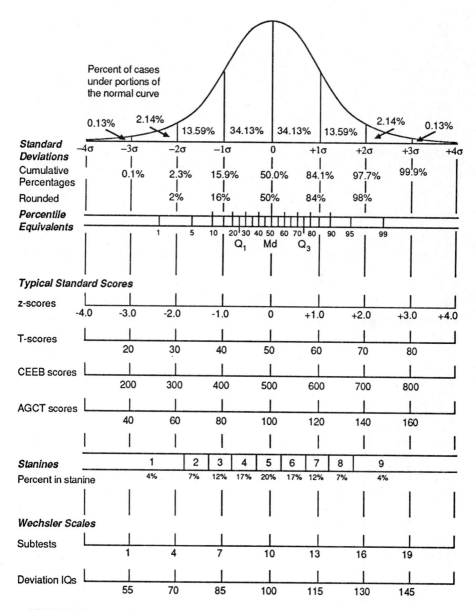

Percent of cases under portions of the normal curve

0.13%	2.14%	13.59%	34.13%	34.13%	13.59%	2.14%	0.13%

Standard Deviations
−4σ −3σ −2σ −1σ 0 +1σ +2σ +3σ +4σ

Cumulative Percentages
0.1%   2.3%   15.9%   50.0%   84.1%   97.7%   99.9%

Rounded
2%   16%   50%   84%   98%

Percentile Equivalents
1   5   10   20 30 40 50 60 70 80   90   95   99
Q₁   Md   Q₃

Typical Standard Scores

z-scores
−4.0   −3.0   −2.0   −1.0   0   +1.0   +2.0   +3.0   +4.0

T-scores
20   30   40   50   60   70   80

CEEB scores
200   300   400   500   600   700   800

AGCT scores
40   60   80   100   120   140   160

Stanines
1   2   3   4   5   6   7   8   9

Percent in stanine
4%   7%   12%   17%   20%   17%   12%   7%   4%

Wechsler Scales

Subtests
1   4   7   10   13   16   19

Deviation IQs
55   70   85   100   115   130   145

NOTE: This chart cannot be used to equate scores on one test to scores on another test. For example, both 600 on the CEEB and 120 on the AGCT are one standard deviation above their respective means, but they do not represent "equal" standings because the scores were obtained from different groups.

FIGURE 3-2
The Normal Curve and Alternative Measurements. Reproduced from p. 8 Test Service Bulletin Nos. 47–49. New York: Psychological Corporation, 1954–1955.

sumption makes sense. But if any of the features cited above are violated (e.g., the test is not valid and/or reliable; test conditions are poor), then the assumption is false. This assumption of correspondence is critical in making inferences about any kind of test. It is largely because this assumption is repeatedly and flagrantly ignored by test users that tests have been used in wrong ways and have thus resulted in invalid inferences. In general, a thorough understanding of statistics and psychological testing is essential for accurate use and interpretation of tests. Therefore, we recommend that this brief summary be supplemented by course work on the nature and methods of both statistics and testing.

AN OVERVIEW OF ASSESSMENT INSTRUMENTS AND TECHNIQUES

In concluding this chapter, we will discuss some representative instruments and techniques that aid human services professionals in identifying target skill deficits. The emphasis in this section will be on instruments that have some direct or indirect relationship to normality and to human skill development (instruments which relate almost exclusively to the determination of mental illness will not be discussed). There are many of these tests, and only a few of the major ones will be identified here. Since new revisions are continually occurring, the reference, in most cases, will be made to the test publisher.

Assessment of Attitudes

Attitudes reflect responses to contextual stimuli that involve more or less enduring dispositions. According to Shaw and Wright (1967), attitude measures are methods of indirectly measuring an individual's beliefs, motives, concepts, and opinions. All are presumably derived from more basic cognitive and emotional processes that are presumably tapped via the rating process. In addition to rating scales, the Q-Sort Technique (Stephenson, 1953) is useful for measuring attitudes. In the Q-Sort, the person is given a pile of cards which contain words, phrases, and other descriptive characteristics and is asked to sort them into piles in accordance with subjective criteria such as "most like me" and "not like me." Although used most often in research, attitude assessment is a potential source for human services professionals to obtain a measure of social issues, relationship to others, and so forth.

Cognitive Ability—Intelligence, Achievement, Aptitude

The concept of intelligence is a hypothetical construct which reflects the aggregate or global capacity of the individual to act purposefully, to think rationally, and to deal effectively with the environment (paraphrased from Wechsler's definition in Matarazzo, 1972, p. 79). From the individual intelligence testing point of view, the Stanford-Binet (Houghton Mifflin) is available and has been revised many times (Sattler, 1974). The most popular individual intelligence test is that of David Wechsler known originally as the Wechsler-Bellevue (Psychological Corporation). Over a number of decades of development, the original instrument has been expanded and revised so that there are currently an adult scale (Wechsler Adult Intelligence Scale—Revised (WAIS-R)), a children's scale (Wechsler Intelligence Scale for Children—Revised (WISC-R)), and a preschooler's scale (Wechsler Preschool and Primary Scale of Intelligence (WPPSI)). In the Wechsler scales, intelligence testing is divided into verbal and performance components. The verbal component includes subtests of information, comprehension, digit span, arithmetic, similarities, and vocabulary. The performance section includes picture arrangement, picture completion, block design, object assembly, and digit symbol. This test yields subtest scores, verbal and performance IQ scores, and a total IQ score. All of these individually administered intelligence tests require special course work and supervision.

In addition, there are several group intelligence tests used to assess intellectual functioning. One of the most popular and extensively used cognitive assessment instruments is *The California Short Form Test of Mental Maturity* (CTMM) (California Test Bureau, McGraw-Hill). This test can be administered in about 40 to 45 minutes, is appropriate from kindergarten through college, and yields three scores—a language IQ, a nonlanguage IQ, and a total score. *The Cognitive Abilities Test* (Houghton Mifflin) provides separate scores for verbal, quantitative, and nonverbal sections. It takes about 40 to 50 minutes of time and is appropriate from preschool to grade 13.

Achievement tests are most often geared to grade levels. They also provide grade-referenced scores for subareas within subject matter such as reading, arithmetic, and language. *The California Achievement Tests* (CAT) (California Test Bureau, McGraw-Hill) are appropriate from lower primary grades up to advanced levels in high school and above (grades 1 to 14). They take anywhere from about 1½ to 3 hours and yield scores in reading vocabulary, reading comprehension, arithmetic reasoning, spelling, and English usage. Another common achievement test is the *Iowa Tests of Basic Skills* (ITBS) (Houghton-Mifflin). This test is also multidimensional and focuses on skills. It is appropriate for grades 3 to 9 and takes from 5 to 6 hours to complete.

Another form of cognitive assessment is related to what are called aptitude tests. *The Differential Aptitude Test Battery* (Psychological Corporation) is available for grades 8 through 12. It provides separate scores for verbal reasoning, numerical ability, abstract reasoning, clerical speed and accuracy, mechanical reasoning, space relations, spelling, and sentences. This battery takes from three to four hours. *The General Aptitude Test Battery* is produced by the United States Employment Service. It can be given in about two hours and is often used for job matching or selection. The subsections of the test are named comparison, computation, three-dimensional space, vocabulary, tool matching, arithmetic reasoning, form matching, mark making, place, turn, assemble, and disassemble. It also includes a number of items and skills relating to manual dexterity.

Another form of cognitive test is the criterion-referenced test. Science Research Associates has a *Diagnostic Test in Reading and Mathematics* available for grades 1 through 6. California Test Bureau/McGraw-Hill has a number of such instruments, such as *The Prescriptive Mathematics Inventory* and *The Prescriptive Reading Inventory,* relating to a bank of items and tests that can be used by elementary and secondary school customers. Most of these assessment instruments are relatively new but are relevant to criterion-referenced trends in school assessment.

Human services professionals utilize a wide variety of these tests. Frequently they administer tests and sometimes they have access to a client's test results and use this information for delivery of service. However, all of these tests need to be studied and understood before being used by counselors.

Personality and Interest Inventories

There are a number of personality and interest inventories that are available to human services professionals. One, *The California Psychological Inventory* (CPI) (Consulting Psychologists Press Inc.), consists of 480 items which are responded to by "true" or "false." It consists of seventeen scales which relate to a number of dimensions such as dominance, psychological mindedness, and style of achievement. The CPI scales fall into categories which make them easy to interpret and understand, and so it lends itself to counseling interpretation with clients. This instrument is appropriate for individuals who are thirteen or older; completion of the instrument requires 45 to 60 minutes.

The Sixteen Personality Factor Test (16 PF) (Cattell, 1949) is another instrument that has had considerable usage and has been applied to many problem areas including clinical assessment, vocational interests, and marriage counseling (i.e., through matching profiles). This instrument was initially developed by Cattell and has alternative versions for high school and elementary students. Testing time for the 16 PF is from 45 to 60 minutes.

The Myers-Briggs Type Indicator (Consulting Psychologists Press) can be used to identify dispositional characteristics. It takes approximately one hour to administer and is appropriate from about grade 9 upwards. This instrument attempts to identify overall temperament characteristics in accord with Jung's rationale: there is a comparison between introversion and extroversion, thinking and feeling, sensing and intuition, and judgment versus perception. Much research has been done with this instrument to identify the characteristics of medical students, health-related professionals, and other groups to determine predominant patterns of thinking and perceiving.

The Barclay Classroom Assessment System (Western Psychological Services) is different from the above tests in that it involves the identification of temperament preferences from self-report ratings, vocational interests, peer sociometric judgments, and teacher ratings. This is an entire system which is appropriate for children from grades 3 to 7. It takes about one and one-half hours to administer. This is a multimethod, multitrait system designed to provide a computer output for teachers, counselors, administrators, special educators, and psychologists who are interested in the early identification of children with learning disabilities, social and behavioral problems, and gifted and creative talents. This system is primarily a prevention system for evaluating the characteristics of children in the classroom environment. It also includes the input of achievement scores.

Aside from personality measures, vocational interest testing assesses the characteristics of an individual in relationship to established patterns of interests shown by professionals in specific fields. Generally, vocational assessment has been done by determining the interest patterns of individuals and matching their individual profile with groups of professionals who are in that particular occupation. The *Kuder Form DD* (Science Research Associates) and the *Strong-Campbell Interest Inventory* (SCII) (Consulting Psychologists Press Inc.) are two of the most popular interest inventories. These surveys provide comparisons for individuals on categories via preferences indicated in outdoor, mechanical, scientific, persuasive, artistic, social service, and clerical areas. In the SCII additional scales have been added that include a General Occupation Theme and Basic Interest Scales based on Holland's (1966) research.

Most of the tests mentioned in this section can be scored by hand or by computer. The test publishers cited with the tests usually provide computer scoring and psychological reports to users. In addition, there are a number of microcomputer programs that will score and interpret some of these tests. However, human services professionals should be aware that, in particular, inferences drawn in microcomputer program scoring routines may be less than acceptable. Despite this, the introduction of the computer into test scoring and interpretation may provide a means to collate meaningfully information obtained from multiple inputs, as described in the Barclay system.

SUMMARY

In this chapter, the basic processes of assessment have been outlined. Assessment is a broader process than just testing. It includes the use of empirical observation using both behavioral and clinical methods. From the interview or counseling sessions, human services professionals can obtain information about the basic needs of clients, problems that they face, and their typical ways of attempting to solve these problems. Once the problem and background information have been identified, tests can be used if there is a purpose for using them. Attitude inventories, intelligence tests, achievement batteries, and personality tests are all useful adjuncts to the process of identification of client needs.

Once the needs have been identified, it is then important to consider the goals desired by the client and what criteria of effective behavior are operative in the given situation. Sometimes criteria of behavior are set too high for the realistic attainment of the client. Sometimes they need to be modified in other directions.

Assessment data should then provide human services professionals with an analysis of the individual as seen by empirical methods and testing. This analysis then becomes helpful in determining with the client the goals of the counseling/therapy process. A recognition of the specific cultural background that a client possesses and a knowledge of whether he or she is a thinking-judging person or a sensing-feeling one helps in selecting the kinds of possible treatments that would be best for this individual.

It would be helpful if some automatic process could be utilized in making integrated assessments. Many tests now do have computerized versions which print out reports. There are also computerized techniques for analyzing social history and background information. Though some of these programs can be helpful in expediting the work of the professional, it should be strongly recognized that assessment in its overall integrative process is and must be done by a qualified diagnostician. If human services professionals aspire to do their own assessment evaluations of clients, they must recognize that much intensive training is required. Assessment is a professional skill that requires considerable attention and specific training. This training is necessary to complement the process of counseling and therapy and becomes a strong part of ethical competency as defined by both the American Psychological Association and the American Association for Counseling and Development.

REFERENCES

Astin, A. W. (1965). Effect of different college environments on the vocational choices of high aptitude students. *Journal of Counseling Psychology, 12,* 28–34.

Barclay, J. R. (1972). *Appraising individual differences in the elementary classroom: A manual of the Barclay classroom climate inventory* (2d ed.). Lexington, KY: Educational Skills Development.

Barclay, J. R. (1983). *The Barclay classroom assessment system manual.* Los Angeles: Western Psychological Services.

Barclay, J. R. (1987). *Conceptual foundations of assessment theory.* New York: Praeger.

Bloom, B. S. (Ed.), Englehart, M. D., Furst, E. J., Hill, W. H., & Krathwohl, D. R. (1956). *Taxonomy of educational objectives: Handbook 1: Cognitive domain.* New York: David McKay.

Cattell, R. B. (1949). *Description and measurement of personality.* New York: World Book.

Cucelogu, D. M. (1967). *A cross-cultural study of communication via facial expressions.* Unpublished doctoral dissertation, University of Illinois, Champaign-Urbana.

Harrow, A. J. (1972). *A taxonomy of the psychomotor domain.* New York: David McKay.

Holland, J. L. (1966). *The psychology of vocational choice.* Boston: Ginn.

Krathwohl, D. R., Bloom, B. S., & Masia, B. B. (1964). *Taxonomy of educational objectives: The classroom of educational goals. Handbook 2: Affective domain.* New York: David McKay.

Matarazzo, J. D. (1972). *Wechsler's measurement and appraisal of adult intelligence* (5th ed.). New York: Oxford University Press.

Powell, G. (1979). *Brain and personality.* New York: Praeger.

Sattler, J. M. (1974). *Assessment of children's intelligence.* Philadelphia: W. B. Saunders.

Shaw, M. E., & Wright, J. M. (1967). *Scales for the measurement of attitudes.* New York: McGraw-Hill.

Shertzer, B., & Linden, J. D. (1979). *Fundamentals of individual appraisal.* Boston: Houghton-Mifflin.

Stephenson, W. (1953). *The study of behavior: A technique and its methodology.* Chicago: University of Chicago Press.

Sundberg, N. D. (1977). *Assessment of persons.* Englewood Cliffs, NJ: Prentice-Hall.

Walberg, H. J. (Ed.) (1974). *Evaluating educational performance.* Berkeley, CA: McCutchan Publishing.

Wolff, W. (1943). *The expression of personality; experimental depth psychology.* New York: Harper.

CHAPTER 4

REMEDIATION AND PREVENTION

Historically, the focus in dealing with mental health problems has been the treatment modality. A problem arises, becomes more serious with time, and ultimately the person or family arrives at the steps of a mental health counselor who works with the person or family to resolve the conflict. The nature of remediation is that it occurs with individual, family, or small group interaction with a helping person, be it a counselor, social worker, or psychotherapist. The goal of the interaction, which may be brief (a few sessions) or lengthy (literally years), is generally for the person, family, or group to begin functioning adequately in society. This model, as you might expect, works well in certain locales and among certain persons. Communities that are fortunate enough to have large numbers of mental health professionals can keep up with treatment demands. Also, persons with money can purchase mental health services privately. However, there are vast areas and millions of persons who are not in a position, geographically or financially, to receive mental health services. Even though the treatment modality is the one that is of primary importance in mental health training programs, the reality of our present situation in the United States demands that changes be made to serve our population adequately.

According to Albee (1984) the problem is worse than most people would suspect. Some 15 percent of the population of the United States exhibit mental conditions that could be labeled as "mental illnesses." Albee (1984) goes on to say that some 32 to 36 million persons in the

United States experience conditions such as depression, incapacitating anxiety, addiction to alcohol and drugs, organic mental disorders including chronic brain syndromes in the elderly, as well as the functional psychoses such as schizophrenia. As you notice, this does *not* include the 6 to 7 million other persons classified as mentally deficient or retarded, the millions of persons with psychosomatic physical conditions like hypertension resulting from stress, or the very large number of other persons experiencing acute emotional upset as a consequence of life crises. Kiesler (1983) brings the situation into uncomfortable focus with the following calculation:

> Today in the United States there are about 45,000 doctoral level service providers in psychiatry and psychology. If you look at the available hours of those 45,000 people as a national resource that could be applied to this problem and you look at the traditional way of applying it—three times a week psychotherapy, assume it goes on for a year—then all of those 45,000 people could handle about 2 percent of the national need. In fact, entirely separate and independent estimates say that's about what they do handle. Phrased another way, if all those psychiatrists and psychologists are viewed as a national resource then they have about two hours a year per person in need. (p. 5)

A search for solutions to the problem that exists in mental health must go well beyond multiplying numbers of treatment personnel and expanding community mental health centers. Clearly, this is a problem of major proportions, and we must look for ways to prevent the incidence of problems, thus lowering the number of persons requiring remediative efforts. According to Lewis and Lewis (1984), the Task Force on Prevention of the President's Commission on Mental Health (1978) identified three strategies or thrusts as having clear promise for the future effectiveness of prevention programs. These are: (1) interpersonal competence building, (2) programs for populations facing life crises, and (3) advocacy directed toward modifying and improving social environments. Strategies such as these are developed and delivered to populations rather than to individuals and their goal is to prevent the onset of symptoms. In this chapter, we will examine both remediation and prevention in the human services. Then later in this text, a training model (Life-Skills Training, see Chapters 1 and 8), that can be applied in either remedial or preventive situations will be described.

REMEDIATION

As mentioned previously, the heart and soul of the mental health professions are the theories, techniques, and strategies that have evolved over the years to treat persons with symptoms of emotional distress. This emphasis has been maintained for many reasons, but probably the most important reason it has lasted is that it works. The reinforcement gained by successfully implementing a change strategy with a person or family encourages mental health persons to implement more of the same to others. Results are tangible, and being tangible, they can be counted and rewarded. People who choose mental health professions by and large want to see the fruits of their labor and implementing remediation strategies allows that to happen. There will always be a place in mental health for remediation, and the many highly effective theories that exist will continue to be utilized. Also, many thousands of practitioners will always be able to find case loads of persons who are suffering with symptoms of emotional distress. The changes that are occurring in the mental health field should not be a threat to mental health practitioners but rather should represent hope that the system will become more efficient, that more of the underserved will find help, and that many thousands of cases will be prevented through preventive efforts.

Remediation Activities

The ever-broadening interests of practitioners has led to a situation in the human services where remediation efforts are applied across a wide range of professions, and particular areas of interest or particular theoretical models are not the exclusive domain of a certain category of mental health professional. The counseling and guidance professionals, for example, who were once primarily school based and served only students, are now working as vocational specialists, rehabilitation specialists, career counselors, family therapists, private practitioners, and the like. These persons now provide services across the settings of school, community, family, and the work place. Social workers are another example. So wide-ranging are their interests and expertise that no satisfactory definition of that profession is even available (Morales and Sheafor, 1983).

In formally defining remediation, then, one has to take into account the fact that a definition should transcend particular professions and be generic enough to cover many situations as they occur across settings. Garfield (1983) seems to satisfy that need with the following definition: "Remediation is a planned intervention, interpersonal in nature, that attempts to help, modify, or improve the status of an individual or group" (p. 226). We can see how this functions by examining remedial strategies that are implemented in the four settings mentioned previously.

Remediation in the Schools   The history of remediation services in the schools is a long one that is anchored by three categories of service providers: school counselors, school psychologists, and school social workers. The arrangement of services in schools varies, of course, from one system to another, but usually services are supervised by superintendents, principals, and other administrators and are governed strictly by federal, state, and local laws. In addition, there are certain remedial functions that are traditionally peculiar to each of the disciplines.

Services delivered by school counselors usually include individual counseling with a student who is having academic difficulties, family counseling in a situation where the family interaction patterns are affecting the student's ability to concentrate in class, desensitization groups for students who experience test anxiety, and individual counseling with a student who walks into the counselor's office in tears. In essence, the school counselor handles the day-to-day problem situations that present themselves in the school and also plans programs to deal with problem situations that seem to be widespread.

The school psychologist position in school systems is one that has changed a great deal during the last decade. Whereas the general public once viewed, and to a great extent accurately, the role of the school psychologist as a person who administered and interpreted tests, the expertise of these professionals is being utilized far beyond testing in many school systems. In keeping with the traditional role, these professionals do typically accept referrals from principals and counselors for assessment and counseling or referral of difficult, confusing, or complicated problem situations. However, presently school psychologists are also involved with other types of remedial activities such as training teachers who are having problems with classroom discipline in techniques that will improve the classroom environment and working with students who have certain learning disabilities to maximize their educational experience. In addition, these professionals may conduct study groups for parents who are experiencing child-rearing problems, and they may be active in designing and administering questionnaires and other information-gathering instruments for use in the school.

In contrast, the school social worker position has usually involved investigative work both *of* the students and their families and *for* the students and their families. Home visits, management of public welfare/assistance programs, and advocacy for students and their families are all within the school social worker's area of responsibility. Examples of remedial services include: (1) attempting to get financial assistance for a family that is struggling to provide the basics for itself, (2) investigating suspected child abuse by visiting a student's house and meeting with parents and other children, and (3) being responsible for locating and helping truants. As these examples indicate, the school social worker handles the many social welfare issues that arise in the school system.

Remediation in the Community   The community setting is where the most obvious need presents itself in mental health. The system of employing persons from all helping professions to meet the needs of community mental health centers has become a frustrating series of increased need each year, requiring additional funding and often supplemental funding to get through a year or to meet emerging crises. The remediation activities of these centers run the gamut of helping services and include individual and group counseling and psychotherapy, day treatment centers, substance abuse programs, psychotropic drug maintenance, and community outreach programs on many topics. A reality of life in many community mental health centers has been that treatment requests exhaust staff time to the point that there is very little time for development of new thrusts such as programs for the prevention of emotional disturbances (more on this later in the chapter).

Remediation in the Family   The programs for remediation activities in families, as in other areas, encompass the entire range of mental health professionals. Whereas historically the social worker was first thought of when one looked for help with family problems, today the involvement is spread between psychiatrists, psychologists, social workers, family counselors, nurses, and others who employ techniques that may or may not have been developed within their disciplines. One umbrella group, the American Association for Marriage and Family Therapy, has established criteria for levels of therapeutic intervention and certifies persons according to these criteria. This type of organization adds order to the field and gives the public a yardstick to use when services are needed.

A host of problem areas are subsumed under the heading of family; these include parenting, family roles, sexuality, finances, communication in the family, recreation and leisure, family planning, and aging. Often these issues are encountered in the context of some form of family counseling. Family counseling is typically conducted with as many of the immediate family members as possible present. Variations include alternating sessions with parents and children seen separately, parents seen separately then together without children, and all combinations in between. Some therapists conduct family counseling in a group setting with audience members questioning the "on-stage" family and interacting back and forth with the therapist. Other methods include psychodramatic techniques in which family situations are "acted out" by family members and discussed in relation to what is said in the interactions or what is communicated nonverbally, below the surface, or symbolically. An important point here is that many techniques work in terms of family members electing to change their behavior in order for the family to function more effectively. The techniques used are a function of the therapist's theoretical orientation, training, and preferences, though the choice of technique might be based on the nature of the concern or the personalities in the family.

Remediation in the Work Place   The work place has experienced a lot of change in terms of mental health remedial activities. Once the domain of industrial/organizational psychologists, many service providers including personnel specialists, rehabilitation counselors, counseling psychologists, clinical psychologists, psychiatrists, and psychiatric nurses are planning interventions within the work setting. Once business and industry were concerned primarily with economic productivity, but the present-day concern of employers and employees includes personal fulfillment, economic and emotional security, and physical well-being.

The most common mode of delivery for activities in the work place is the employee assistance program (EAP). These EAPs were established to coordinate, provide, and refer employees to a wide range of services located either in the organization or, more typically, in the community. Sometimes seen as places where employees are sent when they are suspected of having a drinking problem, many EAPs have expanded to include a wide range of services to their employees.

Current Trends in Remediation Programs

Current remediation efforts and activities in mental health are shaping the nature of both services offered and the professions offering treatment. It seems apparent from already emerging treatment applications that several clear trends have been established and can be predicted as new directions for remedial services. For instance, efforts to serve geriatric populations are on the increase. This thrust, once again cutting across several professional disciplines, is growing in quantity of programs and is, additionally, reflecting a changing perspective of older age from a terminal stage to a developing stage.

There are several other trends that are likely to result in newer directions for treatment and services. Concerns of minorities, including ethnic minorities and women, are receiving attention in remedial services. It is also probable that the chronically mentally ill, long a concern of both the public and the mental health community, will garner additional services as a result of the policies of the National Institute of Mental Health (NIMH), which provides funds for the training of human services personnel. Pardes (1983) reports NIMH funding proposals for the near future focus on treatment of the chronically mentally ill, as well as rural populations and geriatrics. The growth of interest in recreation and leisure will most certainly result in the application of these concepts in remedial treatment in the future (Reitz and Hawkins, 1981). Strain (1978) suggests there is a changing perspective in the relationship of the general physician to the patient that incorporates psychological remedial efforts. The adaptation to chronic pain/illness provides one such instance where psychological components may enter the treatment approaches of the general physician, to engage the patient in pursuit of mental health as well as physical health. Technology provides still another trend area for treatment application.

A major area of change presently occurring and evidencing significant growth relates not to the types of services but to the manner in which they may be provided. The formation of private corporations to offer human services for mental health, based on the private-for-profit model, has recently had significant impact (Forbes, 1982). These large corporations have established facilities throughout the country providing mental health services to clients/patients who can afford their specialized care. The efforts of these innovative groups have been aimed at neglected areas of psychiatric care as well as a primary emphasis on alcohol and substance abuse treatment (Business Week, 1982).

A final trend to be considered here involves not so much specific services or even service providers as it does a changing concept of the goal(s) of treatment. As we noted earlier, the historical development of the human services disciplines was closely related to remedial efforts focused upon individuals or groups that evidenced dysfunction in some dimension of their life. In this traditional approach, the goal of treatment was to relieve the already distressed individual. An alternative approach that has become increasingly attractive is to prevent mental dysfunction. This change of emphasis from treatment to prevention will be the focus of the following section.

PREVENTION

Mental health can find precedent for the shift from treatment to prevention in the medical community. For instance, public health has used the media to saturate the public with information and warnings about diseases and steps that can be taken to prevent them. In addition, medical science has developed medications, e.g., immunizations, that are used for preventive purposes. Following in this tradition, mental health professionals are interested in preventing behaviors that result in mental or emotional stress and thereby affect the effective functioning of individuals in society.

Preventing problems from occurring is a complex, often thankless task that tends to require interdisciplinary efforts. If we look at the history of the preventive movement, we can see that the majority of the involvement has been interdisciplinary in that it has involved public health models, learning theory, social systems theory, the medical model, crisis theory, psychoanalytic theory, self-actualization theory, and educational models (Bloom, 1981; Bronfenbrenner, 1974; Goldston, 1977a). The need for an interdisciplinary effort becomes more evident when we consider the following. Illness and death are more and more related to a combination of physical and psychological factors, so that both areas are necessarily being taken into account in prevention program development. The U.S. Public Health Service along with state and local agencies and organizations concerned with health, both physical and psychological, issue reports that emphasize the need for interdisciplinary cooperation and, more importantly, the need for planned prevention strategies such as the health maintenance organizations that are developed for communities, corporations, or for private subscription.

According to Cowen (1984) there are two major routes that can be taken in primary prevention of emotional problems. One is the analysis and modification of social environments, and the other is competence building. Social environments tend to resist change. As Cowen (1984) explains, "Power structures form, vested interests are protected, and system occupants are threatened by the prospect of change. Thus, rooted systems may not be expected to yield passively and graciously to change..." (p. 73). However, the second route, competence building, is a very attractive option in implementing primary prevention efforts. Murphy and Chandler (1972) have stated that the best possible defense against problems is to "build" resources and adaptive strengths in people from the start. This approach assumes that people become maladjusted because they lack specific skills needed to resolve personal problems. If such skills could truly be taught from the onset, there would be less need ever to engage in maladjustment.

The thrust of the preventive approach is educational rather than restorative, and mass-oriented rather than individual-casualty-oriented. Its key questions are: (1) What core skills undergird positive adjustment? (2) Can curricula be developed to teach young children these skills? (3) Does acquiring a given competence lead to improved interpersonal adjustment? (4) Do adjustive gains, so acquired, endure? Positive answers to these questions would markedly advance de facto primary prevention (Murphy and Chandler, 1972).

Whether the prevention is initiated by psychologists, social workers, nurses, teachers, or counselors, the process involves an educational approach to behavior change. In this educative mode, the burden of responsibility is on the individual rather than on the helping person. As Albee (1984) states, "Prevention results from stress reduction, particularly those stresses arising out of difficult interpersonal relations, and from improved social coping skills and solid support systems" (p. 3).

As discussed in this chapter, the switch from the model of "you're sick, let me give you something to make you feel better" to "you can learn some skills that will help you feel better" is the challenge that faces advocates of prevention as a major mode of treatment. This is an important challenge. Indeed, prevention has been heralded as the "fourth revolution in society's approach to mental illness" (Albee, 1984, p. 3). As we focus on prevention and definition, barriers, programs, and current trends, hopefully the reader will gain enough insight to concur with Albee (1984): "This fourth revolution, if it happens, will identify our society as a *caring society*—one that holds out its hand to its unfortunate members and does all it can to prevent misfortune for those at risk" (p. 5).

Definition

Boundaries   For a term to be useful, it needs to be specific. Accordingly, Klein and Goldston (1977) have identified four parameters that need to be taken into account when defining prevention. A first consideration is that the use of the word prevention should be limited to primary prevention. To refer to early treatment as secondary prevention or rehabilitation activities as tertiary prevention contributes to the confusion and diminishes the usefulness of the term. In addition, we need to recognize that prevention is directed toward reducing the incidence of a highly predictable undesirable consequence, and so the term should not be used interchangeably with "promotion of mental health" or "improving the quality of life." A third parameter is that prevention is a term applicable to populations and not to individuals within those populations. Incidence within a population can be measured and change in incidence can be demonstrated, but it is not possible, with rare exceptions in highly controlled situations, to prove that an individual who did not become the victim of a condition would without question have incurred the condition except for the prevention intervention. Lastly, for an activity to be described as prevention, it should generally include the following elements: (1) a condition which can be observed and recorded in precise terms, (2) an identified population at risk for that condition, (3) a measure of the incidence of the condition in the population, (4) a clearly defined plan of intervention applied to the identified population, and (5) the measurement of incidence following the intervention.

Taking these points into consideration, Goldston (1977a) defines prevention as follows:

> Primary prevention encompasses those activities directed to specifically identified vulnerable high-risk groups within the community who have not been labeled as psychiatrically ill and for whom measures can be undertaken to avoid the onset of emotional disturbance and/or to enhance their level of positive mental health. Programs for the promotion of mental health are primarily educational rather than clinical in conception and operation, with their ultimate goal being to increase people's capacities for dealing with crises and for taking steps to improve their own lives. (p. 27)

With these points and this definition in mind, prevention in mental health can be discussed more in terms of *programs* than any other mode of intervention.

Categories of Primary Prevention   Given that with prevention we are going to be interested in constructing educational activities into a program, it seems appropriate to consider in what areas we can be most effective with our preventive efforts. At a "state of the art" conference on prevention, Goldston (1977a) described four areas of prevention, thereby providing a global view of the arenas in which these programs operate. We will discuss each of these areas including comments and examples.

1 *Primary prevention of the mental illness of known etiology.* This framework involves a medical approach focused on those conditions of *known* etiology which it is possible to prevent by "specific protection" interventions. The goal is to avoid the onset of mental disorders by intercepting the causes of disease before people become exposed. In the medical/psychiatric sphere sufficient scientific evidence exists to prevent some mental disorders, including both acute and chronic brain syndromes, resulting from (1) *poisoning* by certain substances, such as lead-based paints, (2) *infections,* such as encephalitis, rubella, and syphilis, (3) *genetic diseases,* such as phenylketonuria (PKU) and galactosemia, (4) *nutritional deficiencies,* such as pellagra and beriberi, (5) *general systemic* diseases, such as erythroblastosis fetalis and cretinism, and (6) *accidents* and *other physical traumas.* Goldston goes on to say that primary prevention of the mental illnesses of known etiology has become the responsibility of public health and environmental protection agencies. By and large, mental health workers are neither involved in programs aimed at the primary prevention of the mental illnesses of known etiology nor are they generally aware of the multiple opportunities to effect the prevention of many conditions which result in diagnosable mental illness. Perhaps reduction in the incidence of new cases of disorders could be effected if the expertise of mental health workers was brought to bear on these disorders.

2 *Primary prevention of the mental illnesses of unknown etiology.* It is Goldston's feeling that in the absence of scientific research findings on etiology, it is ill-advised to even address issues relating to primary prevention of the mental illness of unknown etiology. Current knowledge of the etiology of the major mental illnesses such as the schizophrenias and the depressions is limited; consequently, generalized, nonspecific efforts purported to be aimed at the primary prevention of these disorders warrant considerable suspicion. Work in this area violates the definition that major investigators in prevention use; that is, all activities must be characterized by *specific* actions directed at *specific* populations for *specific* purposes.

3 *Primary prevention of emotional distress, maladaption, maladjustment, needless psychopathology, and human misery.* This framework that Goldston identified entails a psycho-socio-cultural-educational approach in which crisis theory, crisis intervention, and anticipatory guidance are particularly relevant. Counseling, mental health consultation, community organization, training of vital community caregivers, and mental health education are the major forms of professional intervention. The goal is to reduce or eliminate unnecessary emotional distress, when possible. Understanding emotional responses can lead to less fear and thus better adaptation to life situations.

4 *Promotion of mental health.* The objective here, according to Goldston, is to promote social and functional competence, coping capacities, ego strengths and "positive mental health." This framework is also a psycho-cultural-educational approach with consultative, educational training, and organizational modalities being of major significance. Some examples are family life education and affective education in any number of organizations.

Barriers to Establishment of Prevention Programs

When change takes place, especially when it involves a long-standing structure or long-standing behavior, different "camps" develop representing varying viewpoints. With the introduction of prevention programs, at least three groups have surfaced. Some practitioners reject the training modality and stick exclusively to traditional therapeutic methods. Another group is comprised of practitioners who use traditional therapeutic methods with some patients and training methods with others, or they begin with traditional therapeutic methods and move to training as the patient is ready to move. A third group believes strongly in training as the primary mode of treatment, to the exclusion of traditional methods. With these different camps emerging, we have a situation that provides for a healthy exchange of theoretical positions as well as for a monitoring of successes. It also encourages research in response to criticism. However, these different camps also represent and reflect resistance to the preventive movement. Furthermore, the conflict among professional service providers interacts with other barriers to impede the establishment of prevention programs.

Political considerations have been one major barrier hindering preventive programming. Programs that are designed as preventive have historically been "back burner" items politically. Of course, each program is evaluated according to its own strengths and weaknesses but there are some general very visible political considerations that are worth mentioning. For one, results of prevention programs are not dramatic and do not generally make headlines. When money is invested in a project, particularly tax money, funding sources like to show results quickly and as dramatically as possible. Fixing something that is broken (remediation) many times yields dramatic results that give funding sources (and the politicians behind them) positive visibility. Prevention is slow, and slowness is difficult to fit into the funding game.

In addition, prevention applies to populations as opposed to individuals, and so the impact is "spread thin." The agency or politician looking for an individual to spotlight a "success" as a result of the program would be hard pressed to do so. Populations change slowly, and when the results of evaluation research are interpreted, it is generally in terms of a percentage of the population change as opposed to the expected percentage change if treatment had been introduced. With this type of interpretation, groups, not individuals, are discussed. This condition does not allow politicians to capitalize on the results.

Finally, money has not historically been appropriated for health care when there is no "disease" or "illness" to treat. Prevention deals with potentialities, thus there are no patients, only identified populations containing potential patients. It is easy to see how a funding agency might respond to a request for a preventive program when the request is weighed against a backlog of requests from organizations and individuals representing an identifiable group of sick patients. Many times it seems that politicians and funding sources are overwhelmed with remediation work to the point that prevention is not evaluated according to its merit as much as it is pushed aside by emergencies (remediation).

The absence of a rich research base is another barrier to prevention programming. The mental health field has been dominated since its inception in psychiatry by remedial theories and therapies. This history has resulted in remedial programs getting the larger share of grant monies and dominating the research areas. Moreover, there is a general feeling among opponents of prevention programs that prevention programs are not founded on a research base. In truth, research projects do require a long period of time to complete, and successes are buried in populations where they are difficult to point to specifically. Those professionals, however, who are active in research on prevention are gaining more and more respectability as more sophisticated research designs are developed and as their base of knowledge grows. What can be said with some degree of accuracy is that the research base in prevention is small compared to remediation, but the prevention research that does exist is encouraging.

A third barrier derives from practitioners' motivation. The one thing that attracts most mental health practitioners to the field is patient care. Since preventive programs are primarily educational and require more training than treatment, they are not what most practitioners consider patient care. Individual therapy is the primary mode of treatment in mental health. Since, as we mentioned earlier, prevention is slow with the changes spread out over populations, the effect is not so obvious as a single change which might be quite dramatic. So, remediation might possibly be more rewarding in terms of personal satisfaction and reinforcement provided by the client.

The reward value of remedial care interacts with training to produce new professionals who do not endorse preventive programming. Mental health training programs tend to remain traditional in their philosophy of educating helping persons. There are two main reasons for this. One, they are responding to the demand of students who want to be trained as traditional therapists; and two, they work cooperatively with private and community agencies that supply a seemingly unlimited number of patients who need remediation. In addition, once a person is in the helping profession system and is involved in traditional patient care such as counseling for remediation, few opportunities are available for formal in-service training programs for persons interested in or mandated to get involved in prevention. Because of a lack of training, the programs developed may be ineffective and may fail to effect change. Once discouraged in an attempt to develop a new programming thrust, the helping professional may find it easier to maintain the status quo than to risk failure again. However, the training programs are beginning to look closer at prevention, and students are getting a "pre-service" view of its potential. This seems to be a very positive trend that advocates of prevention can point to as progress.

In addition, when it comes to prevention, community support systems, which have the potential of being preventive when used in conjunction with the communities' mental health professionals, are severely underutilized (Plaut, 1982). The reasons for this lack of cooperation vary, of course, from community to community, but Plaut hypothesizes in a general way two possibilities: (1) mental health professionals view social-psychological support as their own specialized skill and are reluctant to let others, especially nonprofessionals, get involved; and (2) the separation of the world of action, productivity, and achievement from the world of affect, emotion, and personal experience impedes the development of cooperative relationships.

Prevention is also impeded because at the present time there does not exist a national clearinghouse of information on existing prevention programs. A clearinghouse is an efficient way of disseminating information and gathering research evidence from across the country, and without the clearinghouse, researchers and trainers are limited to what they can uncover in the literature, at conferences, or through personal communications. With this limitation there is a great chance for overlapping research and important omissions in reviews of the literature.

One of the most serious barriers to establishing prevention programs is the charge that preventive efforts are not working. Overall, the country has not noticed a significant reduction in mental illness, thus affecting the credibility of prevention programs. However, it also seems that equally rigorous standards are not being demanded for treatment (remedial) activities as for preventive activities. The White House Office on Science and Technology has estimated that no more than 15 percent of generally accepted medical technology (surgery, pharmacological therapy, etc.) has been evaluated and found to be effective (see Plaut, 1982). Charges like this do not, however, affect the use of treatment programs.

Mental health workers have always been associated, in the communities' perception, with mental illness. This perception is changing as community mental health centers, hospitals, universities, and others are engaging mental health professionals to conduct awareness and skill development programs that are available to the general public. The change is slow, but this particular barrier has a chance of fading away as more effort is made to publicize the preventive potential in mental health. All change requires hard work to break down the barriers that tradition and personal perception establish. Prevention programs in helping have made progress and the trend seems to be moving toward them instead of away.

Example Programs in Primary Prevention

Even though prevention in mental health is just coming into its own, sporadic prevention efforts have been underway for years. Though most of the early efforts were not multidisciplinary in design and implementation, they were from a wide range of service providers. The need for interdisciplinary implementation is not a surprise since our mental health is tied into virtually every aspect of our lives, including our physical well-being, our church ties, our family relationships, our work, and our relationships with friends and neighbors in community living. In the following section, we will highlight several prevention programs in a number of disciplines, some very recent developments, and other pioneer efforts in prevention.

Prevention in the Schools   One of the most logical places for prevention programs to be placed is the educational system. School-based programs are able to reach children at a time when primary prevention is possible and in an arena in which a somewhat captive population exists. There are four distinct *types* of primary prevention programs in educational settings (Jason, 1980; see p. 112).

One type of program involves preventing vulnerable populations from succumbing to disorders. Examples include children with schizophrenic parents, children with alcohol or drug-addicted parents, children experiencing the death of a parent, and children with physical handicaps. With a second type of program, we are interested in preventing the onset of carefully defined target disorders. Interventions attempting to prevent school phobias or smoking are examples. In addition, there are programs for promoting and enhancing adaptivity and healthy functioning. Examples of this category are building or strengthening competencies in affective (e.g., social skills, human relations skills), cognitive (e.g., problem-solving abilities), or behavioral (e.g., peer-tutoring skills) modalities. And finally, a last type of program is geared to providing individuals with experiences that ease the impact of traumatic, transitional events in three areas: school (for example, school entrance), family life (for example, parent-child relationships), and work (as in the first part-time job).

One of the early prevention programs in the public schools was developed by Professor R. H. Ojemann at the University of Iowa. Referred to as the Ojemann project, it was started in the early 1940s and continues today. His goal is to reduce emotional conflict in the classroom and increase mutually satisfying relationships among both children and teachers. The program for grades 4 through 12 is delivered by the teachers who receive extensive training in mental health concepts. Ojemann stresses the importance of understanding the "why" of behavior rather than the more common practice of making judgments "about" behavior. Rather than "right" or "wrong," "good" or "bad" behavior, Ojemann stresses the multiple causation of behavior and the importance of establishing a range of values. Ojemann's well-researched project provides convincing evidence that children who are exposed to a teaching and learning experience of this kind are more secure and are more able to develop satisfying relations with others than are children who have not had this experience (Griffin, 1968).

In more recent prevention programs, the Kansas City School Behavior project yielded very interesting results. After sixty sixth-grade teachers were selected from a volunteer pool of ninety, they were divided into experimental and control groups. Experimental group teachers were given summer training in the methods and techniques of small group interaction and were assisted throughout the implementation year by the project team. The approach was multidisciplinary, having been derived from educational sociology, group dynamics, psychology, and psychotherapy. Three central themes were exploration of feelings, use of small groups as a vehicle for social and academic motivation, and the recognition of and dealing with social system and social class differences. The teacher became a resource person and group member, rather than the traditional authority.

Results of the Kansas City project are dramatic. Children said school was more fun, that they had more time for verbal interaction, and they had a better understanding of themselves and others. Peer support was valued highly as were opportunities to lead and to be open. Behavior of both disruptive and withdrawn students improved. Appropriate flexibility seemed to be the general outcome for all of the children. A 3-year follow-up study found the results to be real, lasting, and generalizable to the community. In effect, the project demonstrated that one can do something about what happens to a child in high school, in terms of social behavior, by teaching certain skills to a sixth-grade teacher (Hartley, 1977). A project of this nature could be implemented in a community through a cooperative agreement between the school system and the local mental health center without any significant expenditure of funds.

Prevention in Corrections and Juvenile Delinquency   In the area of corrections, the emphasis through the years has been on remediation. Programs of rehabilitation and programs of gradual reentry into free society (such as halfway houses) followed incarceration only as trends. Just coping with the present situations of prison overcrowding and the cost of incarceration has left little time or money for focusing on primary prevention. Most of the emphasis in this area has been left to the community programs, courts, and colleges and universities.

In the research that has been done in primary prevention of juvenile delinquency, there are frequent findings in a positive direction for counseling and modeling types of interventions (Palmer, 1971; Patterson and Reid, 1970; Persons, 1967). For instance, in one unique study, twenty adolescents who met the criteria of being "antisocial" were treated and have been followed up for the last 15 years (Massimo and Shore, 1963). Briefly, these twenty adolescents were assigned to either a treatment program or a "no-contact" control group. In the treatment program, the contact with the adolescent was in the form of an "outreach," wherein the worker offered help oriented on concrete issues such as getting a job, filling out application forms, or visiting potential employers. After an initial meeting, the service was voluntary. Service was available for 10 months, was provided on a one-to-one basis, and was flexible and individualized for the particular person. The "therapist" attempted to identify with the adolescent and pretended to know very little about the person's truant officer or other information identified with "the establishment." As contact continued, it included vocational counseling, advocacy, remedial education, and psychotherapy—all provided by the same professional.

The follow-up studies in this research have been quite dramatic. In each instance of follow-up, the treatment group has been found to be functioning at a significantly higher level than the control group. This difference is evident in better work histories, including higher pay, higher levels of employment, and more stable employment; better interpersonal relations, including higher rates of marriage and more stable marriages; and less likelihood of later legal difficulties, including lower rates of contact with legal authorities and less serious contact when it does occur. Not every case was successful, but the statistically significant differences between the two groups is dramatic (VandenBos and Miller, 1980).

In summary, there are some general findings in prevention programs for juvenile delinquents. In an extensive review of the literature, VandenBos and Miller (1980) identified several elements as related to the effectiveness of these programs: (1) a genuine interest in and commitment to the adolescents; (2) a nonjudgmental, helpful orientation; (3) multiple foci of problem resolution; (4) tailoring the system to the adolescent, not the adolescent to the system; (5) flexible programming that delivers help when it is needed; (6) strong training components; and (7) ongoing and meaningful program evaluation.

Prevention Programs in Industry   The industrial setting is a prime target for implementation of preventive programs. The staggering loss of time from absenteeism and inefficiency as a result of situations occurring on and off the job is a problem that virtually every organization faces. Family problems, stress, and drug and alcohol abuse are three common problems that impact worker effectiveness.

The industrial setting could lend itself easily to program implementation. Employees are a captive group, at least for about forty hours a week, and industry can exert influence on the individual as a result of the employer-employee relationship. However, prevention programs cost money, and, understandably, industry is disinclined to spend money when there is no evident problem.

Moreover, since what a person does outside the job is not the business of the employer unless it impacts on some phase of the job, industry is, in a sense, handcuffed from doing true primary prevention work. One plan, however, that possibly leads to some degree of primary prevention is to provide a great deal of information to employees and open channels of communication so that employees can seek help on their own. This plan depends on employees studying information and then independently following through—a low probability plan.

In studying industrial intervention programs to determine the extent to which they were primary or secondary prevention, Foote and Erfurt (1980) discovered that they were primarily secondary in nature, and they described four elements that contributed to this. First, most programs are unable to attempt primary prevention because they are overwhelmed with employee problems that have already developed. In addition, the proportion of the work force that industry is able to serve is not usually large enough to make much of an impact on overall plantwide performance figures. Third, industry aid programs are structured to provide a range of treatment services for which technologies exist and are not structured for primary prevention for which the technology is unknown. And finally, prevention of work performance problems is beyond the scope of industry aid programs to the extent that such problems are not caused by underlying health problems that the programs are equipped to address.

Consequently, it is not so surprising that industry is more involved in "secondary prevention." What usually happens is that industry identifies persons based on symptoms that cost the company money and attempts to intervene in the life situations of those individuals through an employee assistance program. Most of these assistance programs operate at three levels. The first level of intervention identifies either a problem behavior or a potential problem behavior, and at this point the person is encouraged to go to the second level, assessment. At this level, data are gathered and decisions made about movement to the third level, referral to an appropriate resource, most likely in the community.

Prevention in Community Mental Health Centers   Organized in the 1960s, the national network of community mental health centers has struggled to develop an identity that is congruent with its mission. The idea that psychological or emotional well-being is the responsibility of the community and not a select group of individuals or a single organization has been a difficult undertaking. The change requires a number of alterations in the "old" way of doing things. For instance, citizens must contribute manpower and funds for a wide variety of activities, money must be appropriated exclusively for prevention, and significant blocks of time must be devoted to developing and managing prevention programs. In addition, community leaders must "join hands" in a cooperative effort to support community-based projects. Finally, mental health professionals must "let go of" some of the responsibility for treatment. This last will entail the professionals' supporting training sessions for volunteers and finding appropriate methods to monitor paraprofessionals.

In spite of there being so many changes necessary to put prevention programs in place, there have been a number of successes in community mental health settings. As a result of the great diversity in client population, there are opportunities for a wide assortment of activities. Examples of populations served by community mental health centers in prevention programs are cited below. Of course, all centers are not engaged in extensive prevention work, but the list below indicates the diversity that exists.

1 Programs for adolescent parents
2 Stress management programs
3 Programs for homosexuals
4 Programs for rape victims

5 Programs for recently bereaved persons

6 Programs for couples who are infertile

7 Programs for divorced persons

8 Programs for pregnant women

9 Parenting skills programs

10 Marital enrichment programs

11 Programs to enhance self-image

12 Interpersonal skills programs

13 Decision-making programs

14 Leadership training programs

15 Educational groups on drug education

This list could go on and on. There are more opportunities for programming than there are staff to present programs. The key to program selection should be community need as opposed to a favorite topic of a presenter.

One noteworthy community health center in rural Kansas has been heavily involved in prevention activities for well over fifteen years. The program at Prairie View Mental Health Center in Newton, Kansas, has been described by Merrill Raber (1977) in the following list. One thing to note in studying this list of eighteen activities is the extensive use of community persons in the sponsorship and the delivery of the programs.

1 Mental health board education: Moving from supporting clinical services only to putting major priority on education, consultation, and prevention.

2 Community-staff study groups: Involving community caregivers as peers in discussing human/mental health issues together.

3 Luncheon groups: Regular meetings at the center for raising community awareness and sensitivity to mental health issues.

4 Community resource councils: Collaborative effort to meet with other agencies as "peers" to coordinate preventive services.

5 Teacher training programs: Include graduate credit for seminars on "teacher effectiveness" and "therapeutic intervention in the community for children with problems."

6 Family life education: Public seminars on topics such as depression, stress, and anger with community persons cosponsoring and leading small group discussions. Also included are county-based family life education councils, family life plays, Mothers' Day Out, and parenting seminars.

7 Community visiting nurse: Full-time effort to be available to intercept and work with families before referrals need to be made.

8 Seminar on counseling: Ongoing case-centered training for community caregivers, with monthly follow-up with therapist/consultant.

9 Child services coordinators: In each of the three counties, coordinators for total services to children to make sure children and their needs do not "fall between the cracks."

10 Jointly sponsored seminars: Relating to public policy and children. Funded by National Committee for the Humanities.

11 Employee assistance program: Training industrial supervisors in dealing with employees' personal problems.

12 Resources fair: Emphasis on collaborating with community and presenting total resources available for wide range of human problems.

13 Socialization groups: Effort to involve nursing home residents in growth-oriented activities with emphasis on training nursing home staffs.

14 Caring Place: Centered in downtown area for anyone needing and/ or desiring support, skill training, and socialization.

15 Worry Clinic: Opportunity for citizens to talk about things on their minds and to get response from resource persons.

16 Church and human relations: Community committee independently funded to work with staff in making local church congregations more effective in areas of prevention.

17 Leadership, Inc. (LINC): Community committee independently funded to work with community and staff in leadership training.

18 Growth Services (Growth Associates): A division of Prairie View totally designed for growth-oriented seminars, workshops, training events, and organization consultation. Examples: Human Experience Series, Weight Control Training, Gestalt Encounter, New Frontiers of Healing, Life Development Lab, Couples' Workshop, Human Interaction Labs, Psychosynthesis, and Fair Fight Training. (See Raber, 1977, pp. 104–105.)

It is obvious that the development and implementation of an array of programs as extensive as the one at Prairie View requires not only a commitment of money and staff time but also a tremendous amount of community support. As Raber noted in his article, "Getting community intellectual support is only half the battle; getting community involvement and participation in the planning and doing has been more difficult" (p. 105).

So, in summary, prevention is mandated for community mental health centers, but because of many constraints the centers have been slow in getting the programs in place. However, as indicated in this section, there are many programs that have been successful. It is apparent that community mental health centers in general are moving in the direction of establishing more prevention programs.

Current Trends in Prevention

Two major trends are noticeable in the field of prevention in mental health. Bloom (1979) has described a shift of interest from predisposing factors to precipitating factors as causal agents in the development of psychological disorders. Instead of searching for preconditions associated with a form of maladaptive behavior, researchers are focusing on stressful life events that appear to be capable of triggering patterns of maladaptive behavior in a proportion of the population that experiences those events. Thus the shift is from "high risk populations" to "high risk situations" (Price, Bader, and Ketterer, 1980). Bloom (1979) states it clearly when he says,

> Four vulnerable people can face a stressful life event—perhaps a collapse of their marriage, or the loss of their job. One person may become severely depressed; the second may be involved in an automobile accident; the third may head down the road to alcoholism; the fourth may develop a psychotic thought disorder, or coronary artery disease. (p. 183)

Even though there *are* populations that are at higher risk than the general population (unemployed, low income, uneducated), the shift from "high risk populations" to "high risk situations" recognizes that in addition to these high risk populations there are millions of others who can potentially be afflicted with similar disorders. Focusing on the generic skill deficits as emphasized in Life-Skills Training allows the prevention program to be delivered wherever the need exists independent of high risk population considerations.

The second development that Bloom describes is a shift of emphasis from the prevention of specific disorders (like schizophrenia and depression) to an interest in health promotion. Health promotion is a general term that refers to prevention that is carried out in a number of modes, such as television, radio, newspaper and magazine stories, and advertisements. The goal of health promotion is to encourage people to take a closer look at what they are doing personally to maintain good health and to give them content information and suggestions of lifestyle changes that will increase the likelihood that they will stay healthy. This, of course, is represented by the countless number of health food stores, exercise classes, weight reduction salons, physical fitness centers, and diet plans that have become popular in the last few years. Since mental health is so closely tied to feeling good about oneself and since these promotions encourage fitness which affects self-esteem, health promotion is potentially preventive in both physical and mental health.

This chapter has attempted to detail the scope of prevention programs in mental health and has discussed issues leading up to the present. Given the present situation, where do we go from here? Reactions to prevention programs range from highly enthusiastic to thoroughly negative—there is no widespread agreement either way. The field, however, seems to be moving toward acceptance, and breakthroughs are occurring in program development and research. The following areas, some summarized from Goldston (1977b), are important if the field of prevention is to continue to gain credibility and acceptance from the professional community and the general public.

Cooperation Between Agencies   In prevention programming, cooperation is the watchword. When projects are in the conception stage, a sponsoring organization has a multitude of possibilities for cosponsorship and shared goals. This approach helps to guarantee support and increases awareness of the effort in the community.

Cooperation Between Disciplines   Historically there has been little in the way of a working relationship between public health/physical health and mental health personnel. As noted earlier in this chapter, prevention programs were first conceived in a public health setting, and physical health situations are so often related to mental health that the linkage seems to be a natural one.

Outreach   Programming where the people are and where the needs are defines outreach. Traditional helping has worked just opposite of this approach: a person sought a program, agency, or helper. The passive, remedial approach must be replaced with high visibility preventive approaches that are taken outside the four walls of an office and into a community.

Focus on Developmental Tasks   Since it is generally agreed that there are optimal times to learn certain tasks, prevention programs could conceivably focus on activities devoted to helping others achieve the developmental tasks associated with their age. This preventive activity could certainly happen in the public schools and also could be a major part of community mental health activities.

Aggressively Seek Funds and Other Support   Four things in this area seem to be crucial for the continued success of prevention programming: encouragement, money, public support, and a clear mandate for prevention activities. Since many prevention programs break with tradition, it sometimes takes assertive leadership to work cooperatively yet deliberately with the holders of the "purse strings."

Establishment of Self-help Groups   Since self-help groups are dedicated to prevention, though they do remedial work also, community organizers and mental health professionals should encourage the establishment of self-help groups in the community. To be most effective, those groups should receive support, encouragement, and cooperation from the mental health community. Most self-help groups are inexpensive, effective, and, with cooperation from other agencies, can have a significant input on the community in the realm of prevention.

In spite of all of the barriers, pitfalls, and political issues, recent happenings show promise in the area of prevention. The President's Commission on Mental Health highlighted the need for a national policy on prevention and health promotion. An Office on Prevention has been established within the National Institute of Mental Health to promote the development of research and policy on prevention. States have begun to develop plans for prevention programming in response to federal intentions to decentralize control of prevention resources to the states. And prevention professionals have begun working with state and federal policymakers to develop better guidelines for prevention programs and to advocate additional resources (Price, Bader, and Ketterer, 1980). These are encouraging signs that keep researchers and prevention practitioners moving forward. Primary prevention, as heralded by Albee (1978), is destined to be the "fourth revolution" in society's approach to mental illness.

SUMMARY

Remediation in mental health is a process used by helping professionals to treat persons who exhibit symptoms of emotional distress. The heart and soul of the mental health system, remedial strategies for any given group or individual may last only a few sessions or extend for years. Taking place in the schools, at the work place, in communities, and in families, remediation involves utilizing one or more of an array of effective intervention strategies available to counselors, social workers, and psychotherapists.

Though firmly entrenched in the training programs as a primary goal, i.e., treatment of symptoms that already exist, remediation is beginning to share the spotlight with preventive strategies designed to reduce the frequency of onset of symptoms in a given population. As a concept, it is rooted in physical health, specifically public health, but it has demonstrated applicability in mental health.

Opponents of primary prevention activities argue that a research base has not been established. Also, they argue that the public will not pay for the services unless there is an identified patient with an identified problem. However, in spite of the theoretical and financial barriers, prevention activities are increasing throughout the country. There are success stories in schools, prisons, industry, and community mental health centers as described in this chapter. As more and more success stories surface, the prevention movement in mental health gains credibility as a legitimate activity for mental health professionals.

REFERENCES

Albee, G. W. (1978). Report of the task panel on prevention. In D. G. Forgays (Ed.), *Primary prevention of psychopathology, Vol. 2, Environmental influences* (pp. 207–249). Hanover, NH: University Press of New England.

Albee, G. W. (1984). A model for classifying prevention programs. In J. M. Joffe, G. W. Albee, & L. D. Kelly (Eds.), *Readings in primary prevention of psychopathology* (pp. ix–xviii). Hanover, NH: University Press of New England.

Bloom, B. L. (1979). Prevention of mental disorders: Recent advances in theory and practice. *Community Mental Health Journal, 15,* 179–191.

Bloom, M. (1981). A working definition of primary prevention related to social concerns. In M. Nobel (Ed.), *Primary prevention in mental health and social work* (pp. 5–12). New York: Council on Social Work Education.

Bronfenbrenner, U. (1974). *A report on longitudinal evaluation of preschool programs, Vol. 2, Is early intervention effective?* Washington, DC: U. S. Government Printing Office.

Charter medical care: Zeroing in on neglected areas in psychiatric care. (1982, July). *Business Week,* 75–76.

Cowen, E. L. (1984). Demystifying primary prevention. In J. M. Joffe, G. W. Albee, & L. D. Kelly (Eds.), *Readings in primary prevention of psychopathology* (pp. 36–51). Hanover, NH: University Press of New England.

Foote, A., & Erfurt, J. C. (1980). Prevention in industrial settings. In R. H. Price, R. F. Ketterer, B. C. Bader, & J. Monahan (Eds.), *Prevention in mental health: Research, policy and practice* (pp. 151–165). Beverly Hills, CA: Sage Publications.

Garfield, S. L. (1983). *Clinical psychology.* Chicago: Aldine.

Goldston, S. E. (1977a). An overview of primary prevention programming. In D. C. Klein & S. E. Goldston (Eds.), *Primary prevention: An idea whose time has come* (pp. 23–42). Washington, DC: U. S. Government Printing Office.

Goldston, S. E. (1977b). Defining primary prevention. In G. W. Albee & J. M. Joffe (Eds.), *Primary prevention of psychopathology* (pp. 18–23). Hanover, NH: University Press of New England.

Griffin, J. D. (1968). Public education and school procedures. In F. C. R. Chalke & J. J. Day (Eds.), *Primary prevention of psychiatric disorders* (pp. 149–161). Toronto: University of Toronto Press.

Hartley, W. S. (1977). Preventive outcomes of affective education with school age children. In D. C. Klein & S. E. Goldston (Eds.), *Primary prevention: An idea whose time has come* (pp. 69–75). Washington, DC: U. S. Government Printing Office.

Jason, L. A. (1980). Prevention in the schools: Behavioral approaches. In R. H. Price, R. C. Ketterer, B. C. Bader, & J. Monahan (Eds.), *Prevention in mental health: Research, policy and practice* (pp. 109–134). Beverly Hills, CA: Sage Publications.

Kiesler, C. (1983). A top-down look at public policy. *APA Monitor, 9,* 5.

Klein, D. C., & Goldston, S. E. (Eds.) (1977). *Primary prevention: An idea whose time has come.* Washington, DC: U. S. Government Printing Office.

Lewis, J. A., & Lewis, M. D. (1984). Preventive programs in action. *The Personnel and Guidance Journal, 9,* 550–553.

Massimo, J., & Shore, M. (1963). The effectiveness of a comprehensive vocationally oriented psychotherapy program for adolescent delinquent boys. *American Journal of Orthopsychiatry, 33,* 634–643.

Morales, A., & Sheafor, B. W. (1983). *Social work: A profession of many faces* (3d ed.). Boston: Allyn and Bacon.

Murphy, L. B., & Chandler, C. A. (1972). Building foundations for strength in the preschool years: Preventing developmental disturbances. In S. E. Golann & C. Eisdorfer (Eds.), *Handbook of community mental health* (pp. 303–330). New York: Appleton-Century-Crofts.

Palmer, T. (1971). California's community treatment program for delinquent adolescents. *Journal of Research in Crime and Delinquency, 8,* 74–92.

Pardes, H. (1983). Health/manpower/policy: A perspective from the NIMH. *American Psychologist, 38,* 1355–1359.

Patterson, G. R., & Reid, J. B. (1970). Reciprocity and coercion: Two facets of social systems. In C. Neuringer & J. Michael (Eds.), *Behavior modification in clinical psychology* (pp. 133–177). New York: Appleton-Century-Crofts.

Persons, R. W. (1967). Relationship between psychotherapy with institutionalized boys and subsequent community adjustment. *Journal of Consulting Psychology, 31,* 137–141.

Plaut, T. (1982). Primary prevention in the '80's: The interface with community support systems. In E. E. Biegel & A. J. Naparstek (Eds.), *Community support systems and mental health* (pp. 86–97). New York: Springer Publishing.

President's Commission on Mental Health. (1978). *Report of the task panel on prevention.* Washington, DC: U. S. Government Printing Office.

President's Commission on Mental Health (1978). *Report to the president from the president's commission on mental health.* Washington, DC: U. S. Government Printing Office.

Price, R. H., Bader, B. C., & Ketterer, R. F. (1980). Prevention in community mental health. In R. H. Price, R. F. Ketterer, B. C. Bader, and J. Monahan (Eds.), *Prevention in mental health: Research, policy and practice* (pp. 9–20). Beverly Hills, CA: Sage Publications.

Raber, M. F. (1977). Involvement of the community in primary prevention. In D. C. Klein & S. E. Goldston (Eds.), *Primary prevention: An idea whose time has come* (pp. 103–105). Washington, DC: U. S. Government Printing Office.

Reitz, A. L., & Hawkins, R. P. (1981). Using volunteer staff to increase severely debilitated nursing home residents' participation in recreation activities. *International Journal of Behavioral Geriatrics, 2,* 5–7.

Strain, J. J. (1978). *Psychological intervention in medical practice.* New York: Appleton-Century-Crofts.

Selling sobriety: Alcoholism treatment for profit. One of the fastest growing markets in health care. (1982). *Forbes, 13,* 59–63.

VandenBos, G. R., & Miller, M. O. (1980). Delinquency prevention program. In R. H. Price, R. F. Ketterer, B. C. Bader, & J. Monahan (Eds.), *Prevention in mental health: Research, policy and practice* (pp. 135–150). Beverly Hills, CA: Sage Publications.

CHAPTER 5

COMMUNITY RESOURCES: ORGANIZATION AND MISSION

The human services professions are a wide array of disciplines that share a common goal: serving people. Primarily developing along independent pathways, the professions made little effort to work cooperatively; consequently, much overlap and territorial ambiguity has developed among service providers. Perhaps as an effect of this, human services programs or community resource programs have been implemented in a fragmented and uncoordinated fashion.

The human services now claim more than 2000 careers in ten major areas including child care, community service, corrections, education, health, housing, law, mental health, social services, and vocational education. As the numbers of people served by these agencies have increased and as cost for services have increased, taxpayers have become aware of opportunities for cooperation among the disciplines, agencies, and programs. Translating awareness of a problem to a workable plan of attack is a formidable task indeed; however, because of dwindling resources and a mandate from the people, efforts at interdisciplinary cooperation are increasing. In this chapter, we will examine, briefly, the history of human services and then explore the problem of coordination of services.

HISTORY OF HUMAN SERVICES

Community resources in the human services area have evolved primarily since the 1940s. It was apparent following World War II that there was a great inequity in terms of who (or, more accurately, what social class) was the primary recipient of services. Those who had the financial means to purchase services received services. The lower socioeconomic classes had to "go it alone," and, consequently, they represented the majority in jails, mental hospitals, and among the unemployed and uneducated. Without money or clout, this larger part of our population was either left out or treated inequitably in medical care, mental health services, legal representation, and education.

In the 1950s, even as more persons were trained professionally in human service areas, the primary recipients of service, apart from the few who were served for training purposes in public institutions, were middle- and upper-class whites. So the system operated with persons who had the greatest need receiving very little in the way of human services.

Because of research data as well as a strong national sense of frustration, there has been constant change in the United States in the direction of services for the needy. During the last three decades, community mental health centers have all but shut down the centralized mental hospitals; legal representation is available through legal aid and other organizations for virtually everyone; health centers provide medical attention for those who cannot afford private medical services; and other social agencies ensure that food, clothing, and shelter are available to the population. With the rapid proliferation of services, with the diversity of professions involved, and with the local, state, and federal jurisdiction differences, the sheer enormity of the system makes for a considerable amount of confusion, overlapping services, and a general lack of coordination.

The social issues that are addressed in our present system of human services delivery had gotten quite out of hand by the time Americans demanded help for the needy. Even today, years after the social programs have been implemented, there remain many problems to be addressed. In detailing some of the present-day dilemmas, Eriksen (1981) mentions the following:

- Thirty-seven percent of hospital beds house mental patients.
- Nine to ten million Americans are alcoholics.
- Two hundred thousand Americans are drug addicts.
- One out of 6 American children will be a juvenile delinquent.
- Organized crime reaps over $7 billion each year.
- The recidivism rate for prisoners is 60 percent.
- At least 1 million children will be abused by their parents this year; over 10 million will be neglected.
- Over 3.5 million Americans are being treated for emotional problems.

Grim figures, but true. And many times there seems to be an insensitivity to the problem by politicians and middle-class Americans. The "out of sight, out of mind" philosophy of many Americans allowed the mental health situation to reach epidemic proportions before anything was done.

The main concept that has grown out of this early social movement is the idea of deinstitutionalization in mental health. The theory here is that keeping persons incarcerated in jails, mental hospitals, and general hospitals far from their homes and families actually impedes their recovery. The resulting program has been a massive effort at rehabilitation through the local human services network *in the individual's community* where more individual attention is possible; where therapy or rehabilitation can be attempted with small groups; and where there is potentially a support system among the person's family, neighbors, and friends.

The concept of deinstitutionalization of services is a good one—on paper. In reality there continue to be major problems in the delivery of services to those who are eligible. Services are in short supply and coordination between service agencies, necessary to implement the concept, is frequently inadequate.

HUMAN SERVICES COORDINATION

Without doubt, the human services network is one of the most difficult to control in terms of one person or agency affecting change throughout the network. In improving delivery, we need to make the services more comprehensive, accessible, effective, and accountable as well as less duplicative and fragmented. In addition, it would be useful to provide more control over programs or impose a different management scheme to the programs. This would enable us to gain flexibility in the use of funds, personnel, and facilities; to make the experience of receiving services easier on the client; and to consolidate budgeting, planning, and information services.

We can accomplish these goals for human resources through coordination. As Dempsey (1982) defines it, coordination is a process, or series of mechanisms, for exchanging, codirecting, and/or pooling resources (by referrals, information, physical space, personnel, and funds) for more efficient or effective goal achievement. Included within this framework are six categories of coordination, some with particular advantages or disadvantages (Dempsey, 1982):

1 *Organizational realignment.* Coordination here many times involves a change in leadership with the "pecking order" being changed internally. Even though on paper the system will operate more effectively with realignment, there is typically a great deal of resistance to it. However, more and more states are moving in this direction by having a single administrator in charge of an umbrella group of human services units.

2 *Interorganizational decision making.* When there is not a single individual "in charge" in human services, it is often the case that representatives come together from different disciplines in human services for the purpose of resolving conflict, building bridges between service areas, and brainstorming ways of making services more accessible to the clientele groups.

3 *Ad hoc response to crisis.* When true crises develop, most states have a system in place that allows them to bypass normal channels to get the job done. This type of "forced coordination" seems to work temporarily—at least until the crisis is resolved.

4 *Allocation of resources (budgeting).* The allocation of resources is probably the most powerful force requiring agencies to formalize coordination efforts.

5 *Efforts to ensure information sharing.* Most communities have at one time or another made an effort to compile a directory of services with comprehensive information of interest to prospective clients. However, this method of coordination is very difficult to maintain because of the constant flux of the organizations. The use of computers should have a positive impact on this problem and allow more communities to provide comprehensive information at one stop.

6 *Efforts to enhance delivery service with "one-stop" centers.* The "co-location" concept allows clients to get many services under one roof, so to speak. This has expanded to a common intake in some communities. The concept does not solve the problem of information sharing, however, as experience has shown that persons do not necessarily know anything about other operations, even if they are just down the hall.

COORDINATION STRATEGIES

As we mentioned previously, fragmentation in the human services has led to a movement of coordination and merging of various agencies in order for the system to operate smoothly. Although some states have let the independent agencies continue to function and work toward building in coordination wherever possible, others have embraced either the integration concept or the generic services concept as methods to coordinate services. The human services integration concept, as Parham (1982) explains, involved the "linking together by various means the services of two or more service providers to allow treatment of an individual's or family's needs in a more coordinated and comprehensive manner" (p. 62). This process is conceptualized as an "umbrella" agency with a central administration responsible for all of the public human services in a state.

A second answer to the fragmentation in the human services is the concept of generic human services. This concept is based on the premise that human problems should be addressed with a problem-solution orientation as opposed to labeling gross symptoms and directing persons to mental health services, health departments, correctional systems, or other specific agencies for a specific problem. The individual who deals with clients in a generic system can be viewed as a generalist change agent. As Mehr (1980) summarizes, the generic field of human services can be defined as follows:

> Human services is the field of endeavor that helps individuals cope with problems in living which are expressed in psychological, behavioral, or legal terminology; and that is characterized by an integrated/pragmatic approach focusing on problem solution within the client's life space utilizing change strategies affecting both the internal person and his/her external environment (p. 53).

This generic approach to human services uses a generalist in the delivery of the services. The focus is on providing service with the least interruption by incorporating a mixture of attitudes, approaches, and behaviors from the other professions. The trade-off here is convenience for the client in place of dealing with a profession-specific person or agency. The hope of generic human service personnel is that someday the subsystems will not exist *per se* and individuals can be dealt with through one system based on problem solutions rather than labels relating to gross problem symptoms.

SUPPORT FOR COORDINATION

For any of the coordination attempts to be successful, particularly the generic strategy, professional disciplines must be able to work together and agree upon the appropriate functions for human service workers. As we have mentioned before in this text, we believe the various mental health disciplines share enough commonality to support effective interdisciplinary cooperation. In particular, people who work with people in a helping role share a common knowledge base that is a prerequisite for developing occupation-specific skills (Erikson, 1981). Grouped into four categories, these prerequisites are identified by Eriksen (1981) as knowledge of history, knowledge of society, knowledge of people, and knowledge of resources. Two of these prerequisites, knowledge of society and knowledge of history, are acquired through comprehensive reading and study of materials that are readily available in books and courses at the college level. These two areas of knowledge, also, are national or international in scope. The other two areas, knowledge of people and knowledge of resources, are region-specific, and successful mastery requires a multimodal approach.

The skill of acquiring knowledge of people requires a combination of life experiences, study, and skill acquisition. Almost everyone has chuckled at the "academic" or "halls-of-ivy" type who seems to have an immense amount of textbook information about a subject, but much of it is unrealistic because it is not tempered with the reality of life, the reality of a region, or the reality of a certain group of people. Data must be analyzed within the context of the situation, and this reality is most important when it comes to learning about people. The extent to which a human services person combines "real world" knowledge with textbook or theoretical information determines, in part, his or her effectiveness with the clientele group. The "real world" orientation also explains, in part, the effectiveness that paraprofessionals have in working with human services clients. Also, the work experience requirement for many human services positions is a recognition of the importance of a mix of theoretical understanding and life experiences. In addition, one of the key factors for success in human services is a knowledge of the community, state, and national resources available to a clientele group. Although some of this knowledge can be acquired through reference books and other academic means (see Appendix B), much of the specialty knowledge required to succeed in utilization of resources is not written in books. The doors open not as a result of a telephone call as much as a personal, face-to-face interaction with representatives of other agencies. In other words, *personal* exploration of community resources allows a human services worker the advantages of (1) knowing the name of a particular individual at the referral site, (2) actually knowing where the resource is located and any features that might be tricky or out of the ordinary, (3) knowing specifically the other agencies' criteria for serving their clientele, and (4) knowing other varied bits of information and nuances that might make it easier for the referral to be successful. Bureaucratic walls are broken down not through additional bureaucratic directives as much as through personal relationship development. Therefore, this factor is a key component in successful community resource utilization by human services. As part of a generic knowledge base, knowledge of people together with knowledge of history, society, and resources enable professionals to communicate, cooperate, and coordinate either across disciplines or in a generic fashion.

Other support for coordination of human services can be construed as developing from the roles and levels of the service workers. With the many service agencies and the wide variety of helping persons, it is not surprising that ambiguity and disagreement have existed with regard to training and job expectations. In an attempt to develop some agreement, the Southern Region Education Board (SREB) undertook a project to put in writing the levels and role functions of human services workers (SREB, 1969). The following resulted from the project:

Levels of Competence
Level I: Entry Level—In-service instructor with little experience.

Level II: Apprentice Level—Substantial formal training or experience (equivalent to 2-year degree).

Level III: Journeyman—Substantial formal training or experience (equivalent to undergraduate degree).

Level IV: Master or Professional Level—Highly competent (equivalent to master's or doctorate).

Role Functions

1 Outreach Worker—Detects problems, refers, follows up.

2 Broker—Helps people get to existing services.

3 Advocate—Works to initiate services, policies, laws for client's benefit.

4 Evaluator—Assesses needs; formulates plans.

5 Teacher-Educator—Performs instructional activities.

6 Behavior Changer—Performs coaching, counseling, casework, and psychotherapy.

7 Mobilizer—Helps to get new resources.

8 Consultant—Works with other agencies regarding their handling of problems, needs, and programs.

9 Community planner—Assesses that community developments minimize emotional stress and strain on people.

10 Caregiver—Provides ongoing support for those in need (for example, day care, financial assistance).

11 Data Manager—Performs all aspects of data handling, tabulating, planning.

12 Administrator—Carries out agency or institution-oriented activities.

13 Assistant to Specialist—Acts as assistant to physician, psychologist, or nurse.

Even though there are variations from state to state as a result of existing organizational structure, more and more of these functions are being accepted as descriptive of the tasks of humans services workers. With levels of competence and roles becoming more standardized, interdisciplinary cooperation can function to impact the barriers to coordination.

BARRIERS TO COORDINATION

If the notion of coordination makes so much sense, why are all human services not coordinated? The answer lies in the enormity of the programs and their resultant bureaucratic red tape, together with the fact that so many different professions are represented. Even so, the citizenry seems to feel that coordination is the key to effective operation of human services systems. As a result, coordination attempts continue to be mandated by legislation.

The primary barriers to coordination in the human services have been outlined by Sauber (1983):

1 *Complexity of agencies.* As an example, there are four main types of health organizations within the health system: Official or public agencies, volunteer or nonprofit agencies, hospitals and nursing homes, and welfare and social agencies. Add to this five mutual self-help groups concerned with health problems, and the organizations becomes so unwieldly that it does not readily lend itself to coordination.

2 *Mixed authority.* Since the autonomous service agencies have their own hierarchy, after coordination who reports to whom? The politics of this inhibits cooperation; thus coordination becomes more difficult.

3 *Specialization.* With so many specialists, all with their own "turf," coordination is a difficult task to accomplish.

4 *Deficient communication.* There are probably as many reasons for this as there are persons in the agencies.

5 *Stereotyped beliefs and attitudes.* Resistance to change and comfort in status quo affect one's ability to coordinate agencies.

6 *Difficulty in defining the primary task.* There are frequently multiple goals that may or may not be compatible. One agency's thinking and action plan may be taking a client in direction *A* while another agency might be steering the client in direction *B*.

The barriers are not different here from most found in any large, diverse organization. With the citizenry behind a move toward more coordination, there should be more and more progress made in this area. As we will mention next, there are many seemingly positive outcomes for making the effort.

COORDINATION BENEFITS

The discussion of coordination is not all negative. There are genuine efforts being made, and the opportunities for coordination are limited only by the imagination of service providers (and externally imposed constraints). The following list developed by Azarnoff and Seliger (1982) indicates the diversity of cooperation and coordination and can be used to generate beneficial efforts:

1 Co-location of staff members
2 Joint outreach and/or intake
3 Consolidation of records on common clients
4 Outstationing of personnel in cooperating agencies, sites, etc.
5 Integrated client support (e.g., transportation)
6 Case consultation or conferencing
7 Sharing of volunteers
8 Information exchange
9 Joint training

10 Centralized accounting or data storage
11 Joint proposal development
12 Consultation
13 Shared equipment purchases and operation
14 Alliances for advocacy and legislation
15 Technology transfers
16 Shared evaluations
17 Shared personnel activities (e.g., transfer benefit packages)

This list is impressive in terms of the potential benefit coordination could have upon the client. Also as a secondary benefit there could be a positive perception of the agency by the clientele group and by the community by virtue of the client-oriented approach.

Even with the barriers, there has been success in coordination efforts. As mentioned previously, the umbrella departments are an attempt at coordination. In addition, there has been an attempt in many states at colocation of services and the use of a common intake form. States, counties, and cities have typically taken these steps. Dempsey (1982) has indicated, however, that a concerted effort by federal, state, and local governments to coordinate programs is much needed yet conspicuously absent. The most probable incident in which coordination takes place is in a crisis situation, but the coordination disappears as the client's symptoms are dealt with by various agencies. Given the maze of human services and the ability level of the majority of their clients, coordination seems like a logical step in the right direction. Time will tell if the system is uncontrollable or whether some logical, rational thought can go into the coordination of services.

SUMMARY

The human services community resources have developed primarily since the 1940s as a result of an obvious deficit of services for those who had no means of obtaining services privately. The term human services encompasses health, education, social services, mental health, child care, corrections, housing, vocational rehabilitation, law, and community service. The fact that there are so many professions represented as well as the fact that their development as community services was splintered as opposed to coordinated has resulted in a great deal of red tape and profession-specific isolationism between services. States have attempted to gain more control over the agencies in order to serve the clientele group more efficiently by forming umbrella agencies at the state level (Department of Natural Resources, for example) in some states and developing generic human services workers in other states. Changes are slow in coming at the national level although there are examples of well-functioning systems in some areas of the country.

There is a strong voice from the people for efficiency in human services delivery. This citizenry demand for coordination and cooperation between agencies in order to serve the clientele group more efficiently and in order to save money may very well impact in a positive way on a system that is unwieldy and in which there is no easy solution.

REFERENCES

Azarnoff, R. S., & Seliger, J. S. (1982). *Delivering human services.* Englewood Cliffs, NJ: Prentice-Hall.

Dempsey, J. T. (1982). Coordination of human services for the 1980's. In H. Orlans (Ed.), *Human services coordination* (pp. 96–114). New York: Pica Press.

Eriksen, K. (1981). *Human services today.* Reston, VA: Reston Publishing.

Mehr, J. (1980). *Human services: Concepts and intervention strategies.* Boston: Allyn and Bacon.

Parham, T. M. J. (1982). Services and coordination in the south. In H. Orlans (Ed.), *Human services coordination* (pp. 62–77). New York: Pica Press.

Sauber, S. R. (1983). *The human services delivery system.* New York: Columbia University Press.

Southern Regional Education Board Community Mental Health Worker Project. (1969). *Roles and functions for different levels of mental health workers.* Atlanta: Author.

CHAPTER 6

PROFESSIONAL ETHICS

Each of the human services professions has a code of ethics that serves to guide its members in the conduct of their relations with clients, interested parties, peers, and the legal system. There are general codes of ethics that are designed to provide basic guidelines to the professions as a whole and there are specialty guidelines and/or standards that address ethical issues germane to each particular profession. The purpose of this chapter is to identify the core ethics and differentiate between the several professions as they diverge from the core ethics. We will discuss the various ethical considerations that are either common to all involved professions or are unique to each organization.

CODES OF ETHICS OF THE HUMAN SERVICE PROFESSIONS

What follows is a listing of the various codes of ethics, specialty guidelines, and standards, together with their sources. A chart (see Figure 6-1) has been provided as an aid to the reader in referencing particular subjects within each code, guideline, or standard.

Professional Codes of Ethics

  I A Ethical Principles of Psychologists (American Psychological Association, 1981a).

 II A Specialty Guidelines for the Delivery of Services by Clinical Psychologists (American Psychological Association, 1981b).

American Psychological Association, Ethical Principles for Psychologists

Ethical codes or guidelines of professionals involved in human services agencies, public and private	1 Responsibility	2 Competence	3 Moral and legal standards	4 Public statements	5 Confidentiality	6 Welfare of the consumer	7 Professional relationships	8 Assessment techniques*	9 Research with human participants	10 Care and use of animals
Ethical Standards, American Personnel and Guidance Association (American Association for Counseling & Development)†	B.4 D.3 E.6 B.10 D.8 F.1 B.11 D.13 G.2 C.11 D.15 G.3 C.12 E.1 G.4 E.4 G.7	A.1 E.3 A.4 G.1 A.7 G.5 C.4 G.6 E.1 G.9	A.2 F.3 A.3 F.4 A.8 F.5 D.11 F.6 E.5	A.6 C.3 D.7 F.2	A.6 B.2 B.5 B.6 D.10	A.2 B.7 C.7 A.5 B.8 E.2 A.8 B.10 E.6 B.1 B.11 G.8 B.4 B.13	B.3 D.12 B.9 D.14 B.14 F.3 D.9 D.11	C.1 C.7 C.2 C.8 C.3 C.9 C.5 C.10 C.6	B.11 D.5 D.1 D.6 D.2 D.7 D.3 D.8 D.4 D.9 D.10	
Code of Ethics for Certified Clinical Mental Health counselors, National Academy of Certified Clinical Mental Health Counselors‡	1a 6b 7e 1b 6c 1c 6g 5d 7c 6a 7d	2a 2c 2d 8d	3a 3c 3d 3e 6b	3a 4e 4a 8g 4b 4c 4d	5a 5g 5b 5j 5c 8g 5e 9j 5f	1e 5h 6a 2e 5i 6f 3e 5j 6h 3f 6a 8h 5g 6d	1a 7e 9f 1f 7f 4g 7g 7a 9b 7b 9e	2d 8d 8a 8f 8b 8g 8c	9a 9g 9b 9h 9c 9i 9d	
Specialty Guidelines for the Delivery of Services by Clinical Psychologists	1.1 3.4 1.2 1.3 1.4	1.5 1.6 1.7 1.8	2.2.2 3.2 2.2.3 3.3 2.2.4 4.1 2.3.4	2.1.2	2.3.5	2.1.1 2.3.1 2.1.3 2.3.2 2.2.1 2.3.3 2.2.2 3.1 2.2.5 3.2 2.2.6 4.1	2.2.5 2.2.6			
Specialty Guidelines for the Delivery of Services by Counseling Psychologists	1.1 3.4 1.2 1.3 1.4	1.5 1.6 1.7 1.8	2.2.2 3.2 2.2.3 3.3 2.2.4 4.1 2.3.4	2.1.2	2.3.5	2.1.1 2.3.1 2.1.3 2.3.2 2.2.1 2.3.3 2.2.2 3.1 2.2.5 3.2 2.2.6 4.1	2.2.5 2.2.6			
Specialty Guidelines for the Delivery of Services by School Psychologists	1.1 1.2 1.3 1.4 3.4	1.5 1.6 1.7 1.8	2.2.2 3.2 2.2.3 3.3 2.2.4 4.1 2.3.4	2.1.2	2.3.5	2.1.1 2.3.1 2.1.3 2.3.2 2.2.1 2.3.3 2.2.2 3.1 2.2.5 3.2 2.2.6 4.1	2.2.5 2.2.6			

Code / Profession								
Speciality Guidelines for the Delivery of Services by Industrial/Organizational Psychologists	1.1 1.2 1.3 1.4	2.1 3.2 2.2 2.3 2.5			2.7	2.1 3.2 2.4 2.5 3.1		2.6
Code of Professional Ethics, American Association for Marriage and Family Therapy	I(1) II(4)	I(6) I(7)	I(2) IV(1) I(3) I(8) III(1)	V**	II(3)	I(1) II(4) I(8) II(1) III(2)	I(4) IV(1) I(5) I(9) III(2)	III(1)
Code of Ethics, National Association of Social Workers	I.C V.M I.D V.N II.I VI.P IV.L	I.B V.O	I.A VI.P I.D II.G V.M		II.H	I.F II.G II.I III.K	III.J III.K V.M	I.E
Standards for the Private Practice of Clinical Social Work, National Association of Social Workers	I.C V.C III.A VI.F III.C VII.E V.B VII.F	I.A I.E I.B VI.E I.C I.D	II III.B V.K III.D VI.B V.A VI.D V.F VI.F	V.6	IV*** V.E VI.C	V.D V.H V.E V.I V.F VII.A V.G VII.C	V.H VII.D V.K VII.E VII.A VII.B	
Principles of Medical Ethics, with Annotations Especially Applicable to Psychiatry, American Psychiatric Association	1(3) 5(5) 2(7) 7(1) 5(3) 7(2) 5(4)	2(3) 2(4) 3(2) 5(1) 5(4)	1(2) 4(2) 1(4) 4(9) 2(1) 4(13) 2(2) 6(1) 3(1) 7(4) 3(2)	7(1) 7(3)	4(1) 4(2) 4(3) 4(4) 4(5) 4(7) 4(9) 4(10)	1(1) 4(7) 2(1) 4(11) 2(2) 4(13) 2(5) 5(5) 2(6) 7(4) 4(6)	2(7) 2(8) 5(2) 7(1)	4(12)
American Nurses' Association Standards: Psychiatric Mental Health Nursing Practice	II X III XII IV XIV	VI XII XIII				II VII V IX VI X	VIII XI	I
Code for Nurses	5 7 8	3 5 7	1	10	2	4 6	9	6

*Does not include separate treatment by APA entitled "Ethical Principles in the Conduct of Research with Human Participants."

**Incorporates set of standards on public information and advertising. AAMFT Code also includes section describing procedures used upon receipt of complaint of unethical practice.

***Appendix I

†APGA (AACD) ethics also include a section on preparation (training of others) standards.

‡NACCMHC codes have 5 subsections (1d, 2b, 3b, 4f, 6c) related to teaching

FIGURE 6-1

A Comparison of Codes of Ethis of Seven Human Services Professions with the American Psychological Association's Ethical Principles.

B Specialty Guidelines for the Delivery of Services by Counseling Psychologists (American Psychological Association, 1981c).

C Specialty Guidelines for the Delivery of Services by Industrial/Organizational Psychologists (American Psychological Association, 1981d).

D Specialty Guidelines for the Delivery of Services by School Psychologists (American Psychological Association, 1981e).

III A Ethical Standards (American Personnel and Guidance Association, (APGA), 1981). (now American Association for Counseling and Development, AACD)

B Code of Ethics for Certified Clinical Mental Health Counselors (National Academy of Certified Clinical Mental Health Counselors, 1980–81).

C Code of Professional Ethics (American Association for Marriage and Family Therapy, n.d.).

IV A Code of Ethics (National Association of Social Workers, 1979).

B Standards for the Private Practice of Clinical Social Work (National Association of Social Workers, 1981)

V A The Code for Nurses: The Ten Points (American Nurses' Association, 1976).

V B American Nurses' Association Standards of Psychiatric Mental Health Nursing Practice (American Nurses' Association, 1976).

VI A Principles of Medical Ethics, with Annotations Especially Applicable to Psychiatry (American Psychiatric Association, 1981).

VII A Ethical Principles in the Conduct of Research with Human Participants (American Psychological Association, 1973).

Common and Unique Features

Because of their general applicability to all persons engaged in providing mental health services (except for psychiatrists who follow their own similar code), the American Psychological Association's Ethical Principles of Psychologists (1981a), hereinafter referred to as the APA Principles, are used here as the standard for comparison with the ethics of other human services professions. These other human service professions include students of psychology, nurses, social workers, counselors, and other people who work in the field of human services either alone or under the supervision of a licensed practitioner.

Persons who are not licensed by their state to practice as psychologists are generally required to work under the supervision of a licensed psychologist or a psychiatrist. These individuals are bound by the ethical principles adopted by the APA and any other professional organization to which they belong. Such principles are intended for the guidance of anyone who is engaged in psychological practice and/or research even though that individual might not be a member of any particular professional organization.

In comparing other codes, standards, and guidelines with the APA Principles, we will utilize the existing division of the APA Principles. More specifically, the APA Principles are divided into ten major areas. Each of the other related codes of ethics will be examined in light of the ten areas set out under the APA Principles. Whenever one code differs significantly from other codes or standards, that fact will be pointed out either in the text or in the "Comments" section of Figure 6-1. In addition, for purposes of brevity, the separate Specialty Guidelines for Clinical, Counseling, School, and Industrial/Organizational psychologists will be referred to as the Specialty Guidelines unless there is a need to discuss any one specialty guideline separately.

Figure 6-1 represents all of the major professional codes of ethics and standards. It is meant to be an easy reference guide to each of the codes and should not be considered an exact representation of what each section of any particular code contains. Notice the ten major headings across the top of the chart. Each of these headings is drawn from and represents the APA Principles. The descending column on the left represents the other major codes of ethics and standards which have been categorized so as to fit within one or more of the ten APA Principles.

Before addressing the codes in a specific manner, a brief review of the chart reveals some general information. For instance, the principles of responsibility to and welfare of the consumer garner most of the attention of these various codes and standards. Some areas, such as public statements and assessment techniques, are hardly addressed by most of the documents while one principle, the care and use of animals, is addressed only by the APA Principles. One area, research using human participants, is dealt with more fully in a document which is separate from all of the codes, including the APA Principles (APA, 1973). The professional distinctions and commonalities will be examined more specifically as we compare codes with each of the ten APA Principles.

APA Principle 1: Responsibility   This principle relates to the responsibility of psychologists to maintain the highest standards of conduct in their profession. Psychologists are charged with the duty to accept responsibility for the consequences of their behavior and with the duty to make sure their services are used appropriately. Principle 1 includes responsibility for work in research, in the sharing of research data, in professional membership standards, in teaching, and in actual practice (public and private).

The Specialty Guidelines for Clinical (1981b), Counseling (1981c), and

School (1981e) psychologists are almost identical in their wording on Principle 1. These guidelines, however, are more specific in that they relate to the responsibility of the psychologists *as a supervisor of others* (who do not meet the requirements for being licensed as psychologists) and as a planner, director, and evaluator of services provided by the psychologist's employer. The guidelines for industrial/organizational psychologists do not address the issues raised by Principle 1.

The American Association for Counseling and Development (AACD) Ethical Standards (APGA, 1981) focus on ensuring that the client receives appropriate care, that testing materials are not misused or mishandled, that consultant relationships are established for the benefit of the client, and that the administrative affairs of public and quasi-public institutions are handled in such a way that the employees and the people being served are benefited the most.

The code of ethics issued by the National Academy of Certified Clinical Mental Health Counselors (NACCMHC, 1980–81) closely follows the language used by Principle 1 and by the AACD Ethics. Like the AACD Ethics, NACCMHC ethics devote several subsections to the responsibilities of those professionals who teach.

The American Association for Marriage and Family Therapy, Code of Professional Ethics (AAMFT, n.d.) addresses the relationship a therapist has with his or her client(s) but does not speak to the areas of administration and teaching. The AAMFT Ethics do have a detailed section on procedures to be used whenever a member is accused of unethical practice. This type of description does not appear in the other codes.

The National Association of Social Workers (NASW) Code of Ethics (1979) describes general responsibility in terms of the social worker's conduct and comportment including the propriety of the social worker's behavior and his or her integrity and impartiality. This code requires social workers to retain ultimate responsibility for the quality and extent of service that they provide, whether that service be direct or through an administrative capacity. The companion set of Standards for the Private Practice of Clinical Social Work (NASW, 1981) focuses on the social worker's behavior while engaged in private practice. These standards closely follow the principles set out in the NASW Ethics.

The Principles of Medical Ethics, with annotations especially applicable to psychiatry, hereinafter referred to as the Medical Ethics, (American Psychiatric Association, 1981), discuss peer review and appeal of decisions in the case of disputes over practice standards. Also, these ethics address the issues of supervision for fee (fee splitting); time spent providing supervision for mental health workers; nondelegation of decision-making responsibility when such requires the use of medical judgment; consultant relations; and the responsibility to participate in activities aimed at contributing to improvements in the general community. Such community involvement includes fostering cooperation among various professions who work in mental health fields and public education through sharing expertise on various psychosocial issues affecting mental health and illness.

The nursing profession utilizes two codes of ethics, the Code for Nurses (American Nurses' Association, ANA, 1976a), and the American Nurses' Association Standards: Psychiatric Mental Health Nursing Practice (ANA, 1976b). On the issue of responsibility, these codes call for nurses to strive continuously to upgrade standards of practice and education and to participate in setting up and maintaining conditions of employment that are conducive to high-quality nursing care.

The ANA Standards also call for the nurse to include clients in the assessment, planning, implementation, and evaluation of their own nursing care programs. The nurse is urged to use the problem-solving approach when developing nursing care programs; to help others achieve satisfying and productive lives through health teaching; to prepare themselves appropriately before beginning the practice of psychotherapy; to be accountable in their practice; to provide leadership, supervision, and teaching for other nurses and nursing care personnel; and to strive to contribute to the field of nursing through innovations in theory and practice and by participation in research.

APA Principle 2: Competence   This principle calls on the individual psychologist to accept responsibility for his or her own competence in providing services and using techniques that have been learned adequately through education and experience. Psychologists must not misrepresent themselves or their capabilities; they should prepare materials carefully when serving as educators; they should seek continuing education and be open to new ideas and procedures; they should be aware of cultural differences and know their own strengths and weaknesses in this regard and act appropriately; they should use test materials judiciously and limit the impact of test results to those areas in which the psychologist has an understanding; and they should be able to recognize that personal problems and conflicts might interfere with effective delivery of service. As a result, they should act to withdraw from situations in which such problems arise and refrain from activities that might lead to potential harm to the client because of any personal problem or conflict.

All other codes treat the subject of competency in much less detail but with more emphasis on what each specialty or particular professional group requires of its members. For example, the Specialty Guidelines (APA, 1981b, 1981c, 1981d, 1981e) call for the psychologists to maintain current knowledge in their specialty, to limit practice to demonstrated areas of competence, and to practice as specialists only after meeting the requirements of their specialty area through a doctoral program in that specialty.

The AACD Ethics (APGA, 1981) address the competency issue in terms of encouraging professional growth and maintaining high standards of conduct. However, unlike the APA Ethics, they include a section on what is termed "preparation standards." These standards relate to the education and training of students in the helping professions. This section is quite detailed as to the level of ethical performance required of an educator and as to the areas that should be taught to all persons entering this field.

With regard to competence, the NASW Standards (1981) include a section on qualification standards for the clinical social worker in private practice. These standards contain specific, minimum educational and direct practice experience requirements as well as the usual admonitions concerning practicing within one's area of competence.

The Medical Ethics (American Psychiatric Association, 1981) attend to a particular and distinct need. In addition to more general statements relating to competency, this code includes a brief section on the practice of acupuncture.

APA Principle 3: Moral and Legal Standards This principle contains general statements about each professional's need to maintain moral and ethical standards of behavior so as to represent the profession in a way that is deserving of the public's trust and that avoids conflict with community standards, regulations, and laws. This principle concerns psychologists who serve as teachers and employers as well as employees, researchers, and private practitioners in the helping professions. It is stated that whenever community standards, regulations, agency rules, or laws are deemed in conflict with the APA Ethical Principles (1981a), psychologists should make known their commitment to their ethical standards and work toward some resolution of the conflict in terms of what is best for the client and in the interest of the general public.

The Specialty Guidelines (APA, 1981b, 1981c, 1981d, 1981e) contain nearly identical language in regard to moral and legal standards. Each guideline addresses this issue from the point of view of the user's personal, legal, and civil rights. Professionals are required to be familiar with and adhere to the requirements contained in the Specialty Guidelines, the APA Ethical Principles (1981a), the APA Standards for Educational and Psychological Tests (1977), and the APA Ethical Principles in the Conduct of Research with Human Participants (1973). These guidelines also require the professional to maintain a system of record keeping and disposition and to observe all federal, state, and local requirements for safety, health, and sanitation.

The AACD Standards (APGA, 1981) call for the professional to review the policies and principles of any institution which seeks to employ the professional to ensure that these standards are not in conflict with the professional's own standards or those of the AACD. The AACD calls on each professional to police the behavior of peers and to attempt to correct any ethical problems that might exist. If such attempts are ineffective, then the professional must take action through the institution, whenever possible, or use the channels established by the AACD. The AACD's subsection on private practice contains detailed requirements as to the professional's behavior when establishing and/or continuing a private practice.

The Certified Clinical Mental Health Counselors' Code of Ethics (NACCMHC, 1980–81) devotes an entire principle to the issue of moral and legal standards, much like the APA Ethical Principles (1981a). However, unlike the APA Principles, where the topic is not dealt with specifically, the Certified Clinical Mental Health Counselors' code specifies that sexual conduct between counselors and clients is in violation of that code of ethics.

The AAMFT Code of Professional Ethics (n.d.) speaks to the same issues as do the APA Principles except that, like the NACCMHC code (1984), the AAMFT also specifies that sexual intimacy with clients is unethical. This code forbids the therapist from using his or her counseling relationship to further personal, religious, political, or business interests.

The NASW Code of Ethics (1979) calls for the social worker to maintain high standards of personal conduct and integrity as well as to work to maintain the integrity of the social work profession. This code also requires the social worker to respect the rights of clients and to make every effort to assist clients in achieving maximum self-determination. Lastly, this code states that the social worker should work toward promoting the general welfare of society through eliminating discrimination, ensuring access of clients to community resources, expanding client choice and opportunity, promoting understanding of cultural differences, helping out in emergencies, advocating changes in laws to improve social justice, and providing informational services to the public to help shape opinion to affect social policy development.

The NASW Standards for the Private Practice of Clinical Social Work (1981) are comprehensive and contain the same basic elements as can be found in Principle 3 and in the AACD Ethical Standards (APGA, 1981). One subsection of this set of standards relates to the composition of the social worker's bill for services rendered and another subsection forbids fee splitting for providing or receiving referrals. One other subsection provides that the social worker can use a collection agency or a small claims court to collect overdue accounts.

The Medical Ethics (American Psychiatric Association, 1981) are quite detailed on moral and legal issues. The pertinent sections are worded in close approximation to the other major codes of ethics. In addition, these ethics include subsections forbidding psychiatrists from taking part in any legally authorized execution, from sexual activity with patients, and from evaluating any adult charged with a criminal act prior to that person's having access to legal counsel. The Medical Ethics also suggest that it may not be unethical to engage in illegal activities such as those concerning the right to protest social injustices so long as such activities do not bear on the image of the psychiatrist or on the ability of the psychiatrist to treat his or her patients ethically and well. There are several subsections that relate to the psychiatrist's responsibility as a witness in court as well as a section on the right of the psychiatrist to refuse to treat an individual, except in cases of emergency; others include the right to select with whom to associate; and the right to choose an environment in which to provide medical services

The Code for Nurses (ANA, 1976a) requires simply that nurses provide services to patients with respect for the dignity of humans and without regard to nationality, race, creed, color, or status. The standards for psychiatric nursing (ANA, 1976b) do not address the issues raised by Principle 3.

APA Principle 4: Public Statements   This principle relates to public statements, announcements concerning services provided, advertising, and promotional activities of psychologists. Such statements and activities are intended to inform the public, to help people make decisions about what they want from a psychologist, and to assist in the selection of a psychologist. This principle goes into considerable detail, especially in the areas of advertising and press relations. The advertising ethics relate both to advertising one's own services and to participating in advertising of other services and/or products.

One paragraph of this ethical concern over public statements is devoted to the behavior of psychologists as teachers. The general point made is that whatever the teacher does to attract students to the course or program of courses should accurately reflect what is going to be taught, how it is going to be taught, who is going to teach the subject(s), the cost(s), and the nature of the experience that the student can expect as a result of having taken the course. This section relates to academic as well as continuing education programs.

The Specialty Guidelines (APA, 1981b, 1981c, 1981e) each contain the same provisions with regard to public announcements. The service unit for each specialty is responsible for providing a written statement of the scope of services and a description of the organization, together with lines of responsibility, supervisory relationships, and the level and extent of each individual's accountability within the unit. The Specialty Guidelines for Industrial/Organizational Psychologists (APA, 1981d) do not address the issue of public announcements.

The AACD Standards (APGA, 1981) deal with the topic of public statements in four different areas. The first to be addressed are public announcements containing information about individuals whose anonymity must be ensured. The second area deals with public statements about tests and testing where the unwarranted use of terms such as IQ and grade equivalent scores should be avoided and where the member should guard against false claims and misleading statements. The third area relates to reporting research results and requires that the reporter make explicit mention of all variables and known conditions that might affect outcomes. Last, the AACD Standards address advertising in much the same manner as can be found in the APA Principles. It should also be noted that the AACD Standards contain an entire section on training and education which addresses the same issues concerning course and program announcements as found in the APA Principles.

The Certified Clinical Mental Health Counselors' Code of Ethics (NACCMHC, 1980-81) addresses the issue of public interaction in several ways. First, the counselor is expected to avoid public behavior that is in violation of accepted moral and legal standards. Next, this code addresses the same concerns as found previously in the APA Principles and the AACD Standards surrounding issues of advertising, endorsements, public talks, and teaching. Last, the NACCMHC Code admonishes counselors not to use the public media for purposes of diagnosis, treatment, or personalized advice when providing counseling services. This provision conflicts with the APA Principles. The latter affords permission so long as the psychologist uses up-to-date relevant data and exercises the highest level of professional judgment, whereas the NACCMHC Code forbids such activity. The NACCMHC Code considers the provision of such services solely by mail as also being unethical.

The AAMFT Code of Professional Ethics (n.d) not only establishes a procedure for filing and hearing complaints made against its members but incorporates, by reference, a set of standards on public information and advertising. These standards cover all aspects of public information, from the information a client might need to select a family therapist to regulations concerning the use of the name, logo, and acronym of the AAMFT. This set of standards is detailed and explicit in describing activities considered to be unethical.

The NASW Code of Ethics (1979) is largely silent on the matter of public statements except for a brief paragraph requiring the social worker to avoid misrepresenting his or her qualifications, competence, services rendered, or expectations of results when advertising to the public. The NASW Standards for the Private Practice of Clinical Social Work (1981) contain essentially the same requirements on advertising as does the NASW Code of Ethics (1979).

The Medical Ethics (American Psychiatric Association, 1981) contain two paragraphs on public information. The first paragraph relates to public statements made by a psychiatrist and to whether that psychiatrist is speaking as an individual or on behalf of some organization. In the same paragraph, psychiatrists are encouraged to foster cooperation among health organizations and to serve society by advising the courts, as well as the legislative and executive branches of government. No particular topic is either included or excluded from the type of advice the psychiatrist is to provide.

The second paragraph of the Medical Ethics pertains to those occasions when a psychiatrist is asked to give the public his or her opinion concerning an individual who has gained some notoriety. The principles forbid the uttering of this type of opinion unless the psychiatrist has conducted an examination of the individual in question and has proper authorization to make such a statement.

The Code for Nurses (ANA, 1976a) requires that the nurse refuse to engage in endorsement and/or advertising of commercial products, services, or enterprises. The standards for psychiatric nursing (ANA, 1976b) are silent on the matter of public statements.

APA Principle 5: Confidentiality   This principle concerns one of the most litigated subjects in the human services field. Confidentiality is one of the most important aspects of the relationship between the professional and the client. Paradoxically, on the surface at least, the subject of confidentiality is given less attention than any other major topic addressed by the APA Ethical Principles (1981a). The APA Principles are brief but to the point and are the product of many years of examination by professional associations and by the courts.

Principle 5 begins with the admonition that confidentiality is the primary obligation of psychologists. Information gained from others as a result of a psychologist's work may only be shared through the consent of the client or the client's legal guardian. The only time this rule can be avoided is when there is a clear danger to the client or to some other person(s) who might come into contact with the client. The psychologist owes the client as well as relevant others a duty to inform them of the potential danger to and/or from the client.

The Specialty Guidelines (APA, 1981b, 1981c, 1983d, 1981e) contain similar language concerning confidentiality. They all make the psychologist responsible for all information concerning clients (users), regardless of its source, and responsible that all persons supervised by the psychologist maintain that confidentiality. These guidelines address the same issues treated by Principle 5—the duty to warn, to release information only with consent, and informed consent. Also, the guidelines discuss the right of the user to have access to psychological records but maintains that the psychologist or the facility where the psychologist works actually owns the records and must be responsible for the records' safekeeping. The guidelines for school psychologists discuss the relationship between the psychologist and the school, the user (student), the parents, and others who might have an interest in the user's records.

The AACD Standards (APGA, 1981) do not significantly differ from the APA Principles. They do relate to the maintenance of confidential information obtained as a result of group practice and to the proper use of confidential information when training counselors.

The Certified Clinical Mental Health Counselors' Code of Ethics (NACCMHC, 1980-81) and the American Association for Marriage and Family Therapy Code of Professional Ethics (AAMFT, n.d.) treat the subject of confidentiality in much the same way as the APA and the AACD. The NACCMHC Code addresses the issue of recording sessions with clients only with the client's written consent and, when working with families, ensuring the rights of each family member are safeguarded.

The NASW Code of Ethics (1979) and the NASW Standards for the Private Practice of Clinical Social Work (NASW, 1981) do not differ from the other major codes and standards on the matter of confidentiality. The NASW Code uses different language from other codes when discussing the need to disclose confidential information. This code uses the term "compelling professional reasons" as contrasted with the APA code's requiring the professional to determine whether there exists a "clear danger to the client or to others." Also, the Standards for the Private Practice of Clinical Social Work discuss the position a clinical social worker might take when ordered by a court to reveal confidences entrusted to the worker by clients. These standards inform the professional that he or she may either comply with the court order or may ethically hold the right to dissent from the court order within the boundaries of the law.

The Medical Ethics (American Psychiatric Association, 1981) do not differ from other codes and standards. The Medical Ethics address the issue of truly informed consent of a person before presenting that person and his or her case to a scientific gathering. Also, this code addresses the need for the psychiatrist to refuse to provide psychiatric evaluative services on any adult charged with a criminal act prior to that person's having access to legal counsel.

The Code for Nurses (ANA, 1976a) indicates only briefly that the nurse must safeguard the individual's right to privacy by protecting confidential information and by sharing only that information which is relevant to the individual's care. The standards for psychiatric nursing (ANA, 1976b) do not address the issue of confidentiality.

APA Principle 6: Welfare of the Consumer   This principle and the treatment by the various codes, standards, and guidelines of the subject of consumer welfare is possibly the most extensive of any of the ethical issues. Perhaps this is because of the nature of the subject—that the welfare of the consumer is of paramount importance to all human service professionals and that the professional must continually exercise judgment over the needs of the client and the professional's own needs (or those of the professional's employer).

This principle is most closely related to what is referred to as consumer law in other areas of trade and industry. It involves a responsibility on the part of the professional to make sure the client (consumer) is fully informed about the nature of the services to be provided, the cost of such services, the conflicts that might arise between the professional's ethics and his or her employer's demands as those conflicts affect the client, and the need to terminate services that are no longer of any real benefit to the client. This issue also relates to the need of psychologists to avoid dual relationships that could negatively affect their professional judgment or create the risk of exploiting the trust and dependency of clients emotionally, economically, and sexually. This principle also designates the practice of accepting any remuneration for referring clients for professional services as unethical.

The Specialty Guidelines (APA, 1981b, 1981c, 1981d, 1981e) speak to this issue with the same or similar language. The welfare of the client is addressed in almost every guideline. Basically, the guidelines reiterate what is contained in Principle 6 and relate the issues found in that principle to each profession's particular setting. The school psychologists' guidelines, for example, relate to the needs of the students, to the student's status as minors, and to the need to relate to the parents of students in such a way as to safeguard the student's welfare (APA, 1981e). In contrast, the Guidelines for Industrial/Organizational Psychologists (APA, 1981d) address the requirement that the psychologist not attempt to gain a competitive advantage for the unit with whom the psychologist is consulting. It is the welfare of the consumer *and* the consumer's competitors that must be protected by the industrial/organizational psychologist.

The AACD Standards (APGA, 1981) deal with the issue of consumer welfare in the same manner as the APA Code. The AACD Standards discuss what the professional must do when confronted with the issue of conflicting standards of conduct between an employer and the professional. These standards also ask that the counselor avoid racial and sexual stereotyping. When engaged in short-term group programs such as marathons and other types of encounters, the professional must ensure that professional assistance is available to the participants both during and after the group program. If a professional is consulting with people who are entitled to consulting services as a benefit of their employment, the professional may not charge or accept any fee or other type of remuneration for providing such consultation.

The Certified Clinical Mental Health Counselor's Code of Ethics (NACCMHC, 1980-81) cautions counselors to be aware of the very important social responsibility they must bear and to be alert to personal, social, organizational, financial, or political situations that might lead to any misuse of the counselor's influence. The counselor should avoid doing anything that would violate or diminish the client's legal and civil rights. One significant aspect of the NACCMHC Code is that there is a reference to test scoring and interpretation services (manual and automated). Such services must be carried out only if it can be demonstrated that the programs used are based on appropriate research establishing their validity. Automated services are to be offered on a professional-to-professional basis.

The AAMFT Code of Professional Ethics (n.d.) deals with consumer welfare as a matter of client relationships. These ethics address the same issues as do the other codes and standards. However, owing to the specific nature of the services provided by professionals of this association, these ethics are particular as to the therapist's responsibility in advising clients that the decision to separate or divorce is the sole responsibility of the client. If separation or divorce occurs during therapy, this code requires that the professional offer continued support and counseling to both spouses and their children during the ensuing period of readjustment.

The NASW Code of Ethics (1979) and the NASW Standards for the Private Practice of Clinical Social Work (1981) contain the same essential elements concerning client welfare as the previously mentioned codes and standards. The main difference between these two sets of ethics is that the general code for social workers relates to traditional work settings and calls for the establishment of fees in accordance with the client's ability to pay. The Standards for the Private Practice of Clinical Social Work, on the other hand, relate specifically to the social worker in nonpublic settings and requires the private practitioner to set fees commensurate with fees charged by mental health professionals in the community and to refer clients who cannot pay the practitioner's fee to other professionals who charge lower fees or to public agencies who use a sliding scale fee system.

The Medical Ethics (American Psychiatric Association, 1981) do not differ from other major codes and standards on the subject of client welfare. There is one section, though, which is not included in any other code or standard listed here. That section states that it is ethical to charge a client for a missed appointment, although it also states that such a practice should be employed only infrequently and always with the utmost consideration for the client and his or her circumstances.

The ANA Code for Nurses (1976a) calls for the nurse to safeguard the patient whenever the patient's care and safety are affected by the incompetent, unethical, or illegal conduct of anyone. The standards for psychiatric nursing (ANA, 1976b) deal with the welfare of patients by ensuring that the nurse engages in proper problem-solving techniques and includes the patient in the assessment, planning, implementation, and evaluation of the patient's nursing care program. The standards also require the nurse to participate in interdisciplinary teams when dealing with clients.

APA Principle 7: Professional Relationships   Principle 7 concerns the interactions of psychologists and the relationship they have with the organizations and associations to which they belong. This principle makes it imperative that psychologists know the competencies of their associates and those in related professions. Psychologists need to have a good understanding of the traditions and practices of other professional groups so they can work and cooperate with them fully. Supervision and training of members from other professions is a special responsibility of psychologists. Care must be taken not to exploit professional relationships with clients, supervisees, students, employees, or research participants. Sexual harassment of these same groups of individuals is considered unethical.

Another area of concern under this principle is the sharing of publication credit when credit is due to others. This part of the principle goes into some detail in an effort to resolve any possible disputes in this area.

The last issue raised by Principle 7 regards what a psychologist should do when confronted with knowledge that another psychologist has violated the Code of Ethics; the ethics do not address the issue of what should be done if a professional who is not a psychologist violates some ethical principle or standard. Most of the process described is of an informal nature, but if it appears that the violation is not amenable to informal treatment, the psychologist is encouraged to bring the matter before the appropriate local, state, and/or national committee on professional ethics and conduct.

The Specialty Guidelines (APA, 1981b, 1981c, 1981e) again respond to Principle 7 in identical ways. They all address the issues of knowing what other services are available, using the network of human services that exists in their communities, and maintaining a cooperative relationship with colleagues and coworkers for the benefit of clients. The only concern for professional relationships in the Guidelines for Industrial/Organizational Psychologists (APA, 1981d) appears to be one of providing a clear statement of the role of the industrial/organizational psychologist to any other psychologist hired for particular services.

The AACD Standards (APGA, 1981) speak to the issues addressed in Principle 7 without much deviation from the APA position. The AACD Standards require that a professional not enter into a counseling relationship with an individual who is already being seen by another professional without first talking to that other professional and obtaining his or her approval. Of course, if a professional discovers after the fact that a client is also seeing another professional, the counselor should immediately make contact to clarify their respective positions and efforts vis-à-vis the client. The AACD Standards also stress that the professional has an obligation to share original research data with qualified others who might want to replicate the study. Lastly, these standards address the issue of professionals forming new or joining existing partnerships or corporations and what must be done to ensure that all members of the organization have a clear understanding as to one another's specialties and particular competencies.

The Certified Clinical Mental Counselors' Code of Ethics (NACCMHC, 1980-81) does not differ from the APA Principles or the AACD Standards. The language used is practically identical with that contained in those two codes.

The AAMFT Code of Professional Ethics (n.d.) treats the subject of professional relationships in much the same way as does the NACCMHC and the other codes. The only difference seems to be that the AAMFT Code, unlike the other codes, goes into specifics about how a complaint of unethical practice will be handled by the Committee on Ethics and Professional Practices.

The NASW Code of Ethics (1979) addresses the issue of professional relationships in terms of respect, fairness, and courtesy toward colleagues. Although this code makes many of the same points as the others, it is interesting to note that the NASW Code calls for mediation or arbitration to settle professional disputes. It also calls for vigorous discussion and criticism from the social work profession in order to protect and enhance the dignity and integrity of the profession.

The NASW Standards for the Private Practice of Clinical Social Work (NASW, 1981) do not differ in any major respect from the other codes and standards in their treatment of professional relationships. They do discuss the need of the social worker who terminates private practice to refer clients elsewhere and of the social worker, when leaving an agency to enter private practice, to abide by that agency's explicit policies regarding the transfer of clients.

The Medical Ethics (American Psychiatric Association, 1981) are practically the same as the APA and AACD codes. However, the Medical Ethics do provide that when a member has been found in violation of the code of ethics by the American Psychiatric Association or one of its district branches, automatic reporting to local authorities responsible for medical licensure should *not* be made. Rather, the decision to report such violations should be made by the American Psychiatric Association based on the merits of the case.

The Code for Nurses (ANA, 1976) addresses the issue of professional relationships by requiring the nurse to work with members of other health professions and citizens interested in promoting community health needs. The standards for psychiatric nursing (ANA, 1976) call for participation with interdisciplinary teams when assessing, planning, implementing, and evaluating individual programs and other mental health activities.

APA Principle 8: Assessment Techniques   This principle is a fairly straightforward treatment of the issues of psychological assessment. The major thrust of this principle is to ensure that the development, publication, and utilization of psychological assessment techniques are all done with the welfare and best interests of the client in mind. Security of test instruments is called for and psychologists are requested to strive to ensure the appropriate use of assessment techniques by others.

The Specialty Guidelines (APA, 1981b, 1981c, 1981d, 1981e) do not address the issue of assessment techniques. Only three of the other associations, the AACD, the NACCMHC, and the ANA, have standards which discuss assessment techniques.

The AACD Standards (APGA, 1981) devote an entire section to assessment. Their treatment relates to measurement and evaluation and cautions professionals to use unvalidated information carefully when modifying interpretations of test results. These standards also call on the professional to recognize the effects of socioeconomic, ethnic, and cultural factors on test scores. Preference is to be given to specific validity, reliability, and appropriateness of tests over general validity and reliability which can be questioned in a court of law and by ethics committees. The remainder of the AACD section on assessment is devoted to the appropriate use of tests and test results and refers the professional to several other sources, including the *Standards for Educational and Psychological Tests,* "The responsible use of tests: A position paper of AMEG, APGA, and NCME," and "Responsibilities of users of standardized tests" (APGA, 1981).

The Certified Clinical Mental Health Counselor's Code of Ethics (NACCMHC, 1984) does not vary significantly from either the APA ethics or the AACD Standards regarding assessment techniques. These ethics do go into significant detail on such technical issues as the development of manuals which should accompany new test instruments and the provision of normative data in test manuals and what the data should describe.

The standards of psychiatric nursing (ANA, 1976) are the only other standards to address the issue of assessment. Here, the ANA merely calls for the collection of data through pertinent clinical observations based on the nurse's knowledge of the arts and sciences, with particular emphasis on the psychosocial and biophysical sciences.

APA Principle 9: Research with Human Participants   This principle deals mainly with the precautions one must take when using humans in psychological research activities. Any psychologist endeavoring to conduct research using human participants must consider alternative directions in which research energy and resources might be invested and should carry out the research with respect and concern for the dignity and welfare of the participants. Aside from the usual precautions that are taken when dealing with human participants, this principle discusses methodological requirements, deception, "minimal risk" versus "at risk" research, and the process of ensuring that the individual participant's freedom to decline or withdraw from the research at any time is respected.

The Specialty Guidelines (APA, 1981b, 1981c, 1981d, 1981e) do not address these issues. Like most other codes and standards, they look to the APA Principles, the AACD Standards, and the Ethical Principles in the Conduct of Research with Human Participants (APA, 1973) for specific guidance in this area.

The AACD Standards (APGA, 1981) refer to the Ethical Principles in the Conduct of Research with Human Participants (APA, 1973) and the Code of Federal Regulations (APGA, 1981) for a detailed review of the proper approach to use of human participants in research. In addition, the AACD calls for the designation of a principal researcher whenever a research project is begun and requires that authors not submit their findings to two or more journals for publication simultaneously.

The way in which other codes and standards treat the issues related to research does not vary significantly. For instance, the Certified Clinical Mental Health Counselors' Code of Ethics (NACCMHC, 1980–81) devotes an entire section to the topic of research with human participants. The AAMFT Code of Professional Ethics (n.d.) refers the researcher to the conditions of the Human Subjects Experimentation as specified by the Department of Health and Welfare guidelines (AAMFT, n.d.). The NASW Code of Ethics (1979) covers briefly the primary obligations of the researcher to any human participants in his or her research. The Medical Ethics (American Psychiatric Association, 1981) require the researcher to (1) advise human subjects of the funding source for the effort, (2) retain his or her freedom to reveal data and results, and (3) follow all appropriate and current guidelines relative to human subject protection. The Code for

Nurses (ANA, 1976a) requires the nurse first to be assured that the rights of individual participants are protected before participating in research activities involving human subjects. No other code, guideline, or standard addresses the issue of research with human participants. Most of these ethics are either silent on the subject or reference other standards and principles that deal directly with the issue.

APA Principle 10: Care and Use of Animals The last APA principle is dealt with only by the American Psychological Association. Not one of the other codes, guidelines, or standards addresses the issues raised by Principle 10, namely the welfare and humane treatment of animals in research. The researcher is directed to conform to all federal, state, and local laws and regulations concerning the acquisition, care, use, and disposal of all animals used in research. The supervising psychologist must ensure that every effort is made to minimize any discomfort, illness, or pain of the animals. When it is appropriate that an animal's life be ended, the psychologist must make certain it is done rapidly and painlessly.

SUMMARY

Throughout this chapter, we have brought together the various codes of ethics and ethical standards for purposes of comparison and explanation. The APA Principles (APA, 1981a) were used as the standard for comparison because they are the most generic to the field and are comprehensive. We suggest that the reader will now be in a better position to evaluate various situations that will be presented either in his or her academic setting or in a work setting that demand an interpretation of one or another standard or ethical statement. At the very least, the reader should now be in a better position to recognize when ethics need to be considered and where to go to get answers.

REFERENCES

American Association for Marriage and Family Therapy. (n.d.). *Code of professional ethics.* Claremont, CA: Author.

American Nurses' Association. (1976a). The code for nurses: The ten points. In F. M. Carter, *Psychosocial nursing: Theory and practice in hospital and community mental health* (2d ed., pp. 515–516). New York: Macmillan.

American Nurses' Association. (1976b). Standards: Psychiatric mental health nursing practice. In F. M. Carter, *Psychosocial nursing: Theory and practice in hospital and community mental health* (2d ed., pp. 503–514). New York: Macmillan.

American Personnel and Guidance Association. (1981). *Ethical standards.* Falls Church, VA: Author.

American Psychiatric Association. (1981). *The principles of medical ethics, with annotations especially applicable to psychiatry.* Washington, DC: Author.

American Psychological Association. (1973). Ethical principles in the conduct of research with human participants. *American Psychologist, 28,* 79–80.

American Psychological Association. (1977). *Standards for educational and psychological tests.* Washington, DC: Author.

American Psychological Association. (1981a). Ethical principles of psychologists (revised). *American Psychologist, 36,* 633–638.

American Psychological Association. (1981b). Specialty guidelines for the delivery of services by clinical psychologists. *American Psychologist, 36,* 640–651.

American Psychological Association. (1981c). Specialty guidelines for the delivery of services by counseling psychologists. *American Psychologist, 36,* 652–663.

American Psychological Association (1981d). Specialty guidelines for the delivery of services by industrial/organizational psychologists. *American Psychologist, 36,* 664–669.

American Psychological Association. (1981e). Specialty guidelines for the delivery of services by school psychologists. *American Psychologist, 36,* 670–681.

National Academy of Certified Clinical Mental Health Counselors. (1980–81). Code of ethics for certified clinical mental health counselors. In *AMHCA News,* (special edition, pp. 1–3). Falls Church, VA: Author.
Monterey, CA: Brooks/Cole.

National Association of Social Workers. (1979). *Code of ethics.* Washington, DC: Author.

National Association of Social Workers. (1981). *Standards for the private practice of clinical social work.* Washington, DC: Author.

CHAPTER 7

LEGAL ISSUES

In addition to the many ethical requirements, the human services professional must face a number of areas of concern that are legal in nature.
Lawyers and courts of law very often use a profession's code of ethics,
standards of practice, or specialty guidelines to explore the issues presented to them by litigants in civil suits. Many of these suits are for malpractice and are based on an individual's claim that the professional failed
to act in a responsible and/or ethical manner when providing services
to that individual. As seen in this light, ethical codes, standards, and
guidelines serve not only to protect the client, but to protect the professional who adheres to them as well.

Many professionals speak of the legal system as "the enemy." They
complain that the courts are usurping the profession's right to police itself,
to take care of its own who fail to live up to already established standards.
Another complaint often heard is that the courts are rewriting professional
codes of ethics and setting professional standards. We suggest here that
while some of these things do happen in the courts, much of what happens in court is either because of the profession's failure to provide
adequately defined standards and ethics (which leads to ambiguous behavior on the part of some professionals) or because of ignorance on the
part of many professionals as to the legal considerations of their work and
the ethics under which they conduct their affairs. The courts do not proac-
tively step into another profession and busy themselves rearranging
codes and rewriting standards. Rather, they passively await litigation that
arises out of disputes between clients and professionals, or professionals
and government, over the provision or nonprovision of services.

The human services professional needs to be aware of the major legal considerations that affect his or her role in order to avoid conflict. Our purpose with this chapter is to help readers discern what is and is not acceptable ethical practice in those areas of special interest to their clients, to persons affected by their clients, and to attorneys representing any or all of these people. To this end, we will review some major court decisions affecting human service professionals in the ethical areas of responsibility, moral and legal standards, confidentiality, and the welfare of the consumer. Our focus is on legal liability, but the reader should be aware that most of these cases would be adjudicated by one or more professional associations' ethics committee, as well. Before completing the chapter, we will address a final area where the professional could expect to interact with the legal system—by serving as an expert witness in a civil or criminal proceeding. For a more detailed follow-up to the material presented here, the reader should refer to those references listed at the end of this chapter.

UNETHICAL PRACTICE

The various associations of the human services professions have developed methods with which to deal with members accused of unethical practice. As will be noted later in this chapter, much of what is considered unethical within the profession can also be considered actionable at law. That is, a person accused of unethical practice can also be sued in a court of law for the same behavior. However, that is not always the case. A human services professional can practice in such a way as to be within the letter of the law but still be unethical.

In a recent article, Widiger and Rorer (1984) explain how a therapist can "help" a client find relief from various obsessional compulsions at the expense of the client's religious beliefs. These authors go on to describe various situations whereby a professional's ethics might not coincide with the requirements of the legal system and vice versa. They suggest that it might be necessary to develop ethical codes for each particular theory of psychotherapy (Widiger and Rorer, 1984). In that way a court could refer to a specific set of ethics, designed for that particular practitioner, when evaluating the merits of the case before it. Also, the human services professional could obtain more specific guidance from his or her specialty area as to what is and is not ethical practice.

To gain some perspective on the nature and size of the problem it is instructive to examine, for example, the American Psychological Association's educative and adjudicative functions. In an article which describes those two functions and gives some indication of the magnitude of the problem, Mills (1984) reports that from five to fifteen inquires (telephone and mail) are received *daily* by the Ethics Office of the American Psychological Association (APA). These inquiries concern ethics and ethical behavior.

The APA Ethics Committee had 130 cases under investigation during 1983. Of those individuals under investigation by the Committee, ten were convicted of a felony, thirty were accused of sexual intimacy with their clients, seventeen were accused of filing fraudulent insurance claims, nine were accused of misrepresentation or sensationalism in either advertising or in public statements, eight suffered complaints for failing to correct misrepresentations, six were complained of for failing to respect other professions, and five each were accused of inappropriate professional practice in the areas of child custody abuses and testing abuse (Mills, 1984). Of those cases, the Committee reached a decision concerning seventy-nine complaints.

It should be remembered that these cases represent only those complaints that were referred to the APA Ethics Committee. Many complaints are handled by the Ethics Office staff and many more complaints go straight to the judicial system for resolution as a matter of civil liability. It should also be kept in mind that this is but one example of one association's experience with complaints of an ethical nature.

LEGAL ISSUES

Most, if not all, of the lawsuits against human services professionals are civil rather than criminal in nature and are claims that the professional engaged in malpractice of one sort or another. Malpractice is best defined as a form of negligent behavior which is applied to professionals who owe their clients a duty of care not to harm them in any way. This duty of care, or standard, is gauged by comparing the professional's behavior to that of any other ordinary and reasonable professional in the same field. For example, a counseling psychologist's behavior should be compared to other ordinary counseling psychologists and *not* to that of psychiatrists or social workers or any other professional. One of the biggest problems that the professional faces is that of trying to decide what *is* the standard of care owed to the client. Rarely do two professionals greet one another with exactly the same techniques and theories about how to conduct a practice.

There are a great number of approaches to the practice of psychotherapy, for instance, so who is to say which practitioner leads the field and sets the standard of care? Fortunately, the law does not show a preference for one method of treatment or approach over any other. The profession, rather than the courts, sets the standard of care. The codes of ethics, guidelines, and standards referred to throughout the previous chapter make up the standards of care for each of the described professions. However, if the professionally set standards are inadequate or outdated, the courts have the power to change those standards.

Most malpractice cases concern a breach of duty owed the client, rather than an attack on the standards themselves. The following discussion focuses on the major areas of litigation in the human services field. Specifically, the decision reached by one court affects the parties in that particular suit. But, on the whole, that court's opinion is constantly looked to by other courts and by professional organizations for guidance in the conduct of the professional's business and as precedent by other courts when attempting to settle similar disputes. It is important to note that while the standard of care is different for each profession, the general principles of law developed out of the cases heard by state and federal courts are applicable to all of the human services professions.

Professional Responsibility Ethic/Client's Right to Treatment

The great majority of case law on this topic centers on the rights of institutionalized people rather than clients of community mental health centers and private practitioners. However, the general principles developed by this body of laws can be applied to all three settings. For the most part, decisions by the courts affecting clients' rights to treatment concern (1) constitutional elements pertaining to the right to treatment, (2) right to refuse treatment, (3) failure to provide treatment, (4) adequacy of care and treatment, and (5) effective treatment.

The primary case in the right-to-treatment area is *Rouse v. Cameron* (1966). The decision in this case was the first to address the right-to-treatment issue. The individual involved was found not guilty of a crime by reason of insanity and was committed to a hospital. After four years this person sued on the grounds that he was not receiving treatment and that he was no longer insane. The court held that there was a statute in effect that required the District of Columbia to provide adequate treatment to Mr. Rouse and others. The court also alluded to the possibility that, had there been no statute involved, Rouse might well be entitled to adequate treatment based on the constitutional requirements of due process, of the prohibition against cruel and unusual punishment (applicable to this case since the person was committed as a result of a criminal trial), and of the equal protection clause of the United States Constitution.

In 1971 a class-action suit was brought by employees terminated from their jobs at a hospital in Alabama because of funding cutbacks (*Wyatt v. Stickney*, 1971). The court decided that there exists a constitutional right to effective treatment. Included in this decision was a set of judicially enforceable standards by which the right to treatment could be objectively measured and practically implemented. These standards included such requirements as minimum staff-to-patient ratios, treatment plans and programs, and nutritional requirements.

Later, in 1975, the U.S. Supreme Court entertained issues brought before the court arising out of a Florida case where a "paranoid schizophrenic" Christian Scientist had been hospitalized for over a decade without any showing that he was dangerous either to himself or to others and without any treatment other than the offer of medication which he refused (*O'Connor v. Donaldson*, 1975). Donaldson had repeatedly demanded his release but was refused. After the lawsuit had been heard by a federal district court (which awarded Donaldson compensatory and punitive damages), the case was appealed. The Court of Appeals for the Fifth Circuit upheld the verdict. On further appeal, the Supreme Court held that nondangerous, involuntarily committed persons cannot be hospitalized without receiving adequate treatment. The court did *not* decide what should or should not be done with those persons who are considered dangerous and who are involuntarily committed to a hospital. The court rested its decision on the right of people to liberty, as guaranteed by the Fourteenth Amendment of the United States Constitution. The court could find no reason for Donaldson's continued hospitalization, especially in light of the fact that Donaldson was not receiving treatment. The defendant would have to provide some acceptable reason, such as a treatment plan to help Donaldson become well, in order to justify continuing to deprive him of his liberty.

While the *O'Connor* case centered on the deprivation of a person's liberty, the case actually hinged on the person's right to treatment. Had Donaldson been receiving adequate treatment, the issue before the court, if at all, would have been whether he was still mentally ill and/or whether he could receive similar treatment in a community setting as opposed to a hospital.

In general, then, the court decisions hold that people do have a right to treatment. This right is most often exercised in situations involving hospitalization. However, the right to treatment exists at the community level as well. Generally speaking, the state and/or local government does not have a duty to provide mental health services to the public. However, if such a service is offered, then all persons have a right to receive equal treatment by whatever facility exists.

As for the private practice of therapy, counseling, and related work, the right-to-treatment issue does not apply directly. This issue becomes one of a right to treatment with the same standard of care as would be rendered by a like professional in the same field but hinges on the right of the private practitioner to refuse to provide treatment in the first place. If the professional refuses to begin treatment, there is no law that can force the issue. Once the professional *accepts* the client for treatment, then the entire body of law relating to treatment can be brought to bear, if and when it becomes necessary.

Legal Standards Ethic/Client's Right to Refuse Treatment

In addition to the right to treatment, the client also has a right to refuse treatment. Again, most of the disputes over this issue have centered on inpatient facilities and their treatment of patients. There does not appear to be any legal principle guiding the courts' response to this issue. The right to refuse treatment is often based on the general right to be left alone (*Olmstead v. U.S.*, 1928). This right, which was articulated by Justice Brandeis in the cited case, is not specified in our Constitution or in the Bill or Rights but is one contemplated by the drafters of the Constitution as an inherent right.

Other approaches to this issue rely on the First Amendment's guarantee of freedom to express one's self and one's ideas. The argument here is that therapy and medication have the power to prevent self-expression and should, therefore, be something that a person not otherwise declared incompetent is free to refuse. Absent a judicial determination that a person is incompetent, the courts have held that a patient does have the right to refuse treatment (*Winters v. Miller*, 1971).

On the other hand, and this seems to be the opposite of the reasoning in *Winters*, courts have held that once a person has been declared incompetent, certain treatments cannot be administered because the person is not legally capable of giving his or her consent. Such was the case where a patient who had been involuntarily committed to a psychiatric facility, through the efforts of guardians, sued in a class action to prohibit treatment by medication in the absence of emergency (*Rennie v. Klein*, 1981). The court held for the patient on the grounds that such unauthorized treatment would be an unconstitutional invasion of the patient's right to privacy.

In the latest case on this issue (*Rogers v. Okin*, 1980), guardians appointed for involuntarily committed patients sued in a class action on the same issues raised in the *Rennie* case. The trial court held that it was up to the guardian to decide on the issue of treatment and that the guardian was to decide as if he or she were the patient functioning competently. The appeals court rejected this notion on the grounds that it was too inflexible. The Supreme Court vacated the decision of the other courts on the grounds that the Supreme Court of Massachusetts had ruled in an unrelated case that state law grants mental patients a right to refuse treatment.

Thus, the courts have said that state law is preferred over court decisions as a method of regulating these issues. Readers should keep this notion in mind and become familiar with those state laws that have a bearing on their practice and on the legal issues raised here and elsewhere.

Welfare of the Consumer Ethic/Informed Consent and Full Disclosure

A closely related subject to that of refusal of treatment is that of informed consent. Informed consent can only be given by a person who has been provided a full disclosure of all matters pertinent to the subject at hand and who is competent to understand and appreciate the importance of the information provided by the counselor or therapist. In separate reviews of this issue Everstine et al. (1980) and Margolin (1982) discussed the competency issue in connection with informed consent and full disclosure. The basic problem is in how to make a determination of whether a person is competent to give consent for treatment. The courts have allowed professionals to assume competence, absent any clear indication to the contrary by the person's behavior or absent a legal declaration that the person is mentally incompetent. If the person is a minor, then that person's parents or legal guardian must give consent. Consent from the incompetent person, in addition to parental or guardian consent, is desirable as an indication of voluntariness on the part of the individual.

Aside from the competency issue, the professional must provide the client with sufficient information to make sure that the client's consent is an "informed" one. The professional needs to explain (1) the procedures to be used and why they will be used, (2) the professional's part in the process, (3) what might happen to create discomfort for the client, (4) any risks that will be involved, (5) what to expect in the way of outcome(s) from the process, (6) what other methods are available that the client might consider, (7) assurance that the client may ask questions about the process at any time, and (8) assurance that the client can withdraw from participation or refuse to be a part of any portion of the process, whether that be counseling, therapy, or testing, at any time (Everstine et al., 1980).

Many professionals prefer not to provide such information in written form. However, as discussed by Noll and Rosen (1982), providing a written consent form containing all pertinent information provides greater protection of the rights of the clients and professionals. The client gets to see the issues clearly and can make a more careful decision about the proposed treatment. The professional's liability is reduced by eliminating the possibility of failure to inform. Thus, with proper informed consent, the possibility of suits arising out of intentional torts (for example, a battery arising out of a particular form of psychotherapy, drug therapy, or electroshock therapy) is greatly reduced (*Cobbs v. Grant*, 1972), while the possibility of suits for negligence remains undisturbed (*Pegram v. Sisco*, 1976). An excellent review of the requirements of the law of consent can be found in a book titled *Informed Consent: A Guide for Health Care Providers* (Rosoff, 1981).

The third element of informed consent and full disclosure is the necessity that the client's consent be voluntary. The essential ingredient here is that the client be afforded true freedom of choice. Coercion precludes the possibility of free choice (*Kaimowitz v. Michigan Department of Mental Health*, 1973). Voluntary consent can only be given by persons who are mentally competent and/or free from any form of coercion, however slight. Thus, a prisoner or an involuntarily confined mental patient cannot "voluntarily" give consent since freedom is usually perceived as something obtainable only by cooperating with the authorities (*Kaimowitz*, 1973).

Welfare of the Consumer Ethic/Use of Somatic Therapies

The use of somatic therapies (e.g., electroconvulsive therapy and psychotropic drugs), while prevalent in institutional settings, does exist at the private, outpatient level as well and needs to be addressed by the human services professional. This type of therapy can result in liability for the professional in several situations.

Electroconvulsive therapy (ECT) can be problematic for the professional in three ways. First, the professional must care for the ECT recipients following its administration because recipients can become dangerous to themselves or to others as a result of their confused and disoriented state of mind (*Brown v. Moore*, 1957). Second, the professional needs to ensure that muscle-relaxing drugs are used to avoid violent thrashing from muscular convulsions, especially since such thrashing can result in bone fractures (*McDonald v. Moore*, 1976). Last, there is the issue of informed consent (see previous section) whereby the recipient needs to be told of the side effects of ECT and the risks involved during administration of ECT.

Use of psychotropic drugs for treating institutionalized persons and clients on an outpatient basis constitutes the other major somatic therapy that can, if not well controlled, create problems for the recipient and liability for the professional. These drugs cannot be administered without a prescription from a physician. However, psychotropic drugs are used both in and out of institutions, and it is often the nonmedical professional who is asked to provide the nondrug therapy that is to work concomitantly with the administration of the drug. Both the physician/psychiatrist and the nonmedical therapist must be alert to the problems inherent in the use of these drugs.

As discussed earlier, clients should have the right to refuse drug treatment, should be fully informed about the possible effects, side effects, and noneffects of the drug(s), and should be monitored carefully so as to help avoid harm to themselves and others from complications including overdosage, problems with motor coordination, combined effects with other drugs/alcohol, or development of severe side effects such as tardive dyskinesia (Cohen, 1979).

Confidentiality Ethic/Right to Confidentiality

The expectation that clients have a right to confidentiality between themselves and the professional is a long established one. The issues are (1) that confidentiality is a necessary precondition to obtain full disclosure from and, thus, effective treatment for the client and (2) that confidentiality is needed to protect the client from those who might not understand or appreciate the client's need for treatment.

It has been suggested that the first issue, confidentiality to elicit the self-disclosure required for effective treatment, is no longer viable. Many nonmedical professionals are treating clients without the "free association" technique that was used by psychoanalysts who argued that confidentiality was necessary to encourage full disclosure (Denkowski and Denkowski, 1982). Moreover, Wilson (1978) found that clients residing in states that do not protect the client/professional relationship from legal inquiry do not seem more reluctant to divulge important personal information about themselves to their therapist.

It is noteworthy that the courts have begun to decide cases more in favor of those who contend that a completely confidential relationship is *not* necessary and possibly not totally effective as a part of the therapeutic climate established by the professional (Denkowski and Denkowski, 1982). The fact remains, however, that confidentiality still exists to a very great extent and that the professional needs to protect the client's utterings and records with the utmost of care.

Even though the courts have weakened the client/professional relationship, there still remains a great deal of valid case law that finds it to be a breach of ethics and a breach of contract to divulge information to unauthorized third parties. The difference here, between what the courts are requiring and what the professional must continue to do, is that the courts are concerned with the client/professional *privilege*, which concerns disclosure of client information in judicial proceedings, while the professional must remain alert to any communication made by him or her to third persons *outside* the courtroom.

The second issue, that of protecting clients from social stigma, is an important one which can lead to a malpractice suit if the professional breaches the confidence. There are two areas of concern that are in conflict with the responsibility of protecting clients from social stigma. These areas receive more attention in the literature and in the courts than any other area related to confidentiality. They are (1) duty to prevent harm to a client by the client himself or herself and (2) duty to warn potential victims of the danger posed by the client.

The first area of concern has been litigated broadly across the country in state and federal courts. In the absence of specific statutory law to the contrary, the general rule of law is that the professional must act to ensure the safety of the client who exhibits a clear and present danger to himself or herself, including informing relatives of the problem and even hospitalization of the client (Schutz, 1982). This professional action is sanctioned in all major codes of ethics and by the courts (Greenberg, 1974; Murphy, 1973; Szasz, 1971).

The second area of concern involves the more recently litigated issue of whether a professional owes a duty to notify persons who might be harmed by the professional's client. The leading case in this area is *Tarasoff v. The Regents of the University of California* (1976). This case concerned the death of a young woman by a client of two mental health employees (a clinical psychologist and a psychiatrist) of the university health service. The client had told his therapist of his intention to kill the young woman. The psychologist informed the campus police of the client's intentions and requested help in having the client committed. The police detained the client but allowed him to go free after a short time. The psychologist was directed by the psychiatrist to destroy all communications (letters and notes) made on the subject of committing the client and to take no further action concerning commitment of the client. Soon afterwards, the client killed the young woman.

The issue in *Tarasoff* was whether or not a special relationship exists between a therapist and his or her client—a relationship that requires the therapist, like a parent or a mental hospital, to protect and control the client. The court, in *Tarasoff*, found that such a relationship does exist and, further, that the duty to protect extends beyond the client to third parties who might be harmed by the client. The court was careful to say that this duty brings with it specific obligations that can only be determined on a case-by-case basis. If a therapist determines that his or her client is a real threat to the safety and well-being of another person or persons, the therapist must exercise *reasonable care* to protect the *foreseeable* victim of the danger posed by the client (*Tarasoff*, 1976 at 25). In the *Tarasoff* case, then, telling the police was not enough. The court decided that the defendants should have warned the decedent, the decedent's family or others who could have kept the decedent from harm.

While the law on this subject is still unsettled, this ruling is being considered in many other states. (The *Tarasoff* case is a California state court decision which has no binding effect outside the state of California.) It would be prudent of the professional not to ignore the client who professes a desire to harm others. The professional should seek immediate counsel from peers and supervisors and should act to avert the danger, if considered real, by contacting the potential victim, his or her family, or others who would be in a position to avert the danger. Notifying the police would appear to be an appropriate action but only when the professional is satisfied that the police have notified the proper parties as to the potential danger.

Moral Standards Ethic/Sexual Relations in Therapy

Our final legal issue concerns the practice of sexual relations between professionals and their clients. There are two surveys that show the number of psychiatrists and psychologists who engage in sexual relations with their clients. In one, the authors report that 5 to 13 percent of physicians (including psychiatrists) report having sexual relations with patients (Kardener, Fuller, and Mensh, 1973). The other survey showed that over 5 percent of all female psychologists responding to the survey engaged in sexual intercourse with their clients (Holroyd and Brodsky, 1977). These numbers suggest that a serious problem exists within the human services professions concerning the unethical practice of having sexual relations with clients. All of the major codes and standards are specific in their position that such practices are unethical.

It seems pertinent to note that the verdict returned against a therapist who had engaged in sexual relations with his client for over five years was severe. The jury awarded the plaintiff $665,000 in compensatory, future mental health care, and punitive damages (*Greenberg v. McCabe*, 1978). The professional who engages in sexual relations with his or her client does so at the risk of losing his or her license to practice and much more. Then, too, there is considerable sentiment that, while sex with one's client may be therapeutic, it is not therapy (Corlis and Rabe, 1969).

SERVING AS AN EXPERT WITNESS

In addition to ethical complications relative to the legal system, the human services professional is "at risk" with the possibility of being called to testify as a party or a witness, sometimes as an expert witness, in a civil law suit or a criminal proceeding. When this happens the human services professional needs to be prepared. We offer here an overview of what ordinarily is a very demanding role. The reader is urged to examine a more comprehensive text on this subject before actually testifying in a trial or administrative hearing.

An expert witness is someone who has more training and experience in a particular subject than does the average lay person. The reason courts look to experts is because some subjects are too technical or too complex for either the judge or the jury to understand without some explanation. There are, therefore, many areas of expertise including real estate, accounting, medicine, engineering, taxidermy, law, education, psychiatry, and psychology. In an excellent description of the psychologist as a witness, Liebenson and Wepman (1964) describe the expert witness as,

> One who possesses special knowledge and experience on matters in issue in a lawsuit.... His function in court is to assist the jurors in arriving at a correct conclusion upon matters that are not familiar to their everyday experiences so that they may arrive at an intelligent understanding of the issues that must be decided. (p. 113)

While this text is very good at describing the function of the expert witness, it is somewhat out of date as to the rules of evidence. The reader should keep that in mind while reviewing the subject and use a more updated version for evidential matters (see, generally, Rosner, 1982).

The key function of the expert witness, aside from assisting the jury in understanding the issues in the case, is that the expert must first and foremost serve the profession which he or she represents. The expert needs to remain impartial regardless of who is paying the fee. When offering testimony concerning an issue, the expert must base his or her opinion on the principles of professional ethics and on training and experience. When two or more experts in the same field differ, it must be on unsettled issues, disputed areas within their profession, and not on biases developed as a result of their affiliation with a particular client. This can be a very difficult position to maintain, especially when the opposing attorney asks a question, the truthful answer to which will damage the client's case in some way.

The expert must be prepared to answer three main questions: (1) What are your qualifications? (2) Do you have an opinion based upon reasonable scientific probability? and (3) What is that opinion? As to qualifications, the expert needs to be able to show that he or she has had specialized training and, more importantly, *experience* in an area in which the average lay person does not have sufficient knowledge. The expert does not necessarily have to possess a Ph.D. or M.D. in order to qualify as an expert. But, the expert must possess the training and experience considered essential by the profession he or she serves. In other words, a high school degree, a bachelor's degree, or a master's degree would be sufficient in many areas of expertise recognized by the courts. The reader should not always think of the "expert" as someone else.

As to the question of whether the expert has an opinion on the issue based on reasonable scientific probability, the important issue centers on the expert's ability to relate his or her opinion to some supporting data usually relied upon by experts in that particular field. If not, the expert must respond that he or she does *not* have an opinion on the issue. This will surely be the expert's most trying moment.

If the expert does have an opinion based on such data, he or she can testify using information concerning the subject and the subject's behavior provided by the subject, by the subject's family and acquaintances, or from data of the type relied upon by experts in the field in forming opinions or inferences concerning the subject. Until recently, the expert could not testify upon the ultimate issue in a case. That is, the expert could not testify as to whether a defendant in a criminal case was or was not criminally responsible. However, this rule was observed more in the breach than in its observance, and the courts have begun to permit the expert to express an opinion on ultimate issues.

Some of the more common issues addressed by experts in the human services field are competency to stand trial, competency or credibility of complaining witnesses (e.g., in rape cases), competency of jurors when placed in issue by a defendant, competency of a person to consent to sexual relations (e.g., when a mentally deficient person claims to have been taken advantage of sexually), insanity, emotional state of mind, emotional impact of personal injury or illness, vocational outlook of persons injured or suffering job related illness, and ability to care for children (e.g., in termination of parental rights proceedings or adoption cases). Regardless of the nature of the testimony, it is imperative that the expert witness be familiar with the judicial process and the rules of evidence (Liebenson and Wepman, 1964; Robinson, 1980; Rosner, 1982). An excellent example of how to handle yourself in the courtroom is provided by William H. Edenfield (1985) in his work on using common sense when in the courtroom. One needs to know the rules of the game, to be prepared, and to use common sense.

SUMMARY

In this chapter, we have provided a general overview of the major areas of legal liability faced by the human services professional. It should be kept in mind that case law, such as described in this chapter, is part of a dynamic process. These cases are used to guide courts in reaching future decisions but only as they can be determined to be similar in nature. New case law is developed as new circumstances, not previously presented to the judicial system, are litigated. Occasionally, courts will overturn existing case law deciding that the logic used in reaching previous decisions is no longer valid in today's world.

The reader must be aware of this judicial decision-making process so as to keep abreast of the current case law as it affects his or her profession. New cases are usually discussed in professional journals or newspapers and can be followed with little or no extra effort. What is important is that the professional be aware of the general areas of potential liability so that he or she can be on the lookout for new developments in the law and for legal potholes that no doubt exist on the road of practice—public or private.

REFERENCES

Brown v. Moore, 274 F.2d 711 (1957), *cert. denied,* 355 U.S. 882 (1957).

Cobbs v. Grant, 8 Cal.3d 229, 104 Cal.Rpter. 505, 502 P.2d 1, 9 (1972).

Cohen, J. R. (1979). *Malpractice: A guide for mental health professionals*. New York: Free Press.

Corlis, R., & Rabe, P. (1969). *Psychotherapy from the center: A humanistic view of change and growth*. Scranton, PA: International Textbook.

Denkowski, K. M., & Denkowski, J. C. (1982). Client-counselor confidentiality: An update of rationale, legal status and implications. *The Personnel and Guidance Journal, 60,* 371–375.

Edenfield, W. H. (1985). Courtroom common sense for the mental health expert. In A. Combs & D. Avila (Eds.), *Perspectives on helping relationships* (pp. 114–134). Boston: Allyn & Bacon.

Everstine, L., Everstine, D. S., Heymann, G. M., True, R. H., Frey, D. H., Johnson, H. G., & Seiden, R. H. (1980). Privacy and confidentiality in psychotherapy. *American Psychologist, 35,* 828–840.

Greenberg, A. (1974). Involuntary psychiatric commitments to prevent suicide. *New York University Law Review, 49,* 227.

Greenberg v. McCabe, 453 F.Supp. 765 (D.C.E.D. Penn. 1978).

Holroyd, J. C., & Brodsky, A. M. (1977). Psychologists' attitudes and practices regarding erotic and non-erotic contact with patients. *American Psychologist, 32,* 843–849.

Kaimowitz v. Michigan Department of Mental Health, 42 U.S. Law Week 2063 (Mich. Cir. Ct., Wayne County) July 10, 1973).

Kardner, S., Fuller, M., & Mensh, I. (1973). A survey of physicians' attitudes and practices regarding erotic and non-erotic contact with patients. *American Journal of Psychiatry, 130,* 1077–1081.

Liebenson, H. A., & Wepman, J. M. (1964). *The psychologist as a witness*. Mundelein, IL: Callighan & Co.

McDonald v. Moore, 323 So.2d 635 (Fla. 1976).

Margolin, G. (1982). Ethical and legal considerations in marital and family therapy. *American Psychologist, 37,* 788–801.

Mills, D. H. (1984). Ethics education and ajudication within psychology. *American Psychologist, 39,* 669–675.

Murphy, G. (1973). Suicide and the right to die. *American Journal of Psychology, 130,* 472.

Noll, J. O., & Rosen, C. E. (1982). Privacy, confidentiality, and informed consent in psychotherapy. In B. L. Bloom & S. J. Asher (Eds.), *Psychiatric patient rights and patient advocacy: Issues and evidence* (pp. 171–195). New York: Human Sciences Press.

O'Connor v. Donaldson, 422 U.S. 563 (1975).

Olmstead v. U.S., 227 U.S. 438 (1928).

Pegram v. Sisco, 406 F.Supp. 776, 779 (W.D. Ark.), aff'd 547 F.2d 1172 (8th Cir. 1976).

Rennie v. Klein, 653 F.2d 836 (3d Cir. 1981).

Robinson, D. N. (1980). *Psychology and law.* New York: Oxford University Press.

Rogers v. Okin, 634 F.2d 650 (1st Cir. 1980).

Rosner, R., (Ed.). (1982). *Critical issues in American psychiatry and the law.* Springfield, IL: Charles C Thomas.

Rosoff, A. (1981). *Informed consent: A guide for health care providers.* Rockville, MD: Aspen Systems.

Rouse v. Cameron, 373 F.2d 451 (D.C. Cir. 1966).

Schutz, B. (1982). *Legal liability in psychotherapy.* San Francisco: Jossey-Bass.

Szasz, T. (1971). The ethics of suicide. *Antioch Review, 31*, 7.

Tarasoff v. The Regents of the University of California, 17 Cal. 3d 425, 551 P.2d 334 (1976).

Widiger, T. A., & Rorer, L. G. (1984). The responsible psychotherapist. *American Psychologist, 39*, 503–515.

Wilson, J. P. (1978). *The rights of adolescents in the mental health system.* Lexington, MA: Lexington Books.

Winters v. Miller, 446 F.2d 65 (2d Cir.), *cert. denied*, 404 U.S. 985 (1971).

Wyatt v. Stickney, 325 F.Supp. 791 (M.D. Ala. 1971), aff'd sub nom. *Wyatt v. Aderholt*, 503 F.2d 1305 (5th Cir. 1974).

CHAPTER 8

THE LIFE-SKILLS
TRAINING MODEL

Recall from our introductory chapter that we believe disciplines, particularly in practice, are united by a common ground. Therefore, we feel it is important to present a comprehensive delivery model that can be implemented by all practitioners, regardless of their disciplinary focus. Life-Skills Training is an eclectic model that can be utilized systematically to fulfill both the preventive and remedial roles of the eight disciplines. In this chapter, we will introduce the model by placing it within a historical context and by emphasizing development and rationale. In following chapters, we will elaborate the model, giving further attention to use and application.

DEFINITION OF LIFE-SKILLS

Life-skills is defined as all of those skills and knowledge prerequisite to development of the skills, in addition to the academic skills, that are necessary for effective living. Obviously this is a very general definition, and it does not imply that academic skills are not very important for effective living. Rather, the focus of the definition is on separating those skills that have been the primary domain of our educational institutions from those that have been, at best, a secondary concern and, at worst, no concern at all.

Whereas the academic curriculum involves reading, writing, arithmetic (mathematics), and more, the life-skills curriculum encompasses four generic life-skills determined in a national Delphi study (Brooks, 1984) — interpersonal communication/human relations, problem solving/decision

133

making, physical fitness/health maintenance, and identity development/ purpose in life. Even though theoretically separated, there is some overlap between what could be considered the life-skills curriculum and the academic curriculum in educational institutions. For example, interpersonal communication/human relations obviously contains some elements of reading, writing, speech, and civics. Elements of problem solving/ decision making can be found in virtually all of the academic skills. Physical fitness/health maintenance includes health education and more. And identity development/purpose in life incorporates philosophy, religion, psychology, and the like.

As an additional point, it is important to note that the word life-skills is deliberately hyphenated. This is to distinguish it from other uses of the term that are somewhat similar yet have different origins and different meanings. In this text and as used elsewhere by the senior author, life-skills connotes (and is related to a training model involving) application in both *prevention* and *remediation* of human problems.

Life-Skills Training (LST) is multifaceted. It refers to the application of the LST model to prevention and remediation of problems as well as to the training of trainers. In this context, the life-skills paradigm represents an innovation in the rapidly developing field of mental health "training" models.

OVERVIEW OF THE TRAINING PARADIGM

The genesis of training models in helping (and their resulting training methods) can be traced to (1) education where actual teaching skills were incorporated into the models, (2) psychology where the impact of behavior modification and social learning theory is obvious, and (3) the group counseling and group dynamics literature. The training model is an educational approach that directly attacks deficits through skills training. This approach is deemed more efficient and more effective (Adkins, 1984b; Goldstein, Sprafkin, and Gershaw, 1976; Lazarus, 1976) but represents a shift from the traditional "treatment" approach. Traditional helping approaches in psychiatry, psychology, and social work have emphasized understanding *causes* of deficit behavior through exploring the past, talking about the present, and planning changes for the future. In contrast, training approaches are concerned with learning. Founded on the belief that there are certain generic life-skills that are important for effective human functioning, these models deemphasize historical information and propose an educational approach to train others in needed skills. It is on this basis that the many training models have developed. (See Table 8-1).

TABLE 8-1
SKILLS TRAINING MODELS

Model	Originator(s)	Primary reference	Primary population	Training methods	Preventive or remedial	Taxonomy development
Structured Learning Therapy	Arnold Goldstein, Robert Sprafkin, N. Jane Gershaw	Goldstein, A., Sprafkin, R., Gershaw, N.J. (1976). *Skill training for community living.* New York: Pergamon Press	Persons with psychological disturbances, skill-deficient adolescents, police managers, teachers	Modeling, role playing, feedback, transfer training	Developed as remedial	59 "modeling tapes" developed
People in Systems	Gerard Egan, Michael Cowan	Egan, G., & Cowan, M.A. (1979). *People in systems.* Monterey, CA: Brooks/Cole Publishing Co.	Anyone	No specific methods developed. References given for recommended existing programs	Developed as preventive	Packages of skill needed to face developmental tasks and crises completely
Canadian	Saskatchewan Newstart	Smith, P. (1982). *The development of a taxonomy of the life skills required to become a balanced self-determined person.* Ottawa, Canada: Employment and Immigration Canada	Economically disadvantaged adults	61 lessons All following 5-phase plan of stimulus evolution, objective skill practice inquiry, skill application, evaluation	Developed as remedial	Product objectives

TABLE 8-1, cont.
SKILLS TRAINING MODELS

Model	Originator(s)	Primary reference	Primary population	Training methods	Preventive or remedial	Taxonomy development
Multimodal Behavior Therapy	Arnold Lazarus	Lazarus, A.A. (1976). *Multimodal behavior therapy.* New York: Springer Publishing Co.	All persons with psychological disturbances	Technical eclecticism Primarily didactic. Each of 7 modalities requires attention	Remedial	Complete taxonomy has been developed around 7 modalities
Life Skills Education	Winthrop R. Adkins	Adkins, W.R. (1984a). Life skills education: A video-based counseling/learning system. In D. Larson (ed.), *Teaching psychological skills: Models for giving psychology away.* Monterey, CA: Brooks/Cole Publishing Co.	Disadvantaged adolescents and adults	Instruction, audio-visual demonstration, discussion (Problem-centered structured inquiry model)	Developed as remedial	"Sets" of prevocational, motivational, and social problems in living

Approach	Author	Reference	Target Population	Method	Orientation	Comments
Developmental Therapy	Mary Margaret Wood	Wood, M.M. (1975). *Developmental therapy.* Baltimore: University Park Press	Emotionally disturbed young children	Psychoeducational classroom approach	Developed as preventive	Complete development of 144 developmental therapy curriculum objectives in 4 curriculum areas: behavior, communication, socialization, academic
Relationship Enhancement	Bernard Guerney, Jr.	Guerney, B.G., Jr. (1977). *Relationship enhancement.* San Francisco, Jossey-Bass	Anyone who is able to master the relationship enhancement skills	Intellectual explanation, discussion of concepts, and teaching skills	Preventive and remedial	Confined to interpersonal relationship skills (developed for improving relationships between family members—now expanded to others)
Structured Groups for Facilitating Development	David J. Drum, J. Eugene Knott	Drum, D.J. & Knott, J.E. (1977). *Structured groups for facilitating development.* New York: Human Sciences Press	Anyone	Educational experiential groups that provide procedures, methods, and systematic techniques	Preventive and remedial	Three areas: Acquiring life skills, resolving life themes, making life transitions. Each has series of workshop topics

TABLE 8-1, cont.
SKILLS TRAINING MODELS

Model	Originator(s)	Primary reference	Primary population	Training methods	Preventive or remedial	Taxonomy development
Human Resources Development	Robert R. Carkuff & Associates	Carkhuff, R.R. (1969). *Helping and human relations: A primer for lay and professional helpers. Vol. 1 & 2.* New York: Holt, Rinehart & Winston	Helpees can be anyone	Helpees go through sequence of involvement, exploration, understanding, action	Developed as remedial	Primarily interpersonal relationships. Also developed a physical fitness/health maintenance program
Psychosocial Adjustment Skills	Robert L. Akridge, Bob L. Means	Akridge, R.L., & Means, B.L. (1982). Psychosocial adjustment skills training. In B. Bolton (ed.), *Vocational adjustment of disabled persons.* Baltimore: University Park Press	Vocational rehabilitation clients	Training group	Remedial	3 competency areas: self-management, interpersonal relations, life planning. "Spheres" of functioning: physical, intrapersonal, ideological, financial, technical

Model	Author(s)	Reference	Target	Format	Type	Basis
Deliberate Psychological Education	Ralph L. Mosher & Norman A. Sprinthall	Mosher, R.L. & Sprinthall, N.A. (1971). Psychological education: A means to promote personal development during adolescence. *The counseling psychologist.* 2(4), 3–82.	Adolescents	Group and classroom instruction by teachers and counselors	Preventive	
Changes	Eugene Gendlin, Kathleen McGuire Boukydis	Gendlin, E.T. (1981). *Focusing.* New York: Bantam Books	Anyone interested in talking about his/her situation in a supportive group of listeners and who is willing to serve also as a listener to others	Weekly 2 to 3 hour meeting for participants to learn listening and focusing skills. Then egalitarian peer-helping takes place in pairs, triads or small groups. No distinction is made between "helpers" and "helpees"	Can be preventive or remedial	Based on the client-centered model as developed by Carl Rogers

TABLE 8-1, cont.
SKILLS TRAINING MODELS

Model	Originator(s)	Primary reference	Primary population	Training methods	Preventive or remedial	Taxonomy development
Life-Skills Training	George M. Gazda	This text	All except actively psychotic or those whose reasoning abilities are impaired by organic brain syndrome	Instruction in skill deficit areas using wide variety of materials and methods according to the following sequence: brief instruction, trainee role play and practice, feedback, homework	Developed with preventive and remedial dimensions Multiple impact training is the name given to the remedial part of the model.	"Families" of life skills suggested. Generic life-skills (GLS) empirically derived are — Fitness/ Health Maintenance Identity Development — Interpersonal Communication/ Human Relations — Problem Solving/ Decision Making. GLS are applied in family, work, school, community

Model Development

It is apparent from an examination of the thirteen models in Table 8-1 that the evolution of the skills training approach in mental health has a relatively short history. Despite the relative newness of the approach, skills training models have progressed from having a very narrow focus to having a strong and broadly based program.

The initial narrow focus was manifested in two ways—in the skills the models addressed and in the populations to be served. Early skills training models and research were confined mostly to the area of interpersonal relationship development (Carkhuff, 1969a, 1969b; Gazda et al., 1973; Pierce, Schauble, and Wilson, 1971). In the early to mid 1970s more comprehensive models that moved beyond interpersonal communication skills and advocated training in more than one dimension began to appear. Of the multidimensional models, the ones with the complete taxonomies are the Canadian, Life-Skills Training, People in Systems, Multi-modal Behavior Therapy, and Developmental Therapy (see Table 8-1). The Canadian and Life-Skills appear to be the most comprehensive although the Canadian model is more focused on career development.

During this period when models were progressing from focus on a particular skill toward focus on a taxonomy of skills, there was a great deal of parallel development that resulted in a number of researchers and practitioners proposing similar programs directed at a variety of populations. Notice in Table 8-1 that many of the training models in use today were narrowly focused in the sense that they were developed for specific populations. However, with few exceptions, either the original developer, his or her students or colleagues, or others have adapted the material for use with additional groups.

One of the earliest training models is Life Skills Education. This comprehensive program was developed by Winthrop R. Adkins for disadvantaged adolescents and adults and was tested in the early 1960s at Project Try in the Bedford-Stuyvesant area of New York. Adkins identifies a handful of variables that describe different target groups. Configurations of the following variables define unique groups and present reasonably accurate predictions of the kinds of emotional problems people are trying to solve: age, sex, socioeconomic status, ethnicity, geographical location, and special conditions of life. Adkins believes there are other problems that can be predicted based on the frequency of their occurrence in the general population. Examples of these are losing a job, raising a handicapped child, or being rejected in love. Adkins's premise in Life Skills Education is that common learning programs can be developed for problems that are experienced in a similar way by a large number of persons and that there are a limited number of workable solutions that can be presented in different combinations. All of this is done in a way that allows individuality by encouraging each person to take responsibility for his or her own learning (Adkins, 1984b). Adkins and his associates coined the term Life Skills to describe this type of learning (Adkins, Rosenburg, and Sharar, 1965). As with other models, the basic model has been adapted for use with many populations by Adkins and his students and associates, even though the primary population is disadvantaged adolescents and adults (Adkins, 1984b).

Deliberate Psychological Education, developed by R. L. Mosher and N. A. Sprinthall, was implemented about the same time as Life Skills Education and was also directed toward adolescents. However, Deliberate Psychological Education was intended as a part of a student's skills experience and was to be delivered by teachers and counselors in the classroom in small groups. Though developed as a preventive model, Deliberate Psychological Education was also expanded to serve a remedial function for those students who had already experienced problems with one or more of the skill areas taught in the program.

Some of the models that specify the population for which they were developed have not been adapted and have remained exclusively for the very narrow population they address. For example, Developmental Therapy developed by M. M. Wood (1975) is still for emotionally disturbed young children, and Psychosocial Adjustment Skills Training developed by Robert Akridge and Bob Means (1982) is used only with vocational rehabilitation clients. The Life-Skills Training model developed by George Gazda also has not been adapted. However, this model departs from the focus on a narrow population; LST is designed for general use with two exceptions—those who are actively psychotic and those whose reasoning abilities are impaired by organic brain syndrome.

In summary, the populations served by training models tend to be very general and in some cases limited only by decisions made by the users. Accordingly, many of the original models which were developed to meet the needs of specific populations were quickly adapted for use with other groups. Adaption was possible because the skills training methodology, derived from related disciplines, is a consistent process, flexible enough to accommodate various skills and populations.

Training Methods

There are similar elements in the training methods of each of the training models examined in Table 8-1 in the sense that they all contain some combination of cognitive and experiential components. The differences lie in the extent to which each component is used in the training and in the specific topics included in the model. Also, there is a tendency in these models to use existing intervention strategies in the experiential phase rather than strategies that are unique to the particular model.

The Relationship Enhancement model of Bernard Guerney, Jr., is illustrative of the training methods used and the process that trainees follow. The initial phase in Guerney's model is *intellectual explanation*. This phase is called the didactic phase by Carkhuff and Lazarus and the instruction phase by Gazda. Basically what happens in this phase is that the trainee is introduced to the skills to be taught, a rationale is given to explain why the skill is important, and the training process is outlined.

Guerney's second phase is *discussion of concepts*. During this phase of training a theoretical overview of the particular skill is given and the training group discusses various aspects of the issue. Since there is a great variance across groups in terms of intellectual curiosity, this phase may be omitted or at least shortened for some groups. Gazda, in Life-Skills Training, limits the discussion of concepts except when the purpose of the group is training trainers. Trainers need the background theory and concepts since they teach others.

The third phase of Guerney's Relationship Enhancement is *teaching skills*. The primary methods used by Guerney and others are modeling by the leaders, role playing by the leaders and the trainees, and feedback by the leader and by the trainees. Others, such as Gazda in Life-Skills Training, add a homework phase which allows trainees to practice particular skills and report on results at subsequent sessions. In this fashion, the trainees learn more effective skills, and as deficits are remedied, they function with fewer problems.

As has been demonstrated in this overview, skills training models have progressed from a focus on a particular skill and/or a particular population to programs that encompass a comprehensive taxonomy of skills applicable to a very general population. The commonality tying these models together is the educational approach evident philosophically and in the training methodology used to implement these programs as helping approaches. In a very brief period of time, there has been successful development of a new approach to mental health. The popularity and rapidly increasing application of the skills training procedures for the prevention and remediation of human problems suggests that we are in the midst of the development of a "fourth force" in mental health prevention and treatment. Life-Skills Training is a comprehensive contribution to this fourth force.

THE DEVELOPMENT AND RATIONALE OF THE LIFE-SKILLS TRAINING MODEL

Historical Development

The LST model has been a progressive development, the product of many years of professional experience of the senior author, George Gazda. The earliest influence on this model was during the 1960s and 1970s when Gazda was actively engaged in the development of group counseling and therapy (Gazda, 1968a, 1968b, 1969, 1971, 1978). During this period, Gazda and his students conducted groups with several different populations including juvenile delinquents, professional educators, psychiatric patients, recovering alcoholics, convicted felons, and adults seeking personal growth, among others. Contact with the developing group procedures for implementing therapeutic intervention and different kinds of contact such as with experimental research, especially in the form of doctoral dissertations, further influenced Gazda's thinking and accounted for his ideas changing.

The result of this experience, of particular relevance to the LST model, was the gradual development of a theory of Developmental Group Counseling. This developmental model for group counseling was especially influenced by the work of developmental theorists such as Erickson (1950, 1963), Havighurst (1953, 1972), Tryon and Lilienthal (1950), Super (1963), Gesell, Ilg, Ames, and Bullis (1946), Piaget (Flavell, 1963; Wadsworth, 1971), Kohlberg and Turiel (1971), Loevinger (1976), and Dupont (1978). A comprehensive framework for the application for Developmental Group Counseling included the holistic view of development of individuals across ages and stages.

Concurrent with the senior author's development of a comprehensive group counseling model, he and his students and colleagues were influenced by the Human Resources Development model of Robert Carkhuff and associates (1969a, 1969b). From this model, Gazda and colleagues developed human relations/communication training applications for educators (Gazda et al., 1973, 1977, 1984), health care practitioners (Gazda, Childers, and Walters, 1982; Gazda, Walters, and Childers, 1975) criminal justice personnel (Sisson, Arthur, and Gazda, 1981), and secondary school students (Gazda, Walters, and Childers, 1981).

A decade of experience in the application of communication and problem-solving skills training to psychiatric patients in a veteran's administration hospital led the senior author and a clinical nurse specialist, Ms. Mildred Powell, to introduce a holistic treatment model—Multiple Impact Training (Gazda, 1981). This approach introduced the idea of providing simultaneous training interventions of multiple generic life-skills. In evaluating this approach, May (1981) found a significant improvement in trained patients over controls in two out of three of the generic life-skill areas in which they were trained. Additional research by Illovsky (1985) also found significant improvement in trained patients over controls on two life-skills variables.

Following this experience with a remedial life-skills approach, the senior author and his students have most recently developed Life-Skill

Training modules that have been applied to elementary and secondary schools for preventive purposes. Research on these programs is promising (Kavkewitz, 1983; Spalding, 1985).

The final development leading to the model proposed in this text was the Delphi dissertation study (Brooks, 1984) of the junior author, David Brooks. Using descriptors of knowledge/skills necessary for successful coping behavior consonant with age and/or stage of development, theorists achieved consensus on the basic life-skills for each age group: childhood, adolescence, and adulthood. These experts also classified the life-skills by generic area producing the four generic life-skills described earlier.

Theoretical Rationale for Life-Skills Training

The viewpoint expressed in the LST model, of an age progressive developmental framework, is consistent with our society and with Western culture in general since the cultures are organized on the basis of expected increments of mastery in the biological, intellectual, vocational, sociological, and psychological realms of their citizens. For example, schools are organized on a preschool and kindergarten, early elementary school, middle school, and high school basis; state laws govern marriage ages of its citizens; and federal laws govern legal employment, retirement ages, and the like (Muuss, 1962).

When building the LST model, we began with how the whole person is constituted developmentally (see Figure 8-1). Notice that there are seven areas of human development represented. It is the theories associated with these seven areas that are the source from which descriptions of skills have been determined. Through the Brooks (1984) Delphi study, these descriptors have been grouped by age and rated as to their importance in human development. Additional descriptors were added by the developmental experts. Each expert classified the descriptors into generic life-skills areas, or families of related knowledge and skills by age groups (see Figure 8-1). The resultant taxonomy (Appendixes D through G) represents what developmental specialists consider to be the essential elements for total human development.

The life-skills taxonomy admittedly represents compromises and certain liberties in interpretations of developmental theoretical models. The greatest liberty assumed was the classification of knowledge/skills descriptors of *stage* theorists into the three general age groupings of childhood, adolescence, and adulthood. Essentially these were the theories of intellectual, ego, moral, and affective development. Even those theories of human development that are age related—namely, psychosocial, physical-sexual, and vocational—contain various gaps, especially at the upper

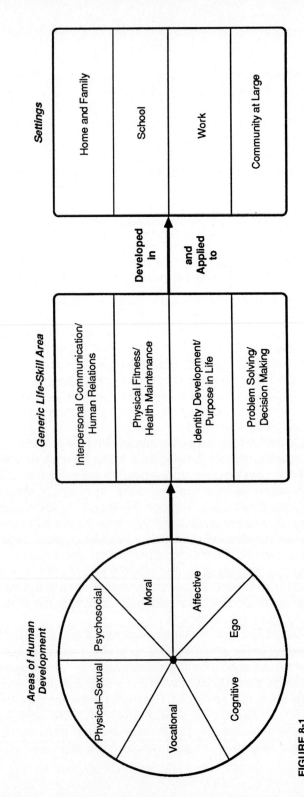

FIGURE 8-1
A Model for the Development and Application of Generic Life-Skills.

end of the age scale. Even with these weaknesses, the life-skills taxonomy represents the first comprehensive attempt using a developmental rationale.

Basic Assumptions

What follows is a listing and brief discussion of basic assumptions underlying the Life-Skills Training model.

1 There are at least seven well-defined areas of human development: psychosocial, physical-sexual, vocational, cognitive, ego, moral, and affective (see Figure 8-1).

Although others may have developed models for areas of human development, seven theorists were selected for the Life-Skills model. These together with their developmental area are as follows: Erikson (1950, 1963), Havighurst (1953, 1972), and Tryon and Lilienthal (1950) (psychosocial); Gesell, Ilg, Ames, and Bullis (1946) (physical-sexual); Super (1963) (vocational); Piaget (cf. Flavell, 1963; Wadsworth, 1971) (cognitive); Loevinger (1976) (ego); Kohlberg and Turiel (1971) (moral); and Dupont (1978) (affective).

2 From the seven well-defined areas of human development, coping behaviors (life-skills) can be determined that are appropriate to age or stage.

Each of the theorists who has developed models included as the seven areas of human development has also specified certain attitudes and behaviors that seem to be necessary for individuals to achieve mastery of a given age or stage. For example, Havighurst (1953, 1972) points out that during middle age (between thirty and sixty) the man and woman must abandon the more strenuous leisure-time activities and develop leisure-time activities that are meaningful, satisfying, and applicable to the physical limitations of their age.

Using the attitudes and behaviors specified by the theorists, the authors have identified approximately 300 life-skills from the seven areas of human development. These 300 life-skills and others contributed by selected developmental experts contacted in the Delphi questionnaire (Brooks, 1984) can be classified into three general age groups: childhood, adolescence, and adulthood. Furthermore, a consensus of developmental experts can be obtained for each life-skill by age grouping. In essence, a taxonomy of life-skills by three general age groupings can be constructed (Brooks, 1984).

3 There are identifiable stages in each of the seven areas of human development through which individuals must progress if they are to achieve mastery of later, more advanced stages.

This assumption can be illustrated by reference to a specific area—moral development. According to Duska and Whelan (1975), stage development is invariant in moral development. In reference to Kohlberg's moral stage development theory, they state, "Moral development is growth, and like all growth, takes place according to a pre-determined sequence" (p. 48).

4 Accomplishment of developmental tasks is dependent upon mastery of *life-skills*, that is, coping behaviors appropriate to stage and task.

This concept may be illustrated by citing a psychosocial developmental task of early childhood followed by the coping behaviors necessary to achieve this task. "Achieving an appropriate dependence-independence pattern" represents the developmental task. The coping behaviors necessary to complete this task require "adjusting to less private attention and becoming independent physically while remaining strongly dependent emotionally." Examples of this would be a child's ability to share parents with his or her new teacher, with peers, and with others while simultaneously learning rules of safety to give greater mobility and physical independence.

5 In general there are certain age ranges when certain coping skills (life-skills) are optimally learned.

A developmental model, whether age- or stage-related, assumes that mastery of concepts and skills at an earlier level is prerequisite to mastery of more advanced concepts and skills. Much of the remedial instruction in education is also based on this assumption. For example, before one is able to master long division, one must first be able to master the multiplication process. In career development, before one achieves the highest position on a career ladder, one must achieve mastery of successive lower positions on the ladder. In achieving a positive self-concept, one must struggle with moments of self-doubt and various degrees of insecurity.

Havighurst (1972) supports this assumption of an optimal learning period with two related concepts: the "teachable moment" and the "developmental task." Concerning the first, he says "when the body is ripe, and society requires and the self is ready to achieve a certain task, the teachable moment has come" (p. 7). In defense of his concept of the teachable moment, Havighurst (1972) refers to Palmer's introduction to a conference on critical periods of development sponsored by the Social Science Research Council:

> In their respective ways, von Sendon, Lorenz, Spitz, and Piaget have observed phenomena which suggest that there may be critical periods in the development of the child—points or stages during which the organism is maximally receptive to specific stimuli. Such stages may exist in the

development of fundamental sensory processes, such as conceptions about size, shape, distance, and in the development of social behavior as well. The critical periods hypothesis asserts that those stages are of limited duration: there may be a finite period of increased inefficiency for the acquisition of experience, before which it cannot be assimilated and after which the level of receptivity remains constant. (p. 6)

Havighurst's (1953) description of the developmental task carries the readiness concept one step further.

A developmental task is a task which arises at or about a certain period of life of the individual, successful achievement of which leads to happiness and success with later tasks, while failure leads to unhappiness in the individual, disapproval by society, and difficulty with later tasks. (p. 2)

The position taken in this text is that the coping skill(s) necessary to complete a given developmental task or series of developmental tasks that may constitute a *stage* of development can be determined across the seven areas of human development cited earlier. In the LST model, these constitute a life-skill or a group of life-skills.

   6 Individuals achieve optimal functioning when they attain operational mastery of fundamental life-skills.

This assumption is dependent on future research. Before comprehensive research can be initiated, however, instruments and other means for assessing life-skills mastery must be developed.

   In the meantime, until life-skill mastery can be shown empirically to be necessary and sufficient for optimal functioning, there is some argument on this issue, stemming from an alternate, more "traditional" frame of reference. Bellack (1979) acknowledges that insofar as the skill model ascribes *some* interpersonal difficulties to specific response deficits these deficits are conceptually responsive to skills training programs. He cautions, however, that there are a variety of other factors that could cause the same pattern of social failures. For instance, anxiety has been shown to interfere with many types of behavior patterns and to serve as an inhibitory function over others (Bellack, 1979; Martin, 1971). In addition, research (Arkowitz, Lichtenstein, McGovern, and Hines, 1975; Wolpe and Lazarus, 1966) indicates that interpersonal anxiety can interfere with effective social performance even in the absence of social skills deficits. Further, cognitive disturbances, such as ones associated with schizophrenia, can interfere with or distort interpersonal communication as well as produce bizarre behavior that results in interpersonal failure (Bellack, 1979; see Bellack and Hersen, 1978). Faculty attributions have also been shown to affect the course of interpersonal behavior independent of skill level (Eisler, Frederiksen, and Peterson, 1978; Warren and Gilner, 1978). And finally, Bellack suggests that people can have response capabilities in their repertoires but fail to emit the response because they have not been reinforced (or have been punished).

7 Neuroses and functional psychoses frequently result from failure to develop one's life-skills.

Kazdin (1979) acknowledges the importance of social behavior in psychotic patients in the following statement:

> Social behaviors occupy an important role in the definition of behavior of psychotic patients as evidenced by withdrawal, irrational statements, blunted affect, and difficulty in communication skills. These behaviors do not begin to exhaust the symptoms of psychiatric patients but illustrate the role of social behavior in identifying psychopathology. (p. 54)

Kazdin (1979) cites the research of Fairweather, Sanders, Maynard, and Cressler (1969), Freeman and Simmons (1963), and Staudt and Zubin (1957) encompassing several somatic, pharmacological, and psychotherapeutic treatments that showed the treatment provided in the hospital had little relationship to community adjustment of psychiatric patients. Research by Greenberg et al. (1975), Linn, Caffey, Klett, and Hogarty (1977), and Paul and Lentz (1977), on the other hand, suggested more favorable results for specific treatments such as *social learning* programs and foster home care.

> The problems in social behaviors that psychiatric patients evidence apparently do not simply emerge immediately preceding their entrance into the career of a patient. Persons later seen in treatment have often shown a history of prior social relations and withdrawal from interpersonal social relationships. Possibly, there would be value in identifying individuals with such interpersonal deficits prior to the point at which this is compounded with additional problems of pathology in order to intervene early. (Kazdin, 1979, p. 65)

Zubin and Spring (1977) have suggested that improvements in *coping skills* in general, and particularly in the area of *social interaction*, are possible factors that might decrease a susceptibility to schizophrenia. The evidence reviewed by Kazdin that persons diagnosed as psychotic have had a long history of interpersonal problems, particularly those with a poor prognosis, suggests the value of training in social skills early in life as an attempt to decrease the risk of psychiatric treatment later in life.

With regard to neurotics, Bryant et al. (1976) found that 28 percent of a sample of neurotic outpatients were regarded as socially unskilled. Argyle (1981) reported that these same neurotic outpatients were low in components of control (assertiveness) and rewardingness and were extremely bad conversationalists. They often suffered acutely from social anxiety and avoided many social situations altogether. Argyle concluded that neurotic patients suffer from all the main kinds of social inadequacy.

> I conclude that SST [social skills training], of various kinds, is useful for neurotics, especially those with social behavior problems, and I believe that it will be most effective if use is made of the principles of social interaction. A valuable recent development, especially in North America, is the administration of SST by nurses, social workers, probation officers, and so on, as well as by psychologists. (Argyle, 1981, p. 283)

8 Instruction and/or training in life-skills that is introduced when a person is developmentally ready to learn given concepts and skills serves the role of preventive mental health.

The position taken in the LST model is that if individuals are taught the subskills of the four generic life-skills during the optimum period for them to be learned, and if in fact they are learned, the cumulative effect would be to enable them to contend effectively with life's problems and therefore be less subject to mental and emotional disturbances. This assumption represents the basis for the preventive mental health contention of this model. Obviously only long-term, longitudinal studies can validate this assumption. Until such time as a comprehensive LST program can be initiated throughout the age span, this assumption will remain unvalidated.

9 Instruction and/or training in life-skills that is introduced when a person is suffering from emotional or mental disturbance, of a functional nature, serves the role of remediation in mental health.

If one assumes that persons suffering from emotional or mental disturbances that are not the result of organic origin are so affected because they lack appropriate coping skills in one or more of the generic life-skills areas, then instruction and/or training that develops coping skills will result in a remediation of these skill deficits, and the person will be able to cope effectively. This assumption can be tested more readily than the previous one because the effects of remedial interventions can be determined immediately following the training.

10 The greater the degree of functional disturbance, the greater is the likelihood that the individual will be suffering from multiple life-skill deficits.

Consultation and research by the senior author in a psychiatric hospital over a period of more than ten years has suggested that hospitalized patients suffer from *multiple* life-skill deficits. Furthermore, remediation of these patients requires multiple life-skill training interventions. These multiple life-skill interventions have been shown by May (1981) to result in improvement by psychiatric patients.

The basic assumptions of the LST model provide the elements that permit the operationalization of the model when combined with the more than 300 specific life-skill descriptors determined from the national Delphi study (found in Appendixes D through G). Our concern now, in the next section, is with outlining the process through which the LST model is implemented.

ISSUES IN ESTABLISHING TRAINING GROUPS

Selection of Members

Since, as mentioned earlier, there are two basic types of training groups—training for prevention and training for remediation—the initial question is whether groups will be composed of prevention or remediation candidates. Although there are situations when two groups are required for effective training, sometimes prevention and remediation candidates will be mixed in the same group. Consider, for example, a population of all ninth graders in a particular school who are being trained in physical fitness and health maintenance skills. Some students would likely be obese or deficient in some physical exertion measure while others would be in the normal or average range on these measures. The students who are in the average range could benefit from the skill training by applying the principles or adopting the lifestyle that will maintain their status as they move through life. Those who are in the remedial category can also benefit from the same information by applying the principles to their lives in a way that allows them to move toward the average and then continue to apply the principles to maintain the position once acquired. In this case, it is not as important to segregate prevention candidates from remediation candidates, since both groups could benefit from the information. Making the decision to segregate the two groups can generally be determined by whether separation is logistically possible, by the way in which the curriculum is written, and by whether the two groups could benefit equally from the experience.

An important factor in member selection is whether or not the potential member is volunteering or is asked to participate by someone else. If practical, groups composed of persons who volunteer to participate are most desirable. The advantage to this arrangement is obvious. A training group can be quickly sabotaged by members who tune out the trainer and training.

Another approach to selection, particularly of reluctant members, is a trial membership in a training group. This is a technique that tends to decrease negative response and gives a group member the option of either staying or leaving after X number of hours or X number of sessions. A good rule of thumb is to ask the person to stay for one-third of the sessions. This allows ample time to understand the nature of the group, the style of the leader, the other participants, and the potential benefit of the training to the person's life. If after the trial period the individual decides to drop out of the group, the decision is based on facts rather than assumptions. In reality, many times, the most resistant member initially becomes the strongest supporter later.

Training Group Composition

There are pros and cons concerning heterogeneity or homogeneity along a number of variables when considering group composition. From experience with hundreds of training groups, though, the authors have developed some guidelines that work most of the time. Sometimes there are budgetary or logistical constraints that dictate a different composition, or a group is preidentified, as in a work group or a school class. When selection for grouping is a possibility, the following guidelines are advocated:

1 In training groups conducted at work sites, keep groups homogeneous with regard to level of position. For example, training groups for hospital personnel work best if all members are functioning at essentially the same level—supervisors in nursing, housekeeping, and business office could be trained together. This arrangement tends to decrease threat and increase verbalization of all members. This also avoids the situation of supervisors in the same training group with their supervisees.

2 Mixing departments in the group representation allows rapport and thus better understanding to develop interdepartmentally. This is a positive residual spin-off of training groups that address a frequent problem— especially in larger organizations. The authors have found that by forcing interaction through participation in the same group, group members frequently develop an appreciation for the problems that departments other than their own experience, resulting in an increase in interdepartmental cooperation and esprit de corps.

3 In many organizations there are employees who respond negatively to any changes or innovations that are introduced. These persons should be spread out over several groups to prevent sabotage of the training group. This guideline, in fact, applies generally across groups of various ages and settings.

4 Mix sexes and races in training groups to approximate the real world.

5 Grouping children in elementary and high school depends to some extent on the training topic, and since there are so many individual differences from school to school, a *rough* guideline is to avoid mixing children with preadolescents and preadolescents with adolescents. However, these categories frequently overlap within the same grade, and so sometimes the decision about mixing these categories must be made at the time of the training, taking into consideration all of the existing factors mentioned in this chapter as well as the trainer's "gut feeling." One approach in the school setting is to assign training groups tentatively with the understanding that changes might be made after the training begins.

If all students understand this from the outset, changes that are made will be more readily accepted.

6 When grouping individuals who require significant remedial training, such as community mental health patients and psychiatric patients, the primary criteria are that they have deficits in the same generic life-skill areas and that they are in contact with reality.

Training Group Size

Since the success of training groups depends upon active participation of group members in the exercises, size is very important. There might very well be a constraint in a particular situation that would dictate either a group too large or too small to be effective. However, when given a choice, a group size of ten to eighteen members seems to be optimal. Fewer than ten might not allow as much peer feedback as desired and might encourage one or two to monopolize the group time. A group larger than eighteen gets unwieldy in terms of controlling the situation and getting everyone involved in the exercise. In the authors' experience, twelve members is optimal because of the possible subdivision available (two groups of six, six groups of two, three groups of four, four groups of three). Also, when working with the entire group, twelve persons can easily participate in each exercise without delaying the process.

Sometimes large groups of individuals (fifty or more people) with minimal deficits are trained by using cotrainers or assistants, or peer helpers who distribute themselves throughout the group to answer questions, aid in role playing or other experiential activity, or simply observe. This model can be effective, and the key to its successful implementation seems to be skilled assistants. This way a trainer can present didactic information as well as model desired behavior, then give assignments to the group, and let the assistants aid in the skill acquisition process. The drawback of this model, in addition to problems associated with weak assistants, is that rapport does not develop as quickly, so participants are likely to be reluctant to become personally involved in the training setting. This could possibly impede gain in skill development.

The Training Group Trainer

The skill and personal qualities of the trainer are of paramount importance to the success of the training experience. While generalists do exist in the training field, it is more common that a trainer will be proficient in one or two skills that thus establish him or her as an "expert" in those areas. However, an additional expertise is required for the LST model. The array of roles the trainer assumes include teacher, model, evaluator, motivator, encourager, facilitator, protector, and training media developer (Gazda,

1984). Trainers must be competent to fulfill these roles across skill areas. The process during which this achievement occurs can be viewed as a "pyramid of training."

The first step in the process is training the prospective trainer in the skills to be taught. This includes essentially putting prospective trainers through an experience similar to the one that they will be expected eventually to lead. The systematic training allows achievement of skills at points along the way in training so that the end result of successfully completing the training is the ability to model the skill effectively. This ability is of paramount importance in training. Included in the training at this stage of trainer instruction is the ability to transfer successfully the modeling of the skills from the training group to everyday life.

The second stage of trainer instruction involves coleadership of a training group with an experienced, effective trainer. This phase allows the neophyte trainer to "fine tune" his or her skills, receive feedback from a significant other in an authentic training setting, and model and adopt techniques that are effective, appealing, and fit compatibly within the neophyte trainer's way of being with people.

The third step in trainer instruction involves allowing the neophyte trainer to train alone under the supervision of an experienced teacher. This can be accomplished in a number of ways including observation through a one-way mirror, videotape or audiotape recordings of the group that are evaluated later, or having the experienced leader participate as a naive group member in the training group. The key here is genuine feedback that will allow the neophyte trainer to fine tune his or her skills even more.

The last stage is when the neophyte trainer trains alone. At this point neophyte may be a misnomer even though this is an anxiety-inducing experience for some trainers. The anxiety is generally short-lived, however, since only the most effective persons progress to this point. Along the way the trainers are taught to encourage group members, give effective feedback in a nonhurtful manner, evaluate the progress of each group member, motivate members to practice the skills outside the group, protect sensitive members from hurt or verbal attack of stronger members, and listen closely to identify barriers, hidden agendas, inadequacies, strengths, fears, or other items that might affect group process or skill achievement.

In addition to the skills mentioned, one important quality of effective trainers is that they allow disagreement or even confrontation without becoming defensive or feeling that their own position needs to be defended. If the trainer is comfortably confident with himself or herself, it is possible to listen to disagreement or confrontation without personalizing it. This difficult stance in a group setting is one of the tests that expert trainers have to pass when implementing the training sequence with groups.

Sequence of Training

The training process takes place in roughly the following sequence:

1 *Theoretical instruction.* This part of training is kept to a minimum in order to devote the majority of time to skill development. However, the extent to which a theoretical rationale and documentation of the technique takes place depends on particular members and the level of the group. Brighter, more articulate group members demand and should receive more communication of the theoretical underpinning of the process, whereas less aware groups will spend the majority of their time in the experiential mode.

2 *Leader modeling.* One of the first experiential activities is initiated by the group leader who models what he or she considers to be appropriate behavior (based on the skill being taught), and group members are thus able to visualize the process. An alternative at this stage is a videotape illustrating the skill in a controlled setting. This is a valuable supplement to a training group since the tape can be designed to communicate some very specific teaching points. It also allows the trainer to focus more on the group without having to do specific modeling at this point.

3 *Demonstration using simulations.* The group leader has a number of options, beginning with using paper and pencil responses as a non-threatening group activity. Other options include a variety of role-playing arrangements from a group role play involving everyone, a role-play demonstration in front of the group, or various configurations of the group in role-play practice. The simulations comprise the heart of the training process and allow members to begin feeling comfortable with the process and with the new skills. It is important when designing the simulations to begin with the least threatening situation and move with each new activity to an increasing level of threat. The threat is induced by being put on the spot in front of others to exhibit a new skill; thus, the trainer might move from anonymous to personal and from hypothetical to real.

4 *Personally relevant interactions.* Toward the end of the training process, the leader, by virtue of skill development and rapport among group members, should be in a position to ask the group to discuss real or personally relevant situations with each other. This is the step immediately preceding generalization of the skill outside the group setting. The trainer can determine readiness at this point by observing the extent to which group members are willing to disclose their feelings and are committed to transferring the information or insight they've gained to a specific situation outside the group.

5 *Transfer of training.* The ultimate effects of training are the degree to which the training transfers to dealing with the problems of daily living. In one sense, this stage is a part of each of the four previous stages as well as a separate or final stage. It is a part of each stage insofar as homework assignments given during each of the stages relate to transfer of the skill being developed to relevant issues in one's life. And, of course, the final goal/stage of training is transferability of laboratory-learned skills to real life situations.

Training Modes

In this section the various training modalities are described. Each modality's strengths, weaknesses, and typical applications are pointed out.

Consultant-Led Training Group   This traditional mode is generally the most expensive means of delivering skill training. In a typical organization an outside trainer comes into the organization and provides X number of hours of training for Y number of dollars. Generally one or two groups are trained: those employees belonging to a department or unit of an organization which is having problems that management feels could be positively impacted upon by skills training or a selected group of managers, directors, or department heads with the idea that what is learned could then be disseminated informally to others by these leaders in the organization. With newer, more efficient, and less expensive modes of delivery available, it is easy to see why this traditional way of delivering training is not seen so often. However, in spite of its cost there are uses for the traditional mode, particularly where specific skill deficit areas involving a relatively small number of persons are uncovered. Another use for this mode is to learn whether or not skill training will truly make a difference before investing in a major training project involving many more employees.

An example of a situation where a consultant might be hired to come in would be a successful company that had begun to get complaints from customers that telephone operators at the company were rude when an inquiry was made about anything out of the ordinary. Provided other departments were operating without significant problems, it would be possible to deal with this situation by hiring a consultant to train only the telephone operators in interpersonal skills as they relate to dealing with customers on the telephone. On the other hand, one of the following plans might be followed if the telephone operator problem turned out to be only a symptom of a larger problem that permeated the company.

Trainer-Led Training Groups   When there are trained trainers on board in an institution or agency, these trainers can be utilized in the same manner as the consultant trainers. Furthermore they can, of course, use the same media for training purposes that are to be described later.

Trainer-led groups are most likely to be in psychiatric hospital settings and educational settings. In the hospital setting, the clientele typically are the psychiatric patients, and group training would be directed toward remediation of life-skill deficits. In educational settings, the clientele would be students, and ideally the group training would be preventive in emphasis.

Consultant-Led Train-the-Trainer Group   The assumption in this training mode is that most organizations have persons already on staff who exemplify the end result management would like from a skills training program. With the aid of a consultant who has developed a train-the-trainer format, high-functioning employees can be selected to become in-house trainers. This training process has two phases: first, one employee must learn the skills to be taught (which, theoretically, only need fine tuning since trainees were screened for these attributes) and the theoretical underpinnings of that particular way of being; and second, the employee must learn training skills or techniques for disseminating the skills in ways that increase the possibility that they will be transferred to the employment situation.

The train-the-trainer approach is gaining popularity as an economical means of training large numbers of employees. An example of this approach is *A Step Ahead in Caring*, a health care training program developed by one of the authors of this text (Childers, 1985). In this media-assisted program, trainers are trained in a 5-day program to deliver a twelve-hour patient relations training workshop to all levels of their institution's staff. As few as two and as many as thirty-six employees from the same hospital have been trained to deliver the skills training program as an in-service program. The number of trainers selected depends upon many factors including the number ultimately to participate in the program, the total number of employees at the institution, and the speed with which all desired employees complete the training. This training approach has been highly successful, but its success depends upon selection of the correct employees to be trainers and upon selection of a consultant who offers a package that is tailored to the specific needs of the organization.

Media-Assisted Training Groups   Generally the media-assisted design involves the use of a trainer together with prepared media presentations that can do any number of things: communicate theory, provide everyday examples, provide training exercises, model appropriate skills, show results of inappropriate behavior, or provide statistical information graphically. The modes run the gamut from overhead projectors to videotape.

As mentioned earlier in this chapter, modeling is a primary part of skills training. Prepared media can sometimes do this more effectively than the trainer, especially if the trainer depends on group members for assistance. Also, by providing a prepared visual mode, the trainer can be free to observe the group members and generally spend more time in facilitation as opposed to instruction and modeling. Of course, this does not eliminate the modeling function of the group leader, but it takes some of the pressure off him or her as the *only* model.

Leaderless Skill Development Groups   The leaderless group, as this design is frequently called, depends upon self-instruction and self-evaluation for success. Since verbal and behavioral skills are determined to be successful or unsuccessful often by subtle changes in facial expression, voice intonation, and word changes, the skill development phase would seem to be more effective with a trained facilitator providing feedback. One way to circumvent the problem is to encourage trainees to give each other feedback in small groups. Again, without a skilled facilitator, the danger is that inappropriate behaviors might be inadvertently reinforced. One way the leaderless group has been effective is when the training is divided into two phases. Phase one includes a presentation of the theory and principles. This material can be communicated successfully through self-instructional manuals or audiovisual media. After this information is mastered, phase two is implemented. Phase two involves the actual skills training based upon the theoretical information learned in phase one. This part is conducted with a trained facilitator, so this approach combines leader and leaderless groups into what could be a cost-effective approach.

Sometimes skills training is conducted using only the experiential phase. Even though the program may be theory-based, some training groups would not be intellectually curious about the basis for training, some would already know the "why" based upon perceived deficit, and still others would omit theory and deal solely with behavior change as a way to save time. Those who do the latter frequently provide a bibliography or other means for interested persons to pursue the theory independently.

Teleconference Training Groups   In a teleconference setting, the originating group or instructor is presented "live," and other groups are receiving and possibly interacting with the leader from remote sites. The possible combinations are one-way audio teleconference (no way to talk to the instructor, listening only); two-way audio teleconference (remote groups can talk via telephone lines to the instructor); video teleconference with one-way audio (remote group sees and hears the instructor but cannot interact); a video teleconference with interactive audio (group can see and hear the instructor and can call in questions via telephone lines); and interactive audio and interactive video teleconference (group can see and hear each other via monitors).

There are obviously many advantages to the use of technology in training, and with adaptions it can possibly become a primary mode of training. However, in its embryonic stage in terms of training groups, techniques are yet to be developed that would make the use of teleconferencing the standard for training. As affordable equipment that will allow cost-effective transmission of audio and video signals is available to the masses, innovations in training designs will follow. At present, the majority of such offerings provide a facilitator at each remote site to do the group process and feedback portions of the training. Obviously, this expense limits the use of teleconferencing and adds considerably to the expense of the production.

Evaluation of Training Process

There are three things to take into consideration when evaluating skill training:

1 The participant's assessment
2 The trainer's assessment
3 Significant others' assessment(s)

The participant assessment is important in terms of the credibility of the program. One negative person can undo other successes by spreading hurtful information into the organization or the community. Trainers should be aware of this potential and work individually as much as possible with those individuals who, for whatever reason, seem disgruntled.

The trainer's assessment goes beyond giving feedback to individual group members. A legitimate question for managers to ask is "Did the training make a difference?" One common method of trainer evaluation is the pre-post test. A sample of behavior is gathered before training begins. This can be accomplished either by observation and rating in the work setting or by asking for a sample that might be videotaped or recorded on paper of each group member's typical response to a specific situation (standard role). An identical sample is taken after training and a determination can be made as to the change, either individually or as a group. Other more sophisticated evaluations, including longitudinal studies, are also appropriate as the training process is being standardized.

The evaluation by significant others may be by supervisors, teachers, parents, friends, or the like who are in a position to observe and contrast behavior. Though this is subjective, it happens whether or not it is orchestrated by the trainer, so it is important for training to be perceived by these persons as having made a positive difference.

Having dealt with establishing training groups, we are now ready to elaborate the Life-Skills Training model in greater detail. In the four chapters that follow, each of the generic life-skills will be presented in separate chapters. The training application of each generic life-skill to each of the three age groups of childhood, adolescence, and adulthood will be illustrated. In addition, the application of each generic life-skill to the four settings of home, school, work, and the community at large will be addressed.

SUMMARY

This chapter was intended primarily to present the theoretical rationale for the Life-Skills Training (LST) model and to illustrate methods for its operationalization. We began with a definition of life-skills and life-skills training and then proceeded to place LST in perspective by comparing it with the other major skills training models.

The historical development of LST is traced to the senior author's early work in developing a group counseling model in the late 1960s and early 1970s, followed by a model for interpersonal communication skills training in the 1970s, and finalized with the development of the LST taxonomy from seven theories of human development. The rationale for LST is developed around the following ten basic assumptions:

1 There are at least seven well-defined areas of human development: psychosocial, physical-sexual, vocational, cognitive, ego, moral, and affective.

2 From the seven well-defined areas of human development, coping behavior (life-skills) can be determined that are appropriate to age or stage.

3 There are identifiable stages in each of the seven areas of human development through which individuals must progress if they are to achieve mastery of later, more advanced stages.

4 Accomplishment of developmental tasks is dependent upon mastery of life-skills, that is, coping behaviors appropriate to stage and task.

5 In general there are certain age ranges when certain coping skills (life-skills) are optimally learned.

6 Individuals achieve optimal functioning when they attain operational mastery of fundamental life-skills.

7 Neuroses and functional psychoses frequently result from failure to develop one's life-skills.

8 Instruction and/or training in life-skills that is introduced when a person is developmentally ready to learn given concepts and skills serves the role of preventive mental health.

9 Instruction and/or training in life-skills that is introduced when a person is suffering from emotional or mental disturbance, of a functional nature, serves the role of remediation in mental health.

10 The greater the degree of functional disturbance, the greater is the likelihood that the individual will be suffering from multiple life-skill deficits.

Implementation of the LST model was outlined through describing how to select trainees, how to group trainees for training, and how to determine the size of training groups. Additionally, trainer qualifications and training modalities were specified. The chapter closed with a discussion of methods for evaluating the training program.

REFERENCES

Adkins, W. R., Rosenburg, S., & Sharar, P. (1965). *Training resources for youth: A comprehensive operational plan for a demonstration training center for disadvantaged youth*. New York: Training Resources for Youth.

Adkins, W. R. (1984a). Life skills education: A video-based counseling/learning system. In D. Larson (Ed.), *Teaching psychological skills: Models for giving psychology away* (pp. 44–68). Monterey, CA: Brooks/Cole.

Adkins, W. R. (1984b). Life-coping skills: A fifth curriculum. *Teachers College Record, 75,* 507–526.

Akridge, R. L., & Means, B. L. (1982). Psychosocial adjustment skills training. In B. Bolton (Ed.), *Vocational adjustment of disabled persons*. Baltimore: University Park Press.

Argyle, M. (1981). The contribution of social interaction research to social skills training. In J. D. Wine & M. D. Smye (Eds.), *Social competence* (pp. 261–286). New York: Guilford Press.

Arkowitz, H., Lichtenstein, E., McGovern, K., & Hines, P. (1975). The behavioral assessment of social competence in males. *Behavior Therapy, 6,* 3–13.

Bellack, A. S. (1979). Behavioral assessment of social skills. In A. S. Bellack & M. Hersen (Eds.), *Research and practice in social skills training* (pp. 75–104). New York: Plenum Press.

Bellack, A. S., & Hersen, M. (1978). Chronic psychiatric patients: Social skills training. In M. Hersen & A. S. Bellack (Eds.), *Behavior therapy in the psychiatric setting* (pp. 169–195). Baltimore: Williams & Wilkins.

Brooks, D. K., Jr. (1984). *A life-skills taxonomy: Defining the elements of effective functioning through the use of the Delphi technique*. Unpublished doctoral dissertation, University of Georgia, Athens.

Bryant, B. M., Tower, P., Yardley, K., Urbieta, H., & Letemendia, F. (1976). A survey of social inadequacy among psychiatric outpatients. *Psychological Medicine, 6,* 101–112.

Carkhuff, R. R. (1969a). *Helping and human relations: A primer for lay and profes-sional helpers: Vol. 1. Selection and training.* New York: Holt, Rinehart & Winston.

Carkhuff, R. R. (1969b). *Helping and human relations: A primer for lay and profes-sional helpers: Vol. 2. Practice and research.* New York: Holt, Rinehart & Winston.

Childers, W. C. (1985). *A step ahead in caring.* Athens: University of Georgia.

Drum, D. J., & Knott, J. E. (1977). *Structured groups for facilitating development.* New York: Human Sciences Press.

Dupont, H. (1978, February). *Affective development: A Piagetian model.* Paper presented at the UAP-USC Eighth Annual Interdisciplinary Conference "Piaget-ian Theory and the Helping Professions," Los Angeles, CA.

Duska, R., & Whelan, M. (1975). *Moral development: A guide to Piaget and Kohlberg.* New York: Paulist Press.

Egan, G., & Cowan, M. A. (1979). *People in systems.* Monterey, CA: Brooks/Cole.

Eisler, R. M., Frederiksen, L.W., & Peterson, G. L. (1978). The relationship of cog-nitive variables to the expression of assertiveness. *Behavior Therapy, 9.* 419–427.

Erikson, E. H. (1950). *Childhood and society.* New York: W. W. Norton.

Erikson, E. H. (1963). *Childhood and society.* (2d ed.). New York: W. W. Norton.

Fairweather, G. W., Sanders, D. H., Maynard, A., & Cressler, D. L. (1969). *Commu-nity life for the mentally ill.* Chicago: Aldine.

Flavell, J. H. (1963). *The developmental psychology of Jean Piaget.* Princeton, NJ: D. Van Nostrand.

Freeman, H. E., & Simmons, O. G. (1963). *The mental patient comes home.* New York: Wiley.

Gazda, G. M. (Ed.). (1968a). *Basic approaches to group psychotherapy and group counseling.* Springfield, IL: Charles C Thomas.

Gazda, G. M. (Ed.). (1968b). *Innovations to group psychotherapy.* Springfield, IL: Charles C Thomas.

Gazda, G. M. (Ed.). (1969). *Theories and methods of group counseling in the schools.* Springfield, IL: Charles C Thomas.

Gazda, G. M. (1971). *Group counseling: A developmental approach.* Boston: Allyn & Bacon.

Gazda, G. M. (1978). *Group counseling: A developmental approach,* (2d ed.). Boston: Allyn & Bacon.

Gazda, G. M. (1981). Multiple impact training. In R. J. Corsini (Ed.), *Handbook of innovative psychotherapies* (pp. 525–533). New York: Wiley.

Gazda, G. M. (1984), *Group counseling: A developmental approach.* (3d ed.). Boston: Allyn & Bacon.

Gazda, G. M., Asbury, F. R., Balzer, F. J., Childers, W. C., Deselle, E., & Walters, R. P. (1973). *Human relations development: A manual for educators.* Boston: Allyn & Bacon.

Gazda, G. M., Asbury, F. R., Balzer, F. J., Childers, W. C., & Walters, R. P. (1977). *Human relations development: A manual for educators.* (2d ed.). Boston: Allyn & Bacon.

Gazda, G. M., Asbury, F. R., Balzer, F. J., Childers, W. C., & Walters, R. P. (1984). *Human relations skills development,* (3d ed.). Boston: Allyn & Bacon.

Gazda, G. M., Childers, W. C., & Walters, R. P. (1982). *Interpersonal communication: A handbook for health professionals.* Rockville, MD: Aspen Systems.

Gazda, G. M., Walters, R.P., & Childers, W. C. (1975). *Human relations development: A manual for health sciences.* Boston: Allyn & Bacon.

Gazda, G. M., Walters, R. P., & Childers, W. C. (1981). *Realtalk: Exercises in friendship and helping skills.* Atlanta, GA: Humanics.

Gendlin, E. T. (1981). *Focusing.* New York: Bantam Books.

Gesell, A., Ilg, F. L., & Ames, L. B. (1956). *Youth: The years from ten to sixteen.* New York: Harper.

Gesell, A., Ilg, F. L., Ames, L. B., & Bulliss, G. E. (1946). *The child from five to ten.* New York: Harper.

Goldstein, A. P., Sprafkin, R. P., & Gershaw, N. J. (1976). *Skill training for community living: Applying structured learning therapy.* New York: Pergamon Press.

Greenberg, D. J., Scott, S. B., Pisa, A., & Friesen, D. D. (1975). Beyond the token economy: A comparison of two contingency programs. *Journal of Consulting and Clinical Psychology, 43,* 498–503.

Guerney, B. G., Jr. (1977). *Relationship enhancement.* San Francisco: Jossey-Bass.

Havighurst, R. J. (1953). *Human development and education.* New York: Longmans, Green.

Havighurst, R. J. (1972). *Developmental tasks and education,* (3d ed.). New York: David McKay.

Illovsky, M. (1985). *The therapeutic effects of two life-skill components in the treatment of psychiatric patients.* Unpublished doctoral dissertation, University of Georgia, Athens.

Kavkewitz, M. (1983). *Assessment of life skills training in communication, appearances, physical fitness, and health maintenance as a substance abuse prevention program for secondary school students.* Unpublished doctoral dissertation, University of Georgia, Athens.

Kazdin, A. E. (1979). Sociopsychological factors in psychopathology. In A. S. Bellack & M. Hersen (Eds.), *Research and practice in social skills training* (pp. 41–74). New York: Plenum Press.

Kohlberg, L., & Turiel, E. (1971). Moral development and moral education. In G. Lesser (Ed.), *Psychology and educational practice* (pp. 410–465). New York: Scott Foresman.

Lazarus, A. A. (1976). *Multi-modal behavior therapy.* New York: Springer Publishing.

Linn, M. W., Caffey, E. M., Klett, J., & Hogarty, G. (1977). Hospital vs. community (foster) care for psychiatric patients. *Archives of General Psychiatry, 34,* 78–83.

Loevinger, J. (1976). *Ego development.* San Francisco: Jossey-Bass.

Martin, B. (1971). *Anxiety and neurotic disorders.* New York: Wiley.

May, H. J. (1981). *The effects of life-skill training versus current psychiatric methods on therapeutic outcome in psychiatric patients.* Unpublished doctoral dissertation, University of Georgia, Athens.

Mosher, R. L., & Sprinthall, N. A. (1971). Psychological education: A means to promote personal development during adolescence. *The Counseling Psychologist, 2*(4), 3–82.

Muuss, R. E. (1962). *Theories of adolescence.* New York: Random House.

Paul, G. L., & Lentz, R. J. (1977). *Psychosocial treatment of chronic mental patients: Milieu versus social learning programs.* Cambridge, MA: Harvard University Press.

Pierce, R., & Drasgow, J. (1969). Teaching facilitative interpersonal functioning to psychiatric inpatients. *Journal of Counseling Psychology, 16,* 295–298.

Pierce, R., Schauble, P. B., & Wilson, R. R. (1971). Employing systematic human relations training for teaching constructive helper and helpee behavior in group therapy situations. *Journal of Research and Development in Education, 4,* 97–109.

Sisson, P. J., Arthur, G. L., & Gazda, G. M. (1981). *Human relations for criminal justice personnel.* Boston: Allyn & Bacon.

Smith, P. (1982). *The development of a taxonomy of the life skills required to become a balanced self-determined person.* Ottawa, Canada: Employment and Immigration Canada.

Spalding, J. (1985). *A comparative evaluation of an Adlerian based program, Individual Education with a traditional program.* Unpublished doctoral dissertation, University of Georgia, Athens.

Staudt, V. M., & Zubin, J. (1957). A biometric evaluation of the somato-therapies in schizophrenia. *Psychological Bulletin, 54,* 171–196.

Super, D. E. (1963). Vocational development in adolescence and early adulthood: Tasks and behaviors. In D. E. Super, *Career Development: Self-concept theory* (pp. 79–95). New York: College Entrance Examination Board.

Tryon, C., & Lilienthal, J. W. (1950). Developmental tasks: I. The concept and its importance. In *Fostering mental health in our schools: 1950 Yearbook of ASCD* (pp. 77–89). Washington, DC: Association for Supervision and Curriculum Development.

Wadsworth, B. J. (1971). *Piaget's theory of cognitive development.* New York: David McKay.

Warren, N. J., & Gilner, F. H. (1978). Measurement of positive assertive behaviors: The behavioral test of tenderness expression. *Behavior Therapy, 9,* 179–184.

Wolpe, J., & Lazarus, A. A. (1966). *Behavior therapy techniques.* New York: Pergamon.

Wood, M. M. (1975). *Developmental therapy.* Baltimore: University Park Press.

Zubin, J., & Spring, B. (1977). Vulnerability—a new view of schizophrenia. *Journal of Abnormal Psychology, 86,* 103–126.

CHAPTER 9

INTERPERSONAL COMMUNICATION/HUMAN RELATIONS SKILLS

When we talk about interpersonal communication/human relations skills, we are concerned most clearly and most frequently with persons' psychosocial development (Erikson, 1950, 1963; Havighurst, 1948, 1953, 1972). Thus, in this generic life-skill area, we are dealing with the person as an individual and, as well, with the person in relationship with other people. If we stop to reflect, it seems intuitively obvious that the quality of our interpersonal communication should impact our development and our general feeling of well-being.

RATIONALE

The importance of interpersonal communication/human relations can be illustrated using the quality of life definition proposed by Flanagan and the American Institution for Research (1978, p. 141). As can be seen by perusing Figure 9-1, this comprehensive definition is comprised of five categories and fifteen subcategories. Notice that one category (Relations with other People) is devoted completely to interpersonal activities. As importantly, the activities of the remaining four categories could not be achieved without effective interpersonal communication/human relations skills.

Since this generic life-skill is fundamental to fulfilling human activities, it should not seem so surprising that this area of skill is a prerequisite to the

Physical and Material Well-being
  Material well-being and financial security
  Health and personal safety
Relations with Other People
  Relations with spouse (girlfriend, boyfriend)
  Having and rearing children
  Relations with parents, siblings, and other relatives
  Relations with friends
Social, Community, and Civic Activities
  Activities related to helping or encouraging other people
  Activities related to local and national governments
Personal Development and Fulfillment
  Intellectual development
  Personal understanding and planning
  Occupational role (job)
  Creativity and personal expression
Recreation
  Socializing
  Passive and observational recreational activities
  Active and participating activities

FIGURE 9-1
Quality of Life Definition

learning and mastery of the remaining three generic life-skills. Examining the core conditions and phases of the helping relationship (see Figure 9-2) helps to convey how effective communication and human relation skills underlie the development of effectiveness in the three remaining life-skill areas.

In the helping relationship, effective communication is necessary (especially from the helper) to move a person through the phases: from self-exploration through increased understanding and commitment to appropriate action. And in many cases, if not most, the client's exhibiting appropriate action involves skill development in other generic life-skills. The helper, therefore, may be instrumental in facilitating problem solving/decision making, physical fitness/health maintenance, and/or identity development/purpose in life skills. Since teaching the action (behavior) is interdependent with effective communication, primary emphasis on interpersonal communication/human relations skills is necessary to accomplish the goals of the helping relationship. In this chapter, we will explore a model for interpersonal communication/human relations. In keeping with Life-Skills Training's focus on both remediation and prevention, we will see how remedial efforts may need to begin with communication skills while preventive efforts can be directed toward teaching all of the generic life-skills concurrently.

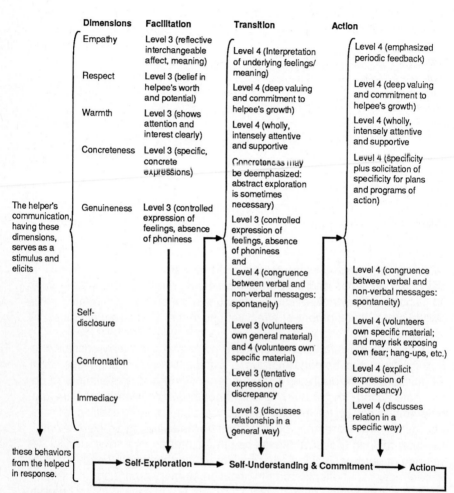

FIGURE 9-2
Core Conditions and Phases of the Helping Relationship.

A MODEL FOR INTERPERSONAL COMMUNICATIONS/ HUMAN RELATIONS

The model for interpersonal communication/human relations training described in this chapter originated within the field of psychotherapy, based on the original work of Carl Rogers (1957). Truax and Carkhuff (1967), first working with Rogers at the University of Wisconsin and then independently, developed a training model starting with Rogers's original "core" conditions of a helping relationship—accurate empathy, nonpossessive warmth, and genuineness. As research progressed, several new dimensions were discovered, and scales for rating the dimensions of helping relationships were developed (Carkhuff, 1969; Carkhuff and Berenson, 1967; Truax and Carkhuff, 1967). Carkhuff (1969) renamed and standardized the scales and developed a model for effective functioning.

The strength of the Carkhuff (1969) model is evident in the research it has generated and in its versatility. Cash (1984), in the most recent review of the research on this model, cites numerous studies on its effectiveness. And regarding adaptations, the model, developed originally from research on the therapist-client relationship, has been modified for numerous populations. For instance, the senior authors and others adapted it to teachers/educators (Gazda et al., 1973; Gazda et al., 1977, 1984); health practitioners (Gazda, Walters, and Childers, 1975; Gazda, Childers, and Walters, 1982); secondary school students (Gazda, Walters, and Childers, 1981); and criminal justice personnel (Sisson, Arthur, and Gazda, 1981). No other model for interpersonal communication/human relations has been so thoroughly adapted and researched as has this one. Therefore, it is offered here with considerable confidence regarding its effectiveness.

The interpersonal communication/human relations model outlined in this chapter consists of three parts: (1) a system for classifying messages, (2) attending, and (3) the act of responding. Although this model is intended for the human services professions, the illustrations that are included at the end of this chapter show how it can be applied for the lay person in the settings of home, school, work, and community. Emphasis will be on the spoken word and nonverbal communication; however, these facilitative modes can also be translated to the written message.

System for Classifying Helpee Requests

In order for the communicator/facilitator/helper to be able to discriminate the request/message of the sender, some system for classifying these requests/messages is necessary. As shown in Figure 9-3, there are four message categories to be utilized by the person who wishes to operationalize the generic life-skill of interpersonal communication/human relations.

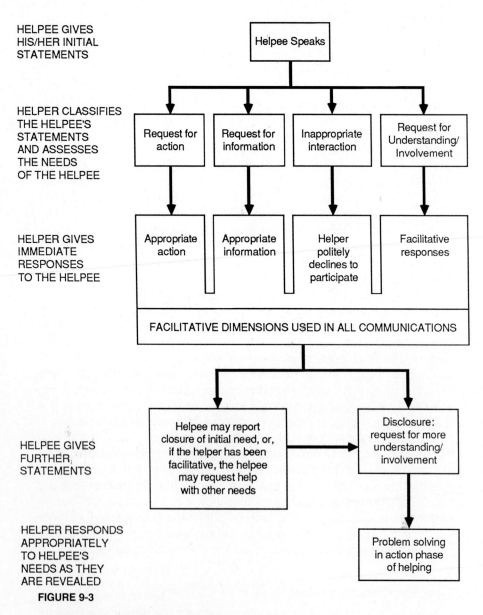

HELPEE GIVES
HIS/HER INITIAL
STATEMENTS

Helpee Speaks

HELPER CLASSIFIES
THE HELPEE'S
STATEMENTS
AND ASSESSES
THE NEEDS
OF THE HELPEE

Request for action

Request for information

Inappropriate interaction

Request for Understanding/ Involvement

HELPER GIVES
IMMEDIATE
RESPONSES
TO THE HELPEE

Appropriate action

Appropriate information

Helper politely declines to participate

Facilitative responses

FACILITATIVE DIMENSIONS USED IN ALL COMMUNICATIONS

HELPEE GIVES
FURTHER
STATEMENTS

Helpee may report closure of initial need, or, if the helper has been facilitative, the helpee may request help with other needs

Disclosure: request for more understanding/ involvement

HELPER RESPONDS
APPROPRIATELY
TO HELPEE'S
NEEDS AS THEY
ARE REVEALED

Problem solving in action phase of helping

FIGURE 9-3

System for Classifying Helpee Requests.

Reprinted by permission from *Human relations development: A manual for educators* (3d ed.) G.M. Gazda, F. Asbury, F.J. Balzer, W.C. Childers, & R.P. Walters. Boston: Allyn and Bacon, Inc., 1984, p. 36.

Request for Physical Help/Action   This category of requests refers to statements from the sender that convey the need or desire for some physical action on the part of the receiver. For example, an older person may request physical assistance such as a helping hand as he or she ascends a stairway. In such instances, the request for assistance may be transmitted verbally or nonverbally. Sometimes, sensitive facilitators/ helpers may actually anticipate the need of the other person and volunteer to help without waiting for a verbal or nonverbal request from the sender/ helpee. This anticipating-helping response is, of course, frequently necessary when attending to babies and young children or to persons who are incapacitated either emotionally or physically.

Request for Information   This type of message is similar to the sender's request for action, but nothing physical beyond a verbal response is required from the facilitator. An example would be the sender asking the facilitator for directions, such as, "Could you give me directions to the First National Bank?" This request could be satisfied by giving clear directions or sending the person to someone who can give the directions. Once again, the sensitive facilitator can anticipate this need if he or she notices that someone appears to be lost and respond by volunteering to help them find their way. In other words, the request need not be actually verbalized.

Request for Inappropriate Interaction   Not all requests or messages from the sender are appropriate. For instance, the message may be for the recipient to engage in gossip, rumor spreading, or belittling of others. Of course, the facilitator should politely decline to become involved in gossiping, rumor spreading, and the like. Such situations are easy to recognize, but some requests may not be verbalized. For instance, the sender may be attempting to establish an unhealthy dependency relationship with the facilitator. If this is so, the facilitator, needing to avoid the development of an unhealthy dependency relationship, should also be aware that this type of request can be disguised in requests for action and information. The facilitator will need to evaluate each request to determine if by fulfilling it, the sender will become too dependent. It may be more effective to encourage the sender to perform the task or get the information on his or her own.

Request for Understanding/Involvement   This category of requests includes all verbal and nonverbal requests for assistance with personal problems of both minor and great significance to the sender. A person may simply be seeking to clarify his or her position on an issue or may, in fact, be seeking assistance with a problem of great concern such as his or her illness. In either case, the facilitator's responses should follow the helping format outlined in Figure 9-2.

Attending Skills

Prerequisite to facilitating any relationship is attending to the other person(s). In many respects, attending is one of the most powerful communication/human relations skills. For one thing, attending skills have a potent effect on the speaker, especially in setting the tone for the interaction through the first impression that the speaker receives. Furthermore, unless the facilitator attends fully, he or she will not be able to respond appropriately; we cannot respond to what we have not attended to enough to see or hear. Because attending is such a powerful skill, the general guidelines provided in Table 9-1 are worthy of careful study. It will be useful to remember these guidelines as we discuss how the cues gleaned through careful attending can affect interpersonal communication/human relations.

Noticing and paying attention to the physiological cues expressed in another person's visage and physique is a way of identifying emotional responses that the other person is experiencing internally. For instance, observing the facial responsiveness and the body language of other individuals is an important contribution to understanding the person, and the world in general. Indeed, the face of another person is the single most intriguing and meaningful stimulus in a human's physical environment (Singer, 1976), although other areas are important too. Bandler and Grinder (1979) have identified four cues—skin color, lip size, muscle tone, and breathing—that reflect the internal emotional processes and their concomitant physiological changes. By observing the subtle changes in these and related areas, it is possible to evaluate the impact of personal interaction on other persons (Haynie, 1982). Haynie (1982) elaborates as follows:

> Skin color sometimes is expressed in language that describes the feeling state both metaphorically and physiologically: red with rage, white with fear (or pain), black with fury. Lips flush with an increased flow of blood when an individual is excited or aroused; they become narrow and white or purple with terror or tension. Muscle tone in the face causes drooping and lifting of the mouth, chin, and cheeks. Breathing patterns are rapid and shallow in states of excitement or tension, deep and rhythmic in a relaxed state, or arhythmic in a depressed state. Fluctuation in skin temperature and moisture content are other cues. These and pulse rate are monitored by an individual's kinesthetic external sensory channels.... Voice tone and tempo are processed through the auditory ex-

TABLE 9-1
GUIDELINES FOR HELPERS IN USING ATTENDING SKILLS

	Attending skills	
Ineffective use (Any of these behaviors probably will close off or slow down the conversation)	**Nonverbal modes of communication**	**Effective use (These behaviors encourage talk because they show helper's acceptance and respect for the other person)**
Spread among activities	Attention	Given fully to talker
Distant; very close	Space	Approximate arm's length
Away	Movement	Toward
Slouching; rigid; seated leaning away	Posture seated leaning slightly	Relaxed, but attentive; toward
Absent; defiant; jittery	Eye contact	Regular
Slow to notice talker; in a hurry	Time	Responds at first opportunity; time shared with talker
Used to keep distance from the talker	Feet and legs (in sitting)	Unobtrusive (in sitting)
Used as a barrier	Furniture	Used to draw persons together
Does not match feelings; scowl; blank look	Facial expression	Matches own or other's feelings; smile
Compete for attention with helper's words	Gestures	Highlight helper's words; unobtrusive; smooth
Obvious; distracting	Mannerisms	None, or unobtrusive
Very loud or very soft	Voice: volume	Clearly audible
Impatient or staccato; very slow or hesitant	Voice: rate	Average, or a bit slower
Apathetic; sleepy; jumpy; pushy	Energy level	Alert; stays alert throughout a long conversation
Sloppy; garish; provocative	Dress, grooming	Tasteful

Source: Reprinted by permission from *Amity: Friendship in Action.* R.P. Walters. Kentwood, Michigan: Christian Helpers, Inc. 1980, p. 31.

ternal channel.... These physiological cue changes are expressed externally and are observable responses to the facilitory and inhibitory influences from the limbic system of the brain. (p. 31)

There seems to be an interesting connection between the brain, in particular the limbic system, and the way we respond to others' externalized emotional cues. The limbic system consists of the structures in the brain that are believed to be essential to emotion. The limbic structures can be thought of as a response-modulation system that ranges on a continuum from inhibition to facilitation of consummatory behavior to meet physiolog-

ical needs (McCleary, 1966). In addition, the limbic system has connections with the visual structures of the brain through the prefrontal cortex
and in the occipitotemporal lobe and the fusiform gyrus. Furthermore,
there is evidence to suggest that these connections between the limbic
system and visual structures function to help individuals gain insight into
the feelings of others or to see with feeling (Haynie, 1982).

If there is a physiological base to seeing with feeling, we may wonder
then why we do not all "see" the same feelings in others' externalized
cues. According to Haynie (1982), all normal humans are endowed with
essentially equivalent sensory organs and structures, both anatomically
and physiologically. The neurological pathways and projection areas that
serve the sensory mechanisms also are considered to be similar in all
human brains. Yet, despite sensory and anatomical similarity, no two
persons understand a particular occurrence in exactly the same way.
Differences are learned through selective attention to particular sensory
input channels and through variations of the experiences we have with the
senses (Bandler and Grinder, 1975; Bateson, 1972; Korzybski, 1958).
More specifically, the visual judgment channel is more accurate than the
channels for making auditory and gustatory judgments. Nevertheless,
each person learns to depend on one of these systems. Through the
idiosyncratically determined primary sensory system, the person perceives the world and records his or her understanding of experience
through the channel into language and memory.

It seems obvious, then, that attending to the external cues of another
person is a complex process and requires considerable self-discipline and
practice. Effective communication depends on noting the other's external
cues; the process is further complicated because these external cues
must be translated through our own internal sensory mechanisms. Then,
as we shall see in the next section, the follow-through of attending, the act
of responding, is required to use these cues to complete the communication process.

Communicating Through Verbal Responding

The purposes of effective interpersonal communication are numerous, but
one of the more important purposes is to help people to learn about themselves and to make good decisions based on this knowledge. Through
appropriate sharing and self-monitoring of words and actions, this is possible. But facilitating communication includes knowledge of a process.
The propositions that follow are intended to help explain this process.

*Proposition 1.   Both individuals involved in an interaction are mod-
ified by the interaction.* The helper influences the helpee, *and* the helper
is also being influenced by the helpee.

Proposition 2.   Responses may be verbal or nonverbal, but are usually a combination of both. Verbal responses almost always have nonverbal components even though they may not be discernible.

Proposition 3.   The real message is more likely to be transmitted by the nonverbal responses because they are often involuntary reactions transmitted by the autonomic nervous system. Often we transmit more that we intend by our body posture, tone of voice, gestures, eye movement, and the like. Mehrabian (1968) has found that facial expressions alone transmit over 55 percent of the meaning of a message.

Proposition 4.   Verbal responses are generally composed of two parts: content and feeling. Content refers to the topic or theme being discussed whereas feeling refers to the emotion(s) surrounding the topic.

Proposition 5.   "When individuals' expressed messages in verbal... and non-verbal...language are received, understood, and expressed by other persons, communication occurs" (authors' emphasis) (Haynie, 1982, p. 35).

Relative to this last proposition, we would like to elaborate on a neurolinguistic approach to improving communication. Recall from our previous discussion that physiological processes are involved with producing external cues for us to attend to when trying to communicate effectively with others. Although concerned with a different set of cues than these we addressed in the last section, neurolinguistics can be thought of as picking up from the point of attending and being used for the purpose of completing communication in a manner consistent with our fifth proposition.

Broadly conceived, neurolinguistics is the "study of how people receive information through the senses, process the information in neurons and neural pathways of the brain including the language areas, and express information in language and behaviors" (Haynie, 1982, pp. 34–35). Within this framework, Neurolinguistic Programming (NLP)(Bandler and Grinder, 1975; Grinder and Bandler, 1976) is a systematic approach to improving communication by identifying how people structure their language. One point of focus is on the representational system, that is, the preferred use of sensory modalities. Individuals who favor the visual modality express themselves more often with process words and predicates (verbs and adjectives) such as see, perspective, visualize, bright, and the like. Those who prefer the auditory mode express themselves more frequently through words such as hear, sound, noise, loud, and resonate. Finally, persons who prefer the kinesthetic mode use words such as feel, grasp, handle, tough, soft, and the like. When the listener matches predicates with the speaker in responding to the speaker, improved communication is presumed to occur. For example, if the speaker says, "I can *see* that I cannot be very *clear* about what I want," the listener would match predicates in responding with something like, "Your *perception* is that you have been *foggy* about what you want."

In addition to working with the speaker's representational system, the listener can also concentrate on the speaker's transformational grammar as a tool to facilitate efficient communication. When using the term transformational grammar, we are referring to the use of nominalizations, generalizations, and deletions that may lead to imprecise communication. With "nominalization" we find the person has restructured language so that the process or action word (a verb) has been transformed into an event word or noun. The effect of this is to change the action of experience to a passive condition, and, thus the process is seen as an accomplished and irreversible event. For example, if one is expressing a feeling such as, "My confusion keeps me from making a decision," one would denominalize or remove the distortion in this expression by saying something like, "Your being confused tends to keep you from deciding." The "event" is brought into appropriate perspective as the process it actually is, and the affective energy can become neutralized.

A different kind of transformation occurs with generalization. Should the speaker say "I cannot do math" instead of the accurate "I have difficulty remembering my multiplication tables," then, in the communication, the speaker has universalized an event and robbed it of its specificity. Since the expression is imprecise, effective communication has not occurred. Generally, universal qualifiers such as every, all, any, never, none, nothing, and no one, being nonspecific, detract from effective communication, except when further explanation is provided.

The last transformation we will discuss is deletion. In this restructuring, portions of the original experience have been removed, and so a full linguistic expression of the deep meaning is missing. The communication is incomplete because portions of the full statement or explanation have been deleted. When a speaker deletes information, the listener may be able to improve the communication by guessing about the missing data. If someone says, "I feel inadequate," the listener may respond with "You feel unable to perform to your satisfaction in important areas of your life." In this example, what was missing from the speaker's response is "inadequate in what respect." If previous communication had specified the area(s) of inadequacy, the listener, of course, would not have to guess and communication would have occurred. In contrast, in situations such as our example, when information is not specified, listener guesses have to be verified by the speaker before understanding (communication) has occurred.

Returning to our original point (proposition 5), communication occurs when messages are received, understood, and expressed by others.

From our short discussion on NLP, it is easy to understand that

> By matching language to the modality, it is possible to communicate with rapport, empathy, and trustworthiness. Appreciation of the different processing styles of other persons can encourage respect for them and their responsibility and right to make their own decisions. Knowing these rules of transformational grammar can guide facilitative individuals to be more specific and honest with others. (Haynie, 1982, p. 36).

Having presented the framework of the communication process, we can now consider how Life-Skills Training incorporates prevention and remediation in the model of interpersonal communication/human relations. We will then conclude the chapter with a section on application that includes specific examples for training.

Prevention

The basic assumption underlying the application of our interpersonal communication/human relations model to prevention is the need for extra education. If we take a look at how schools approach communication, we notice that the traditional academic methods of instructing individuals in communication skills only indirectly focus on the interpersonal communication/human relations domains. Even though spelling classes, English literature, and foreign language courses supplement instruction, learning how to write complete sentences in grammar courses and how to give a speech in a speech course constitutes the communications training that students receive in the traditional school curriculum. Little, if any, emphasis is placed on assisting individuals in developing the effective listening and verbal responding skills that are so crucial to interpersonal communication and the establishment and maintenance of effective interpersonal relationships. Whereas there are rules of grammar in guiding speaking and writing, there are no rules taught in traditional classes on how to respond to others' affective domains. Though these skills are essential to enhancing interpersonal communication/human relations, no models are taught for these functions, which constitute the majority of interactions among individuals.

The model outlined earlier in this chapter presents an emphasis that builds upon and extends the traditional curriculum. The implicit assumption is that individuals can learn effective components of interpersonal communication/human relations in a fashion similar to the ways they learn rules of grammar and speaking. If we take into account the person's developmental level and readiness to learn, the concepts of the model can then be taught with increasing degrees of complexity to children, adolescents, and adults by using the coping skill and developmental task descriptors (see Appendix D). For the reader's convenience, concrete examples of this teaching process are included at the end of this chapter.

Remediation

Recall that Life-Skills Training is also appropriate for remedial interventions. In this chapter remediation efforts focus on people who are debilitated in interpersonal communication/human relations to a serious degree. Moreover, as mentioned earlier, the trainee typically is deficient in more than one generic life-skill.

Since dysfunction reflects a deficit of generic life-skills, the task is to teach the person the lacking skills so that he or she may use the skills to cope more effectively. When the person suffers deficits in more areas than interpersonal communication/human relations, in remediation, it is best to teach the communication skills first. They can, however, be taught concurrently with other generic life-skills. Gazda (1982, 1984) has described this procedure elsewhere as Multiple Impact Training.

When interpersonal communication/human relations is taught as remedial intervention, the trainer is usually a mental health professional. The training may be one-to-one or in a small group, in an inpatient or outpatient setting. Inasmuch as treatment for psychiatric patients is typically intensive, so too skills training is frequently provided on a daily basis or at least two or three times per week for inpatients and at least weekly for outpatients. Some trainees may be functioning in society but are behind in their development of generic life-skills. For these individuals, training may take place outside a mental health setting. The training materials are essentially the same when applied to prevention or remediation; the difference is primarily one of frequency or intensity of training. Therefore, the sample training units found in the following section may be adapted for both prevention and remediation.

APPLICATION

Based on the national Delphi study by Brooks (1984), four settings were determined wherein life-skills are both learned and implemented. These include the family, school, work, and the community at large. In this section, we want to illustrate how strategies (see Table 9-2) and interpersonal communication/human relations skill descriptors (see Table 9-3) can be developed into applications for children, adolescents, and adults in the defined settings. To encourage further the reader's application skills, a model for developing training units is included in Appendix C and all descriptors (objectives for training) for the interpersonal communication/human relations generic life-skills are included in Appendix D.

TABLE 9-2
INTERPERSONAL COMMUNICATION/RELATIONSHIP STRATEGIES

	Family	School	Work	Community
Prevention	As a parent, practice giving high level empathy responses to your children, including responding to their feelings. Practice listening and attending skills with all family members. Teach your children how to attend, listen, and respond to others' requests through indentifying the type of request for information, action, inappropriate interaction, involvement/ understanding. Use family council as a practice opportunity for attending, listening, and responding.	Implement Life-Skills Training courses throughout all grades in elementary and secondary schools by developing a curriculum in Life-Skills Training. Counselors should coordinate this curriculum.	Provide Life-Skills Training workshops in interpersonal communication/ relationship skills for managers, middle managers, and workers. Develop continuous evaluation and training for all managers and workers through the personnel office and/ or industrial psychologist.	Utilize the community mental health facility to provide classes in the interpersonal communication/relationship skill training for all age groups in the community.
Remediation	Use family council to evaluate each member's communication/relationship skills and provide corrective suggestions for those whose skills are lacking.	Arrange for remedial Life-Skills Training groups led by counselors and other mental health professionals to assist those students who are not developing their skill satisfactorily.	Arrange for a skilled private practitioner to assist those with significant communication/relationship problems.	Incorporate Life-Skills Training as a primary treatment modality offered by the mental health professionals in the community mental health facility.

TABLE 9-3
INTERPERSONAL COMMUNICATION/HUMAN RELATIONS SKILLS[a]

Childhood	Adolescence	Adulthood
Communicates affect through language expressions.	Responds with empathy to the problems of others.	Relates to others with appropriate openness.
Masters social tasks within one's immediate environment.	Employs perspective-taking in interpersonal relations.	Manages intimacy with close friends.
Works and plays cooperatively with age-mates	Relates comfortably with members of the opposite sex.	Uses one's peer group for support while still maintaining one's individual autonomy.
Differentiates positive and negative feedback.	Forms interpersonal relationships based on mutuality and respect for individual indentity.	Maintains continuous satisfying relationships with family members.
Views interpersonal relations from the perspective of others.	Utilizes language to represent complex concepts with increasing accuracy.	Gets along with both superiors and peers on the job.
Develops and nurtures peer relationships.	Is assertive in interpersonal relationships.	Communicates one's wants and needs effectively.
Uses interpersonal skills in social situations.	Copes successfully with peer pressure.	Is able to listen so well to another that one's response reflects the original statement in both content and feeling.
Listens attentively to others.	Understands to some degree the problems and difficulties of others.	Reflects empathically and effectively to one's children (if any) at all developmental stages.
Responds empathically to others.	Responds to the feelings of others; is able to express one's own feelings.	

[a]Skills necessary for effective communication, both verbal and nonverbal, with others, leading to ease in establishing relationships, small and large group and community memberships and participation, management of interpersonal intimacy, clear expression of ideas and opinions, and ability to give and receive feedback. See Appendix D for a complete listing of interpersonal communication/human relations skills.

Interpersonal Communication/Human Relations Skills Training: Example 1

I Setting: Work/Adults

II Life-Skill Objectives: Ability to get along with both superiors and peers on the job; listen well to another; that one's response reflects the original statement in both content and affect; manage conflicts on the job and at home; recognize and respect the individual rights, personal worth, and uniqueness of others.

III Activity: Learn to differentiate among types of requests made of middle managers.

    A Procedure:

1 Generating questions

    a Have the whole group generate a list of thirty random questions. A volunteer should write these on the chalkboard. These questions will be used in Activity 3.

2 Minilecture on types of questions

    a Teach the four types of questions: (1) request for action; (2) request for information; (3) inappropriate interaction; (4) request for understanding/involvement. These are explained in G. Gazda et al. (1984) *Human Relations Development*. Chapter 3, pp. 24–49.

3 Classifying questions/requests

    a Have the group classify the questions generated in Activity 1 according to the four types.

Interpersonal Communication/Human Relations Skills Training: Example 2

I Setting: Home/All ages

II Life-Skill Objectives: Children—ability to view interpersonal relations from the perspective of others, follow or lead in a group depending on the circumstances, recognize other points of view, listen attentively to others.

Adolescents—ability to employ perspective-taking in interpersonal relations, be open to opinions and actions of others, appreciate diversity in personalities and activities, relate positively with significant persons in one's immediate environment.

Adults—ability to tolerate and respect those of different backgrounds, habits, values, and appearance; manage conflict at home; relate empathetically and effectively to one's children at all developmental stages.

III Activity: The family members, especially the children, will practice listening attentively to others.

    A Procedure:

        1 The family chooses a TV program* that they would be willing to watch for at least 20 to 30 minutes. During the first 10 minutes, the family watches the TV without sound. At the end of 10 minutes, the TV is turned off and the family members share what they observed, especially the general theme of the interaction.

        2 After 10 minutes of discussing the various themes that were shared and how each determined the theme, the TV is turned on

---

*This is especially nice with a videotaped program. Then no program content is lost during the short discussion periods.

again without the picture and the family members listen to the program. After 10 minutes, the TV is turned off and family members again share their understanding of the theme(s) as well as confirm their earlier theme determined from observing the TV without sound.

3 At the conclusion of theme presentations following only listening to the TV, the family members each discuss what nonverbal behaviors they used to help them understand the TV characters' messages such as tone of voice, for example, when they could only hear the character.

4 The family concludes the exercise sharing personal observations of each other's verbal and nonverbal cues used in their communication. Also, they help each other evaluate the strengths and weaknesses of each other's listening skills.

Interpersonal Communication/Human Relations Skills Training: Example 3

I Setting: Community/Adults

II Life-Skill Objectives: Ability to establish and enjoy relationships within social groups; recognize and respect the individuals rights, personal worth, and uniqueness of others; tolerate and respect those of different backgrounds, habits, values, and appearance.

III Activity: Through a program in the mental health center, learn the components of effective listening skills and practice effective listening skills.

   A Procedure:

   1 Generate list of good listening characteristics

   a The group will discuss the characteristics of a good listener and generate a list. Write these on the chalkboard.

   2 Interviewing in dyads

   a Have persons choose a partner whom they do not know well. Each partner is to take about five minutes to tell the other about him/herself using items such as: how long they've lived here, where they were born, information about their families, outside interests, one behavior they value in themselves. The listener then repeats the information, which the speaker corrects if necessary. Then roles are reversed.

   3 Introducing a person to the group

   a Bring the group back together and ask each person to introduce his/her partner to the group. When all persons have participated, discuss the activity, starting with the question, "What did you find out about others in the group?" or "What did you learn about your listening skills?"

4 Homework: Instruct persons to observe the nonverbal listening behaviors of others and be prepared to share this with the group at the next session.

Interpersonal Communication/Human Relations Skills Training: Example 4

I Setting: School/Adolescents

II Life-Skills Objectives: Ability to respond with empathy to the problems of others; respond reciprocally in interpersonal relationships; recognize the feelings and motives behind interpersonal actions; respond to the feelings of others; express one's own feelings.

III Activity: Classroom exercise using didactic and experiental techniques to enhance students' communication skills.

  A Procedure:

  1 Mini-lecture. Say the following or, using your own words, convey the same ideas: One type of request studied in the previous two sessions was a request for understanding. Suppose you realize that someone is asking for understanding. How can you respond, letting that person know you understand? You can do that by (1) reflecting feelings and content, (2) focusing exclusively on him/her, (3) asking appropriate questions, and (4) communicating warmth nonverbally. There is a strong inclination to give advice and to look for solutions to a problem. These behaviors are inappropriate at this time.

  Let's look at each way of responding to let a person know you understand. (Make a chart of these, put them on the chalkboard, or use an overhead projector transparency.)

  a Reflecting feelings and content. As a person is talking, listen for feelings and the reasons for those feelings. "You feel _____ when _____ ," is a formula for a reflecting response. To help you do this more easily, I've prepared two handouts, one on communications leads and one on feeling words. We'll use these in a few minutes when we practice.

  b Focusing exclusively on the speaker. This means that for now you're going to leave your experiences and feelings out of the conversation and talk just about him or her.

  c Asking appropriate questions. Questions may help the speaker understand his/her situation better if used sparingly and carefully. You are not interrogating. You may use questions to clarify feelings or to pinpoint information. It is better to ask open-ended questions and to avoid the use of "why." That word usually sounds like an accusation.

d Communicating warmth nonverbally. This you do by using the listening skills you learned earlier, including sitting attentively, frequent eye contact, and smiling when appropriate.

2 Practice in communicating understanding. Break into triads and practice letting a person know you understand. You may find these sheets on communication leads and feeling words helpful. (Distribute handouts with communication leads (e.g., You feel ..., As you see it, etc.) and feeling words (e.g., annoyed, furious, elated, blue, fearful, etc.). The speaker should talk about something that he/she has strong feelings about. The listener will reflect feelings, communicate warmth, and ask appropriate questions. The observer will watch and make comments about what was done well and what could be done better next time. Rotate roles until all have taken each part.

3 Homework: Listen for people who are communicating understanding at home and around school. Make notes about good responses you hear.

SUMMARY

This chapter contains the rationale and model for the generic life-skill interpersonal communication/human relations. As appropriate for the Life-Skills Training paradigm, the application of the model to prevention and remediation is described and sample training materials are included to illustrate how descriptors obtained in a national Delphi study are applied as training objectives for the age groups childhood, adolescents, and adults and to the settings of home, school, work, and community.

Suggested readings are included at the end of the chapter to provide the reader with resources for additional study. The entire list of interpersonal communication/human relations descriptors obtained in the national Delphi study are provided in Appendix D for those individuals who would like to develop their own training materials. Likewise, Appendix C is provided to illustrate a model for developing these training materials.

SUGGESTED READINGS

Bellack, A. S., & Hersen, M. (1979). *Research and practice in social skills training*. New York: Plenum Press.

Brammer, L. M. (1979). *The helping relationship: Process and skills* (2d ed.). Englewood Cliffs, NJ: Prentice-Hall.

Carkhuff, R. R., & Anthony, W. A. (1979). *The skills of helping*. Amherst, MA: Human Resources Development Press.

Curran, J. P., & Monti, P. M. (Eds.). (1982). *Social skills training*. New York: Guilford Press.

Danish, S. J., & D'Auguelli, A. R. (1983). *Helping skills II.* New York: Human Sciences Press.

Drum, D. J., & Knott, J. E. (1977). *Structured groups for facilitating development: Acquiring life skills, resolving life themes, and making life transitions.* New York: Human Sciences Press.

Egan, G. (1975). *The skilled helper.* Monterey, CA: Brooks/Cole.

Gazda, G. M., Asbury, F. R. Balzer, F. J., Childers, W. C., & Walters, R. P. (1984). *Human relations development: A manual for educators.* (3d ed). Boston: Allyn and Bacon.

Gazda, G. M., Childers, W. C., & Walters, R. P. (1982). *Interpersonal communication: A handbook for health professionals.* Rockville, MD: Aspen.

Goldstein, A. P. (1981). *Psychological skill training: The structured learning technique.* New York: Pergamon.

Guerney, B. G., Jr. (1977). *Relationship enhancement.* San Francisco: Jossey-Bass.

Larson, D. (Ed.). (1984). *Teaching psychological skills: Models for giving psychology away.* Monterey, CA: Brooks/Cole.

Marshall, E. K., & Kurtz, D. (1982). *Interpersonal helping skills.* San Francisco: Jossey-Bass.

Smith, P. (1982). *The development of a taxonomy of life skills required to become a balanced self-determined person.* Ontario, Canada: Employment and Immigration Canada, Occupational and Career Analysis and Development.

Spence, S., & Shepherd, G. (Eds.) (1983). *Developments in social skills training.* London: Academic Press.

REFERENCES

Bandler, R., & Grinder, J. (1975). *The structure of magic I.* Palo Alto, CA: Science and Behavior Books.

Bandler, R., & Grinder, J. (1979). *Frogs into princes.* Moab, UT: Real Peoples Press.

Bateson, G. (1972). *Steps to an ecology of mind.* New York: Ballatine Books.

Brooks, D. K., Jr. (1984). *A life-skills taxonomy: Defining elements of effective functioning through the use of the Delphi technique.* Unpublished doctoral dissertation. University of Georgia, Athens.

Carkhuff, R. R. (1969). *Helping and human relations* (Vols. 1-2). New York: Holt, Rinehart & Winston.

Carkhuff, R. R., & Berenson, B. G. (1967). *Beyond counseling and therapy.* New York: Holt, Rinehart & Winston.

Cash, R. W. (1984). The human resources development model. In D. Larson (Ed.), *Teaching psychological skills* (pp. 245–270). Monterey, CA: Brooks/Cole.

Egan, G., & Cowan, M. A. (1979). *People in systems.* Monterey, CA: Wadsworth.

Erikson, E. H. (1950). *Childhood and society.* New York: W. W. Norton.

Erikson, E. H. (1963). *Childhood and society* (2d. ed.). New York: W. W. Norton.

Flanagan. J. C. (1978). A research approach to improving our quality of life. *American Psychologist, 33.* 138–147.

Gazda, G. M. (1982). Multiple impact training. In A.J. Corsini (Ed.), *Handbook of psychotherapy* (pp. 525–533). New York: Wiley.

Gazda, G. M. (1984). Multiple impact training: A life-skills approach. In D. Larson (Ed.), *Teaching psychological skills* (pp. 87–103). Monterey, CA: Brooks/Cole.

Gazda, G. M., Asbury, F. R., Balzer, F. J., Childers, W. C., & Walters, R. P. (1977). *Human relations development: A manual for educators* (2d ed.). Boston: Allyn & Bacon.

Gazda, G. M., Asbury, F. R., Balzer, F. J., Childers, W. C., & Walters, R. P. (1984). *Human relations development: A manual for educators* (3d ed.). Boston: Allyn & Bacon.

Gazda, G. M., Asbury, F. R., Childers, W. C., Desselle, E., & Walters, R. P. (1973). *Human relations development: A manual for educators*. Boston: Allyn & Bacon.

Gazda, G. M., Childers, W. C., & Walters, R. P. (1982). *Interpersonal communication: A handbook for health professionals* Rockville, MD: Aspen Systems.

Gazda, G. M., Walters, R. P., & Childers, W. C. (1975). *Human relations development: A manual for health sciences*. Boston: Allyn & Bacon.

Gazda, G. M., Walters, R. P., & Childers, W. C. (1981). *Realtalk: Exercises in friendship and helping skills*. Atlanta, GA: Humanics.

Grinder, J., & Bandler, R. (1976). *The structure of magic II*. Palo Alto, CA: Science and Behavior Books.

Havighurst, R. J. (1948). *Developmental tasks and education*. Chicago: University of Chicago Press.

Havighurst, R. J. (1953). *Developmental tasks and education* (2d ed.). New York: Longmans, Green.

Havighurst, R. J. (1972). *Developmental tasks and education* (3d ed.). New York: David McKay.

Haynie, N. A. (1982). Learning how to learn. In G. M. Gazda, W. C. Childers, & R. P. Walters, *Interpersonal communication: A handbook for health professionals* (pp. 21–39). Rockville, MD: Aspen Systems.

Korzybski, A. (1958). *Science and sanity* (4th ed.). New York: Science Press.

McCleary, R. A. (1966). Response-modulating functions of the limbic system: Imitation and suppression. In E. Steller & J. M. Sprague (Eds.), *Progress in physiological psychology* (pp. 209–272). New York: Academic Press.

Mehrabian, A. (1968). Communication without words. *Psychology Today 2*, 52–55.

Rogers, C. R. (1957). The necessary and sufficient conditions of personality change. *Journal of Counseling Psychology, 21*, 95–103.

Singer, J. L. (1976). *Daydreaming and fantasy*. London: George Allen and Unwin.

Sisson, P. J., Arthur, G. R., & Gazda, G. M. (1981). *Human relations for criminal justice personnel*. Boston: Allyn & Bacon.

Truax, C. B., & Carkhuff, R. R. (1967). *Toward effective counseling and psychotherapy*. Chicago: Aldine.

CHAPTER 10

PROBLEM SOLVING/ DECISION MAKING

"Making decisions is like speaking prose—people do it all the time, knowingly or unknowingly" (Kahneman and Tversky, 1984, p. 341). In addition, "decision making is one of the most important recurrent human activities" (Hogarth, 1980, p. ix).

It is interesting that "decision making" and not "problem solving" is presented as a pervasive and meaningful activity. With regard to personal "problems," this seems sufficiently anomalous to lead us to question what the distinction is between decision making and problem solving. However, an answer is not readily available. Both the research and applied literature deal with problem solving and decision making without distinguishing between the two. Moreover, the process of decision making as encountered in the research literature seems synonymous with the process of problem solving as delineated by professional helpers. Some clarity can be provided by Fischhoff's distinction (Personal communication, May 17, 1984). Accordingly, *problem solving* as a term is more accurately applied to a task that has a definite solution that is known to be right or wrong. In contrast, *decision making* is more appropriately defined as dealing with issues in which the solution cannot be specified as right or wrong. To reiterate, the consequences of the solution may be viewed as desirable or undesirable, but there exists no objectively correct or incorrect solution. From this perspective, the issues that people face and define as problems are more appropriately termed decisions. More importantly, people approach professional helpers for help with these personal decisions. This book is aimed at the professional human services worker who will be called upon to facilitate persons' coping skills. Therefore, the terminology and model used for decision making will accommodate the lay definition of problem solving and thereby provide an interfacing of problem solving/decision making that will be useful as a means of enabling clients to reframe "problems" as decisions to which they will apply coping skills.

Decision making involves a judgment or a choice between alternatives (Hogarth, 1980), and as such it is the commitment to a plan of action (Janis, 1968). However, it can also be conceived as a stage in the process of problem solving.

A problem exists when the individual is confronted with a task (Simon and Newell, 1971). Whether the problem is expressed as an obstacle blocking progress toward a goal or, more simply, as a situation confronting the individual (Maier, 1970), the conditions that elicit the need for problem solving also present the conditions for decision making. Effective decision making is implicit in productive problem solving (Maier, 1970). This chapter focuses on the problem solving/decision making process as a life-skill.

RATIONALE

Problems and decisions are an inevitable and pervasive part of living (Hogarth, 1980). While some problems are minor and their decision aspects routinized (such as choosing items from a restaurant menu), others involve more complex and personally vital issues (such as choosing a career or choosing a marriage partner) (Janis and Mann, 1977). In addition, some decisions proceed from problems that carry implications and consequences that affect many other persons and even society in general. For instance, managerial or organizational problems/decisions (such as whether to shut down a plant) as well as political problems/decisions (such as the one President Kennedy was embroiled in when approving the Bay of Pigs invasion) affect many people aside from the individual solving the problem (Janis and Mann, 1977). In most contexts, implementing a decision commits the person to an action that has consequences, possibly unforeseen, that have an impact on either an individual or a group on a professional and/or a personal level.

Life can be conceived of as a series of problems with concomitant decisions ranging from what time to get up in the morning, to whom to marry, to what action to take in a relationship, to a national decision of how to counter foreign aggression. Since problem solving/decision making is a frequent necessity, one would assume that people would be practiced, proficient, and well educated in the skills utilized in solving tasks or coping with situations through appropriate decisions. However, there is evidence that, frequently, decisions are difficult for people (Miller, 1978, 1981), particularly when resolution requires an unusual or innovative response (Maier, 1970). Moreover, across trivial and important issues, people do not regularly demonstrate effective decision making (Hogarth, 1980; Janis and Mann, 1977). The problem-solving/decision-making process seems in real-life situations to be unstructured and intuitive (Hogarth, 1980). It is, however, a process that can be studied and taught, and such teaching can improve people's problem-solving/decision-making skills (Hogarth, 1980; Maier, 1970). For instance, research has demonstrated that training improved young children's ability "to think through and solve real-life interpersonal problems" (Shure, 1981, p. 178).

Before proposing procedures for improving these skills, it will be useful to examine more closely the problem-solving/decision-making process. The emphasis will be on individual problem solving, but the reader should remain aware that problem-solving skills are important in groups such as business, families, and politics as well.

A MODEL FOR PROBLEM SOLVING/DECISION MAKING

In this section, the problem-solving/decision-making process will be described with respect to the various functions and attendant biases inherent in the process. In general, the problem-solving/decision-making process occurs in five theoretical stages: recognizing a problem, defining the problem, producing alternatives as solutions, weighing and selecting from the alternatives a course of action, and assessing feedback from implementation of a particular alternative. After a more detailed presentation, the model will be summarized and then prevention and remediation elements related to problem solving/decision making will be considered. Applications of the model for children, adolescents, and adults in family, school, work, and community settings will be explored in a later section.

Recognizing a Problem   To solve a problem, the person must first perceive that the present situation does in fact constitute a problem. Not all conditions that require a solution *are* problem situations nor should these non-problems engage the problem-solving/decision-making process. In particular, problem situations differ from recall situations in that "problem situations introduce a selectivity in stored information that is unique and different from recall situations" (Maier, Thurber, and Julius, 1970, p. 49). For instance, in school we are presented with tasks that involve remembering the answer. But life presents questions for which school did not teach the answer (Maier, 1970), and so answers have to be generated and selected, not recalled, from stored knowledge. Thus, a problem situation exists when the person recognizes that he or she is in a situation requiring the generation of an action because progress toward a goal is blocked or because progress involves choosing between two or more alternative actions (Miller, 1981).

Defining the Problem   Beginning the problem-solving procedure involves exploring the problem (Carkhuff, 1973). The purpose of this phase is to define the relevant elements of the problem, both in terms of the person and the context of the environment (Carkhuff, 1973; Maier, 1970; Miller, 1978). In essence, the problem is represented in internal memory, and a function of the problem assessment is to distinguish between the task environment and the way the task is represented (Simon and Newell, 1971). It is important at this stage to get beneath the surface representation of the problem because previous experience with similar problems may aid efficient solution, but only if the situations are actually similar. Without exploring the problem, seeming similarities may lead to past experience being misleading and producing inefficient solutions. Good problem solving demands using the process that suits the problem at hand (Maier, 1970). Once the problem is placed accurately within the context of the person and the environment, the problem is understood (Carkhuff 1973). At this point it becomes possible to define the problem (Gagne, 1966).

Defining the problem means specifying its essential and relevant features and the concomitant goal (Carkhuff, 1973). More specifically, this means to state the problem in a way that generates a search that will determine the goal and explore obstacles to the goal (Maier, 1970). This process may be helpful in uncovering previously overlooked factors and possible actions (Fishburn, 1972). It is essential, as with understanding the problem, to consider personal and societal factors as well as task features (Miller, 1978). In particular, personal values, assets, and limitations are essential determinants of desirable outcomes. In addition, societal attitudes and pressures impact the acceptability of particular solutions. As importantly, effective problem solving involves the ability to collect and select the information that is really necessary in order to solve the dilemma (Maier and Burke, 1970). In this regard, definition and goal setting may involve gaining supplementary information or experience (Miller, 1978). The end result is not an absolute, "right" solution, but an individualistically-based desirable solution.

Because problem solving/decision making is a life-skill and because the process is subject to inefficiencies and errors (Nisbett and Ross, 1980), we need to examine this process more deeply at the level of the functioning of internal mechanisms. Internally, the problem features, as a pattern of information, are encoded and represented in memory in such a way that the problem is related to other knowledge (Pitz and Sachs, 1984; Simon and Newell, 1971). The task for the person is to combine beliefs about probable outcomes with preferences (values) to determine a "best" course of action. In this regard, determining the best solution involves applying rules to search the stimuli associated with information and knowledge (Simon and Newell, 1971). Therefore, problem solving/decision making can be conceived of as an information processing task (Gagne, 1966) with task features, past experience, personal values, and societal issues constituting the relevant information.

Alternatives   With the problem coded or defined and the goal specified, the problem-solving process interfaces with the decision-making process. The activity shifts from constructing the representation of the problem to solving the problem (Simon and Newell, 1971) in that alternatives are generated and an action is produced.

As an initial activity, the person searches for and formulates hypotheses or alternatives (Carkhuff, 1973; Gagne, 1966; Janis, 1968). Several issues are relevant at this stage where decision making begins to interface with the problem-solving procedure. For instance, it is useful to brainstorm alternatives without evaluating their potential usefulness (Carkhuff, 1973). Individuals can store and use information in three different ways: through associative bonds, through fragmentation (making pieces of previously bonded information), and through reorganization of pieces of information (Maier and Burke, 1970). Since individuals differ in this preferred storage method and since all persons are capable of using information in all three ways, brainstorming, with evaluation held in abeyance, may help to produce the elements in such a way as to facilitate combining past experience (information) into a new integrative, "creative" solution.

In more generalized mechanistic terms, the person as an information processor with limited short-term memory applies rules or heuristics to the problem features to generate solutions, that is, possible actions (Simon and Newell, 1971). The person's search proceeds in sequential or step-like fashion and is influenced by the individual's store of knowledge, including his or her knowledge of rules to manipulate information (Gagne, 1966). Effectiveness of the search process depends on factors such as the ability to distinguish relevant problem features (problem definition), flexibility in forming possible solutions, and ease of recall. In particular, ease of recall is subject to interference (Gagne, 1966). Moreover, intense emotion can interrupt the information-processing/decision-making system (Fiske and Taylor, 1984). Research (Bower, 1983) suggests that the experiencing of particular emotions primes associated "concepts, words, themes, and rules of inference" (Bower, 1983, p. 395). More specifically, when the person is emotional,

> His emotional state will bring into readiness certain perceptual categories, certain themes, certain ways of interpreting the world that are congruent with his emotional state; these mental sets then act as interpretative filters of reality and as biases in his judgment. (Bower, 1983, p. 395)

In sum, the person's emotional state may systematically bias the alternative solutions produced. The next step then, weighing the alternatives for a best action/solution may be implemented without access to a sufficiently wide range of alternatives, and so inefficiency or bad judgment may result.

Decision   Once the search has delineated the possible solutions, it is necessary for the person to choose a specific course of action (Carkhuff, 1973; Gagne, 1966; Janis, 1968). The choosing involves searching through the alternatives and weighing them or judging them according to their probability of success as well as their desirability as courses of action (Carkhuff, 1973; Miller, 1978). One strategy for weighing the alternatives is to manipulate mentally each proposed solution to its predicted conclusion (Maier, 1970; Simon and Newell, 1971). This evaluative procedure serves to eliminate some alternatives and to give priority to others as possibilities based on the perceived positive versus negative outcome (Janis, 1968). However, the perceived outcome of each alternative retains some degree of uncertainty regarding actual consequences (Janis and Mann, 1977).

To the extent a judgment or decision-making task is characterized by uncertainty of outcome, the person's decision reflects a prediction about the likelihood of particular outcomes and may also entail an assessment of risk (Hogarth, 1980; Pitz and Sachs, 1984). In making such predictions, people utilize particular heuristic principles that "reduce the complex tasks of assessing probabilities and predicting values to simpler judgmental operations" (Tversky and Kahneman, 1974, p. 1124). While these heuristics account for efficient inferential processes and are effective over a wide range of problems, they also lead to systematic errors or biases in judgment (Nisbett and Ross, 1980; Tversky and Kahneman, 1974).

An example may help to clarify how a heuristic can usually be effective but in particular instances can lead to biased judgment. In some situations "people assess the frequency of a class or the probability of an event by the ease with which instances or occurrences can be brought to mind" (Tversky and Kahneman, 1974, p. 1127). This particular search rule is termed the availability heuristic. Research has documented that easily recalled or vivid classes or instances will seem more numerous than those that are less easily retrieved from memory (see Nisbett and Ross, 1980; Tversky and Kahneman, 1974). For instance, different groups of people were presented with different lists of well-known men and women and asked to judge which gender appeared more frequently. In some lists the men were relatively more famous, while on other lists the women were relatively more famous. Most of the people erroneously judged that the gender that had the more famous names was more numerous altogether. It seems the famous people were more easily recalled and so their gender was judged as more frequent. Imagine also the frequency with which the letter r appears at the beginning of a word as opposed to being the third letter in a word. Since it is easier to search for words beginning with r, most people erroneously conclude r is more frequent as a beginning letter. In actuality, it occurs more often as the third letter of a word. In sum, the rule which in many instances produces accurate judgment also in some situations leads to biased decision making.

Relatedly, a person's mood may affect prediction and assessment of the best solution. According to Clark and Isen (1982), assessing the costs and rewards of a particular solution may be a function of mood operating in conjunction with the availability heuristic. Specifically, a good mood may facilitate thinking of rewards and concurrently impede thinking of costs when evaluating alternatives. In addition, research suggests that a good mood pervasively influences the problem-solving/decision-making process (Isen, Means, Patrick, and Nowicki, 1982):

> All else equal, a person who is feeling happy will be more likely than at other times to reduce the load on working memory: to reduce the complexity of decision situations and the difficulty of tasks, by adopting the simplest strategy possible, considering the fewest number of alternatives possible, and doing little or no checking of information, hypotheses, and tentative conclusions. (p. 258)

Although these same authors' research further suggests that this tendency to simplify and possibly impair performance is mitigated when there is feedback on the task and when the task is extremely important, the research (Bower, 1983; Clark and Isen, 1982; Isen, Means, Patrick, and Nowicki, 1982) suggesting systematic biases in decision making because of the influence of one's current emotional state are noteworthy. Given that weighing and assigning priority to solutions involves retaining alternatives despite some degree of uncertainty of actual outcome, a biased search and selection procedure seems akin to double jeopardy. In addition, perception of risk may be influenced by mood. Experimental manipulation of mood (Johnson and Tversky, 1983) indicated that negative mood produced a pervasive increase in assessment of risks, while positive mood produced a global decrease in perception of risk. It seems evident that these mood-influenced perceptions could have a profound and biasing effect, possibly leading to inefficient decisions.

As previously stated, besides predicting the likelihood of outcomes, effective decision making entails preferences (Pitz and Sachs, 1984). In fact it seems some value is at the basis of any decision (Miller, 1981). Janis and Mann (1977) point out that "seemingly irrational choices sometimes make good sense once we realize that a person may be willing to renounce utilitarian and social rewards in order to avoid the pain of self-disapproval for violating internalized standards" (pp. 8–9).

It is important that preferences reflect the values of the present and immediate future (Bell and Coplans, 1976). Also the value system being considered needs to be person-specific, that is, represent and reflect the preferences of the decision maker—whatever his or her preferences are. Awareness of the value system is particularly important to decision making (Miller, 1978, 1981). Regardless of the person's level of awareness, values affect one's goals, the information one attends to and selects as relevant or critical to the decision situation, the risks one is willing to take, and the assessment of the decision outcome. Therefore, effective decision making entails establishing priorities and maintaining awareness of personal values.

As an additional note, it seems worthwhile to reiterate that decision making involves some ambiguity in that there is an element of uncertainty regarding the hoped-for outcome (Janis and Mann, 1977). As a result, persons often experience difficulty in choosing between alternatives and may respond with "defensive avoidance." Accordingly, persons may procrastinate or avoid choosing, or they may try to resolve the doubts attendant to the choices through rationalization. It also is important to remember that difficulty with decision making may reflect fear—fear of making a mistake (Miller, 1981). This latter source of difficulty may be a result of the person not being aware of having developed skills for competent decision making as well as a result of deficient skills. More importantly, the difficulty with problem solving may result in frustration if the problem is too difficult for the person's skill level, if there is pressure to solve the problem, if the person is unable to escape the problem, or if there is no substitute goal (Maier, 1970). Such frustration could result in behavior that is characterized by fixation, aggression, and regression. More specifically, problem solving/decision making is impeded. Therefore, to lessen future difficulties and frustration, a final component of the problem-solving/decision-making process is to obtain feedback and assess outcomes resulting from decisions.

Assessing Feedback   Once the decision is implemented as action, it is important to process the outcome so as to further develop decision skills (Miller, 1981). Such assessment may be difficult. In particular, the outcome or consequence of the decision may be the only source of feedback (Einhorn and Hogarth, 1978). Further, the issue may be complicated because "evidence about outcomes contingent on the action not taken is missing, or if outcomes are available, attention is not paid to them" (Einhorn and Hogarth, 1978, p. 401). In this respect, it may be difficult for us to learn from our errors, as errors or more effective decision outcomes may not be obvious. It is in this area that specific training and education in problem solving/decision making may be most useful, as it seems experience may not be an effective teacher.

To recapitulate, problem solving/decision making is a process that can be conceptualized in five stages (see Figure 10-1):

1 Recognizing a problem exists
2 Defining the problem
3 Producing alternatives as solutions
4 Weighing and selecting a course of action
5 Assessing feedback from the outcome

Given the delineation of the basic process, it is now possible to consider the relevance of Life-Skills Training in terms of prevention and remediation.

Prevention

According to Pitz and Sachs (1984), "Judgment and decision skills develop along with other abilities" (p. 154). In addition, "efforts to debias judgments should focus on extended skills training" (Pitz and Sachs, 1984, p. 155). In sum, prevention relative to problem solving/decision making needs to emphasize a developmental approach to account for learning and maturation of skills and to include training to lessen bias in the procedures. This seems consistent with the Life-Skills Training model, and it would seem that preventive training would be useful in a designated educative program, such as an academic facility or school.

Relative to training, research by Brooks (1984) has defined particular skills necessary for problem solving/decision making. These are expressed within a developmental framework for childhood, adolescence, and adulthood (see Table 10-1). In addition, attention to some general educative strategies might be beneficial, especially as an approach to integrating particular skills as well as for defusing judgmental biases.

In this regard, trainer's knowledge of Life-Skills Training would be useful to enable appropriate implementation of strategies. For instance, trainers should remain aware that there are important individual differences in problem solving/decision making. More specifically, problem solving will be more effective for the person who possesses more information (e.g., through verbal and quantitative rules stored in memory) and/or is free from recall interference (Gagne, 1966). Moreover, it is helpful for trainers to recognize that judgmental skills require learning, maturation, and abilities such as memory and knowledge of rules and heuristic strategies (Fischhoff, 1980). Students must be functioning at an appropriate level before they are capable of responding to particular strategies.

There are also content issues that are relevant to strategies for implementing Life-Skills Training. Course work introducing school children to inferential concepts and strategies as well as programs designed to increase people's awareness of inferential errors would be useful in augmenting Life-Skills Training (Nisbett and Ross, 1980). Moreover, using "concrete, vivid, and anecdotal information" (Nisbett and Ross, 1980, p.

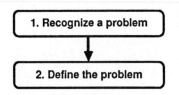

FIGURE 10-1
Model of Problem Solving/Decision Making.

1) What are the situational elements?

2) What are the personal elements?

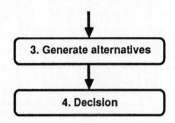

1) Most desirable action?

2) Action with most probability of success?

3) Implementation/action

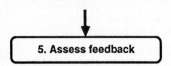

TABLE 10-1
PROBLEM-SOLVING/DECISION-MAKING SKILLS[a]

Childhood	Adolescence	Adulthood
Anticipate possible consequences of actions through personal reflection.	Maintain balance between awareness of one's own opinions and those of others in making decisions.	Resolve conflicts, make decisions, and encounter new situations through effective problem-solving strategies.
Develop and carry out a complex intention.	Identify and define personal problems and goals.	Assess evidence with detachment and objectivity.
Make perceptual judgments involving one variable.	Generate alternative problem solutions based on pertinent information.	Set personal goals and plan for their implementation.
Utilize objective data in making judgments.	Demonstrate personal values as the basis for making decisions.	Set goals and apply personally chosen performance standards to their achievement.
Understand and relate tasks to goal achievement.	Manipulate and apply abstract ideas in problem solving.	Decide and act based on one's judgment.
Stick with tasks to completion.	Compare and analyze patterns of thought.	Think creatively.
Follow directions in situations involving multiple tasks.	Distinguish between supported opinions and those without support.	Assess and analyze one's commitments on an ongoing basis and order one's priorities and goals accordingly.

[a]Skills necessary for information seeking, information assessment and analysis, problem identification, solution, implementation, and evaluation; goal setting; systematic planning and forecasting; time management; critical thinking; and conflict resolution. See Appendix E for a complete listing of problem-solving/decision-making skills.

281) could help make problem-solving/decision-making strategies more salient and more memorable. Also, deliberate training in a problem-solving attitude would be productive for facilitating skill development. Attitudinal focus would involve trainers specifying the construction of a social environment in which "students" expected disagreement, welcomed all points of view, placed no blame, emphasized the problem rather than an already desired solution, and perceived differences as a result of the problem situation (Maier, 1970). Such a problem-solving attitude could be particularly useful for combating bias due to mood fluctuations. And finally, it should be noted that decision aids and simulation techniques would be viable skill-training strategies (Maier, 1970; Pitz and Sachs. 1984).

To summarize, prevention as related to Life-Skills Training is an educative/academic mode. Information and skill training is provided by trained personnel on the basis of developmental readiness. Other training programs are necessary, however, when persons experience the need for help with their problems.

Remediation

A remedial approach to problem solving/decision making becomes relevant when a person is experiencing frustration and is blocked in the decision process. In this situation, a professional helper can facilitate the problem solving by defusing the frustration (Maier, 1970). In relation to this, the helping professional simultaneously pursues two goals: "(1) to help the helpee develop strategies for solving the immediate problem, and (2) to help the helpee learn problem-solving skills that the helpee can continue to use in future situations" (Gazda, et al., 1984, p. 200). Even in remediation, the emphasis is on the person learning life-skills.

There are several basic themes pertinent to remediation. For one, exploring values enables the person to realize, own, and place a priority on his or her individual preferences (Carkhuff, 1973). This in turn will help determine the goal of the problem situation and enhance the effectiveness of the problem resolution (Carkhuff, 1973; Miller, 1978).

The helper can also be effective by helping persons recognize that they do have choices or alternatives. (Miller 1978). According to Miller (1978), people "who fail to make choices when they have the opportunity are not necessarily backing away from the choices. *They may simply not recognize that a choice does exist*" (p. 29). If the fact that there is a choice is not perceived, alternative actions are not considered, and satisfactory resolution of the problem situation (be it acceptance of the situation or a change through action) may be impeded. As a specific example, consider the person who "has to" get up and go to work each day. There is a choice: the person could stay home and not work (Miller, 1978). Although the consequences of the alternative action are not positive or desired, it is useful to recognize that there is a choice and a decision was implemented.

In the helping situation, it is also productive to reframe the problem situation. For instance, a person may perceive that having problems with other people is an indication of personal inadequacy and failure (Maier, 1970). Altering the problem statement to "finding ways to improve relationships with others" can lead to constructive consideration of the problem rather than faulting the blaming self. In this fashion, the emotional components are reduced and a problem-solving attitude can be achieved.

In general, the goal of remediation is similar to the goal of prevention—to teach people life-skills relative to problem solving/decision making. The helper provides the training in skill development by facilitating the person's resolution to the particular immediate problem situation. With this in mind and having explored the procedural model and provided some insight into prevention and remediation, we can now consider applications of the model.

APPLICATION

Life-Skills Training is provided in four settings according to developmental parameters: in the family, at school, at work, and in the community for children, adolescents, and adults. This section will provide examples of strategies that can be used to implement the training model in the various settings (see Table 10-2). In addition, a strategy from each of the settings will be presented in detail in order to explicate fully how the various aspects of the Life-Skills Training model are related within problem solving/decision making. To this end, the following activities are intended as illustrations of the model in action. Persons utilizing the Life-Skills Training orientation are encouraged to refer to Appendix E for a list of descriptors and then to exercise their own problem-solving/decision-making skills to create techniques useful for their own situation.

Problem-Solving/Decision-Making Skills Training: Example 1

I Setting: Family/All ages
II Life-Skill Objectives: Children—ability to be goal-directed, understand cause and effect relationships, use cognitive and perceptual processes in problem solving, formulate future plans on a limited basis, understand and relate tasks to goal achievement. Adolescents—maintain balance between awareness of one's own opinions and those of others in making decisions, generate alternative problem solutions based on pertinent information, compare and analyze patterns of thought, distinguish between supported opinions and those without support. Adults— assess evidence with detachment and objectivity, think creatively, set personal goals and plan for their implementation, decide and act based on one's best judgment.
III Activity: Family meeting (Dinkmeyer and McKay, 1982; Dreikurs, 1964). Set up a family meeting or council where all members of the family meet at a regularly scheduled time to make decisions relative to family problems.
  A Rules:
    1 All family members contribute at all levels.
    2 Children and parents have equal votes.
    3 Decisions are enforced for one week.

TABLE 10-2
PROBLEM-SOLVING/DECISION-MAKING STRATEGIES

	Family	School	Work	Community
Prevention	Allow children to make age-appropriate decisions (such as what to wear each day); this provides practice in decision making and parents can help process feedback about consequences (such as wearing shorts on a cold day). Family conferences can help resolve problems and provide a forum for children to learn decision making from trial and error as well as through imitation.	Course work on inferential and statistical methods. Curriculum activities geared to presenting artificial and vivid problem situations could structure the learning of skills through practice and feedback in situations where outcomes could be varied and alternate consequences recognized.	Training programs in decision making with emphasis on the company's philosophy and chain of command. Train managers to implement decision making to resolve conflict within the work setting. Institute periodic meetings to review and resolve problems relative to work performance, including organizational procedures and work climate.	Programs through organizations such as the PTA to provide training for parents in utilizing decision-making skills for determining solutions to problems encountered in raising/disciplining children. Lectures and special classes designed to enhance adults' understanding of inferential strategies. Training through public agencies in modeling and use of problem-solving skills applied to daily problems such as child rearing and stress reduction.

| Remediation | At family meetings, rework the previous week's decisions that have not proved effective. | Availability of a school counselor for those students experiencing personal or school-related problems. Teachers model problem solving to initiate behavior modification programs to resolve classroom difficulties. | A private helping professional on staff to assist employees experiencing "problems" relative to self or work | Private and public mental health facilities provide remediation for individuals and groups. |

B Procedure:
  1 Pinpoint issues. Recognize and define problems from the aspect of each family member.
  2 Brainstorm solutions. Encourage everyone to contribute ideas regardless of how "silly" they might sound.
  3 Explore and evaluate the implications and consequences each of the possible solutions has relative to each family member. Consider each person's attitude and values about the various solutions.
  4 Try to obtain a consensus before opting for a majority-rule solution.
  5 Implement the decision for one week.
  6 Reevaluate the decision at the next meeting. Assess how the decision has worked out for each family member.

Problem-Solving/Decision-Making Skills Training: Example 2

 I Setting: School/Adolescents
 II Life-Skill Objectives: Ability to analyze multiple variables in problem solving, to learn to use an effective approach to decision making, to do critical task analysis as an initial step in problem solving.
 III Activity: Curriculum in problem solving. Present students with a fictitious newspaper article. For example:

> Singer Jay Geally has been fired from the title role in the hit Broadway musical *Rowing Along the Mississippi*. Apparently no one told him the show must go on, and he had missed twelve performances since taking over the role on November 2—and he also missed his originally scheduled opening performance in September. Understudy Dan Dickson will perform until a new star is found. Absenteeism also cost Jay a TV series, "Hard Rock." The reason given was emotional problems because of the breakup of his marriage to superstar Brenda Beaconson.

  A Procedure:
  1 Have students identify the problem.
  2 Ask students to define the problem and delineate any subproblems.
  3 Students can generate possible solutions.
  4 Ask the student to role play and decide which of the solutions would be most appropriate.
  5 As a group, students can discuss their individual decisions and "imaginatively" assess the possible outcomes of the various solutions.

Problem-Solving/Decision-Making Skills Training: Example 3

I Setting: Work/Adults

II Life-Skill Objectives: Ability to assess evidence with detachment and objectivity, to think clearly and solve problems, to think creatively, to set goals and apply personally chosen performance standards to their achievement.

III Activity: On-the-Job Training. Given a conflict situation such as school assessment personnel being dissatisfied with the organization's designated format for report writing, management can facilitate problem solving by setting up a committee comprised of assessment personnel to revise the format.

  A Procedure:

    1 Pinpoint the elements to be included in reports.

    2 Brainstorm various ways to incorporate these elements into report styles.

    3 Weigh the pros and cons of each alternative.

    4 Choose the most desirable format.

    5 Report to management and implement the new format.

    6 Together employees and management evaluate the usefulness of the chosen style one month after implementation.

Problem-Solving/Decision-Making Skills Training: Example 4

I Setting: Community/All ages

II Life-Skill Objectives: Children—utilize intuition in making judgments, stick with tasks to completion, try new methods of problem solving, follow directions in situations involving multiple tasks, develop and carry out a complex intention. Adolescents—identify and define personal problems and goals, demonstrate personal values as the basis for making decisions, manipulate and apply abstract ideas in problem solving. Adults—assess evidence with detachment and objectivity, resolve conflicts, make decisions, encounter new situations through effective problem-solving strategies.

III Activity: At an organizational meeting such as a Cub Scout pack meeting, role play a sibling, peer, and/or parent-child conflict using organizational participants as actors and audience.

  A Procedure:

    1 Have audience (individually first, then together) define the problem.

    2 Have audience generate possible solutions.

    3 Weigh alternatives and choose an action.

4 Role play the chosen action.
5 Assess the consequences.
6 Role play an alternate action and assess those consequences.
7 Throughout the procedure, the leader can point out or lead a short discussion on parts of the decision-making process (e.g., attention to values, possible biasing components).

SUMMARY

This chapter has presented a model of problem solving/decision making that is relevant to Life-Skills Training. As such, a five-stage process is proposed: recognizing a problem exists, defining the problem, generating alternatives, making a decision (choosing an alternative) and assessing the feedback from the consequences of the decision. The model emphasizes that both situational and personal elements are important for effective decision making. In addition, discussion reviewed the possibility of biased and noneffective decisions arising from various components such as mood.

In Life-Skills Training, education according to developmental readiness as provided by trained personnel is viewed as a preventive function. Remediation retains the goal of teaching the person life-skills relative to decision making but includes as well the professional's facilitating resolution of the immediate problem situation. Finally, the chapter provided illustrative examples of how to apply the model in the four settings (family, school, work, and community) for the three age groupings (childhood, adolescence, and adulthood).

SUGGESTED READINGS

Bell, R., & Coplans, Jr. (1976). *Decisions, decisions*. New York: W. W. Norton.
Carkhuff, R. R. (1973). *The art of problem-solving*. Amherst, MA: Human Resource Development Press.
Gazda, G. M., Asbury, F. R., Balzer, F. J., Childers, W. C., & Walters, R. P. (1984). *Human relations development: A manual for educators* (3d ed.). Boston: Allyn & Bacon.
Hogarth, R. M. (1980). *Judgment and choice*. New York: Wiley.
Isen, A. M., Means, B., Patrick, R., & Nowicki, G. (1982). Some factors influencing decision-making strategy and risk taking. In M. S. Clark & S. T. Fiske (Eds.), *Affect and cognition: The seventeenth annual Carnegie symposium on cognition* (pp. 243–261). Hillsdale, NJ: Lawrence Erlbaum Associates.
Janis, I. L., & Mann, L. (1977). *Decision making: A psychological analysis of conflict, choice, and commitment*. New York: The Free Press.
Maier, N. R. F. (1970). *Problem solving and creativity: in individuals and groups*. Belmont, CA: Brooks/Cole.

Miller, G. P. (1978). *Life choices*. New York: Thomas Y. Crowell.

Shure, M. B. (1981). Social competence as a problem solving skill. In J. D. Wine & M. D. Smye (Eds.), *Social Competence* (pp. 158–185). New York: Guilford Press.

Tversky, A., & Kahneman, D. (1974). Judgment under uncertainty: Heuristics and biases. *Science, 185*, 1124–1131.

REFERENCES

Bell, R., & Coplans, J. (1976). *Decisions, decisions*. New York: W. W. Norton.

Bower, G. H. (1983). Affect and cognition. *Philosophical Transactions Royal Society of London* B 302, 387–402.

Brooks, D. K., Jr. (1984). *A life-skills taxonomy: Defining elements of effective functioning through the use of the Delphi technique*. Unpublished doctoral dissertation, University of Georgia, Athens.

Carkhuff, R. R. (1973). *The art of problem-solving*. Amherst, MA: Human Resource Development Press.

Clark, M. S., & Isen, A. M. (1982). Toward understanding the relationship between feeling states and social behavior. In A. Hastorf & A. M. Isen (Eds.), *Cognitive social psychology* (pp. 73–108). New York: Elsevier North-Holland.

Dinkmeyer, D., & McKay, G. D. (1982). *The parent's handbook: Systematic training for effective parenting*. Circle Pines, MN: American Guidance Service.

Dreikurs, R. (1964). *Children: The challenge*. New York: Hawthorne.

Einhorn, H. J., & Hogarth, R. M. (1978). Confidence in judgment: Persistence of the illusion of validity. *Psychological Review, 85*(5), 395–416.

Fischhoff, B. (1980). For those condemned to study the past: Reflections on historical judgment. In R. A. Sweder & D. W. Fiske (Eds.), *New directions for methodology of behavioral science: Fallible judgment in behavioral research* (pp. 79–93). San Francisco: Jossey-Bass.

Fischhoff, B. (1984, February). Personal communication.

Fishburn, P. C. (1972). Personalistic decision theory exposition and critique. In H. S. Brinkers (Ed.), *Decision-making: Creativity, judgment, and systems* (pp. 19–41). Columbus: Ohio State University Press.

Fiske, S. T., & Taylor, S. E. (1984). *Social cognition*. Reading, MA: Addison-Wesley.

Gagne, R. M. (1966). Human problem solving: Internal and external events. In B. Kleinmuntz (Ed.), *Problem solving: Research, method, and theory* (pp. 128–148). New York: Wiley.

Gazda, G. M., Asbury, F. R., Balzer, F. J., Childers, W. C., & Walters, R. P. (1984). *Human relations development: A manual for educators* (3d ed.). Boston: Allyn & Bacon.

Hogarth, R. M. (1980). *Judgment and choice*. New York: Wiley.

Isen, A. M., Means, B., Patrick, R., & Nowicki, G. (1982). Some factors influencing decision-making strategy and risk taking. In M. S. Clark & S. T. Fiske (Eds.), *Affect and cognition: The seventeenth annual Carnegie symposium on cognition* (pp. 243–261). Hillsdale, NJ: Lawrence Erlbaum Associates.

Janis, I. L. (1968). Stages in the decision-making process. In R. P. Abelson, E. Aronson, W. J. McGuire, T. M. Newcomb, M. J. Rosenberg, & P. H. Tannenbaum (Eds.), *Theories of cognitive consistency: A sourcebook* (pp. 577–588). Chicago: Rand McNally.

Janis, I. L. & Mann, L. (1977). *Decision making: A psychological analysis of conflict, choice, and commitment.* New York: The Free Press.

Johnson, E. J., & Tversky, A. (1983). Affect, generalization, and the perception of risk. *Journal of Personality and Social Psychology, 45,* 20–31.

Kahneman, D., & Tversky, A. (1984). Choices, values, and frames. *American Psychologist, 39*(4), 341–350.

Maier, N. R. F. (1970). *Problem solving and creativity: In individuals and groups.* Belmont, CA: Brooks/Cole.

Maier, N. R. F., & Burke, R. J. (1970). Test of the concept of "availability of functions" in problem solving. In N. R. F. Maier, *Problem solving and creativity: In individuals and groups* (pp. 155–161). Belmont, CA: Brooks/Cole.

Maier, N. R. F., Thurber, J. A., & Julius, M. (1970). Studies in creativity: III. Effect of overlearning on recall and usage of information. In N. R. F. Maier, *Problem solving and creativity: In individuals and groups* (pp. 44–49). Belmont, CA: Brooks/Cole.

Miller, G. P. (1978). *Life choices.* New York: Thomas Y. Crowell.

Miller, G. P. (1981). *It's your business to decide.* Boston: CBI.

Nisbett, R., & Ross, L. (1980) *Human inference: Strategies and shortcomings of social judgment.* Englewood Cliffs, NJ: Prentice-Hall.

Pitz, G. F., & Sachs, N. J. (1984). Judgment and decision: Theory and application. *Annual Review of Psychology, 35,* 139–163.

Shure, M. B. (1981). Social competence as a problem solving skill. In J. D. Wine & M. D. Smye (Eds.), *Social competence* (pp. 158–185). New York: Guilford Press.

Simon, H. A. & Newell, A. (1971). Human problem solving: The state of the theory in 1970. *American Psychologist, 26*(2), 145–159.

Tversky, A., & Kahneman, D. (1974). Judgment under uncertainty: Heuristics and biases. *Science, 185,* 1124–1131.

CHAPTER 11

PHYSICAL FITNESS/ HEALTH MAINTENANCE

The importance of physical fitness/health maintenance as a generic life-skill area is reflected in the pattern of "sickness care" exhibited in national statistics. During a time that medical science has been able to control infectious diseases by immunizations (e.g., measles, polio, smallpox) and reduce death from certain illnesses through antibiotics (e.g., pneumonia), American's health-care spending has reached almost unmanageable proportions. As a nation, we spend more than 200 billion dollars annually, and the percentage of our gross national product spent for health care has increased from 4 percent in 1940 to 9 percent in 1979 (Gibson, 1980) to 10.5 percent in 1983 (Opatz, 1985). This increased expenditure does not, however, beget a proportionate return in improved health since the current highest threats to nondisabled functioning derive from unhealthy lifestyles and environments, with the former being the greatest.

It is the choices we make in the way we live our lives that are currently most responsible for death and disability. If we look at disease, it is the *disease of choice* that is the leading cause of death. Both cardiovascular disease, the number one killer of Americans, and cancer, the second leading cause of death, are responsive to lifestyle modification. Of the risk factors associated with cardiovascular disease—age, gender, familial history, levels of cholesterol, blood pressure, tobacco usage, obesity, stress management, and exercise habits—only chronological age, familial history, and gender cannot be controlled or altered by an individual's choosing a different lifestyle. Similarly, choices about diet, weight, stress management, and tobacco usage influence the likelihood of the occurrence of cancer. In addition, the probability of deaths related to vehicles can be decreased by controlling "drinking" drivers, by using seat belts, and by enforcing lower speed limits. Thus, a close look at the three leading causes of death suggests that choosing a healthy lifestyle contributes to health maintenance. In this chapter, we will examine how physical fitness/health maintenance is implemented through a life-skills perspective.

RATIONALE

We *can* lead healthy lives. In doing so, we live a life in which we have learned to enjoy pleasures that increase both our own and others' well-being, not one in which we have been deprived of our pleasures. A discussion of the seven precepts basic to developing a healthy lifestyle will help to illustrate this point. It is important to realize that acceptance of those precepts leads to approaching health as total well-being.

1 *Holism.* A healthy lifestyle involves all aspects of our lives—the physical, intellectual, emotional, social, occupational, and spiritual areas. We are total beings and each area affects every other area. For example, choices we make about our work affect our social well-being, positive and negative emotional feelings are frequently felt physically, and our physical fitness affects our intellectual productivity (Bloomfield and Kory, 1980).

2 *Control.* We are in control of much that happens in our lives. We are always in control of our response to events. It is the values, beliefs, and attitudes we choose to accept and maintain that determine how we live our lives.

3 *Responsibility.* As persons in the process of becoming, we assume more and more responsibility for ourselves and for our well-being (Ardell, 1977).

4 *Choices.* Our control and responsibility are expressed by the choices we make. We choose the directions we take in life as well as the environment in which we live. In addition, we choose our attitudes toward work, play, ourselves, and others. Because the small daily choices we make turn into habits, they are very important.

5 *Changes.* Changes made in one area are frequently followed by changes in other areas. For instance, a smoker who begins a cardiovascular exercise program often quits smoking; as a person becomes more fit, he or she usually experiences positive psychological changes; and when one person in a family behaves differently, the other family members are likely to change their behaviors. Sometimes such changes occur in a ripple pattern, such as that made by a stone thrown into water. Other times the pattern is a chain, as dominoes falling (Jones, 1983).

6 *Healthy lifestyle.* A healthy lifestyle is a process rather than a goal.

We are in the process of becoming. Although none of us will achieve a high level of well-being in all dimensions and maintain that high level for any period of time, we may choose an acceptable level in four or five dimensions and concentrate on making changes in one or two dimensions. As long as we are in the process of becoming more healthy, we know we are on the right course (Hettler, 1983).

7 *Social beings.* We are social beings, and thus we affect each other. We have responsibility for the effect we have on those around us. Realizing that we are likely to behave like the people around us may help us choose those people. In situations where choice is limited, we may choose to limit the degree of influence accorded those people (Allen, 1981).

In considering how to facilitate acceptance of a healthy lifestyle, it is useful to reflect upon the role of social norms. Even though social norms are powerful determinants of behavior, it is not necessary to accept them without question. More importantly, norms can be changed. Such changes can happen gradually, unconsciously, or consciously. For example, the social norm concerning smoking behavior has been deliberately changed in recent years. Now, fewer adults smoke, and, consequently, fewer nonsmokers are exposed to smoking's noxious effects, especially in public places. It is noteworthy that education was a useful strategy for implementing a more healthy lifestyle.

This chapter is designed to stimulate the service provider's interest in physical fitness/health maintenance. In reading, it will be useful to reflect on how physical fitness/health maintenance life-skills pertain to one's own personal fitness. Our concern in this chapter is with how each of us, human service provider and client, can develop a healthy lifestyle. Therefore, we will examine elements that contribute to our health. The areas of attention include physical fitness, nutrition, stress management, and discriminating drug usage. The life-skills approach involves objectives, assessment, and implementation in these areas within three age groups (childhood, adolescence, and adulthood) and in four settings (family, work, school, and community).

A MODEL FOR PHYSICAL FITNESS/HEALTH MAINTENANCE

Recall from the discussion of the seven precepts that we view fitness and health holistically and as a process that reflects lifestyle. Consistent with this assumptive base, we propose that there are five objectives which, if accomplished, will culminate in a healthy lifestyle. They are:

1 That persons feel good and have a zest for life.

2 That persons be physically fit; that is to say, they achieve and maintain an appropriate level of cardiovascular fitness, that they be sufficiently

strong to handle tasks routinely encountered, that they achieve and maintain a high degree of flexibility.

3 That people become free of communicable diseases.

4 That we as a society minimize the occurrence and intensity of chronic disease.

5 That persons live a life free of accidents and violence.

In order to meet these objectives, each person needs adequate life-skills in areas such as physical fitness, nutritional maintenance, stress management, drug usage, prevention of communicable diseases, motor development and coordination, and sexuality (see Table 11-1). In the following sections, we will focus on physical fitness, nutrition, stress management, and appropriate drug usage—for children, adolescents, and adults—as we dis-

TABLE 11-1
PHYSICAL FITNESS/HEALTH MAINTENANCE SKILLS[a]

Childhood	Adolescence	Adulthood
Ability to demonstrate muscle control and coordination.	Ability to understand what is normal and natural about sexual arousal and expression.	Ability to cope with age-related decline and illness.
Acquisition of self-help skills requiring muscular coordination.	Ability to be a participant in competitive, cooperative, and/or individual sports.	Ability to promote physical fitness through appropriate regular exercise and dietary habits.
Ability to set reasonable and safe limits of physical activities.	Ability to understand and decide how to control one's rapidly changing body in positive ways.	Ability to maintain positive body image as physical changes occur.
Ability to understand the nature of physical maturation.	Ability to understand menstruation as a normal physical phenomenon.	Ability to incorporate appropriate health and fitness activities into one's lifestyle.
Ability to perform fine motor skills with greater consistency.	Ability to accept as normal various physiological changes associated with puberty.	Ability to conceptualize one's health in terms of wellness rather than simply in the absence of illness.
Ability to relate the function of sexual organs to one's understanding of reproduction.	Ability to cope with occasional undesirable side effects of physical maturation.	

[a]See Appendix F for a complete listing of physical fitness/health maintenance skills. Skills necessary for motor development and coordination, nutritional maintenance, weight control, physical fitness, athletic participation, physiological aspects of sexuality, stress management, and leisure activity selection.

cuss how the Life-Skills Training model operates in the physical fitness/ health maintenance generic area.

Physical Fitness

Adequate physical fitness means the individual has attained age-appropriate levels of cardiovascular fitness, of body composition, and of flexibility. Concerns in this area include assessment of these elements and strategies for developing and maintaining fitness. Generally, an indication of fitness level is provided by measuring heart rate and/or blood pressure. For men, a resting heart rate below 58 is considered good; for women, below 60 is good. Although acceptable blood pressure varies by sex and age, 120/80 is within normal limits. To obtain one's minimum exercise heart rate, subtract your resting heart rate from your estimated maximum heart rate, multiply this number by .65, and add your resting heart rate to the number just obtained: minimum exercise heart rate = [(220 − age) − resting heart rate] × .65 + resting heart rate. Exercise at this level. Although you may increase your intensity if you wish, do not exceed 85 percent of your maximum heart rate reserve. In addition, exercise from three to six times per week beginning with twenty minutes of aerobic activity and gradually increasing to forty-five minutes. As a "daily" routine, this strategy can ensure adequate cardiovascular fitness.

Body composition is a measure of percentage of body fat and is a more accurate indicator of fitness than is total body weight. This measure provides a ratio of lean body weight to fat body weight. Its accuracy as a measure of fitness is easy to understand if we reflect that two people of the same weight and height may vary considerably in fitness if one exercises frequently and the other leads a sedentary lifestyle. To measure body composition, either underwater weighing or a methodology using calipers to measure skin-fold thickness may be employed. (Protocols for these procedures may be found in the suggested readings.) Acceptable ranges of body fat are 15 to 19 percent for adult males and 18 to 24 percent for adult females. The reader is referred to the American Alliance for Health, Physical Education, Recreation and Dance (AAHPERD) manual mentioned in suggested readings to obtain appropriate percentages for children and adolescents.

Flexibility as a physical fitness term refers to a person's range of motion. It can be measured by a sit-and-reach technique (see AAHPERD manuals). Increasing flexibility, and therefore fitness, involves a gentle stretching of all muscle groups. It is important when working on flexibility to avoid stretching to the point of actual pain and to avoid bouncing stretches. For the interested reader, sources of specific stretching exercises may be found in the suggested readings—see especially Cooper (1977), Fixx (1977), and Lance (1977).

As indicated by the skills listed in Table 11-1, the focus of physical fitness development changes from childhood to adolescence to adulthood. Most children enjoy active playing, and so most exhibit a high level of physical fitness. For young children, guidance toward physical fitness may be as simple as encouraging physical activity and its attendant skill development. For those children who prefer a sedentary lifestyle, parents can facilitate physical fitness skill development through systematic activities such as dancing classes, organized sports, or individual activities. Since behavior modeled by parents is important in influencing young children, family outings that include hiking or swimming create an opportunity for pleasure associated with an example of a lifestyle that contributes to being physically fit and active. In addition, parents may choose to limit the amount of time their child/children spend(s) in nonphysical activities such as television viewing.

During adolescence, physical activity may become more performance oriented as organized sports assume importance. Because of this shifting emphasis, peer groups may split into dichotomous camps—highly trained individuals and spectators. To facilitate continued physical fitness development and maintenance for all adolescents, schools could deemphasize competitive athletics and provide programs that encourage individual development. With parental encouragement, the school curriculum could include assessment of individuals' fitness levels and design of appropriate programs based on models such as the Life-Skills Training program outlined in this text. Community recreation programs could also be a source for activity opportunities.

Physical fitness for adults involves personal responsibility for obtaining an assessment of current levels of fitness and providing for time, opportunity, and activities appropriate for improvement and maintenance. Social norms, whether of the family, peers, work group, or community, can influence the successfulness of the individual's fitness efforts. For instance, a supportive and exercising spouse increases the chance of a new exerciser making fitness a permanent change. Also, an industry that provides exercise facilities and encourages employees to exercise contributes to employees' personal health and fitness. Similarly, wellness-oriented communities make it easier for individuals to incorporate healthy lifestyle changes.

Nutrition

The concern in this area is with providing the body with the nutrients it needs for effective functioning while maintaining an appropriate level of body weight. Ideal body weight, as in determining fitness, is better determined by the percent of body fat desired. Although determining ideal weight through this method requires the use of skin-fold calipers and a knowledge of measurement and calculation techniques, it is a preferred method because it reflects lean body weight, unlike the more traditional method of estimating ideal weight.

The purpose of skills in this area is to learn how to provide the body with nutritionally balanced caloric intake that is appropriate to need according to the person's size, activity level, and metabolic rate. Eating a nutritionally balanced diet means that fats represent no more than 25 percent of total caloric intake, carbohydrates no more than 60 percent, and proteins no more than 15 percent. In addition, simple sugars, salt, and cholesterol intake should be minimized, and empty calorie consumption, such as alcohol, soft drinks, and highly processed foods, should be limited. Other strategies for good nutrition include: (1) eat four or more servings of fruit and vegetables each day; (2) eat fresh, frozen, or low sodium products rather than canned goods as the latter are usually high in salt; (3) since extra protein is turned into fat, avoid overeating of protein (approximately four ounces per day is sufficient for an adult); and (4) eat whole grain breads and cereals as they are more nutritious than "enriched" products. Two other points are worth remembering. First, if a balanced diet is eaten, then vitamin and mineral supplements are not generally needed, with the possible exception of iron for menstruating women. Second, adjustments to ideal weight are best accomplished by gaining or losing at a rate of one pound per week. If losing weight, the person should not reduce caloric intake below 1000 calories a day. Also, it is useful to remember that losing weight may be facilitated by increasing exercise and decreasing calories simultaneously.

Aside from these general considerations, there are some specifics that apply to particular age levels. Childhood nutrition is especially important for establishing lifetime eating habits and preferences as well as for physical growth. Therefore, it is especially important that parents be aware that they are behavioral models for their children. In addition, a healthy diet for children is one that minimizes animal fats, and so *low-fat* milk, lean meat, fish, and poultry are especially important during childhood.

During adolescence, nutrition is still particularly important for the body's growth. However, with the advent of adolescence, habits may change suddenly. For instance, the ten-year-old who loved a big breakfast may at thirteen want to eat nothing before noon. It is useful to remember that quarrels over eating may be attempts to establish independence. Parents can facilitate growth and good nutritional habits during this age by modeling effective nutritional habits, providing accurate nutritional information, and encouraging the adolescent to assume responsibility for his or her own nutritional choices. Then in adulthood the person should be adequately prepared to eat appropriate amounts of food that maintain ideal body weight and to make quality choices of food so that the body obtains a sufficient supply of carbohydrates, fats, proteins, vitamins, and minerals.

Stress Management

Each of us has some level of stress in our lives. Since some level of stress is useful (for instance, to help motivate us) the goal of stress management is not to eliminate stress. Rather, we need to keep stress at a level that is within healthy parameters. Through the appropriate regulation of stress, we can be responsible for enhancing our health.

Assessing our level of stress is necessarily subjective. Each of us reacts to the same event in different ways, and so it is important that we learn to listen to our body's messages. By being aware of the tension and anxiety that we experience, we can have some knowledge of when we are exceeding the limits of a healthy level of stress. If we monitor our stress level, then we are able to adjust the level before harmful effects occur. Therefore, we find ourselves in the position of making conscious and deliberate choices based on an understanding of and responsibility for the consequences of those choices.

To make choices that are consistent with maintaining an appropriate level of stress, it is necessary to have available strategies for managing stress. Effective stress management involves self-awareness in relation to recreation and especially relaxation. Relaxation counters stress and can be obtained in several ways, for instance, through engaging in activities that regenerate energy. In addition, specific training in relaxation, such as deep muscle relaxation, and imaging techniques can provide each person with a learned method of physically relaxing the body according to a conscious decision. Such techniques enable the person to design idio syncratic stress management programs as an ongoing part of their lives. Other parts of a program would include regular participation in activities that provide fun and pleasure as well as knowledge of a range of strategies that could be implemented on a day-to-day or as needed basis. Such strategies might involve aerobic exercise (three to five times per week), building and maintaining a strong support system, choosing commitments, adjusting performance levels, and being aware of choice dynamics, such as the choices available and their benefits and drawbacks. At the same time, it is important to be wary of activities such as smoking, drinking, taking drugs, and procrastinating. Such activities may seem to provide relief but are nonproductive ways of handling stress.

As with the other areas within the physical fitness/health maintenance model, there are some special stress considerations for children, adolescents, and adults. Most importantly, we need to be aware that children *do* experience stress and anxiety. Therefore, families, schools, and communities need to help children learn stress management skills. This involves teaching responsible use of leisure time and can include basic relaxation techniques. With adolescents, education can address how to develop useful coping techniques and can simultaneously teach the risks attendant to implementing noneffective coping techniques such as alcohol use, drug use, use of caffeine and sugar to obtain quick energy, and use of excitement for diversion. In adulthood, we need to experience a productive sense of playfulness. If the person needs to regain this skill, then he or she should find pleasurable activities and pay attention to the joyful experiences that occur in his or her life.

Drug Usage

Using drugs as a way to feel better has become an accepted behavior in the American lifestyle. As a society, we use caffeine to wake us up, alcohol to relax us, and sleeping pills to help us sleep. The acceptability of drug usage is reflected in the numerous television commercials devoted to selling drug products and by the fact that Americans spent $4,250,850,000 on over-the-counter drugs in drug stores alone during 1983 (Chi, 1984). To produce a healthy lifestyle, we need to become aware of the frequency of drug usage and, when appropriate, decrease that frequency.

It is important to emphasize that some drug usage may be healthy and/or necessary to living an effective and productive life. However, the authors' position is that minimal drug usage is the best drug usage. While pain and suffering are not advocated, awareness of the effects and amount of drug usage as well as awareness of the least invasive, effective treatment approach can minimize the unnecessary use of drugs. Certainly medical conditions requiring treatment should not be ignored, but, when possible, correcting the underlying problem is preferable to treating the symptom. For instance, exercise, diet, and relaxation techniques are preferable to a lifetime of hypertensive drug therapy, although medication may be required early on to control the acute problem (and in some cases may be necessary on a continuous basis). As individuals, each of us can exercise responsibility for our own health by choosing physicians who consider minimal medication coupled with less invasive treatment and by becoming cognizant of how drugs affect our everyday lives.

Obtaining information about drugs is a major means for determining what products and how much use of such products is conducive to health. For instance, caffeine and alcohol are potentially habit-forming drugs. When used excessively, these drugs are a menace to health, though, at present, it seems there may be no inherent harm in moderate use. Therefore, unless a person has ulcers, cardiovascular disease, or fibrocystic disease, moderate usage of these drugs may not be harmful.

This means limiting usage to the following amounts: caffeine intake of less than the amount found in three cups of coffee and one alcoholic drink per day.

Some drugs have harmful effects when combined with other drugs; for example, a prescribed drug may have an interactional effect when combined with alcohol. Other drugs, such as antibiotics and steroids, must be continued for a certain period, while others may be taken only as needed for symptom relief. Asking questions of the physician and/or the pharmacist is a responsible "drug" behavior.

It seems obvious that drug education is needed along with parental modeling of appropriate and effective behaviors. Using drugs as little as possible, whether for prescribed medical reasons or for recreational purposes, is a value that can be transmitted through family norms. In addition, schools can contribute with direct instruction about drugs, including goals and strategies for decreasing the use of drugs. With adults, monitoring of drug usage, particularly the situations involved with drug usage, can produce decreased intake and effective health life-skills.

APPLICATION

The Life-Skills Training model involves both prevention and remediation in four settings—in the family, in the school, at work, and in the community (see Table 11-2). Throughout the previous section, we have emphasized the preventive aspect of this model. Prevention involves teaching physical fitness/health maintenance skills both directly through planned experiences and indirectly through planning and implementing attitude and institutional changes. Both approaches are necessary. The specific skills need to be taught, and the practice of those skills needs to be supported by groups. If the group norms support healthful behavior change, then changes are likely to be maintained, and we, as individuals and as a society, will experience more healthy lives.

The alternative aspect of this model involves remediation. The people who need remediation of this generic life-skill area either have a physical disease, have difficulty managing stress, or have difficulty with drug usage. Depending upon the particular problem, a physician and/or human services professional may be involved in treatment, and treatment may include changes in lifestyle as well as the administration of drugs. When a change in lifestyle is required, the helping professional becomes involved with the strategies for teaching more effective life-skills. These may be very similar to those strategies utilized in prevention—in teaching life-skills in the home, at school, at work, and in the community. Some examples of activities that can be useful for operationalizing the life-skills training are provided in the following pages.

TABLE 11-2
PHYSICAL FITNESS/HEALTH MAINTENANCE STRATEGIES

		Setting		
	Family	School	Work	Community
(1) Physical fitness				
Prevention	Model appropriate aerobic exercise. Plan activities involving exercise. Limit passive entertainment. Provide many opportunities for involvement in physical activities such as dancing, individual sports, team sports, hiking.	Fitness assessment. Teach fitness fun with emphasis on sports that are likely to be continued throughout life. Maintain individual achievement levels. Build in much movement during day. Encourage flexibility and stress management with frequent stretch breaks.	Fitness modeled by top management. Time and facilities available to workers at all levels. Fitness assessment and aerobic exercise programs available on site. Stress on cardiovascular fitness.	Programs for all ages and preferences, including organized sports, walking groups, community facilities such as bike trails, cross-country skiing trails, indoor jogging tracks, and pools. Emphasis on cardiovascular conditioning and fun of exercise.
Remediation	Assess fitness levels. Write exercise prescription. Plan workable program that is fun. Plan for family support.	Assess; plan programs for students who are below acceptable fitness levels. Encourage participation in many movement activities. Counteract competitiveness with stress on individual achievement.	Assessment and special programs planned for those whose fitness is far below acceptable levels. Focus on slow progress, lifestyle changes.	Cardiac Rehabilitation programs, programs for stroke patients, diabetics, and patients with hypertension. People encouraged to reduce medication by exercise and diet.

TABLE 11-2 (continued)
PHYSICAL FITNESS/HEALTH MAINTENANCE STRATEGIES

	Setting			
	Family	School	Work	Community
(2) Nutrition				
Prevention	Each family member involved in planning appropriate quantity and quality of foods. Healthy snacks. Emphasis on lifestyle habits.	Health education curriculum K-12 designed to teach basics of nutrition, appropriate choices. School breakfast and lunch programs should emphasize healthy eating; fruits, vegetables and whole grains maximized; minimal servings of red meat, sugars, animal products, salt, and highly processed foods. Coin operated machines should contain only healthy foods.	Food served on site is healthy. Management models appropriate eating habits and desirable weight. Education programs and nutrition information offered on a regular basis.	Encourage availability of fresh products, through co-op buying if necessary. Serve less meat and sweets at community functions. Education programs aimed toward healthier eating can be provided by many community agencies. Food sections of local newspapers are another educational forum.
Remediation	As needed for fat loss, diabetes, hypertension, modify diets and exercise habits. Encourage family members to support member who is making changes.	Health curriculum of high school levels could include special diets designed to reduce hypertension and control diabetes.	Weight loss programs and classes in nutrition for hypertension and diabetes offered regularly.	Community agencies such as hospitals, the Heart Association, and the Cancer Society can offer classes in special nutrition. Meal programs for the elderly can provide special diets.

(3) Relaxation/ Recreation/Stress Management

Prevention	Parents can plan for relaxation and recreation for the family, as a group, and as individuals, being sure that children learn to enjoy numerous ways of relaxing. Choosing levels of stress can be taught to help children balance activity schedules with free time.	Teacher can balance stressful situations with brief periods of relaxation. Techniques of deep muscle relaxation, stretching, exercising vigorously, and use of imagery can be taught.	Provision of recreation programs. Keep job stresses to an acceptable level. Train supervisors and managers in human relation skills to minimize imposed stress. Use of quality circle management techniques to increase involvement. Require vacation use. Encourage wellness days occasionally rather than use of sick leave.	Provision of numerous opportunities for use of leisure time. Encouragement of creativity. Provide stress management education programs, relaxation skills group.
Remediation	A more deliberate approach may be needed if severe stress is a problem. Consultation with a counselor trained in stress management would be useful.	Counselors can help students in need of more specific skills by providing structured experiences and opportunities to practice relaxation and stress management skills.	Education programs in relaxation, stress management skills. Strongly encourage wellness counseling for any workers who are hypertensive.	Stress management group, relaxation groups.

TABLE 11-2 (continued)
PHYSICAL FITNESS/HEALTH MAINTENANCE STRATEGIES

		Setting		
	Family	School	Work	Community
(4) Drug use				
Prevention	Adults model minimal use of drugs, including caffeine, alcohol, and nicotine. Drugs used to treat illness used only as prescribed; alternate treatment considered.	Educational programs designed to counteract media advertising of drugs. Effects of caffeine, alcohol, and nicotine on the body taught at all grade levels. Proactive "feeling good" methods taught, such as exercise, positive problem solving skills.	Education programs provided on site. Extensive information in newsletters. Ban smoking in all working areas. If alcohol is served at company functions, limit the amount served and serve an alternate beverage. Offer bonuses for those who quit smoking.	Work to ban smoking in public buildings and businesses. Support legislation encouraging responsible drinking, enforcing drunk driving regulations. Prevent the sale of alcohol and other drugs to those under age. Work to create non-drinking recreation opportunities in the community.
Remediation	If a family member chooses to reduce or eliminate use of a drug, the support and encouragement of other family members is very important. It is suggested that the other members ask what behaviors would be helpful.	Diagnosis and referral for substance abuse. Community agencies may provide programs housed in schools.	Identify workers with drug problems early. Provide treatment programs, either on site or through community agencies. Confront absentee problems and poor work early.	Provide smoking cessation programs, Alcoholics Anonymous, and other substance abuse programs.

220

**Physical Fitness/Health Maintenance Skills Training:
Example 1**

I Setting: Community/Adults
II Life-Skill Objectives: Ability to cope with age-related physical decline
and illness, to promote physical fitness through appropriate regular
exercise and dietary habits, to incorporate appropriate health and fitness activities into one's lifestyle.
III Activity: Nutritional analyses to improve healthful eating. The local hospital, through its education department, may offer a nutrition course for
persons at high risk for those already known to have cardiovascular
disease. Persons diagnosed as having hypertension, those with a family history of heart disease, and those having elevated cholesterol
levels are likely to be interested in making dietary changes. It is
suggested that spouses be encouraged to attend the group, also.
  A Procedure:
    1 Discuss the importance of eating in relation to heart disease. En-
list group members' interest and cooperation in analyzing their
present eating habits and developing a plan for healthy eating.
    2 Contract with group members to keep a dietary record for one
week, including the quantity of each food eaten. Analyze this information, perhaps by computer using the DINE software system or
a similar program. The analysis can be interpreted to group members in terms of (1) overall score, (2) appropriateness of caloric intake to activity level, (3) nutritional content—percentages of fats,
proteins, and complex carbohydrates, (4) salt content, (5) alcohol
content, and (6) sugar content.
    3 Using exercises such as the following (Where's the Salt?), teach
desired changes and help members plan to make those changes.
Members are presented with lists of "offenders" or foods high in
salt: most canned foods, highly processed foods, shellfish, pick-
les, bacon, diet drinks, and more. Each is asked to note the
worst offenders in his or her diet. Then each is asked to rank
order the offenders in terms of ones he or she is willing to eliminate or reduce. Suggest that changes be made as an experiment for one week.

**Physical Fitness/Health Maintenance Skills Training:
Example 2**

I Setting: Family/all ages
II Life-Skill Objectives: Children—ability to maintain a high level of
energy and stamina. Adolescents— ability to cope with occasionally
undesirable side effects of physical maturation. Adults—ability to cope
with age-related physical decline and illness; ability to conceptualize

one's health in terms of wellness rather than simply the absence of illness.

III Activity: Family Members Drug Usage. Leadership for this activity may
be taken by an older child, an adolescent, or an adult. It is intended as
a preventive activity, but could also be used for remediation. Each family member will (1) define a drug as a chemical substance taken to alter
body processes, to relieve symptoms, and/or to treat disease; (2) become aware of all drugs he or she uses; (3) become aware of the benefits and disadvantages of drugs he or she uses; and (4) choose if he or
she wishes to change any pattern of drug usage.

A Procedure:

    1 Recordkeeping. Each family member will keep a record of drugs
used for a week. This activity may be continued for a longer
period, or permanently. (See suggested form below.)

    2 Evaluation of records. The family will share records. This sharing
will be more effective if it is voluntary and If it is begun when children are young. It will not work as a policing activity for older children. The nature of the interaction needs to be supportive, with
each member assuming responsibility for himself or herself, and
with other members acting as encouragers once goals are established.

Drugs I have used

Name _____

Prescription drugs:

Name	Date	Times per day	Purpose

Over-the-counter drugs:

Name	Date	Times per day	Purpose

Alcohol:

Type of drink	Date	Times per day	Total number of calories	Purpose

Caffeine:

Type of drink	Date	Times per day	Purpose

Nicotine:	Date	Times per day	Purpose

Other Drugs:	Date	Times per day	Purpose

Each member may wish to review drug usage in reference to these questions:

Prescription and over-the-counter drugs
  1 Was this medication the least invasive way of responding to this need?
  2 What side effects occurred?
  3 Was the medication effective?
  4 Was there an interaction effect with other drugs?
  5 Is there anything I can do to avoid the need for this medication in the future?

Alcohol
  1 Is the quantity of my drinking acceptable to me?
  2 What percentage of my daily caloric intake comes from alcohol?
  3 What effect does my use of alcohol have on my safety and the safety of others?
  4 Am I modeling appropriate behavior for those I influence?

Caffeine
  1 Is the quantity of my caffeine consumption acceptable to me?
  2 In what situations do I need a stimulant?
  3 Am I using a stimulant when a noncaffeinated beverage would be acceptable?
  4 Are there less invasive ways of achieving the effects of caffeine?

Nicotine
  1 Is the quantity of my nicotine use acceptable to me?
  2 How am I affecting others by my use of nicotine?
  3 Is there a less invasive way of meeting the needs I feel nicotine satisfies?

( ) I am satisfied with my use of drugs in the past week.
( ) I would like to do something differently.
I would like to change my use of _____ in this way:
(Be as specific as possible.)
Here is how I will do that:

  1
  2
  3

Here's how others may choose to help me:

  1
  2
  3

( ) I will report results of my change in one week to _____.

**Physical Fitness/Health Maintenance Skills Training:
Example 3**

I Setting: Work/Adults
II Life-Skill Objectives: Ability to incorporate appropriate health and fitness activities into one's lifestyle, to conceptualize one's health in terms of wellness rather than simply the absence of illness.
III Activity: Relaxation, recreation, stress management: Set up methods through one of the employer's departments for stress management programs to be offered systematically through the work setting. Employees can be provided with an overview of positive ways to handle stress and then encouraged to choose other areas/programs for further learning.
  A Procedures:
    1 An overview of positive ways to handle stress may be given as part of a stress management group, as an introduction to a series of stress management mini-courses, as a videotape shown during breaks, or as an insert included (see following) in pay envelopes.
      a Ten ways of managing stress positively (insert)
        (1) Choose your level of activities and responsibilities.
        (2) Exercise vigorously three times a week.
        (3) Eat well-balanced meals emphasizing complex carbohydrates, minimizing sugar, salt, and animal fats.
        (4) Give some of your time to making your world a better place.
        (5) Have three close friends in whom you confide. One may be a relative.
        (6) Sleep seven and one-half to eight hours every night.
        (7) Have a hobby that gives you pleasure.
        (8) Balance time each day: time at work, time with important others, time alone.
        (9) Spend time in prayer or meditation every day.
        (10) Tend to troubled relationships.
    2 The personnel or wellness department at the work site may wish to offer stress management programs (see below) to employees. Staff members or consultants may lead the programs which could be announced as follows:
      a Balancing stress levels and stress management skills—learn to assess various types of stress, make changes where possible, and increase stress management skills so that there's a comfortable balance in your life.
      b Relaxation techniques—a sampler—learn and practice a deep muscle relaxation, yoga, imagery, self-hypnosis.

c Developing and nurturing close relationships—learn how to establish and maintain satisfying friendships and love relationships that are close, interdependent, and respectful. Learn to ask for what you want and to give in caring, nonmanipulative ways.

d Leisure time fair—set up exhibits of hobbies, crafts, and groups that are available in the community.

e Volunteer opportunities—list needs in company newsletter. Feature volunteers in various settings.

f Nutrition and well-being—provide groups that offer information and support for appropriate eating.

g Recreation opportunities—provide for team sports, family fun days, weekend trips, company sponsored YWCA or YMCA memberships, exercise/recreational facilities.

h Wellness lifestyling group—take control, take inventory, plans for changes. Focus on how you would like for your life to be better.

Physical Fitness/Health Maintenance Skills Training: Example 4

I Setting: School/Adolescents

II Life-Skill Objectives: Ability to be a participant in competitive, cooperative, and/or individual sports; to understand and decide how to control one's rapidly changing body in positive ways: to accept as normal various physiological changes associated with puberty.

III Activity: Fitness Assessment.

A Procedures:

1 Students will become aware of their level of cardiovascular fitness and participate in developing their own fitness plan. As an integral part of the school's physical education program, each student will be assessed annually for cardiovascular fitness, flexibility, and strength. The student will be given a record of his or her fitness test results, and a copy will be kept by the school. It is suggested that the school use a standard assessment procedure such as the one outlined in the AAHPERD publication, *Lifetime Health Related Physical Fitness Test Manual*. (See bibliography.)

2 Students, in their physical education classes, can be divided into small groups (see 4).

3 Using the results of the fitness assessment, students can share results and plan for changes.

4 Under the instructor's supervision, students can make contracts (see example) to improve or maintain their levels of fitness. Con-

tracting can encourage students to take responsibility for changes, allow the instructor to be used as a resource person for specific strategies for improvement/maintenance, and provide for students' choices and preferences in how to implement fitness skills.

CONTRACT FOR FITNESS

Date _____

My present level of cardiovascular fitness is
( ) excellent
( ) good
( ) average
( ) below average
( ) poor

My present level of flexibility is
( ) excellent
( ) good
( ) average
( ) below average
( ) poor

My present level of strength is
( ) excellent
( ) good
( ) average
( ) below average
( ) poor

I choose to make these changes
1
2
3

Here is how I plan to make those changes
1
2
3
4

I am pleased with my present level of fitness. I intend to maintain it by

1

2

3

I want _____ to help me by

1

2

3

I will report my progress
( ) weekly
( ) monthly

My reward for achieving/maintaining my chosen level of fitness will be

_____ .

SUMMARY

In this chapter, we have discussed the generic life-skill area physical fitness/health maintenance. In accord with this model, we proposed seven precepts for developing a healthy lifestyle: (1) *holism*—a healthy lifestyle involves all aspects of our lives including the physical, intellectual, emotional, social, occupational, and spiritual, (2) *control*—we control much of what happens to our lives, (3) *responsibility*—as persons in the process of becoming, we assume more and more responsibility for our well-being, (4) *choices*—our control and responsibility are expressed by the choices we make, (5) *changes*—changes made in one area are frequently followed by changes in another, (6) *healthy lifestyle*—a process, and (7) *social beings*—through our social aspects, we affect each other.

Through the remainder of the chapter we emphasized the objectives and functioning of the Life-Skills Training model. This included assessment and implementation of physical fitness, nutrition, stress management, and drug usage as they are applied, for prevention and remediation, to childhood, adolescence, and adulthood in the four settings of family, work, school, and community. Some examples of application are supplied to stimulate the service provider's rendering of the model.

SUGGESTED READINGS

American Alliance for Health, Physical Education, Recreation and Dance. (1980). *Lifetime health related physical fitness manual.* Reston, VA: Author.

Bailey, C. (1977). *Fit or fat?* Boston: Houghton Mifflin.

Benson, H. (1975). *The relaxation response.* New York: William Morrow.

Cooper, K. (1977). *The aerobics way.* New York: Bantam Books.

Fixx, J. E. (1977). *The complete book of running.* New York: Random House.

Jacobson, E. (1957). *You must relax.* New York: McGraw-Hill.

Lance, K. (1977). *Running for health and beauty.* New York: Bobbs-Merrill.

National Dairy Council. (n.d.). *Source book on food practices with emphasis on children and adolescents.* Rosemont, IL: Author.

Queen, S. (1986). *Wellness for children.* Lifeworks: Columbia, MD, 21045, P. O. Box 2668.

Sinning, W. E. (1975). *Experiments and demonstrations in exercise physiology.* Philadelphia: W. B. Saunders.

Shapiro, D., & Walsh R. (1980). *Mediation: Self-regulation strategy and altered state of consciousness.* New York: Aldine.

REFERENCES

Allen, R. F. (1981). *Lifegain.* New Jersey: Human Resources Institute.

Ardell, D. F. (1977). *High level wellness.* New York: Bantam Books.

Bloomfield, H. H., & Kory, R. B. (1980). *The holistic way to health and happiness.* New York: Simon & Schuster.

Chi, J. (1984, July). "Drug Topics, 36th annual report on consumer spending—1983: 'It was a very good year.'" *Drug Topics: The Magazine for Today's Pharmacies,* pp. 22–24.

Cooper, K. H. (1979, June). Running clinic presentation sponsored by Liberty Life Insurance Company, Greenville, SC.

Gibson, R. M. (1980). Demonstrations and statistics, national health expenditures, 1979. *Health care financing review* (Health Care Financing Administration Publication No. 03054). Washington, DC: U.S. Government Printing Office.

Hettler, G. W. (1983, July). *Introducing wellness to the uninitiated.* Paper presented at the Wellness Promotion Strategies Conference, Stevens Point, WI.

Jones, J. P. (1983). The effects of increasing physical fitness levels on the locus of control, self-concept, and reported changes in lifestyle dimensions. Unpublished doctoral dissertation, University of Georgia, Athens.

Opatz, J. P. (1985). *A primer of health promotion.* Washington, DC: Oryan Publications.

CHAPTER 12

IDENTITY DEVELOPMENT/ PURPOSE IN LIFE

The development of individual identity and purpose in life is a lifelong process. There are certain "marker events" that call attention to identity development at various times during the life span. For instance, the "terrible twos" are well known to parents and others who function as caregivers to children. Adolescence is another major life period during which individual struggles to define identity and purpose in life are familiar to parents, teachers, researchers, and, often, law enforcement officials. Recent attention to "midlife crises" by scholarly and popular media has focused on midlife career changes, women reentering the work place after child rearing, and the increasing number of couples seeking divorce after 20 or more years of marriage. Such phenomena as these are only the more dramatic manifestations of an ongoing process of developing a personal identity and purpose in life.

RATIONALE

Philosophers through the ages have speculated about the essence of human nature, religious thinkers from all traditions have focused their attention on the nature of the soul, and psychologists in the last century have attempted to bring modern scientific theory and methodology to bear on the study of personality and the measurement of its presumed components. In Chapter 3, J.R. Barclay described personality as the composite of responses, skills, traits, aptitudes, and temperaments. Other theorists, especially during the last forty years, have presented significant models of human nature that are based on a developmental perspective and are derived from clinical and experimental observations. Four of these conceptualizations are particularly relevant as background for the model of identity development/purpose in life that will be described later in this chapter.

Erikson's Psychosocial Development

Erik Erikson (1950, 1963) has his theoretical roots in the psychoanalytic school. As we mentioned in Chapter 2, Freud (1923/1961) proposed psychosexual stages of development as a key dimension of his personality theory. Maintaining the psychoanalytic tradition, Erikson built on Freud's stages, transforming them from intrapsychic formulations that were limited to childhood and early adolescence to a life-span stage theory. Erikson's focus is on the ego, which he views as a selective, integrative, coherent agency that enables the individual to relate to the environment.

The ego develops according to what Erikson calls the epigenetic principle; that is, the ego unfolds according to its own logic. Psychosocial stages are conceptualized in terms of a series of crises that occur when physical, cognitive, and social needs converge to present the individual with a developmental task to be resolved. Resolution of a crisis leads the individual to greater life satisfaction and a higher probability of coping successfully with subsequent crises. In chronological order, stated in polarities, these stages are basic trust versus mistrust, autonomy versus shame and doubt, initiative versus guilt, industry versus inferiority, identity versus role diffusion, intimacy versus isolation, generativity versus stagnation, and ego integrity versus despair. Erikson allows for the possibility of variability in progression from one stage to the next according to differences in one's epigenetic operations. He sees individuals confronted with new life crises whether the issues of previous crises have been resolved or not and admits that persons sometimes retreat to earlier stages when an inability to cope with a later one becomes overwhelming.

For Erikson, a person's identity (and consequently his or her purpose in life) is developed as the ego interacts with the environment. Successful resolution of the eight life crises by the ego progressively enhances one's identity, while unsuccessful attempts at resolution shape identity in less optimal ways.

Kohlberg's Moral Development

Lawrence Kohlberg's (1973) stage model of the development of moral judgment constitutes another perspective on the development of identity/

purpose in life. Kohlberg's formulations are in the cognitive-developmental tradition originally conceptualized by Jean Piaget. Cognitive developmental theorists regard stage progression as invariant, cumulative, qualitatively different from one stage to the next, and irreversible. While this view contrasts with Erikson's rather dramatically, it does not diminish the value of this perspective for identity development/purpose in life skills.

Kohlberg's six stages of moral development are closely linked with the person's cognitive development. The stages are as follows: heteronomous morality, in which the individual follows rules to avoid punishment; instrumental purpose, in which one consciously seeks to meet one's own needs while being aware of others' rights to do the same; interpersonal conformity, in which "right" is judged in terms of the Golden Rule; social system and conscience, in which individual relations are considered in terms of their place in the social system; social contract, in which ideals such as life and liberty are actively valued; and universal ethical principles, in which individuals follow self-chosen ethical principles that they hold to be harmonious with universal moral principles.

The way in which one makes moral judgments is an expression of one's identity and purpose in life. Since Kohlberg's stages are progressive in nature, the person's identity develops as he or she moves from one stage to the next. Kohlberg does not maintain that all persons achieve the higher stages in his system, estimating that the level of moral judgment of most Americans is somewhere around the third level, interpersonal conformity. Thus the moral dimension of identity is likely to stabilize and remain fairly constant relatively early in the individual's life span.

Although Kohlberg's initial research was conducted with a sample of men, he contends that his model is applicable to both sexes.

Loevinger's Ego Development

Jane Loevinger's theory of ego development is considered by many (Aubrey, 1980; Rodgers, 1980; Schlossberg, 1984) to be a cognitive developmental paradigm. She herself disagrees (Loevinger, 1976). While she does not dispute the validity of constructs such as those of Kohlberg, her own work has a decidedly neo-Freudian tone. Focusing on the ego as the "master trait," Loevinger has, through extensive research, formulated developmental stages of the ego. These ten stages are: presocial, symbiotic, impulsive, self-protective, conformist, self-aware, conscientious, individualistic, autonomous, and integrated. Each of these stages represents a milestone of development as the ego proceeds from the simple to the complex along a path that is irreversible, invariant, and hierarchical. Ego structures, developed in these stages, are the means by which the individual interacts with the environment. Although Loevinger's initial research (1966) was conducted with a sample of women, she contends that her model is applicable to both sexes and to all ages.

For Loevinger, then, the ego structure corresponding to a given stage is the core of an individual's identity and purpose in life. She sees her theory as integrating several dimensions of human development, namely cognitive complexity, interpersonal relationships, and moral and ethical development. Under the direction of the master trait, these integrated dimensions develop concurrently "in some more or less coherent way" (Loevinger, 1976, p. ix).

Rogers's Actualizing Tendency

Carl Rogers is not usually viewed as a developmental theorist, but as the reader will recall from Chapter 2, Rogers has addressed the issue of the developing self in considerable detail. For Rogers, the basic life-force is the actualizing tendency, which moves the individual to ever more advanced levels of awareness and wholeness. Rogers (Meador and Rogers, 1979; Rogers, 1951, 1961) sees the actualizing tendency in all life forms, but especially in human beings. Under optimal conditions, individuals naturally strive toward mastery of their environments and toward self-actualization, or becoming the best that they can become. These optimal conditions are an openness to experiencing, trust in the organism, internal locus of evaluation, and a willingness to be a process. Rogers maintains that these are the natural conditions of humankind. When individuals experience these conditions, they grow and develop according to the actualizing tendency, which is not dissimilar to Erikson's idea of the epigenetic principle. Deprived of such conditions, persons may, at worst, develop psychopathological symptoms or, at best, cope with life situations in a marginal fashion. For Rogers, individual identity/purpose in life is the product of the actualizing tendency as it interacts with an environment that provides growth-inducing conditions in varying degrees.

A MODEL OF IDENTITY DEVELOPMENT/PURPOSE IN LIFE

Of the four generic life-skills areas presented in this text, identity development/purpose in life is perhaps the most complex. The preceding discussion of various theorists' conceptualizations of psychosocial development, moral development, and the actualizing tendency provides a rich theoretical background for understanding this life-skill area. It is from this background that we will abstract several dimensions relevant to identity development/purpose in life.

Development is Cumulative

The stages postulated by Erikson, Kohlberg, Loevinger, and other developmental theorists point to the cumulative nature of identity/purpose in life development. Although Erikson specifically focuses on identity in only one of his developmental crises, identity is a continuous theme throughout the life span. The young child's attempts at individuation are early stirrings of this theme, stirrings that approach resolution only in the rewarding life review of the elderly. Similarly, in Kohlberg's scheme, an individual at one stage of moral judgment builds on the awareness of all previous stages as he or she strives to meet the challenges preparatory to being able to function at the next highest level.

Development is Interactive

Individuals do not define identity/purpose in life in a vacuum. There are numerous external reference points that interact with each other and with the internal structures of an individual's genetic endowment to contribute to the development of identity/purpose in life.

Obviously, the young child's interaction with his or her parents is an early contributor to developing identity/purpose in life. The process of individuation, through which the infant learns to distinguish between self and other, is perhaps the earliest building block of identity and purpose in life development. Peer interactions become salient as the child grows older. Feedback from the significant persons in one's environment is a major factor in the development of self-esteem.

A major theme in these early interactions is the formation and stabilization of gender identity. While there is some disagreement as to how this process operates, it is generally believed that a genetic component is involved. There can be no doubt, however, that gender identity develops to a considerable extent as the result of interaction with parents, peers, siblings, and surrogate caregivers.

Similarly, the development of a value system occurs through interaction with significant others. The child soon learns the statements and actions that are valued in the immediate culture and those that are condemned (cf. Rogers's conditions of worth). Later, in adolescence and beyond, these early learnings are reexamined and redefined, but rarely by the individual in isolation. The interaction may occur in many contexts—in a dormitory bull session, a Bible study group, a singles' bar, or a consciousness-raising group focusing on women's issues. In most cases, the individual and his or her values are shaped in interaction with others.

Closely related to values is that component of individual identity connected with one's ethnicity or geographic origins. Again there are external reference points. The music, the food, the dances, the native costumes, and the rituals of a Polish wedding communicate to a child part of what it means to be Polish American. In innumerable other rituals, other children learn what it means to be Jewish, black, or from the South. The reference points are multiple, and the individual interacts with them according to his or her unique patterns of processing information.

Children spend an ever-increasing portion of their time observing and mimicking adults. The work that adults do is particularly fascinating to them. As individuals approach adolescence, the issue of vocational choice becomes salient. Adolescents tend to value the work done by those they admire, whether the object of admiration is a heart surgeon, a rock singer, a professional athlete, or a fashion model. As they ponder career decisions, adolescents interact with each other, as well as with parents, teachers, counselors, neighbors, and the media. Incorporation of career into one's identity and purpose in life usually comes after much exploration, trial and error, and often the intervention of unforeseen events. Vocational choice, too, is the result of interaction between the individual and many elements in the environment.

Development is Idiosyncratic

No two individuals are alike. The celebration of individualism is a tradition of long standing not only in contemporary American culture but also in the Judeo-Christian heritage from which much of the American value system has emerged. And just as each individual is unique, the process of identity and purpose in life development in each person has idiosyncratic characteristics as well.

We know that each person's genetic endowment is unique. Because of this, each person's developmental process is unique as well. Erikson (1968) uses the term *epigenetic principle* to describe this uniqueness. Accordingly, there is a developmental "game plan" that is unique to each organism. Each part arises to its ascendancy according to a master schedule that is idiosyncratic to the individual. The sequence of the events dictated by the epigenetic principle is the same for all members of a species, but the timing and salience of development vary from individual to individual.

Rogers's actualizing tendency (1951, 1961) is another theoretical construct that supports the idiosyncratic aspect of identity and purpose in life development. Regardless of how optimal or how detrimental conditions may be, the actualizing tendency moves the person toward whatever higher levels of functioning the environment will permit.

Concepts such as the epigenetic principle and the actualizing tendency are only part of the equation in identity development/purpose in life. The other major elements are the environment and the person-environment interaction. It is this combination of elements that further delineates the idiosyncratic nature of identity development/purpose in life and makes it amenable to intervention by an approach such as Life-Skills Training.

Identity Development/Purpose in Life: A Working Definition

In a recent study that developed a taxonomy of life-skills, Brooks (1984) presented the following definition of identity development/purpose in life skills:

> Skills and awareness necessary for ongoing development of personal identity and emotional awareness, including self-monitoring, maintenance of self-esteem, manipulating and accommodating to one's environment, clarifying values, sex role development, making meaning, morals/values, dimensions of sexuality, etc. (p. 362)

Combining this definition with the dimensions of identity development/purpose in life presented earlier yields a working definition for purposes of this chapter and for conceptualization of identity development/purpose in life within the context of the Life-Skills Training model. *Identity development/purpose in life is the component of total life span development that incorporates the interaction of genetic endowment and feedback from the environment such that the individual derives personal values, self-esteem, emotional expression, capacity for interpersonal intimacy, career direction, and a sense of place and purpose in life.* It is an ongoing process that underlies the other three generic life-skills areas of interpersonal communication/human relations, problem solving/decision making, and physical fitness/health maintenance. In many respects, identity development/purpose in life, as we have defined it, is similar to the concepts discussed earlier, namely Erikson's (1950, 1963) psychosocial development and Loevinger's (1976) ego development constructs. It differs from these conceptualizations in that no "master trait" is posited (or denied) in the role played by intentional intervention in the form of training.

Recall from Chapter 8 when the theoretical foundations of the Life-Skills Training model were presented that underlying these is the basic principle that human development throughout the life span is a learning process. Failure to learn certain skills at developmentally appropriate times or stages frequently results in deficits that cause problems in living. These problems vary in magnitude and in their impact on individuals' lives. Identity development/purpose in life skills are learned in ways similar to skills in the other three generic areas and can be taught both for purposes of prevention and remediation of problems. A sample of the identity development/purpose in life life-skills identified by Brooks (1984) appears in Table 12-1. A complete listing of these skills is contained in Appendix G.

Prevention

As stated earlier, identity development/purpose in life as a skill area is a cumulative, interactive, and idiosyncratic process. Put another way, indi-

TABLE 12-1
IDENTITY DEVELOPMENT/PURPOSE IN LIFE SKILLS[a]

Childhood	Adolescence	Adulthood
Expresses appropriately the emotions of anger, fear, happiness, and sadness (ages 4 to 5). Understands that one's perspective is often different from that of others (ages 4 to 5). Obeys rules in the absence of authority (ages 4 to 6). Understands that individual differences are normal and acceptable (age 10).	Understands and accepts the development of secondary sex characteristics (age 10; preadolescence). Is able to indentify the role of personal values in one's feelings (age 16; middle adolescence). Deals with uncertainty in relations with authority (age 16; middle adolescence).	Examines and resolves differences between personal beliefs and social norms (young adulthood). Fully participates in intimate sexual relationships (young adulthood). Views objectively the aspirations one has for one's children. (early middle age). Maintains one's sense of occupational competence in the face of competition from younger workers (later middle age).

[a]Skills and awareness necessary for ongoing development of personal identity and emotional awareness, including self-monitoring, maintenance of self-esteem, manipulating and accommodating to one's environment, clarifying values, sex-role development, making meaning, morals/values, and dimensions of sexuality. See Appendix G for complete listing of identity development/purpose in life skills.

viduals are constantly defining their identity and purpose based on past experiences, in light of present interactions with a variety of environmental referents, and in ways that are unique to themselves. Many of the skills of identity development/purpose in life are acquired more or less naturally in the course of one's life, without intentional intervention. Assuming a nurturing early environment, enlightened, caring parents, positive early educational experiences, healthy peer relationships, normal physical development and sound nutrition, opportunities for development of interests, and acquisition of cultural values, most persons experience ongoing development of identity and purpose in life in a relatively nontraumatic fashion.

It is often the case, however, that one or more of these conditions is either missing or present to an insufficient degree in a person's life. A physical handicap, malnutrition, abusive or alcoholic parents, educational disadvantage, a harmful social environment, or cultural indifference may put an individual at risk of deficient development of identity and purpose in life. Similarly, all of the desirable and positive ingredients may be present, but other factors may operate against them such that a comparably deficient outcome results. The possibility of either situation points to the necessity of deliberate programming to ensure positive development.

The most obvious setting for preventive training in identity development skills to occur is in the K through 12 school curricula. This is the surest approach for reaching the broadest possible audience. Not only would the identity development/purpose in life skills of children and youth, ages 5 to 18, be enhanced, but the foundation for later learning in skills appropriate to more mature tasks would be laid. Numerous opportunities exist at all grade levels for incorporating identity development/purpose in life skills training as a separate curriculum and/or for incorporating this skills training into present curricula such as English, social studies, and science classes, as well as providing various extracurricular activities.

Student development programming practices on many college campuses offer another ideal vehicle for skills training with a young adult population. The many settings in which adult education programs are offered provide yet another opportunity for extending identity development/purpose in life skills training upward in the life span. Even though the coverage is less uniform in these settings, learners tend to be more motivated than is the case in elementary and secondary schools.

Many opportunities for training also exist in settings other than purely educational ones. Churches, civic groups, labor unions, fraternal organizations, charitable agencies, youth organizations such as boy and girl scouts, and senior citizen centers are just a few of the settings in which identity development/purpose in life skills training programs could be implemented on a preventive basis.

Remediation

We observed in the previous section that the factors necessary to ensure positive identity development/purpose in life are not always present in an individual's life. Deficits in development occur because of the absence of these factors and because of the presence of actively noxious elements in life experience. When such deficits are severe enough and when the opportunities for preventive intervention are inadequate, individuals develop a variety of problems in living that can result in the need for remediation.

Again, there are a variety of settings in which remedial skills training can occur. Community mental health centers, youth development centers, hospitals, psychiatric clinics, hospices, adult correctional institutions, and rehabilitation centers all serve populations that may be deficient in identity development/purpose in life skills and for whom remedial skills training would be appropriate. Most of these facilities support a variety of in-house educational programs, and incorporating skills training as part of such programs would possibly yield substantial results.

Identity development/purpose in life skills training follows the same procedures discussed elsewhere in this book. It is pertinent, however, to point out a particular dimension of training in this life-skill area. Issues such as intimacy, values, emotional expression, and developing purpose in life have strong affective components. Yet, individuals effect change in these areas through cognitive processes. It is therefore important that training include experiences designed to create cognitive dissonance, while at the same time providing a supportive environment.

APPLICATION

There are a number of ways of implementing skills training for identity development/purpose in life. In Table 12-2, several strategies for training are presented as examples. In this section, more detailed examples of skills training modules for identity development/purpose in life in family, school, work, and community settings are provided.

**Identity Development/Purpose in Life Skills Training:
Example 1**

I Setting: Family/Children

II Life-Skill Objectives: Ability to obey rules in the absence of authority, to face problems with confidence in one's ability to solve them, to understand one's place within one's immediate environment, to understand that one's perspective is often different from that of others.

III Activity: Give children this situation: An extraterrestrial being wants to live with our family for awhile. Parents agree, but only if children take the responsibility for teaching the extraterrestrial earth manners.

    A Procedure:

      1 Let children discuss this novel situation among themselves for awhile.

      2 Ask children to brainstorm what manners they would teach the extraterrestrial. Then ask them to discuss why they chose the particular manners they did.

      3 Ask children how they would teach the extraterrestrial the manners identified.

      4 Contract with the children to practice no more than three of the chosen manners for the coming week.

      5 Ask children at week's end to evaluate how well the extraterrestrial would have learned manners during the preceding week.

      6 Identify new sets of manners to be taught to the extraterrestrial during the following week.

TABLE 12-2
IDENTITY DEVELOPMENT/PURPOSE IN LIFE STRATEGIES

	Family	School	Work	Community
Prevention	Encourage children to express and label feelings. Provide appropriate toys to encourage fantasy in play situations. Assign and reward completion of appropriate household chores. Express affection physically—HUG! Use logical consequences for misbehavior.	Encourage creativity through a variety of artistic media. Make frequent use of group work in which leadership roles are shared and exchanged. Encourage development of special talents through a variety of extracurricular offerings.	Institute quality circles or other means of encouraging involvement in work tasks. Provide opportunities and rewards for creative approaches to solving problems. Provide opportunities for leadership training to enhance career advancement. Institute sabbatical leave program.	Seek out opportunities for community service in satisfying tasks. Become a "big brother" or "big sister" to a disadvantaged youngster. Become involved in environmental issues. Donate two days each month for volunteer work with elderly. Contribute to community charitable fund drives
Remediation	Enter family therapy with whole family participating, even though only one member may be experiencing problems.	Institute special group counseling program for students exhibiting low self-esteem.	Institute employee assistance program (EAP) with special focus on Life-Skills Training.	Provide Life-Skills Training program for youths judged to be predelinquent.

**Identity Development/Purpose in Life Skills Training:
Example 2**

I School/Adolescent

II Life-Skill Objectives: Ability to incorporate a variety of learnings about oneself into one's self-image; incorporate feelings about one's maturing body with other elements of one's emerging self-image; develop a clearer and more realistic self-identity; appreciate one's own development and that of one's peers as representative of a broad range of individual differences; act responsibly in decisions, actions, and relationships.

III Activity: Within the high school social studies or physical education class, students will develop a realistic positive body image and learn how to get feedback from others on physical characteristics.

A Procedure:

1 Have students draw a full-length picture of themselves wearing their favorite clothes.

2 Give a brief mini-lecture on body image. Explain to students what body image is—that it's in people's heads. Different people have different body images, some positive and some negative. What's most desirable is an *accurate* body image, one that changes as we change. One way of correcting a faulty body image is to check it out with friends and for them to respond honestly. That gives us data upon which we can plan some changes, if necessary.

3 Devise a worksheet on which students can rate their overall opinion of how they look (on a 10-point scale); describe their best feature(s); make judgments about their weight, physical condition, height, hair, skin, posture, and how well they select clothes.

4 Ask students to talk about how to give honest feedback to friends. Then role play several situations in which students can see honest feedback demonstrated.

5 Have students review their worksheet to select items they would like to receive honest feedback on. Then divide them into pairs to discuss these items. Combine pairs into groups of four and ask for additional feedback.

6 Based on the feedback, have each student select one thing about their appearance that they would like to change. Ask them to write a contract with themselves that contains the objective and reasonable strategies for effecting the desired change. Have the contract witnessed by a friend who agrees to give them feedback on a weekly basis.

7 Taking account of the weekly feedback, students will either adhere to their original strategies or develop new ones more suitable to their objectives.

8 As objectives are reached, ask students to write a brief theme describing how they feel about themselves now.

9 Optional: Ask them to share the theme with their feedback partner or with you.

Identity Development/Purpose in Life Skills Training: Example 3

I Setting: Work/Adults

II Life-Skill Objectives: Ability to identify values in particular occupations, manage one's emotions in constructive ways, act with independence and awareness of likely outcomes, assess objectively one's strengths and weaknesses for various life roles, maintain one's identity and self-esteem as occupational involvement changes.

III Activity: Performance evaluation for management trainees. In, for example, the corporate branch office, a consultant can provide training for employees to improve their self-assessment skills and to increase their ability to utilize feedback to improve performance.

A Procedure:

1 Ask trainees to brainstorm as a group the criteria upon which their first performance evaluation will be based.

2 Ask each trainee to devise a form based on the brainstormed criteria. The form will be used to evaluate one of their peers in a role-play situation.

3 Divide the group into triads. One member of each triad will play the role of evaluator, a second will role play the person being evaluated, and the third will observe the role-play evaluation and give feedback on the process.

4 After 10 minutes for role play and 5 minutes for feedback from the observer, have the trainees change roles. Repeat this process until each person has played all three roles.

5 Reassemble the large group for sharing. Go once around the group, asking the trainees to share one thing that they learned about themselves.

6 Distribute to the group for the first time the *real* performance evaluation form. Ask each trainee to rate himself/herself on this form.

7 With a volunteer, role play in front of the group a performance evaluation using the real form. After 10 minutes, ask the group for feedback.

8 Immediately following each trainee's actual evaluation, ask them to complete a brief survey describing the process from their perspective and their relative rating of the benefits of the training session prior to the actual event.

9 Based on the feedback, modify procedures for future activities of this type.

Identity Development/Purpose in Life Skills Training: Example 4

I Setting: Community/Adults

II Life-Skills Objectives: Ability to find purposeful and satisfying activities in all stages of life, maintain one's identity and self-esteem as occupational involvement changes, maintain an integrated and positive sense of self as one moves through the life span.

III Activity: Orientation of new residents to retirement community. Program designed to be implemented by staff member, coordinator of volunteer services, to help new residents to become oriented to the community. In addition, the new residents are provided an opportunity to commit themselves to regular volunteer service in their new community.

A Procedure:

1 Each new resident will be paired with a previous graduate of the course who has become an active volunteer.

2 Each graduate volunteer will give his or her new resident partner a very limited but intensive tour of part of the community.

3 The new residents will assemble as a group and be given a list for a scavenger hunt that can be successfully completed only if they cooperate with each other, since each has only partial information about the community.

4 Following the scavenger hunt, the new residents assemble again. They are administered an inventory concerning the community, with a special focus on areas of need that they observed, to assess what they learned.

5 Each is asked to commit a block of time each week to serving as a volunteer in the area of greatest interest to them.

6 After 6 weeks, assess the usefulness of the program according to the following questions: (1) what percentage of each class of new residents actually become involved in community volunteer work? (2) what is their level of satisfaction with this work as measured by a simple quarterly questionnaire? (3) how does their adjustment to community living compare with those who choose not to become volunteers? and (4) how do the volunteers and nonvolunteers interact with each other?

SUMMARY

In this chapter, we have presented identity development/purpose in life as the fourth and most complex of the generic life-skills areas. We noted that identity development/purpose in life is cumulative, interactive, and idiosyncratic. We have defined identity development/purpose in life as the component of total life span development that incorporates the interaction of genetic endowment and feedback from the environment such that the individual derives personal values, self-esteem, emotional expression, capacity for interpersonal intimacy, career direction, and a sense of place and purpose in life.

In addition, we discussed Life-Skills Training as a medium for promoting the development of skills in both preventive and remedial dimensions. Four sample training modules were presented that demonstrated applications of identity development/purpose in life skills training in family, school, work, and community settings.

SUGGESTED READINGS

Erikson, E. H. (1963). *Childhood and society* (2d ed.). New York: W. W. Norton.

Erikson, E. H. (1968). *Identity: Youth and crisis*. New York: W. W. Norton.

Gould, R. L. (1978). *Transformations: Growth and change in adult life*. New York: Simon & Schuster.

Kegan, R. (1982). *The evolving self*. Cambridge, MA: Harvard University Press.

Loevinger, J. (1976). *Ego development: Conceptions and theories*. San Francisco: Jossey-Bass.

Rogers, C. R. (1961). *On becoming a person*. Boston: Houghton Mifflin.

Vaillant, G. E. (1977). *Adaptation to life*. Boston: Little, Brown.

REFERENCES

Aubrey, R. F. (1980). Technology and counseling and the science of behavior: A rapprochement. *Personnel and Guidance Journal, 58*, 318–327.

Brooks, D. K., Jr. (1984). *A life-skills taxonomy: Defining elements of effective functioning through the use of the Delphi technique*. Unpublished doctoral dissertation, University of Georgia, Athens.

Erikson, E. H. (1950). *Childhood and society*. New York: W. W. Norton.

Erikson, E. H. (1963). *Childhood and society* (2d ed.). New York: W. W. Norton.

Erikson, E. H. (1968). *Identity: Youth and crisis*. New York: W. W. Norton.

Freud, S. (1961). The infantile genital organization: An interpolation into the theory of sexuality. In J. Strachey (Ed.), *The standard edition of the complete psychological works of Sigmund Freud* (vol. 19, pp. 141–149). London: Hogarth Press. (Original work published 1923.)

Kohlberg, L. (1973). Continuities in childhood and adult moral development revisited. In P. B. Baltes & K. W. Schaie (Eds.), *Lifespan developmental psychology: Personality and socialization* (pp. 179–204). New York: Academic Press.

Loevinger, J. (1966). The meaning and measurement of ego development. *American Psychologist, 21*, 195–206.

Loevinger, J. (1976). *Ego development: Conceptions and theories.* San Francisco: Jossey-Bass.

Meador, B. D., & Rogers, C. R. (1979). Person-centered therapy. In R. J. Corsini (Ed.), *Current psychotherapies* (2d ed.) (pp. 131–184). Itasca, IL: F. E. Peacock.

Rodgers, R. F. (1980). Theories underlying student development. In D. G. Cramer (Ed.), *Student development and higher education: Theories, practices, and future directions* (pp. 10–95). Cincinnati: American College Personnel Association.

Rogers, C. R. (1951). *Client-centered therapy.* Boston: Houghton Mifflin.

Rogers, C. R. (1961). *On becoming a person.* Boston: Houghton Mifflin.

Schlossberg, N. K. (1984). *Counseling adults in transition.* New York: Springer.

The Evolution of Counseling

Table A-1: Evolution of Guidance and Counseling/Vocational Guidance

1890   James McKeen Cattell published an article, using the term *mental tests* for the first time; psychological measurement of the era was limited to sensory and motor task evaluation.

1895   George Merrill developed vocational guidance activities at the California School of Mechanical Arts, San Francisco.

1896   The first psychological clinic was established by Lightner Witmer at the University of Pennsylvania. Later, in the early 1920s, one of Witmer's students, Morris Viteles, began a vocational guidance clinic as part of the general clinic.

1898   Jesse B. Davis conducted class counselor activities at Central High School, Detroit.

1899   William Rainey Harper, first president of the University of Chicago, spoke on guidance specialists in universities.

1905   Frank Parsons established Breadwinners' College at Civic Service House, a settlement house in Boston.

1906   Eli W. Weaver, principal of Boys' High School in Brooklyn, New York, published the book *Choosing a Career.*

1908   Frank Parsons opened the Vocation Bureau in Boston.

        Jesse B. Davis organized a program of vocational and moral guidance in the schools of Grand Rapids, Michigan.

1909	Frank Parsons's *Choosing a Vocation,* in which the term "vocational guidance" was first used, was published posthumously.
1910	The first national conference on vocational guidance was held in Boston. Leaders were David Snedden, Frank Thompson, and Meyer Bloomfield.
1911	Meyer Bloomfield taught the first university level vocational guidance course at Harvard.
	The Vocational Guidance News-Letter, the first American journal devoted to vocational guidance, was published by the Vocation Bureau.
	Three groups, established to improve opportunities for blacks, merged to form the National League on Urban Conditions Among Negroes, later the National Urban League.
1913	The National Vocational Guidance Association (NVGA) was formed in Grand Rapids, Michigan, with Frank M. Leavitt of the University of Chicago as first president.
	The American edition of Hugo Munsterberg's *Psychology and Industrial Efficiency* was published, demonstrating the application of experimental psychology to vocational choice.
	The U. S. Department of Labor was formed.
1915	The *Vocational Guidance Bulletin* was first published.
	The Division of Applied Psychology was established at the Carnegie Institute of Technology. It was the first academic division to conduct vocational training and research.
1916	L. M. Terman published a revision of the Binet scales standardized on a population of American students, including the concept of "intelligence quotient."
1917	E. L. Thorndike and Robert Yerkes developed the Army Alpha and Army Beta tests for military screening.
	The Smith-Hughes Act provided reimbursement for vocational education.
1918	The Vocational Rehabilitation Act became law. The Rehabilitation Division for Disabled Soldiers was established, under the Federal Board for Vocational Education.
1919	John Brewer served as the director of Vocational Guidance at Harvard.
1920	The George-Reed Act provided reimbursement for vocational guidance activities.
1925	Harry Kitson published *Psychology of Vocational Adjustment.*
1926	New York was the first state to require certification for guidance workers.
1927	Clark L. Hull published *Aptitude Testing.*
	E. K. Strong, Jr., published the *Strong Vocational Interest Blank.*
	Elton Mayo and a team from Harvard University began a series of studies on industrial behavior at the Western Electric Company, Hawthorne plant.

1931	The Minnesota Employment Stabilization Research Institute was established by Donald G. Paterson, from the University of Minnesota, and others.
1932	John Brewer published *Education As Guidance.*
1933	The U. S. Employment Service was created by the Wagner-Peyser Act.

1933 The U. S. Employment Service was created by the Wagner-Peyser Act.

The National Occupational Conference was formed under the sponsorship of the American Association for Adult Education. Its publications included *Occupations, The Vocational Guidance Magazine,* the *Occupational Index,* and *Occupational Abstracts.*

The Civilian Conservation Corps was formed to provide training and employment for unemployed youth.

1934 The George-Ellzy Act provided reimbursement for vocational guidance activities.

The NVGA and five other societies joined to form the American Council of Guidance and Personnel Associations. Harry Kitson was its first president.

1935 The Works Progress Administration was created as a federal agency. One division, the National Youth Administration, provided occupational counseling, placement, and follow-up for underprivileged youth.

Robert Hoppock published *Job Satisfaction* for the National Occupational Conference.

1936 The George-Dean Act provided reimbursement for vocational guidance activities.

1937 Walter V. Bingham published *Aptitudes and Aptitude Testing* for the National Occupational Conference.

1938 The Occupational Information and Guidance Service was established with George-Dean Act funds in the Division of Vocational Education, U. S. Office of Education.

The American Council on Education published the experimental edition of the *Tests of Primary Mental Abilities* by Louis L. and Thelma G. Thurstone.

The B'nai B'rith Vocational Service Bureau opened in Washington, D. C.

1939 The *Dictionary of Occupational Titles* was published by the Bureau of Labor Statistics, U. S. Department of Labor.

The Jewish Occupational Council was formed to coordinate all Jewish vocational agencies.

1930s During this 10-year period, William Proctor's perspectives of guidance were extended by Koos, Kefauver, and Hand to include two major functions: (1) distribution—helping students to find educational/vocational opportunities effectively, and (2) adjustment—helping students to adjust to environmental requirements. The economic depression also led to an emphasis on replacement in vocational guidance.

1940 The Occupational Outlook Service was established in the Bureau of Labor Statistics.

1941   World War II efforts led to contributions by the Personnel Research Section of the Adjutant General's Office including the Army General Classification Test, various new psychomotor tests, improved methods of assessing reliability and validity, and the stanine method of converting raw scores to standard scores.

1942   John M. Brewer published *History of Vocational Guidance.*

Carl R. Rogers published *Counseling and Psychotherapy,* a work which ultimately forged a stronger link between vocational and other forms of counseling.

1943   E. K. Strong, Jr., published *Vocational Interests of Men and Women.*

The Barden-LaFollette Act expanded civilian vocational rehabilitation.

The Disabled Veterans Rehabilitation Act provided vocational counseling services for disabled servicepersons.

1944   The G.I. Bill extended education and training benefits as well as counseling services to all veterans of World War II.

The Army Separation-Classification and Counseling program was established under the War Department for returning veterans.

1945   The U. S. Employment Service began experimental use of the General Aptitude Test Battery.

Ira Scott published the *Manual of Advisement and Counseling,* used widely in Veterans Administration guidance centers after World War II.

1946   The George Barden Act provided salaries, travel expenses, and other guidance-related support for vocational counselors.

1947   The American Psychological Association established separate divisions. Vocational psychologists were principally affiliated with Divisions 17 and 5, Counseling and Guidance, and Evaluation and Measurement, respectively.

1948   The *Occupational Outlook Handbook* was first published.

1940s   During this period guidance techniques expanded and eclectic models became abundant. Jones, Myers, and others introduced the concept of guidance as decision making. Myers contended that differences among individuals and differences among choices were two areas of concern for guidance and that other areas such as social, health, and recreational guidance should be assigned to instruction.

1951   The National Vocational Guidance Association, American College Personnel Association, National Association of Guidance Supervisors and College Trainers, and the Student Personnel Association for Teacher Education merged to form the American Personnel and Guidance Association (APGA).

Donald Super initiated the Career Pattern Study.

Ginzberg, Ginsburg, Axelrad, and Herma conceptualized occupational choice as a developmental process.

1952   The American School Counselors Association (ASCA) was organized.

The *Vocational Guidance Quarterly* was first published.

1953	The American School Counselors Association became a division of the APGA.
	The School Counselor was first published.
1954	The research and demonstration program of the Office of Vocational Rehabilitation was initiated under the Rehabilitation Amendments.
1956	*Estimates of Worker Trait Requirements for 4,000 Jobs,* developed by the U. S. Employment Service, was published.
1957	Donald Super's *Psychology of Careers* was published, emphasizing career development theory as related to life stages.
	The American Board on Professional Standards in Vocational Counseling was created by the American Personnel and Guidance Association to evaluate and certify vocational counseling agencies.
1958	The National Defense Education Act (NDEA) was created. Title V-A required states to submit plans to test secondary school students, to identify talented students, and to encourage talented students to enter higher education programs, particularly the physical sciences. Funds were provided for support and development of local school guidance programs. Title V-B provided funds for the training of secondary school counselors, resulting in significant increases in the number of school counselors.
1959	In *The American High School Today,* James B. Conant recommended one full-time counselor or guidance office for every 200 to 300 high school students.
	The National Association of Guidance Supervisors and Counselor Trainers began a 5-year project to develop standards for the education of secondary school counselors.
1950s	During the decade of the 50s, education's role in national defense was recognized. As a result, school counselors were given an important role and state certification of school counselors became the rule. Career- and vocational-development theories appeared in the writings of Eli Ginzberg, Donald Super, Anne Roe, Robert Hoppock, John Holland, and David Tiedeman.
1961	The Association for Counselor Education and Supervision (ACES) was founded.
1962	C. Gilbert Wrenn published *The Counselor in a Changing World,* under the sponsorship of The Commission on Guidance in American Schools. This landmark work outlined the forces acting on individuals in society and the potential role of the school counselor.
	The Manpower Development and Training Act provided for guidance services to the economically displaced and the underemployed.
	Mathewson described guidance as a developmental process with the goal of personal mastery.
	Tiedeman and Field proposed guidance as the science of purposeful action within education.
1963	The Vocational Education Act Amendment of 1963 provided for voca-

tional guidance and counseling for students already enrolled or planning to enroll in vocational-education courses.

1964   Amendments to the NDEA provided for guidance and counseling in elementary schools and postsecondary (nonbaccalaureate) education.

The Economic Opportunity Act indirectly affected the development and expansion of guidance with the establishment of the Job Corps, Vista, and Head Start programs.

The ACES *Standards for Counselor Education in the Preparation of Secondary School Counselors* was adopted on an experimental basis.

On the fiftieth anniversary of NVGA, Henry Borow edited *Man in a World at Work*.

1965   The Elementary and Secondary Education Act (ESEA) of 1965 designated funds for guidance and counseling.

The first computer-based guidance system was initiated.

1966   *The Elementary School Guidance and Counseling Journal* began publication.

1967   Peters, Farwell, and others proposed guidance as a developmental process with the goal of achievement of personal mastery, an approach requiring teachers, counselors, administrators, and pupil personnel specialists to function as team members.

1968   The Vocational Education Act Amendment of 1968 advocated career programs, programs for the disadvantaged and handicapped, and extension of guidance and counseling into elementary schools.

1969   The NDEA V-B and the ESEA III funds were combined into one appropriation for guidance.

1960s   During the decade of the 1960s, guidance and counseling faced the upheavals in values created by the Vietnam War, the civil-rights and women's rights movements, and an overall concern with racial, social, and sexual stereotyping. Counselor education programs experienced a period of major expansion. Group counseling and other group procedures gained in popularity.

1971   Career education was introduced as a priority of the U.S. Office of Education.

1974   The Educational Amendments of 1974 legislated career education and initiated the Office of Career Education in the U. S. Office of Education.

The Buckley Amendment to the Family Educational Rights and Privacy Act called into question the validity of certain guidance information and opened school counselor records for parent inspection.

1975   The APGA introduced into Congress the Career Guidance and Counseling Act of 1975.

P.L. 94-142 required mainstreaming of special education students and involved elementary school counselors, in particular, in the development of Individual Education Programs.

1976   The Educational Amendments of 1976 included support for guidance and counseling through Titles I, II, and III. Title II provided support for vocational guidance. Title III, Part D, authorized an administrative unit in the Office of Education to assess the status of guidance and counseling in the schools, coordinate legislation on guidance and counseling, and consult with the Commissioner of Education about guidance and counseling.

1970s   During this period, performance- and competency-based counselor education models were developed. Mosher, Sprinthall, and others proposed the concept of guidance as psychological education for preventive mental health and psychological development.

1983   The APGA changed its name to the American Association for Counseling and Development to emphasize its prominent focus on counseling.

RESOURCES

Borow, H. (Ed.). (1964). *Man in a world at work.* Boston: Houghton Mifflin.
Brewer, J. M. (1942). *History of vocational guidance.* New York: Harper & Brothers.
Herr, E. L. (1979). *Guidance and counseling in the schools: The past, present, and future.* Falls Church, VA: American Personnel and Guidance Association.
Kroth, J. A. (1973). *Counseling psychology and guidance: An overview in outline.* Springfield, IL: Charles C Thomas.

Table A-2: Evolution of Counseling Psychology

1946   Following suspension of annual meetings during World War II, the American Psychological Association (APA) held its first convention in Philadelphia at the University of Pennsylvania. A merger had been effected between the APA and the American Association of Applied Psychologists and the APA was reorganized into divisions. Carl Rogers was president-elect of the APA.

      The first annual business meeting of Division 17 of the APA (then called the Division of Personnel and Guidance Psychologists) was held in Philadelphia, Pennsylvania. E. G. Williamson became the first president and John G. Darley the first secretary-treasurer.

      The American Board of Examiners in Professional Psychology was established.

1950   The *Annual Review of Psychology,* a review of theoretical and research advances, was first published.

1951   The Northwestern Conference emphasized the role of the counseling psychologist and produced statements on doctoral training and practicum standards in counseling psychology.

      The title "Counseling Psychology" for Division 17 of the APA was adopted.

The National Vocational Guidance Association, American College Personnel Association, National Association of Guidance Supervisors and College Trainers, and the Student Personnel Association for Teacher Education merged to form the American Personnel and Guidance Association (APGA). Many individuals were active in both Division 17 of the APA and the APGA and a close relationship existed between the *Journal of Counseling Psychology* and the *Personnel and Guidance Journal.*

1952   The Division of Counseling and Guidance, Committee on Counselor Training, published "The Practicum Training of Psychologists," and "Recommended Standards for Training Counseling Psychologists at the Doctoral Level," in the *American Psychologist,* recommending training standards for doctoral level counseling psychologists, (*American Psychologist,* 1952, 7, 182–188 & 175–181). Edward S. Bordin chaired the committee that produced standards for training at the doctoral level and Donald E. Super chaired the committee that produced recommendations for practicum training.

The Veterans Administration established two major psychological positions: "Counseling Psychologist (Vocational)" and "Counseling Psychologist (Vocational Rehabilitation and Education)."

1953   The APA adopted and published *Ethical Standards of Psychologists.*

Division 17 officially became the "Division of Counseling Psychology."

1954   *The Journal of Counseling Psychology* was published with C. Gilbert Wrenn as the first editor.

Donald Super published "Career Patterns As a Basis for Vocational Counseling," a work which subsequently served as a research guide in vocational psychology.

Meehl and McArthur published works arguing the relative merits of clinical and statistical prediction.

The Vocational Rehabilitation Act, in creating a demand for counselors, prompted APA and APGA cooperation in obtaining funds for training master's level of rehabilitation counselors.

The Executive Committee of Division 17 commissioned C. Winfield Scott to write a history of the Division. The final report was submitted to the Executive Committee in 1963.

1955   The American Board of Examiners in Professional Psychology established the diploma in Counseling Psychology to replace the earlier diploma in Counseling and Guidance.

Donald Super published "Transition: From Vocational Guidance to Counseling Psychology," (*Journal of Counseling Psychology, 2,* 3–9), exploring the origins of counseling psychology.

Milton E. Hahn published "Counseling Psychology," (*American Psychologist, 10,* 279–282), a statement of definitions for counseling psychology, subsequent to the Northwestern Conference and the Committee on Counselor Training recommendations of 1952.

The Stanford Conference for Training in Counseling Psychology explored the general question of training in psychology and the particular interest of counseling psychology in mental health.

1956   The APA published "Counseling Psychology As a Specialty," (*American Psychologist, 11,* 282–285). Harold B. Pepinsky chaired the committee that produced this statement.

1958   Passage of the National Defense Education Act (NDEA) encouraged further cooperation between the APA and the APGA in procuring funds for the training of primary and secondary school counselors, resulting in the NDEA Guidance Institutes.

The Miami Conference on Graduate Education in Psychology focused on program content. Outcomes indicated a tendency to move toward more specialized curricula.

1959   The APA Education and Training Board appointed an ad hoc committee to report on the status of counseling psychology as a specialty; committee members were Irwin Berg, Harold B. Pepinsky, and Edward J. Shoeben. Their report claimed a decline in the specialty, particularly in the area of empirical research, and proposed several remedial alternatives.

1960   The Executive Committee of the Division of Counseling Psychology appointed three members of the division to report on the status of counseling psychology. Their findings emerged as "A Report of a Special Committee of the Division of Counseling Psychology, 1961," by Leona Tyler, David Tiedeman, and C. Gilbert Wrenn, and emphasized a professional focus on encouragement of individual growth and development.

The Division of Counseling Psychology, Committee on Internship Standards, reported *Recommended Standards for Internships in Counseling Psychology.*

1963   Brayfield produced a seminal statement on the problems confronting counseling psychology, particularly those of status and focus (*Annual Review of Psychology, 14,* 319–350).

1964   The Greyston Conference was held with Albert Thompson and Donald Super as conference planners and editors of conference proceedings. Outcomes of the conference were organized under four headings: (1) roles, (2) content of training, (3) organization of training, and (4) unity and diversity. History and implications were incorporated within these headings.

The Civil Rights Act of 1964 was passed. Title VII had distinct implications for psychologists engaged in psychometrics.

1965   The Cubberley Conference focused on implications of the behavioral sciences for guidance, particularly the possibilities for participation of counseling psychologists in the schools.

The Invitational Conference on Government-University Relations in the Professional Preparation and Employment of Counselors focused on problems arising from government pressure on universities for specialized education.

1967	The APA acquired the *Journal of Counseling Psychology.*

The Bromwoods Conference was held with the purpose of evaluating and refocusing the research literature in counselor characteristics and effectiveness, client characteristics and implications for selection and treatment, and outcome assessment.

Enneis published "Discrimination: Planned and Accidental," (*Counseling News and Views,* 1967, *19*(2), 5–10) outlining the implications of the Civil Rights Act of 1964 for psychologists.

1968   The APA published a revised statement of ethical standards (*The American Psychologist,* 1968, *23,* 357–61).

Jordaan, Myers, Layton, and Morgan published a comprehensive definition of counseling psychology, sanctioned by the Professional Affairs Committee of Division 17 and the Executive Committee (*The Counseling Psychologist,* Washington, D.C., American Psychological Association).

1969   *The Counseling Psychologist* began publication with J. M. Whiteley as founding editor.

1973   The APA published *Ethical Principles in the Conduct of Research with Human Participants.*

The Vail Conference, with funding from the National Institute of Mental Health, focused on the training of professional psychologists.

1975   Division 17 published "The Licensing and Certification of Psychologists—A Position Statement." (*The Counseling Psychologist,* 5(3), 135.)

1976   Ivey produced an alternative definition of counseling psychology (*The Counseling Psychologist,* 1976). While this statement, like the earlier version by Jordaan et al. (1968), emanated from the work of the Division 17 Professional Affairs Committee (1974), it did not receive official sanction.

1977   The first issue on professional identity was published in *The Counseling Psychologist.*

Division 17 published *The Defining Characteristics of Counseling Psychologists,* (Washington, D.C.: APA).

1980   *The History of Counseling Psychology,* edited by John Whiteley, and *The Present and Future of Counseling Psychology,* edited by John Whiteley and Bruce Fretz, were published, comprising the most comprehensive treatment of the past, present, and predicted future of the profession.

1981   The APA published "Ethical Principles of Psychologists," "Specialty Guidelines for the Delivery of Services," and "Specialty Guidelines for the Delivery of Services by Counseling Psychologists," (*American Psychologist,* 36(6), 633–638, 639–651, 652–633).

1982   Kagan initiated the Next Decade project of Division 17 (*The Counseling Psychologist,* 1982).

1985   The APA published "Casebook for Providers of Psychological Services," (*American Psychologist, 40,* 678–684).

RESOURCES

Borow, H. (Ed.). (1964). *Man in a world at work.* Boston: Houghton Mifflin.

Brown, S. D., & Lent, R. W. (1984). *Handbook of counseling psychology.* New York: Wiley.

Whiteley, J. M. (Ed.). (1980). *The history of counseling psychology.* Monterey, CA: Brooks/Cole.

Whiteley, J.M., & Fretz, B. R. (Eds.). (1980). *The present and future of counseling psychology.* Monterey, CA: Brooks/Cole.

Table A-3: Evolution of School Psychology

1885   James McKeen Cattell employed the term "mental tests" in articles appearing between 1885 and 1900, and in 1896 he published the results of a series of tests given to Columbia College freshmen.

1896   Lightner Witmer, head of the psychological laboratory at the University of Pennsylvania, applied psychological techniques to children with deficiencies in subject matter. (Along with the development of the Child Study Center in the Chicago public schools, Witmer's work is generally credited with the beginning of school psychology in America.)

1899   The Chicago public schools, through the efforts of Walter S. Christopher, established what has come to be known as the Bureau of Child Study.

1905   The Binet-Simon Scale was introduced into the United States.

1908   Clifford Beers published *A Mind That Found Itself.*

1910   Edward C. Elliott developed a test that was probably the first attempt to measure personality characteristics objectively and quantitatively.

1910   Clarence W. Stone and Stuart A. Courtis developed the first scientifically established American achievement tests. These were arithmetic tests with grade norms.

1911   Henry H. Goddard adapted the Binet for American students.

1912–
1913   Hugo Munsterberg of Harvard developed tests for the selection of streetcar motormen and telephone operators.

1915   Dr. Arnold Gesell was appointed as a school psychologist to the Connecticut State Board of Education to make mental assessment of backward and defective children and develop methods for their care in public schools.

1916   Lewis M. Terman popularized the intelligence quotient (IQ) concept.

1917   The Army Alpha and Army Beta group intelligence tests were developed

	for classifying military recruits for World War I. These tests were the first standardized group intelligence tests.
1918	Arthur S. Otis published the first group battery of intelligence tests standardized on students in American schools from grade 4 to college level. Army psychologists developed trade and aptitude tests.
1919	Louis M. Terman developed the first aptitude tests administered under controlled conditions. These tests were made for prospective telegraphers, office clerks, and engineering students.
	Robert S. Woodworth published a psychoneurotic questionnaire designed to screen out soldiers based on neurotic symptoms.
	The Progressive Education Association and movement began in America with John Dewey as one of the chief spokespersons.
	The State Education Department of Missouri provided that candidates for special classes should be psychologically tested.
1920	Child guidance clinics were being established throughout the country. They were expanded beyond the original interest in juvenile delinquency to include community education and treatment programs in mental health.
	Sidney L. Pressey designed the first unified battery of achievement tests for different areas of instruction which produced a pooled or total score. These second-grade tests included the areas of spelling, arithmetic, reading, vocabulary, and sentence meaning.
1923	The first individual test of general mechanical ability was developed by John L. Stenquist, founder of the Bureau of Educational Research of the Baltimore public schools.
1936	Delaware was the first state to mandate individual psychological examinations on a statewide basis.
1947	Division 16, School Psychology, was established in the American Psychological Association (APA).
1952	The APA identified the school psychologist as an individual with clinical and educational skills who practiced in an educational setting.
1954	The Thayer Conference on the Functions, Qualifications, and Training of School Psychologists was held.
1955	The Thayer Conference Report *School Psychologists in Mid-century* was published. A statement defining the school psychologist was published. This definition recognized the school psychologist as a psychologist who had training and experience in education and who used his or her knowledge of assessment, learning, and interpersonal relationships to assist school personnel in the growth and development of all students and also to be able to recognize and treat exceptional children.
1958	An APA committee produced *The Psychologist on the School Staff; Report of the Committee on Reconsideration of the Function of the School Psychologist.* This publication provided a consensus on the functions of the school psychologist. Twenty types of essential activities of the school psychologist and other pupil personnel specialists were outlined.

1967	Forty-one states had certified school psychologists.
1969	The National Association of School Psychologists (NASP) was organized as a reaction to the APA position that the entry level for independent practice and licensure for psychologists was the doctorate. NASP contended that school psychology is a profession in its own right and that the entry level for independent practice is subdoctoral.
1977	The APA published the revised *Standards for Providers of Psychological Services* in which the professional psychologist was considered by the APA to be the doctoral psychologist.
1978	The "NASP Position Paper" committed the NASP to establishing independent practice rights for school psychologists in as many states as possible and authorized the Council on Postsecondary Accreditation to represent school psychology as the accrediting unit under the National Council for the Accreditation of Teacher Education (NCATE).
1981	The Olympia Conference on the Future of School Psychology was held.
	Proceedings of the Spring Hill Symposium on the Future of Psychology in the Schools was published in the *School Psychology Reviews.* The goals emanating from this symposium stressed the need for coordination among the overlapping state and national organizations (i.e., APA Division 16 and NASP) and improved differentiation of the purposes of these organizations. Another goal was to develop united fronts in areas of mutual concern.
	J. Grimes and R. Grubb's report for NASP on state school psychology association presidents' concerns for their profession.
1982	A special issue on the Olympia Conference was published in the *Journal of School Psychology.*

RESOURCES

Gray, S. W. (1963). *The psychologist in the schools.* New York: Holt, Rinehart & Winston.

Holt, F. D., & Kicklighter, R. H. (1971). *Psychological services in the schools.* Dubuque, IA: Wm. C. Brown Company.

Hynd, G. W. (Ed.). (1983). *The school psychologist.* Syracuse, NY: Syracuse University Press.

Magary, J. F. (Ed.). (1967). *School psychological services.* Englewood Cliffs, NJ: Prentice-Hall.

Table A-4: Evolution of Clinical Psychology[1]

1793	Pinel unchained the inmates and founded moral treatment in asylums.
1796	Tuke established the York Retreat to provide a "refuge" and a humane physical and social environment for lunatics.

[1]This table is from Kendall, P. C., & Norton-Ford, J. D. *Clinical psychology.* New York: Wiley, 1982. Reproduced by permission of John Wiley & Sons.

1824	Todd founded the Retreat to offer moral management as milieu therapy.
1840	Dix began a 40-year crusade to establish humane mental hospitals.
1869	Galton published *Hereditary Genius,* commencing the study of individual differences that led him to later develop tests of simple abilities such as reaction time.
1870s	William James and Wilhelm Wundt were separate founders of the first psychology laboratories.
1887	Hall founded the *American Journal of Psychology* for experimental research in psychology.
1890	J. M. Cattell introduced the concept of "mental tests and measurements" that aimed at discovering constancies in mental processes that differentiate among individuals.
1891	Bernheim described treatment by hypnosis.
1892	Hall, James, Cattell, Ladd, Jastrow, Fullerton and Baldwin founded the American Psychological Association (APA).
1895	Breuer and Freud described transference in the therapist-client relationship.
1896	Witmer founded the first psychological clinic, University of Pennsylvania.
	Witmer advocated pedagogical treatment in psychology clinics.
1900	Freud described dream analysis and free association as therapy methods.
1905	Binet and Simon published the first objective test of intelligence.
	Worcester and Pratt initiated group therapy.
	Franz began teaching brain-damaged patients with speech loss to recover their speech skills.
	Binet and Simon presented validity evidence for their intelligence test.
1906	Janet proposed relearning of competing responses as a treatment for impulse problems.
	Prince founded the *Journal of Abnormal Psychology* for experimental research, theory, and case reports in clinical psychology.
	Franz reported experimental data from monkeys to demonstrate that the brain's frontal lobe controls sensory associations, and that habits that are lost due to brain damage can be relearned.
	Prince and Coriat described examples of therapy, based on a reeducation process guided by scientifically derived principles of learning.
1907– 1909	Jung presented between-groups experiments to demonstrate that persons with different psychological problems manifest different psychophysiological responses.
1908	DuBois advocated talking therapy to persuade clients to master their psychological symptoms and problems.
1909	Healy and Fernald founded the Juvenile Psychopathic Institute, spurring the child guidance movement in the United States.

1912	Witmer founded the journal *Psychological Clinics* to represent clinical practitioners.
1913	Jelliffe described countertransference in therapy.
1915	APA recommended that only qualified psychologists use psychological tests.
1915–1918	Psychologists developed the Army Alpha (verbal intelligence) and Beta (nonverbal intelligence) tests and the Personal Data Sheet (personality) to screen recruits for the armed forces during World War I.
1916	Terman reported updated norms for the Binet-Simon intelligence test.
	Terman revised the Binet-Simon, incorporating the IQ.
1917	Hollingworth founded the American Association of Clinical Psychologists.
1919	McDougall used "sympathetic rapport" to treat shell-shocked soldiers.
	APA established a Clinical Section to represent clinical psychologists.
1920	Watson and Rayner described a case of conditioned fears.
1921	Rorschach inkblot test was published, representing the first major projective test.
	J. M. Cattell founded the Psychological Corporation.
1922–1928	Adler and Dreikurs pioneered therapy interviews with entire families.
1925	Gesell published developmental schedules describing the normal developmental attainments of 3- to 30-month-old infants.
1926	Thurstone suggested that Deviation Quotients be used in intelligence tests rather than the MA/CA ratio.
1927	Edward K. Strong, Jr., published the Strong Vocational Interest Blank for Men.
1928	Anna Freud described psychoanalytic play therapy with children.
1930	Tulchin advocated therapy as a legitimate function of clinical psychologists.
1932	Moreno introduced the concept of "group therapy."
1934	Allen described "passive therapy," forerunner of Rogerian therapy.
	G. Frederick Kuder published the Kuder Preference Record - Vocational.
1935	Doll published the Vineland Social Maturity Scale.
	APA Clinical Section established standards for clinical training and practice.
1936	Louttit published the first text on clinical psychology.
1937	American Association of Applied Psychologists was founded for clinical psychologists as an alternative to American Psychological Association.
	Journal of Consulting Psychology was founded.
	Mathews reported the first experimental study in the *Journal of Consulting Psychology.*

	Terman and Merrill published the revised Stanford-Binet.
1938	Bender-Gestalt test was introduced.
	Levy described "relationship therapy," forerunner of behavior therapy.
1939	Wechsler-Bellvue test was introduced.
	Wechsler reported validity evidence for his intelligence test for adults.
1940	Hathaway and McKinley developed the Minnesota Multiphasic Personality Inventory (MMPI).
	Hathaway and McKinley reported validity evidence for the Minnesota Multiphasic Personality Inventory (MMPI).
	Slavson summarized his principles for group therapy.
1941	Korzbyski popularized "semantic therapy."
1942	Rogers formulated "client-centered therapy."
1943	Sarbin contrasted clinical versus statistical prediction.
1944	Clinical psychologists rejoined a reorganized APA.
1945	Thorne founded the *Journal of Clinical Psychology.*
1946	Cronbach described the problem of response sets in clinical assessment.
	Alexander and French described brief psychoanalytic therapy based on the "corrective emotional experience."
	National Institute of Mental Health, United States Public Health Service, and Veterans Administration began funding clinical training and service.
	Virginia became the first state to certify clinical psychologists.
	APA and American Psychiatric Association created a joint committee to promote cooperation.
1947	APA Committee on Training in Clinical Psychology reported training standards.
	Snyder reported an early study of the process of individual therapy.
	Halstead introduced a test battery for neuropsychological assessment.
	Peres reported an early study of the process of group therapy.
	American Board of Examiners in Professional Psychology (ABEPP) was established to certify professional psychologists.
1948	Lewin, Bradford, Benne, and Lippit introduced T-groups.
	Bettleheim and Sylvester popularized "milieu therapy."
	MacCorquodale and Meehl distinguished between hypothetical constructs and intervening variables.
	Hamlin and Albee reported one of the first quasi-experimental studies of therapy.
1949	Wechsler Intelligence Scale for Children was introduced.
	Salter described *Conditioned Reflex Therapy* in book of same name, forerunner of desensitization and assertiveness training.
	Boulder APA National Conference endorsed a scientist-practitioner training model.

1950   Dollard and Miller offered a synthesis of psychoanalysis and learning theory.

1951   Powers and Witmer reported one of the first controlled evaluations of counseling.

Perls introduced gestalt therapy.

1952   Eysenck criticized psychotherapy and therapy research.

1953   Frankl introduced logotherapy, an existential approach to therapy.

Warne et al. reported an early controlled study of a psychological intervention.

Skinner provided a blueprint for the application of operant conditioning to therapy and social change.

Sullivan described the "interpersonal" approach to psychotherapy.

1954   American Psychological Association published standards for psychological tests.

Meehl provided a seminal review of the clinical-statistical prediction issue.

Rogers and Dymond reported one of the first controlled studies of Rogerian therapy.

1955   Cronbach and Meehl described construct validity in clinical measurement.

U. S. Mental Health Study Act mandated a national health program and established the Joint Commission on Mental Health (JCMH).

1957–
1963   Cowen pioneered preventive psychological intervention.

1958   Ackerman described family therapy.

Wolpe pioneered desensitization in *Psychotherapy by Reciprocal Inhibition.*

Ellis introduced Rational Emotive Therapy.

1960   Fairweather et al. reported an early controlled study of milieu therapy.

1963–
1970   Masters and Johnson pioneered research on sexual therapy.

1963   Community Mental Health Centers Act evolved from the JCMH report.

1964   Berne introduced his book *Transactional Analysis* (TA).

Beck introduced cognitive therapy for depression.

1964–
1969   Fairweather pioneered experimental social innovation.

1965   Separate training for professional psychologists was first proposed.

Boston Conference on Community Mental Health was held.

1966   Paul reported one of the first controlled studies of behavior therapy.

1967   Rogers et al. reported one of the first controlled studies of individual therapy with schizophrenic clients.

1968   Behavioral assessment was sparked by Mischel and described by Goldfried and Pomeranz.

Langsley et al. reported major comparative outcome study of family therapy versus inpatient hospitalization.

Ayllon and Azrin introduced *The Token Economy* in book of same name.

1973   APA National Conference at Vail reaffirmed scientist-practitioner professional training but also endorsed Psy. D. training in clinical psychology.

Virginia and Maryland passed freedom of choice legislation providing insurance reimbursement for services provided by independent clinical psychologists.

1974   APA National Conference at Austin established standards for community psychology training.

1975   *Donaldson v. O'Connor* suit before Supreme Court established right of non-dangerous persons to treatment when confined.

1980   Fourth U.S. Circuit Court of Appeals decides against Blue Cross/Blue Shield's refusal to honor freedom of choice legislation.

RESOURCES

Garfield, S. L. (1983). *Clinical psychology.* New York: Aldine.
Kendall, P. C., & Norton-Ford, J. D. (1982). *Clinical psychology.* New York: Wiley.
Reisman, J. M. (1976). *A history of clinical psychology.* New York: Irvington.
Sahakian, W. S. (1975). *History and systems of psychology.* New York: Wiley.
Sundberg, N. D., Tyler, L. E., & Taplin, J. R. (1973). *Clinical psychology.* New York: Appleton-Century-Crofts.

Table A-5: Evolution of Social Work[1]

1843   The New York Association for Improving the Conditions of the Poor (AICP) was established and served as a model for many general relief societies in the 1840s and 1850s and also developed principles that approximated charity organizations. Visitors were expected to distinguish between the worthy and unworthy poor and to provide moral exhortation.

1863   Samuel Howe and Frank Sanborn provided the leadership for the founding of the Massachusetts State Board of Charities which became the forerunner of the public welfare system and which provided a base of operation for social work practice.

1886   The Neighborhood Guild was formed in New York under the leadership of Stanton Coit.

1887   S. H. Gusteen was instrumental in the formation of the Buffalo Charity

[1]The following reference was the primary source for the historical development of social work: Lubove, R. (1965). *The professional altruist: The emergence of social work as a career 1880–1930.* Cambridge: Harvard University Press. Reproduced by permission of Harvard University Press.

Organization Society in Buffalo, New York. It spread to about 125 cities in the United States with such leaders as Edward Devine and Mary Richmond. This organization provided for legitimate social work practices.

1889 The Hull House was formed in Chicago under Jane Addams. This settlement house and those of the Neighborhood Guild provided service to immigrants both individually and through community action.

1898 The New York Charity Organization Society inaugurated formal social work education by establishing its summer school of philanthropy, called New York School of Philanthropy.

1899 The Chicago Juvenile Court was founded. It was the first court to combine probation, separate hearings, and a special judge in legal treatment of youthful offenders.

1904 Adolf Meyer's wife became one of the first psychiatric social workers.

1905 Dr. Richard C. Cabot introduced medical social service at Massachusetts General Hospital to overcome the hospital's depersonalization and isolation from social sources of disease.

1906 The "visiting teacher" concept of casework was originated in New York City, followed quickly by other major cities. By 1913 boards of education began to provide official status to the visiting teacher whose function it was to socialize the school and individualize the child in response to the depersonalization of the public school.

1909 William Healy headed the Juvenile Psychopathic Institute in Chicago, a forerunner of child guidance clinics and a site for the early study of juvenile offenders. From Healy and his staff's research, multiple causes but no simple solutions were found to differential diagnosis of delinquency.

The National Committee for Mental Hygiene was founded by Clifford Beers, a former mental patient, which led to public enlightenment and legislative reform in mental patient treatment.

1912 Massachusetts General helped the Boston School of Social Work organize a 1-year course for medical social work that included 10 months of supervised hospital work and school lectures and conferences.

Henry Goddard's *The Kallikak Family: A Study in Heredity of Fee-blemindedness* alerted social workers to the role mental defects played in a client's difficulty.

1913 The Cleveland Federation was the first modern community chest (now the United Way) and marked the real beginning of the "federated" movement in the United States.

1915 Abraham Flexner's address to the National Conference on Charities and Corrections was "Is Social Work a Profession?"

1917 Mary Richmond's casework classic *Social Diagnosis* was published. It was to represent the beginning professionalization of social work on a scientific professional basis distinguishing social workers from volunteers.

World War I established the prestige and acceptance of psychiatry in the treatment of war neuroses and along with it that of psychiatric social work, whose workers functioned under the auspices of the Red Cross and the U. S. Public Health Service.

1918   The training school for psychiatric social work was established at Smith College under the auspices of the National Committee for Mental Hygiene. Casework also began to pass into a phase emphasizing psychological aspects of disability, and the study of personality versus the environment began to achieve a prominent role in social work. Jessie Taft predicted the eventual establishment of a "new psychological foundation for all case work."

The American Association of Hospital Social Workers (AAHSW) was founded under Mary Jarrett's leadership. It restricted members to paid workers and, in 1925, to graduates of schools of social work.

1919   The American Association of Visiting Teachers was organized.

The Association of Training Schools for Professional Social Work was organized, and was renamed in the 1920s as the Association of Professional Schools of Social Work (APSW).

1920   Minimum criteria for medical social workers were defined including knowledge of social elements of disease, major groups of diseases dealt with by hospitals, and problems of hygiene and public health.

By 1920 social workers had begun to extricate themselves from their earlier affiliations with philanthropy, charity, sentimentalism, and paternalism and had begun to accept a professional attitude and role of "authority and impersonal friendliness." In addition, the social worker had begun to view himself or herself as the professional representative of an agency rather than of the "middle class."

1921   The Division of Delinquency under the National Committee of Mental Hygiene was inaugurated by the Commonwealth Fund to find methods to prevent delinquency. The division worked closely with social agencies and hastened the acceptance of a psychiatric point of view among caseworkers. Many caseworkers received their training in child guidance clinics associated with the division's programs, and they were able to participate in the translation of mental hygiene from theory into reality.

The American Association of Social Workers (AASW) was organized growing out of the Intercollegiate Bureau of Occupations and the National Social Worker's Exchange. It formulated professional goals and standards of competence for social workers, and it embodied the vision of social work as a professional community with a singular function and generic skills.

1922   The psychiatric social workers created a section of psychiatric social work of the AAHSW and in 1926 it formed a separate American Association of Psychiatric Social Workers.

Mary Richmond wrote *What is Social Casework?* in which she set forth her theory of differential casework as the foundation of social work skill and technique and social evidence as a unique form of insight into personality.

1923   The high school in LaSalle, Illinois, established a Bureau of Educational Counsel with a psychiatric social worker in charge. Just as the child guidance social workers found the mother and family important in the mental hygiene of the child, so too the visiting teacher or school social worker found the teacher's attitude to be a significant factor in a student's school adjustment. Schools were viewed as a mental hygiene laboratory and a few schools began to hire school social workers.

1926   The American Association of Psychiatric Social Workers formed.

1927   The Institute for Child Guidance was established by the Bureau of Children's Guidance at the completion of the Commonwealth Fund's 5-year Division of Delinquency experiment. Child guidance became a highly sought service and the institute developed training programs for psychiatric social workers at the New York School of Social Work and Smith College where students were able to apply casework therapy under psychiatric supervision. Psychiatry influenced the practice and theory of social work through the child guidance clinics.

1929   The Milford Conference Report reflected the attitude of the social work leaders to accept a generic form of social casework regardless of the form it took in the different casework fields.

By 1929 community organization was largely dominated by and applied to social work agencies in order to coordinate the activities of these agencies toward greater efficiency.

1930   Virginia Robinson wrote *A Changing Psychology in Social Case Work.* Robinson was critical of the past functions of social workers and propounded a casework role based on the practice of psychotherapy rather than the sociologic manipulation of the environment.

1930s   George Stevenson and Lawson Lowrey actively promoted the mental hygiene point of view in social work. Wilhelm Rank and Jessie Taft championed "functional" casework through the Pennsylvania School of Social Work and Philadelphia children agencies and child guidance clinics, breaking with the Freudian emphasis and recommending limited therapy adapted to the "agency function and procedure." This functionalism served only to obscure rather than to clarify the social worker's distinctive function.

1932   The APASW adopted a minimum curriculum for the first graduate year of professional education.

1933   A National Committee on Volunteerism Social Work was created.

1936   The American Association for the Study of Group Work was formed to identify a distinct methodology for group work practice. Social group work emerged as a speciality within social work.

1939   The APASW based accreditation upon the establishment of 2-year graduate programs in social work, although provisions were made for institutions with 1-year programs that continued until 1952.

1952   The Council on Social Work Education (CSWE) was formed to accredit graduate social work education.

1955   The merger of the specialized social work organizations with the AASW led to the creation of the National Association of Social Workers (NASW).

1958   The "Working Definition of Social Work Practice" was published in 1958 from a unified effort to establish a domain for social work and to identify the common elements of the profession.

1960s   By the 1960s, social work had been restructured to incorporate the breadth of its practice activities. Nevertheless, because social work did not possess an adequate theoretical base to support a unitary approach to social work practice, the field continued to define practice in a somewhat circular manner by the methods that were used, such as casework, group work, and community organization. It was recognized, however, that many social workers used several methods in their practice and should be equipped to do so. Educational programs were organized to make it possible for students to become multimethod practitioners. (Morales and Sheafor, 1983, p. 10)

1974   The CSWE assumed accreditation of undergraduate baccalaureate programs in social work.

1978   *Guidelines for the Selection and Use of Social Workers* drafted by the NASW and approved for distribution.

1979–
1980   NASW *Task Force on Labor Force Classification.*

1981   *Guidelines* (noted previously) published in final form by the NASW. *Standards for the Classification of Social Work* published by the NASW. The Seventh Professional Symposium of the NASW was held, addressing the theme "Social Work Practice in a Turbulent World."

RESOURCES

Bracht, N. F. (Ed.). (1978). *Social work in health care.* New York: The Haworth Press.

French, L. M. (1940). *Psychiatric social work.* New York: The Commonwealth Fund.

Levine, M., & Levine, A. (1970). *A social history of helping services.* New York: Appleton-Century-Crofts.

Morales, A., & Sheafor, B. W. (1983). *Social work: A profession of many faces.* Boston: Allyn & Bacon.

Table A-6: Evolution of Industrial/ Organizational Psychology

1901   Walter Dill Scott introduced industrial psychology (I/O) into America by showing how psychology could be applied to advertising and selling.

1903   Dr. Walter Dill Scott published *The Theory of Advertising*—the first book that involved the application of psychology to business. Scott is considered to be the first industrial psychologist.

1911   Taylor wrote *Principles of Scientific Management* in which he pointed out the effects of social influence on production and rejected unionism. He also recommended the *Taylorizing of tasks,* a job design strategy in which all decisions were made in advance by management without any input from the worker. The repetitiveness of this approach in the modern assembly line has been related to poor motivation and physical problems.

1913   Hugo Munsterberg wrote *Psychology and Industrial Efficiency* in which he introduced psychology into the study of the worker. Some consider Munsterberg to be the first industrial psychologist.

Edward K. Strong, Jr., added the vocational guidance dimension to I/O psychology through his research on vocational interest.

1915   Walter Van Dyke Bingham established the first school of industrial psychology in America at the Carnegie Institute of Technology.

1917   The *Journal of Applied Psychology* was first published, and colleges began to offer applied psychology courses.

Whiting Williams wrote *What's on the Worker's Mind* and *Mainsprings of Men* which started an emphasis on studying the worker, an emphasis that remained until the 1960s.

1919   The first consulting psychology company, the Scott Company, was formed in Philadelphia.

The post World War I years produced industry's first interest in industrial psychology with several firms forming their own personnel research programs.

1921   The Psychological Corporation was the second psychological consulting enterprise formed. It was organized by Cattell and other prominent American psychologists.

1923   Scott and Clothier's *Personnel Management* was the standard work of the personnel movement, and its revised editions are still the standard.

1927   Mayo, Dickson, Roethlisberger, Homans, and Whitehead began the Hawthorne (Chicago plant of Western Electric) studies designed to determine the relations between conditions of work and employee reactions. These studies were to have a tremendous impact on the growth and development of industrial psychology.

1934   Viteles did early studies on the problems of the aging worker and warned against the stereotype that they are inefficient. He also recognized the need to reduce stress and its effect on fatigue and job satisfaction.

1935   Robert Hoppock pioneered job satisfaction research.

1937   The American Association for Applied Psychology was formed as the official organization of industrial psychology (later to become Division 14 of the American Psychological Association (APA)).

1939	Roethlisberger and Dickson published *Management and the Worker* based on the Hawthorne studies. It focused on the refinement of methodological approaches and the induction of new human behavior problems as others were resolved. The Hawthorne studies led to many changes in research methodology and in the focus of research. The studies began to show the need for indirect versus direct interviewing methods, a revised view of leadership, the importance of social organizations and their effect on production, and the problems involved in communication. The Hawthorne studies are considered by many to be the beginning of industrial counseling.

The first edition of the *Dictionary of Occupational Titles* was published by the U. S. Employment Service.

1941–1945	World War II became a major factor in the development of psychology in industry. Like psychologists in World War I, World War II psychologists also developed tests for screening and classifying recruits, developed selection programs for officers, did job analysis, and used performance evaluation techniques, among other services.
1948	Post–World War II saw the growth of several new APA divisions with industrial psychology interests: Division 19 (Military Psychology), Division 21 (the Society of Engineering Psychologists), and Division 23 (the Division of Consumer Behavior).

The Human Factors Society was a non-APA society formed after World War II to meet the needs of applied psychologists with interest in human engineering.

Personnel Psychology was first published. This journal included reports of psychological studies in training, job analysis, selection, evaluation, motivation, morale, work conditions, and equipment design.

1950	Likert emphasized the need for organizations to consider human resources as capital and to give as much attention to maintenance of human resources as is given to financial capital.
1952	Dr. Caroll Shartle published *Occupational Information* in which he demonstrated the need for occupational information in education, industry, and the community at large.
1954	Flanagan developed the critical incidents methodology which led to the identification of behavioral requirements of different jobs.
1956	The first assessment center in American industry was established. It was designed for research purposes only.
1957	Argyris described how formal organizations treated employees as children rather than mature adults.
1960	McGregor developed his Theory X and Theory Y of management.
1964	The passage of the Civil Rights Act contained within it equal employment opportunities (Title VII).
1965	Cronbach and Gleser emphasized the importance of utility in personnel decision making.

1966	The first Equal Employment Opportunity Commission (EEOC) "Guidelines on Employee Selection Procedures" were issued.
	Herzberg popularized the concept of job enrichment.
1967	Likert propounded a theory of participative management.
1971	John Campbell in his *Annual Review* chapter was most optimistic about the application of behavioral modification to industrial settings.
	In Griggs et al., a Duke Power Company case, the Supreme Court held that when a test has a disproportionate impact on minorities, then the burden of proof is on the employer to demonstrate that the test performance is related to job performance.
1972	Fleishman, McCormick, and Owens developed taxonomies of human performance that linked performance to task requirements.
1974	Stogdill completed an exhaustive literature search on leadership and concluded that research results were inconclusive.
	Hively applied domain (criterion) referenced testing to organizational psychology.
	Friedlander and Brown in their chapter in the *Annual Review* pointed out the importance of action research as an avenue for advancing knowledge in organizational psychology.
1975	Locke presented the results of management by objectives (MBO) research in the *Annual Review*.
1976	Publication of *Handbook of Industrial and Organizational Psychology*, edited by M. D. Dunnette.
1978	Levinson and colleagues established a basic model of adult development that included the notion that different variables become important in making career and job change decisions in different life stages.
	The Equal Employment Opportunity Commission published a "uniform" set of employment guidelines, defining standards for employment testing.
1980	The Division of Industrial-Organizational Psychology (APA-Division 14) published *Principles for the Validation and Use of Personnel Selection Procedures.* Employment appraisal extended from selection to promotion, advanced training, early retirement, and more.

RESOURCES

Bass, B. M. (1965). *Organizational psychology.* Boston: Allyn & Bacon.

Korman, A. K. (1971). *Industrial and organizational psychology.* Englewood Cliffs, NJ: Prentice-Hall.

Muchinsky, P. M. (1983). *Psychology applied to work.* Homewood, IL: The Dorsey Press.

Schein, E. H. (1980). *Organizational psychology.* Englewood Cliffs, NJ: Prentice-Hall.

Table A-7: Evolution of Psychiatric Nursing[1]

1873	Linda Richards graduated from the New England Hospital for Women and Children in Boston and was later called the first American psychiatric nurse because of her pioneer work in developing nursing care in psychiatric hospitals and for organizing nursing services and educational programs in state mental hospitals in Illinois. She was skilled in assessing the physical and emotional needs of her patients.
1882	McLean Hospital in Waverly, Massachusetts, opened. It was the first school to prepare nurses to care for the mentally ill. It had a 2-year program based primarily on custodial care with little attention given to psychological skills.
1800s	Until the end of the 1800s, psychological care of psychiatric patients consisted of being kind and tolerant to them and looking after their physical needs. The emotional and physical needs of patients were separated and nursing education reflected this insofar as nurses were taught either in the general hospital or the psychiatric hospital.
1913	Johns Hopkins was the first school of nursing to include a fully developed course for psychiatric nursing in their curriculum. However, it was not until the late 1930s that nursing education recognized the importance of psychiatric implications in all illnesses.
1933	A superintendent of nursing from a state hospital identified the three most pressing needs of psychiatric nurses at that time as more nurses, better prepared nurses, and cooperation and understanding of the nursing organizations.
1935	Insulin shock therapy was introduced for psychiatric patients.
1936	Psychosurgery was introduced. The somatic therapies made patients more amenable to psychotherapy, and nurses became more involved in the therapy and also began the struggle to define their role as psychiatric nurses.
1937	Electroconvulsive therapy was introduced.
1945	The post–World War II period was one of major growth and change in psychiatric nursing. The increase in treatment programs, especially the Veterans Administration hospitals, resulted in a significant increase in the need for psychiatric nurses with advanced preparation. Graduate programs, however, were still few in number.
1946	The National Mental Health Act was passed authorizing the National Institute of Mental Health to promote training and research of psychiatric and mental health personnel, including federal funding of nursing education.

[1]The following reference was the primary source for the historical development of psychiatric nursing: Stuart, G. W., and Sundeen, S. J. *Principles and practice of psychiatric nursing.* (2d ed.) St. Louis: C. V. Mosby, 1983. Reproduced by permission of the C. V. Mosby Company.

1947   By 1947 eight graduate programs in psychiatric nursing had been initiated.

M. O. Weiss published an article in the *American Journal of Nursing* in which she described "attitude therapy." The directed use of the nurse's attitude, she claimed, led to the patient's recovery. The nurse's therapy consisted of careful observation, treating the patient as a unique human being, and demonstrating acceptance, respect, and understanding. She believed that the physician, however, should prescribe the appropriate attitude.

1949   Santos and Stainbrook advocated that nurses should perform "psychotherapeutic tasks" and understand concepts related to therapy such as transference.

1950   The National League for Nursing required that nursing schools provide an experience in psychiatric nursing to be accredited.

Drug treatment for mental illness began in the early 1950s.

1951   Bennett and Eaton wrote an article in the *American Journal of Psychiatry* in which they identified three problems affecting psychiatric nurses: the scarcity of qualified psychiatric nurses, the limited use of their abilities, and the limited practice of psychiatric nursing in otherwise good psychiatric hospitals. Bennett and Eaton described the responsibilities of psychiatric nurses as including joining mental health societies, consulting with welfare agencies, working in occupational clinics, practicing preventive psychiatry, engaging in research, and helping to educate the public. The most controversial proposal was that psychiatric nurses should practice psychotherapy and that they should be a member of the psychotherapy team of psychiatrists, psychologists, and social workers.

1952   Peplau published *Interpersonal Relations in Nursing.* This was the first systematic theoretical framework developed for psychiatric nursing. In it she defined nursing as a "significant therapeutic process" and characterized the relationship by four overlapping and interlocking phases: orientation, identification, exploitation, and resolution. Peplau proposed the following roles for nurses: resource person, teacher, leader in local, national, and international situations, surrogate parent, and counselor.

1953   The National League for Nursing published "A Study for Desirable Functions and Qualifications for Psychiatric Nurses." The following desirable functions were included: (1) collecting data relevant to the problem, (2) making judgments regarding patient's behavior, (3) acting on the judgments to effect patient change, and (4) evaluating the process regarding the effectiveness of the intervention.

M. Jones published *The Therapeutic Community* in which he proposed that the patient's social environment should be used to provide the therapeutic experience. Therapeutic communities became the preferred environment for psychiatric patients and the psychiatric nurse's role was identified by Gregg in 1954 as that of assisting to create an environment in which the patient will be able to develop new behaviors and make a better adjustment to life. The nurse-patient relationship was expected to produce growth, which had not been found in the previous more custodial and protective environment. The introduction of psychotropic drugs in the 1950s also facilitated the development of the therapeutic community approach and increased the need for more therapists, thus further expanding the therapy functions of psychiatric nurses.

1955   The 1955 National Mental Health Study Act established the Joint Commission on Mental Illness.

1958   Hays conducted a review of the literature and reported that the following functions of psychiatric nurses were described: managing patient's problems of attitude, mood, feeling-tone, and interpretation of reality; exploring patient's disturbing and conflicting thoughts and feelings; facilitating psychophysiological homeostasis, counseling patients in emergencies, and strengthening the healthy components of the patient.

1962   Maloney published an article raising the question of independent functioning of psychiatric nurses. She identified one clear area of independent functioning as the management and supervision of a patient's environment; however, this function could be either therapeutic or mechanical and clerical depending on the goals of the nurse.

Peplau in "Interpersonal Techniques: The Crux of Psychiatric Nursing" identified the heart of psychiatric nursing to be in the role of counselor or psychotherapist. Other functions were considered to be subroles. Peplau also differentiated between the roles of general practitioners or staff nurses and psychiatric nurses. She stressed the unique clinical competence based on the interpersonal techniques of the graduate psychiatric nurse versus the staff nurse.

1963   Two new nursing journals were published: *Perspectives in Psychiatric Care* and the *Journal of Psychiatric Nursing and Mental Health Services* (changed to the *Journal of Psychosocial Nursing and Mental Health* in 1981). Both journals deal with psychiatric nursing practice.

Congress passed the Community Mental Health Centers Act of 1963 (P.L. 88-164). Federal monies were made available to states to plan, construct, and staff community mental health centers. Multidisciplinary treatment teams of many professionals were developed.

1965   Federal legislation extended funding for community mental health services through 1968.

1970   Community mental health funding was extended including funds for adolescents and children, for drug and alcohol abuse, and for mental health consultation.

1973   The Council of Specialists in Psychiatric and Mental Health Nursing of the American Nursing Association (ANA) published the *Standards of Psychiatric and Mental Health Nursing Practice* (revised in 1982).

1975   Amendments to the 1963 Community Mental Health Centers Act (Amendment P.L. 94-63) reemphasized the goals of the 1963 legislation and added seven additional mental health services: follow-up care, transitional (living arrangements), children and adolescent treatment and follow-up, screening, alcohol abuse, and drug abuse.

1976   The Council of Specialists in Psychiatric and Mental Health Nursing also published *The Statement on Psychiatric and Mental Health Nursing Practice,* which defined psychiatric nursing, identified types of practitioners, and described the scope of practice.

1978   The 1978 report of the President's Commission on Mental Health addressed some of the problems and inadequacies of the mental health services system. The report emphasized the need for community-based services that would include treatment and support services to include long- and short-term care, access to and continuity of care, coordination with the network of other human services (such as education and social services) to provide comprehensive care, adaptation to meet changing conditions and needs of special populations, and adequate financing with public and private funds. The report also stated that the tension among mental health professionals was detrimental to patient care. Increased funding was also proposed. This report was the first official high-level document to recognize the professional competence of nurses in mental health.

1979   *Issues in Mental Health Nursing* was published.

1980   The Mental Health Systems Act of 1980 was passed in support of the 1978 report of the President's Commission on Mental Health. This act represented a landmark piece of legislation because it established a federal role in mental health for the 1980s. The legislation focused on services for children, youth, the elderly, minority populations, and the chronic mentally ill. In 1981, however, the Reagan administration repealed this act and the 1982 budget severely cut federal funds for psychological and social services.

1982   Revision by the ANA of the *Standards of Psychiatric and Mental Health Nursing Practice* included both generalist and specialist practices.

1984   Koldjeski suggested differentiating the field of psychiatric nursing into three areas: community mental health nursing, mental health nursing, and psychiatric nursing.

1985   *The Clinical Specialist in Psychiatric Mental Health Nursing* was published. It was edited by D. L. Critchley and J. T. Maurin. New York: Wiley.

RESOURCES

Critchley, D. L., & Maurin, J. T. (1985). *The clinical specialist in psychiatric mental health nursing.* New York: Wiley.

Kalkman, M. E., & Davis, A. J. (1974). *New dimensions in mental health-psychiatric nursing.* New York: McGraw-Hill.

Manfreda, M. L., & Krampitz, S. D. (1977). *Psychiatric nursing.* Philadelphia: F. A. Davis Company.

Stuart, G. W., & Sundeen, S. J. (1983). *Principles and practice of psychiatric nursing* (2d ed.). St. Louis, MO: C. V. Mosby Company.

Table A-8: Evolution of Psychiatry

1773   The first public hospital exclusively for mental patients was established in Williamsburg, Virginia.

1783   Benjamin Rush joined the staff of physicians at the Pennsylvania Hospital in Philadelphia. This event is often referred to as the actual beginning of American psychiatry. He introduced "moral" treatment and was the first American physician to approach the investigation and treatment of mental disorders from a scientific viewpoint.

1800–
1860   Psychiatric activity was centered on the mental hospital. Emphasis was on description and classification of mental diseases, devising a "moral therapy," and studying brain anatomy.

1812   Rush published *Medical Inquiries and Observations upon Diseases of the Mind.* Principal remedies were purgatives, emetics, and bloodletting.

1838   Isaac Ray wrote the *Treatise on the Medical Jurisprudence of Insanity.* This book established Ray as a pioneer in medicolegal matters and forensic psychiatry.

1841   Dorothea Dix began her crusade to clean up the mental hospitals.

1844   The Association of Medical Superintendents of American Institutions was organized. It became the American Medico-psychological Association in 1893 and the American Psychiatric Association in 1921.

1860–
1920   The university psychiatric clinic became the center of psychiatric activity. The development of psychiatric systems was emphasized. From the study of neuroses, schools of dynamic psychiatry developed.

1869   George Beard introduced the concept of nervous exhaustion (neurasthenia).

1883   Emil Kraepelin published the first edition of *Psychiatrie,* which changed the entire classification of mental disorders.

1895   Freud replaced hypnosis with his method of free thought association and dream interpretation. Offshoots from Freudian thought resulted in modification theories by Jung, Adler, Rank, Stekel, Rado, Franz Alexander, Horney, and Harry Stack Sullivan.

The Pathological Institute of the New York State Hospitals was established. The establishment of the institute was the first large-scale attempt at psychiatric research.

Adolf Meyer recognized the school as an excellent place to detect and treat mental illness in children.

1905   J. H. Pratt introduced group psychotherapy in Boston, Massachusetts.

1908   The National Committee for Mental Hygiene (now called the National Committee for Mental Health) was organized. Its charter members included psychologists as well as psychiatrists.

1909	William Healy created child guidance clinics in Chicago. (The term child guidance clinic was not coined until 1922.)
1910–1941	Adolf Meyer was professor of psychiatry at The Johns Hopkins University. He formulated the reaction type of behavior and his concept of social adjustment. He brought the term "psychobiology" into the foreground.
1912	Elmer Southard developed the psychopathic hospital idea and also brought into the foreground the training of social workers in psychiatry.
1915	Harry Stack Sullivan and his associates systematically developed the theme of interpersonal relationships. They proposed that neuroses were products of cultural environment and distorted interpersonal relationships rather than being based on the preformed instincts, as Freud thought.
	Thomas W. Salmon demonstrated during World War I that psychiatry could contribute a great deal to the efficiency of the armed services by recognizing and treating the war neuroses.
1920s–1930s	Psychiatry entered the mainstream of social work theory and practice through the child guidance clinic.
1920–present	A psychiatric explosion occurred with tremendous widening of the field and development of subspecialties.
1930	W. Gantt founded the Pavlovian Laboratory at Johns Hopkins University.
1937	By this time an "American school" of psychiatry had developed that proceeded along the following lines in treating patients:

1 The correction of all recognized defects in the soma of the patient.
2 The establishment of adequate rapport between physician and patient.
3 The careful study and evaluation of familial, economic, and social situations.
4 The detailed investigation of the personality problem.
5 The attitude of adjustment to reality.
6 The ventilation of conflicts and desensitization of the patient.
7 The institution of reeducational training.
8 The formation of adequate philosophy of life.
9 The desirability of follow-up studies.

1930s	Insulin, metrazol, and electric convulsion shock therapies were introduced into the United States.
1942	The Vocational Rehabilitation Act was passed.
1946	F. Alexander and T. French in *Psychoanalytic Therapy* recommended shortening of psychotherapy.
	The National Mental Health Act was passed, which led to the creation of the National Institute of Mental Health.

1949	The Society for Clinical and Experimental Hypnosis was formed.
	The National Institute of Mental Health was begun, its purpose being research, training, and assistance in developing mental health programs.
1940s	W. Freeman and Y. Watts introduced psychosurgery into the United States.
1953	The introduction of the concept of "therapeutic community" by Jones in England led to greater patient involvement.
1955	The Mental Health Study Act was passed which provided for the creation of the Joint Commission on Mental Illness and Health.
1958	Nathan Ackerman published *The Psychodynamics of Family Life* and founded the Family Institute in New York City in 1960. Ackerman was a pioneer in family therapy.
1959	*Action for Mental Health* was published by the Joint Commission on Mental Illness and Health. This document was to pave the way for a shift from institutional to community care of the mentally ill.
1950s	Chemotherapy was introduced on a large scale for the treatment of the mentally ill.
1962	Maslow's *Toward a Psychology of Being* was representative of a "third force" in psychology, between behaviorism and psychoanalysis.
1963	The Community Mental Health Act was passed and in 1965 funds were allocated for staffing community mental health centers designed to offer a comprehensive program of prevention, treatment, and rehabilitation throughout the country.
1968	The *Diagnostic and Statistical Manual II (DSM II)* was published by the American Psychiatric Association.
1970s	E. R. Torrey of the National Institute of Health reported a general decline in the field of psychiatry marked by a decline of persons entering the field (e.g., 3300 graduates of psychiatric residency programs in 1972, 2900 in 1975); a decline in psychiatrists' employment in Veterans Administration and community mental health care (CMHC) settings (during 1970–1982, psychiatrists administering CMHCs declined by 50 percent); a decline of federal support (64 percent decline in real dollars since 1969); increased government regulation of psychiatric practice (e.g., required second opinions for electric convulsion therapy (ECT), citizen control groups); and a potential loss of status as a medical specialty.
1980	Publication of *DSM III* by the American Psychiatric Association.
	Publication of *Comprehensive Textbook of Psychiatry III* - in three volumes, edited by H. Kaplan, A. M. Freedman, and B. J. Sadlock.

RESOURCES

Alexander, F. G., & Selesnick, S. T. (1966). *The history of psychiatry.* New York: Harper & Row.

American Psychiatric Association. (1944). *One hundred years of American psychiatry.* New York: Columbia University Press.

Deutsch, A. (1959). *The mentally ill in America* (2d ed.). New York: Columbia University Press.

Kaplan, H. I., & Sadlock, B. J. (Eds.). (1985). *Comprehensive textbook of psychiatry/IV* (4th ed.). Baltimore, MD: Williams & Wilkins.

Kraepelin, E. (1962). *One hundred years of psychiatry.* New York: Philosophical Library.

Schneck, J. M. (1975). United States of America. In J. G. Howells (Ed.), *World history of psychiatry.* London: Baillière Tindall.

Wallace, E. R., & Pressley, L. C. (Eds.). (1980). *Essays in the history of psychiatry.* Columbia, SC: Wm. S. Hall Psychiatric Institute.

Zilboorg, G. (1941). *A history of medical psychology.* New York: W. W. Norton.

SOCIAL SERVICE RESOURCES FOR HUMAN SERVICES WORKERS

The services listed in this appendix deal with issues about which a helper might need information and referral sources. They are divided into broad content areas with subheadings listed in parentheses next to each category.

Many of the service agencies, groups, and governmental agencies have local offices which are listed in local telephone books or social service directories. If not, the national organizations can provide information concerning the appropriate local resources.

The U. S. government addresses which occur more than once in this appendix are listed separately at the end of the appendix. Listings and addresses appropriate to the agency referral source can be found under the U. S. listings.

There are many groups not covered in this appendix. These include, among others, those devoted to the environment, political action, citizen's actions, and community affairs. Complete listings for these and others can be found in *Social Services Organizations and Agencies Directory* and *The Help Book.*

Additionally, there are information offices in each state. To obtain information about any federal government program or service, one should write or call the Federal Information Center (FIC) in one's own state. Many states have toll-free numbers.

The following are the books from which this material was drawn and to which the reader should refer for greater detail:

Barkas, J. L. (1979). *The help book.* New York: Charles Scribner's Sons.
Conrad, James H. (1982). *Reference sources in social work, an annotated bibliography.* Metuchen, NJ: The Scarecrow Press.

Congressional Quarterly. (1985). *Washington information directory 1985–86.* Washington, DC: Author.

Gruber, K. (Ed.). (1985). *Encyclopedia of associations, 1986.* Detroit, MI: Gale Research.

Haimes, N. (Ed.). (1974). *Helping others: A guide to selected social services agencies and occupations.* New York: The John Day Co.

Kruzas, A. T. (Ed.). (1982). *Social service organizations and agencies directory.* (1st ed.). Detroit: Gale Research Co., Book Tower.

National Association of Social Workers. (1980). *Directory of agencies: U. S. voluntary, international voluntary, intergovernmental.* Washington, DC: Author.

National directory of private social agencies. (1983). Queens Village, NY: Croner Publications, Inc.

Romanofsky, P. (Ed.). (1978). *The Greenwood encyclopedia of American institutions, social service organizations.* Connecticut: Greenwood Press.

Weinstein, A. (Ed.). (1983). *Public welfare directory.* Washington, DC: American Public Welfare Association.

Services to Children (Adoption, Foster Care, Participation Groups)

All states have agencies for child protection and child advocacy.

U. S. Department of Health and Human Services
Administration for Children, Youth and Families
Information and referral requests.

National Center for Child Advocacy
Children's Bureau
Office of Child Development
P. O. Box 1182
Washington, DC 20013
Information clearinghouse.

Child Welfare League of America, Inc.
67 Irving Place
New York, NY 10003
(212) 254-7410

F.A.C.E., Inc. (Families Adopting Children Everywhere)
P. O. Box 28058, Northwood Station
Baltimore, MD 21239
National adoptive parents organization; information for home and abroad adoptions.

National Foster Parent Association
P. O. Box 7596
Hampton, VA 23666
Clearinghouse and activist organization for foster parents.

Big Brothers/Big Sisters of America
117 S. 17th St., Suite 1200
Philadelphia, PA 19103
See local telephone directory.

Boy Scouts of America
Girl Scouts of America
Boy's Clubs of America
See local telephone directory.

Services to the Elderly

Administration on Aging (AOA)
National Clearinghouse on Aging
Office of Human Development Services
U. S. Department of Health and Human Services
Health and Human Services—North Building
330 Independence Ave., S.W.
Washington, DC 20201
(202) 245-0724

American Association of Homes for the Aging
1050 17th St., N.W.
Washington, DC 20036
(202) 296-5960

American National Red Cross
17th and D Streets, N.W.
Washington, DC 20006

National Council on Aging, Inc. (NCOA)
600 Maryland Ave., S.W., West Wing 100
Washington, DC 20024
Information clearinghouse; there are several institutes within the organization.

National Senior Citizens Law Center (NSCLC)
1302 18th St., N.W., Suite 701
Washington, DC 20036
Helps the elderly resolve legal problems.

There are a variety of self-help groups, such as Gray Panthers, as well as agencies for which the volunteer services of elderly persons are needed. These can be located through the clearinghouses. Health care facilities as well as homemaker services can usually be identified through the groups listed above. The reader might check the local telephone directory for the nearest office. Each state has a Commission or Council or Office on Aging. For crimes against the elderly and what can be done, contact your police department.

Consumer Affairs

There is a consumer protection division in every state which serves as a consumer complaint clearinghouse and makes appropriate referrals. On the federal level, call 800-555-1212 for the toll-free telephone number of:

Consumer Affairs/Complaints
Director, Office of Consumer Affairs
U. S. Department of Health and Human Services
1725 I St., N.W.
Washington, DC 20201
(202) 634-4267

Civil Rights and Discrimination

Equal Employment Opportunity Commission
2401 E. St., N.W.
Washington, DC 20507
Contact the nearest district office to file charges of individual discrimination.

Office of Civil Rights
Health and Human Services—North Building
330 Independence Ave., S.W.
Washington, DC 20201
(202) 472-4256
Enforces civil rights laws.

U. S. Department of Labor
Employment Standards Administration
200 Constitution Ave.
Washington, DC 20210
Requires equal pay for equal work. Contact the nearest Wage and Hour Division Office in the U. S. Government section of the telephone book to file a written complaint of alleged discrimination.

American Civil Liberties Union (ACLU)
132 W. 43rd St.
New York, NY 10036
Information clearinghouse affiliates throughout the U. S., concerned with constitutional rights.

Anti-Defamation League of B'nai B'rith
823 United Nations Plaza
New York, NY 10017
Working against discrimination for all peoples.

Association on American Indian Affairs, Inc.
95 Madison Ave.
New York, NY 10016

Center for Constitutional Rights (CCR)
853 Broadway, Suite 1401
New York, NY 10003
Works with a variety of social movement groups and individuals in the legal defense of their constitutional rights.

International League for Human Rights
263 E. 46th St.
New York, NY 10017
A coalition of groups with broad concerns for human rights, including civil liberties groups such as ACLU, NAACP, and the American Jewish Committee affiliates.

National Association for the Advancement of Colored People (NAACP)
186 Remsen St.
Brooklyn, NY 11201
Working against segregation and discrimination. There are local groups in most cities throughout the U. S.

National Committee Against Discrimination in Housing (NCDH)
733 15th St., N.W., Suite 1026
Washington, DC 20005
A clearinghouse also providing legal information and advice.

National Urban League
500 East 62nd St.
New York, NY 10021
Working against discrimination in employment, education, housing, and social welfare; there are local groups in many cities throughout the U. S.

Operation P.U.S.H.
930 East 50th St.
Chicago, IL 60615
An outgrowth of the civil rights movement, this is an action-issue oriented group working with local people trying to deal with economic and political issues.

Women's Action Alliance, Inc.
370 Lexington Ave.
New York, NY 10017
An information clearinghouse and resource center against sex discrimination.

Working Women's Institute
593 Park Ave.
New York, NY 10021
An information clearinghouse on sexual harassment.

Crisis/Emergency Situations (Emergencies and Disasters, Missing Persons, Suicide Prevention)

Federal Disaster Assisting Administration (FDAA)
U. S. Department of Housing and Urban Development
Contact your state or regional office.

National American Red Cross
Disaster Relief Program
Contact your local office of the American Red Cross.

National Clearinghouse for Poison Control Centers
5401 Westbard Ave.
Bethesda, MD 20016

Poison Surveillance and Epidemiology Branch
Parklawn Building
Room 15B-23
5600 Fishers Lane
Rockville, MD 20857
There are local poison control centers throughout the U. S.

National Safety Council
444 North Michigan Ave.
Chicago, IL 60611
Information clearinghouse.

The Salvation Army.
See local telephone directory.

Center for Studies of Suicide Prevention
National Institute of Mental Health
Alcohol, Drug Abuse, and Mental Health Administration
Public Health Service
A government-sponsored education program in suicide prevention.

Local areas have suicide prevention centers, usually including a hotline.

Runaway Hotline
105 Sam Houston Building
Austin, TX 78711
Toll-free, 24 hours hotline: (800) 231-6946; in Texas, (800) 392-3352
Offers referrals and information for runaway youth around the country. This
provides a neutral channel through which to make contact with their families.

National Youth Work Alliance (NYWA)
1346 Connecticut Ave., N.W.
Washington, DC 20036
For information about runaway shelters. They work with youth services staff offering education and technical assistance.

Runaway Switchboard
2210 North Halsted
Chicago, IL 60614
Toll-free, 24 hour hotline: 800-621-4000
In IL: 800-972-6004
A liaison between parents and children. Services are completely confidential.
They make referrals to appropriate social service agencies.

Domestic and Personal Violence (Child Abuse, Spouse Abuse, Rape and Sexual Assault, Victims)

Child Abuse

Each state has a division or department of protective services.

National Center on Child Abuse and Neglect
U. S. Children's Bureau
U. S. Department of Health and Human Services
P. O. Box 1182
Washington, DC 20013
(202) 245-2859
Information clearinghouse.

Child Welfare League of America, Inc.
(See Services to Children)

Salvation Army

Odyssey Institute
817 Fairfield Ave.
Bridgeport, CT 06604
Child abuse and neglect information and clearinghouse, and research.

Parents Anonymous, Inc.
22330 Hawthorne Blvd., Suite 208
Torrance, CA 90505
Volunteer self-help group with professional assistance, education, and referral.

Spouse Abuse

Many local areas have shelters for battered women and their children. A local referral agency, Salvation Army, rape crisis center, or state department of family and
children's services would have this information.

Center for Women Policy Studies
2000 P. St., N.W., Suite 508
Washington, DC 20036
National information clearinghouse on sexual and physical abuse of women
and children.

Rape and Sexual Assault

Many local areas have a rape crisis center, rape crisis line, sexual abuse center, or the equivalent with information, referral, and support.

National Center for the Prevention and Control of Rape
National Rape Information Clearinghouse
National Institute of Mental Health
(See National listing) or
5600 Fishers Lane
Parklawn Building
Rockville, MD 20857
(202) 443-1910
Information and educational materials for rape prevention and treatment.

Center for Women Policy Studies (See *Spouse Abuse*)

Feminist Alliance Against Rape
P. O. Box 21033
Washington, DC 20009
International clearinghouse on issues related to violence against women, particularly rape and wife abuse.

Please note that there are victim witness and victim's assistance programs in many cities. Some states also have violent crime victim compensation programs.

Education

Each state has a department of education, a state superintendent of education, and each county has a superintendent and a board of education.

U. S. Department of Education
Secretary of Education
400 Maryland Ave., S.W.
Washington, DC 20202
For information on regional and local offices for direct services on educational matters.

Association for Childhood Education International (ACEI)
11141 Georgia Ave., Suite 200
Wheaton, MD 20902
Information clearinghouse on all education matters related to children, with branches throughout the country.

Employment

Each state has a department of labor where one can seek employment opportunities, a part of the U. S. Department of Labor. Each state has a workmen's compensation division or commission in case of a work-related injury.

JOBS Program
National Alliance of Business (NAB)
1015 15th St., N.W.
Washington, DC 20005
National effort to place disadvantaged youths in summer and part-time jobs.
Also work to place former offenders in permanent positions.

Family Services (Childbearing, Family Planning, Parenting, Sex Education and Therapy)

U. S. Department of Health and Human Services
Maternal and Child Health Service, Public Health Service and
National Clearinghouse for Family Planning Information.
Each provides information on family planning.
(See U. S. Government listings)

National Institute for Child Health and Human Development
Office of Research Reporting
National Institutes of Health
(See U. S. Government listings)

Education for Parenthood
National Center for Child Advocacy
U. S. Department of Health and Human Services
P. O. Box 1182
Washington, DC 20013
Children's Bureau
Administration for Children, Youth and Families
Information on various aspects of family life is available.

National Clearinghouse for Family Planning Information
U. S. Public Health Service
(See U. S. Government listings)
Offers a clearinghouse and information to the public about family planning and
sex education.

American Association of Sex Educators, Counselors, and Therapists
(AASECT)
11 Dupont Circle, N.W., Suite 220
Washington, DC 20036
An information clearinghouse and referral source.

Association for Voluntary Sterilization, Inc.
122 E. 42nd St.
New York, NY 10168

Birthright, U.S.A.
686 N. Broad St.
Woodbury, NJ 08096

The Compassionate Friends
P. O. Box 1347
Oak Brook, IL 60521
A national self-help group with local chapters throughout the country for be-
reaved parents who have lost a child or children.

National Genetics Foundation, Inc. (NGF)
555 W. 57th St.
New York, NY 10019

Planned Parenthood Federation of America, Inc.
810 Seventh Ave.
New York, NY 10019
(212) 541-7800
Information, guidance, and referral for all areas of family planning.

Reproductive Freedom Project
American Civil Liberties Union Foundation (ACLU)
132 W. 43rd St.
New York, NY 10030

Resolve, Inc.
P. O. Box 474
Belmont, MA 02178
Self-help support groups and referrals for infertile people.

Council For Sex Information & Education (CSIE)
Box 72
Capitola, CA 95010
A national clearinghouse on sexuality and related topics.

Zero Population Growth, Inc.
1346 Connecticut Ave., N.W.
Washington, DC 20036
A free referral source for birth control and venereal disease.

Health Concerns/Physical (General Health, Specific Illnesses, Food and Nutrition, Handicaps and Disabilities, Mental Retardation and Learning Disabilities)

Each state has a public health department.

Center for Studies of Schizophrenia
National Institute of Mental Health
5600 Fishers Lane
Rockville, MD 20857

The U. S. Department of Health and Human Services maintains the following divisions:

Alcohol, Drug Abuse, and Mental Health Administration
Center for Disease Control
Food and Drug Administration
Health Care Financing Administration
Health Resources Administration
Health Services Administration
National Institutes of Health

The reader can write to the director of public information at the appropriate agency.

Childhood Cancer Foundation
2025 I St., N.W., Suite 1011
Washington, DC 20006
Self-help for families of children and adolescents with cancer.

Make Today Count, Inc.
P. O. Box 222
Osage Beach, MO 65065
A national organization for persons with life-threatening illnesses and for their families.

The following is a partial listing of groups organized for specific illnesses:

American Cancer Society
American Diabetes Association, Inc.
American Heart Association
American Parkinson Disease Association
American Narcolepsy Association, Inc.
Anorexia Nervosa Aid Society, Inc.
The Arthritis Foundation
Better Sleep Council
Committee to Combat Huntington's Disease
Digestive Diseases Information Center
Epilepsy Foundation of America
Juvenile Diabetes Foundation
Leukemia Society of America, Inc.
Mended Hearts, Inc. (a national organization of recovered heart surgery patients)
Muscular Dystrophy Association
Myasthenia Gravis Foundation
National Association of Patients on Hemodialysis and Transplantation (NAPHT)
National Cystic Fibrosis Research Foundation
National Foundation for Ileitis and Colitis, Inc.
National Foundation of the March of Dimes
National Genetics Foundation
National Hemophilia Foundation (NHF)
National Multiple Sclerosis Society
National Operation Venus Program (venereal disease hotline, information, and referral)

National Psoriasis Foundation
National Retinitis Pigmentosa Foundation
National Sickle Cell Disease Research Foundation, Inc.
National Tay-Sachs and Allied Diseases Association, Inc.
Spina Bifida Association of America
United Ostomy Association

Food and Nutrition

The reader could contact their local agricultural extension service or the home economics department of a nearby college or university for information on various foods and nutrition.

Community Nutrition Institute
2001 S. St., N.W.
Washington, DC 20009
Information clearinghouse on food and nutrition.

U. S. Government Addresses:

U. S. Department of Agriculture
Food and Nutrition Service
3101 Park Center Dr.
Alexandria, VA 23302
(703) 756-3276
Contact with information and/or complaints about meat and poultry products; free booklets are available.

U. S. Department of Commerce
Consumer Goods and Services Division
Bureau of Domestic Commerce
Room 1104
Washington, DC 20203
Publishes booklets and fact sheets on various foods and condiments.

U. S. Department of Commerce Consumer Affairs
14th Street and Constitution Ave., N.W.
Washington, DC 20230
(202) 377-5001
Publishes booklets and fact sheets on various foods and condiments.

U. S. Department of Health and Human Services
Public Health Service
Food and Drug Administration
Office of Public Affairs
5600 Fishers Lane
Rockville, MD 20857
Offers pamphlets on food and drug safety, medical devices, cosmetics, biologics, and veterinary products.

National Association to Aid Fat Americans, Inc. (NAAFA)
P. O. Box 43
Bellerose, NY 11426
An organization to fight discrimination against fat people.

Overeaters Anonymous
2190 W. 190th St.
Torrance, CA 90504
A self-help group in all states modeled after Alcoholics Anonymous.

Weight Watchers International, Inc.
800 Community Dr.
Manhasset, NY 11030
Check local telephone book.

Handicaps and Disabilities

Each state maintains an office for rehabilitation or employment of the handicapped. They are titled differently in each state. Check your telephone book.

Clearinghouse on the Handicapped
Office of Handicapped Individuals
U. S. Department of Health and Human Services
200 Independence Ave., S.W.
Room 338D
Washington, DC 20201
Serves as a clearinghouse with a directory of national, state and local resources, information for the handicapped, and referrals for assistance.

Goodwill Industries of America (GIA)
9200 Wisconsin Ave.
Bethesda, MD 20814
Provides rehabilitation services in local communities.

Closer Look
1201 16th St., N.W.
Washington, DC 20036
A national information center for parents of children with mental, emotional, and physical handicaps; assistance in finding special programs, services, and resources; provides a link with local organizations.

American Foundation for the Blind

National Association for the Deaf

National Easter Seal Society of Crippled Children and Adults

National Foundation of the March of Dimes

United Cerebral Palsy Association, Inc.

Mental Retardation and Learning Disabilities

Contact your city or county department of mental retardation or education; contact the state department of mental retardation for information and referrals.

Association for Children and Adults with Learning Disabilities (ACLD)
4156 Library Road
Pittsburg, PA 15234
Information and referral to nearest local chapter.

Division of Mental Retardation
Council for Exceptional Children
1920 Association Drive
Reston, VA 22091
Information clearinghouse on educational programs for mentally retarded children.

Family Service Association of America
44 East 23rd Street
New York, NY 10010
Offers counseling through member agencies.

National Association of Private Residential Facilities for the Mentally Retarded
6269 Leesburg Pike, Suite B-5
Falls Church, VA 22044
(703) 536-3311

Association for Retarded Citizens
P. O. Box 6109
Arlington, TX 76011
See local telephone listing for the nearest chapter. Information clearinghouse.

National Society for Autistic Children
1234 Massachusetts Ave., N.W., Suite 1017
Washington, DC 20005

Orton Dyslexia Society
724 York Road
Baltimore, MD 21204
For the study and treatment of dyslexia.

Mental Health

Each state has a department of mental health and each county has a mental health unit.

Clearinghouse of Mental Health Information
National Institute of Mental Health
U. S. Department of Health and Human Services

Center for Studies of Schizophrenia
National Institute of Mental Health (see Health Concerns/Physical)
Information clearinghouse.

National Association for Rural Mental Health (NARMH)
425 Lowell Hall
Madison, WI 53706

National Council of Community Mental Health Centers
6101 Montrose Rd., Suite 360
Rockville, MD 20852
Information and job clearinghouse focusing on clinical, research, consultation, education, and administrative aspects of rural mental health.

National Mental Health Association (NMHA)
1021 Prince St.
Arlington, VA 22314
Information clearinghouse to promote citizen interest and activity on behalf of the mentally ill and for the cause of mental illness. Many local areas have chapters.

National Self-Help Clearinghouse
c/o Graduate Center, City University of New York
33 West 42nd St.
New York, NY 10036
For the exchange of information for self-help group members, self-help practitioners, and theoreticians.

National associations working in the area of mental health:

American Academy of Child Psychiatry
American Association of Marriage and Family Therapists (AAMFT)
American Association of Pastoral Counselors
American Association of Counseling and Development
American Orthopsychiatric Association, Inc.
American Psychiatric Association
American Psychological Association
American Mental Health Foundation, Inc.
Family Service Association of America (FSAA)
National Association of Community Health Centers
National Association of Prevention Professionals
National Association of Social Workers
Contact state offices of all of the above for information and referrals.

Offenders and Former Offenders (includes Juvenile Delinquency and Legal Rights)

Each state has a department of corrections and a board of parole (or equivalent).

U. S. Department of Justice
Bureau of Justice Assistance
633 Indiana Ave., N.W.
Washington, DC 20531

Bureau of Prisons
U. S. Department of Justice
320 First Ave., N. W.
Washington, DC 20534
(202) 724-3198

Office of Personnel Management
Recruitment and Job Information
1900 E. St., N.W.
Washington, DC 20415
Provides information on employment with the federal government.

American Bar Association
750 N. Lake Shore Drive
Chicago, IL 60611
Has several programs to help offenders and former offenders including Project
ADVOCATE and National Volunteer Parole Aide Program.

National Alliance of Business (NAB)
Ex-Offender Employment Program
(see Employment)

National Council on Crime and Delinquency
77 Maiden Lane
San Francisco, CA 94180
Sponsors a variety of local programs to help offenders and former offenders.

National Yokefellow Prison Ministry, Inc.
112 Old Trail North
Shamskin Dam, PA 17876
Provides counseling for incarcerated men and women; referrals to counselors,
lawyers, and other social services; conducts rap sessions; serves religious
needs; helps bridge the gap between inmates and the community; offers
emergency housing.

Prison Pen Pals
Box 82188
San Diego, CA 92138

Correctional Service Federation, U.S.A.
436 W. Wisconsin Ave.
Milwaukee, WI 53203
Affiliated with the International Prisoners Aid Association. Coordinates services
to prisoners and former inmates. Information clearinghouse about volunteer
correctional service agencies.

Salvation Army

Jaycees

Juvenile Delinquency

Each state has a department related to juvenile delinquency such as a department of corrections, division of youth services, or equivalent.

Legal Rights

Juvenile Rights Project
American Civil Liberties Union
132 W. 43rd St.
New York, NY 10036
National information clearinghouse. Contact the local ACLU office for direct assistance.

Legal Aid and Defenders Society
Each person has a right to an attorney. Contact the local legal aid society or state public defender office.

Safety

Each state has a division of occupational safety. In addition, federal offices include the National Safety Council, U. S. Consumer Product Safety Commission, Occupational Safety and Health Administration, and the National Highway Safety Administration.

Self-Help Groups

There are many self-help groups throughout the United States, such as Divorce Anonymous, Alcoholics Anonymous, Parents Without Partners, and The Compassionate Friends. To find the self-help group most appropriate to the individual's needs, contact the National Self-Help Clearinghouse and/or the local university, mental health center, family counseling center, or women's center for self-help groups in one's own area.

National Self-Help Clearinghouse
Graduate School and University Center/CUNY
33 West 42nd St., Room 1227
New York, NY 10036
For information about self-help groups throughout the country.

Gamblers Anonymous
1543 W. Olympic Blvd., Suite 533
Los Angeles, CA 90015
Modeled on Alcoholics Anonymous.

Homosexual Information Center
6758 Hollywood Blvd., Suite 208
Los Angeles, CA 90028
National information clearinghouse.

Social Welfare (Financial Assistance, Housing)

Each state has a department of social services, welfare department, or equivalent which provides various kinds of support payments for those in need. The requirements to be accorded assistance vary from state to state and one should check with the county office of the department.

Aid to Families with Dependent Children (AFDC)
Assistance Payments Administration
2100 2nd St., S.W.
U. S. Department of Health and Human Services
Washington, DC 20201

Food Stamp Program
U. S. Department of Agriculture
Food and Nutrition Services
3101 Park Center Drive
Alexandria, VA 22302
Applications for food stamps are available from the Food Stamp Certification office in each county of the U. S.

Social Security Administration
U. S. Department of Health and Human Services
6401 Security Boulevard
Baltimore, MD 21235
Applications should be made to the local Social Security office.

National Center for Urban Ethnic Affairs (NCUEA)
P. O. Box 33279
Washington, DC 20033
Information and clearinghouse providing technical assistance and support activities for revitalizing neighborhoods.

National Committee Against Discrimination in Housing (NCDH)
733 15th St., N.W., Suite 1026
Washington, DC 20005
Information clearinghouse.

U.S. Department of Housing and Urban Development (HUD)
451 Seventh St., S.W.
Washington, DC 20410
Direct inquiries to the nearest office.

Substance Abuse (Alcohol, Drugs, Smoking)

Each state has an alcohol and drug program usually located in the department of mental health, health or human resources, or equivalent.

Alcohol

Alcoholics Anonymous, Inc. (AA)
General Service Office
468 Park Ave. S
New York, NY 10016
(212) 686-1100
Al-Anon and Alateen, (P. O. Box 182, Madison Square Station, New York, NY 10010) are part of the umbrella organization. There are local chapters through-out the U. S.

National Clearinghouse for Alcohol Information
1776 E. Jefferson St.
Rockville, MD 20852

National Council on Alcoholism, (NCA)
12 W. 21st St.
New York, NY 10010
Clearinghouse with local offices. Provides education on alcoholism.

The Salvation Army
Contact your local affiliate.

Drugs

Food and Drug Administration
U. S. Department of Health and Human Services
Public Health Service
To complain about specific drugs.

National Clearinghouse for Drug Abuse Information (NCDAI)
Linked to the Alcohol, Drug Abuse and Mental Health Administration and the National Institute on Drug Abuse (NIDA)
5600 Fishers Lane
Rockville, MD 20857

Families Anonymous
P. O. Box 528
Van Nuys, CA 91408
A national organization with local branches. A self-help group based on the principles of AA.

Odyssey Institute (Child Welfare)
817 Fairfield Ave.
Bridgeport, CT 06604
Provides research, education, and childrens' advocacy programs on issues of serious concern to children such as giftedness and child abuse. Has children's resource library. Also offers addresses for educational services and family cooperatives. Runs a number of drug abuse treatment programs in Louisiana, Minnesota, New Hampshire, New York, and Utah.

Smoking

American Cancer Society
777 Third Ave.
New York, NY 10017
(212) 371-2900

American Heart Association
7320 Greenville Ave.
Dallas, TX 75231
(214) 750-5300

American Lung Association
1740 Broadway
New York, NY 10019
(212) 245-8000

Veterans

There are many national military organizations listed in the United States Almanac which are too numerous to name here.

Veterans Administration (VA)
Information Service
810 Vermont Avenue, N.W.
Washington, DC 20420
For information on referrals, benefits, and more. A toll-free number is available to 90 percent of the population. Call 800-555-1212 for that number. Most cities, counties, and states have a department of veteran's affairs.

American Friends Service Committee (AFSC)
1501 Cherry St.
Philadelphia, PA 19102
Maintains ten regional offices.

Central Committee for Conscientious Objectors (CCCO)
National Headquarters
2208 South St.
Philadelphia, PA 19146
An agency for military and draft counseling.

Fellowship of Reconciliation (FOR)
P. O. Box 271
Nyack, NY 10960
National education project in nonviolence and peace.

National Interreligious Service Board for Conscientious Objectors (NISBCO)
800 18th St., N.W., Suite 600
Washington, DC 20006
Provides professional counseling and literature for anyone interested in conscientious objectors.

The American Legion

Disabled American Veterans (DAV)

Paralyzed Veterans of America (PVA)

Volunteers

There are a myriad of volunteer programs and groups throughout the United States. A local information and referral agency or family counseling center could be helpful in locating the appropriate volunteer group to meet individual needs, be it for assistance or to become a volunteer.

Volunteer—The National Center for Citizen Involvement (VNCCI)
111 N. 19th St., Suite 500
Arlington, VA 22209
Provides information, consultation, assessment, evaluation, and training to the leaders of volunteer programs in all human service areas. Seeks to encourage citizen involvement and volunteer administration.

Volunteers of America
National Headquarters
340 West 58th St.
New York, NY 10024

U. S. Government Addresses

National Institute for Child Health and Human Development
Office of Research Reporting
9000 Rockville Pike, Room ZA-32
Bethesda, MD 20205

U. S. Department of Agriculture
Food and Nutrition Service
3101 Park Center Drive
Alexandria, VA 22302
(202) 756-3276

U. S. Department of Agriculture
Science and Education Administration
Technical Information Systems
Food and Nutrition Information Center
National Agricultural Library Building
Beltsville, MD 20705
Books, journal articles, audiovisual materials, and other items dealing with food and nutrition.

U. S. Department of Education
Special Education and Rehabilitation Services
Office on Information and Resources for the Handicapped
Clearinghouse for the Handicapped
330 C. St., S.W.
Washington, DC 20202
(202) 732-1723

U. S. Department of Health and Human Services
Administration for Children, Youth and Families
P. O. Box 1182
Washington, DC 20013

U. S. Department of Health and Human Services
Health Services Administration
Bureau of Community Health Services
Maternal and Child Health Office
5600 Fishers Lane
Rockville, MD 20857

U. S. Department of Health and Human Services
National Clearinghouse for Family Planning Information
P. O. Box 2225
Rockville, MD 20852
(301) 881-9400

U. S. Department of Health and Human Services
Public Health Service
200 Independence Ave., S.W.
Washington, DC 20201
(202) 245-6867

U. S. Department of Health and Human Services
Public Health Service
Alcohol, Drug Abuse, and Mental Health Administration
Parklawn Building
5600 Fishers Lane
Rockville, MD 20857
(301) 433-3783

U. S. Department of Health and Human Services
Public Health Service
National Institutes of Health
9000 Rockville Pike
Bethesda, MD 20205
(301) 496-5787

U. S. General Services Administration
Office of Consumer Affairs
Consumer Information Center
Pueblo, CO 81009
Publishes *Consumer Information Catalog.*

SAMPLE TRAINING MODULE

Earlier, in chapters 9 through 12, we provided examples demonstrating how the Life-Skills Training Model could be implemented in the settings of home, school, work, and community. Now we would like to illustrate a more detailed approach to creating training modules. The earlier and the present styles of operationalizing Life-Skills Training are similar, and, of course, both are appropriate. The present style is included (1) to make more obvious the steps used in creating the previous examples and (2) to illustrate a style that in its systematization may be more useful for those who are involved in ongoing, comprehensive preventive or remedial programs.

In order to develop the training units/exercises, the trainer makes an assessment of the level of functioning of a given group on the life-skills appropriate to their age group. Next, the appropriate descriptors are operationalized into goals or objectives; then appropriate activities and materials are incorporated into the unit and subsequently into each lesson within a unit. An evaluation is developed for each unit, so that "student" areas of weakness can be identified; additional practice is provided until the weakness is overcome.

Within a given lesson, an attempt is made to devote at least half of the time to practice and to keep the didactic component to a minimum. Furthermore, each training/class session is devised so that the training modalities will relate to the auditory, visual, and kinesthetic styles of learning and, when relevant, include the cognitive and affective components of Bloom's taxonomy (1956). Homework or extended practice beyond the training period is frequently included to facilitate the generality of the new response(s).

In keeping with our purposes in this appendix, the following is provided as a detailed example of the translation of life-skill descriptors (goals/objectives), obtained from the national Delphi study, into a skills training unit for a generic life-skill. The life-skill utilized is Interpersonal Communication/Human Relations. This example represents only one training (class) period for grades 3, 4, and 5. Although this example has been developed for elementary school children, the same descriptors can be applied to adolescents and adults; however, the exercises were developed to be relevant for the given age group. A comprehensive training program would include training units involving all of the life-skills descriptors (goals/objectives) for all age groups.

I Life Skill: Interpersonal Communication/Human relations

II Unit 1: Introduction to Communication

III Session 1: Introduction to Communication

IV Learner's Objectives: Communicates affect through language
> Works and plays cooperatively with peers
> Follows or leads in a group depending upon circumstances
> Listens attentively to others

V Grade 3

  A Activity 1: Mini-Lecture/Discussion, "What is Communication?" Say the following or, using your own words, convey the same ideas: "Today we are going to start talking about what communication is and how we communicate with each other. We will be spending much of our time learning what good communication is and practicing how to do it." Using the following question(s) or questions of your own that are similar, discuss the following topics:

    1 "What do you think communication means?" (Write "communication" on the chalkboard and list responses underneath it.) Emphasize, from the examples, that communication is a process of giving (sending) messages and getting (receiving) messages.

    2 "What are some ways we communicate?" (List responses on chalkboard.) Show that these responses represent the way we *give* messages.

    3 "What are the ways we get messages from others?" (List responses on chalkboard—Alternative question: "What senses do we use to get messages?") Show that many senses are used to get messages. Then say the following: "A message is made up of the words we use, the way we sound, the way we look, and the way we move. Whether we are giving a message or getting a message, each of these things—words, sounds, expressions, and gestures—is important."

  B Activity 2: Gossip. Divide the students into groups of about eight. Line up each group. Instruct students that the first student in each line will be whispered a message by you only once. Then each student is responsible for whispering the same message, only once, to the next person in line. The last student in each line will say the message out loud. An example of a message is: "My fluffy white dog likes to eat liver and chocolate when she goes for a ride in the boat" or "My goldfish would rather watch TV than listen to me read a story because the jokes are funnier when you can see them." Each can be given the same message or a different message. After the last person in line has given the message out loud, compare that message with the original message(s). Point out that each student did two things: get a message and give a message. Discuss how easy it was to distort a message and suggest that through these activities, they will practice being better communicators.

C Activity 3: Verbal and Nonverbal Components of Messages. Divide the class into dyads. The first student in each dyad will pick a message that they will first gesture (signal) to their partner, then write to their partner, and finally speak to their partner. Examples: "hello," "goodbye," "come here," "I love you." Model an example of this for the students. When the first student is done, have the students reverse roles. Discuss the activity in terms of the different verbal and nonverbal channels of communication.

D Summary and Homework: Review the concepts of giving and getting messages and verbal and nonverbal channels of communication. For homework, have students watch TV for 5 minutes without sound and 5 minutes with sound but with no picture (with their backs facing the TV) with instructions to note the differences between the two.

VI Grade 4

A Activity 1: Use Mini-Lecture/Discussion from Grade 3.

B Activity 2: Gossip. Use Activity 2 from Grade 3, substituting these messages: "When we want Mom to listen to us, my brother and I pretend to argue about chocolate chip cookies, but only when they're made with oatmeal." "My father drove his purple car to the fire station, then rode to work on the green truck, holding the Dalmation in one hand and a balloon in the other."

C Activity 3: Verbal and Nonverbal Components of Messages. Use Activity 3 from Grade 3.

D Summary: Same as Grade 3.

E Homework: Make a list of how your family sends you messages and how you send messages to your family.

VII Grade 5

A Activity 1: Use Mini-Lecture/Discussion from Grade 3.

B Activity 2: Gossip: Use Activity 2 from Grade 3, substituting appropriate messages, such as: "We would have won the soccer game, but the opposing team had a spotted goat butting the ball and our players." "While I was watching the movie, an elephant sat in the seat next to me and shared her peanuts with me, then she ate my popcorn."

C Activity 3: Verbal and Nonverbal Components of Communication. Have students sit in a circle. Give each student a card with one feeling written on it (e.g., furious, confused, happy, terrified). Have each student act out that feeling without using words. The rest of the students guess that feeling. Continue around the circle and then discuss what it is like to communicate without words. Stress that even when we use words, we also use other ways—voice tone, gestures, expression—to communicate as well.

D Summary: Same as Grade 3.

    E Homework: Have each student watch 10 minutes of TV with the sound off. Have students write down what happened, what feelings were expressed, and how they knew they were expressed.

VIII Resources

    A Grade 3: Chalkboard, chalk.

    B Grade 4: Chalkboard, chalk.

    C Grade 5: Chalkboard, chalk, cards with feeling words.

  IX Learning Styles: Auditory, visual, kinesthetic.

   X Bloom's Taxonomy:

    A Cognitive: Knowledge, comprehension, application, analysis.

    B Affective: Receiving, responding.

REFERENCE

Bloom, B. S. (Ed.). (1956) *Taxonomy of educational objectives: The classification of educational goals, by a committee of college and university examinees.* New York: Longmans, Green.

INTERPERSONAL COMMUNICATION/HUMAN RELATIONS SKILLS

The items in this appendix are taken from the national Delphi study that identified life-skills descriptors for childhood, adolescence, and adulthood, and grouped these descriptors into generic categories. The list is not exhaustive, but it is comprehensive in its coverage. The descriptors below were judged by panels of experts who then assigned them to the categories. Where possible, normative age ranges are attached to the descriptors that indicate the approximate time in a person's life when the skill is usually acquired.

Interpersonal Communication/Human Relations Skills

Definition: Skills necessary for effective communication, both verbal and nonverbal, with others, leading to ease in establishing relationships; small and large group and community membership and participation; management of interpersonal intimacy; clear expression of ideas and opinions; giving and receiving feedback; and so forth.

Descriptor

In childhood, the individual:

Functions with age-appropriate independence outside the home (ages 2 through 4).

Understands and acts on established rules of conduct (ages 2 through 4).

Masters social tasks within one's immediate environment (ages 2 through 5).

Interacts with age-mates (ages 2 through 5).

Communicates affect through language expression (ages 2 through 7).

Differentiates positive and negative feedback (ages 2 through 7).

Accords equal justice to one's peers and oneself (ages 2 through 7).

Gives and receives affection in appropriate ways (ages 3 through 6).

Follows or leads in a group depending upon the circumstances.

Develops meaningful relationships with age-mates.

Maintains relationships with peers.

Relates to members of both sexes in play situations (ages 4 through 6).

Responds with affect to peers and adults in an age-appropriate fashion (ages 4 through 10).

Develops and nurtures peer relationships (ages 4 through 10).

Recognizes other points of view (ages 4 through 10).

Meets personal goals through cooperative play (ages 5 through 7).

Works and plays cooperatively with peers (ages 6 through 8).

Uses interpersonal skills in social situations (ages 6 through 14).

Values personal privacy and respects that of others (ages 7 through 8).

Applies abstract principles such as fairness to interpersonal relations (ages 7 through 9).

Values democratic processes in group decisions (ages 7 through 11).

Understands and follows rules in games (ages 7 through 11).

Views interpersonal relations from the perspective of others (ages 7 through 12).

Establishes primary identification with peers (ages 8 through 10).

Values others for their own sake.

Listens attentively to others.

Responds empathetically to others.

Resolves interpersonal disputes through negotiation.

Finds "no-lose" solutions to conflicts.

Differentiates assertiveness from aggression.

Differentiates competition from conflict.

Differentiates leadership from dominance.

In adolescence, the individual:

Responds with empathy to the problems of others (ages 8 through 10).

Is able to initiate, maintain, and, when appropriate, terminate friendships (ages 8 through 10).

Understands and accepts as healthy the interpersonal communication of sexual attraction (ages 8 through 11).

Utilizes language to represent complex concepts with increasing accuracy (ages 9 through 13).

Employs perspective-taking in interpersonal situations (ages 10 through 13).

Understands that accomplishment of group goals may require compromise and reevaluation of personal goals (ages 10 through 13).

Forms interpersonal relationships based on mutuality and respect for individual identity (ages 10 through 15).

Relates positively with significant persons in one's immediate environment (ages 10 through 15).

Undertakes cooperative enterprises involving individual responsibility (ages 11 through 12).

Is independent in many relationships (ages 11 through 14).

Shows reasonable respect for legitimate authority (ages 11 through 14).

Understands the value of social order (ages 11 through 14).

Appreciates diversity in personalities and activities (ages 11 through 15).

Is able to resolve conflicting loyalties.

Tolerates differences of opinion without being afraid of holding to a divergent view.

Appreciates a sense of community with peers (ages 11 through 15).

Relates comfortably with members of the opposite sex (ages 12 through 14).

Is able to be objective about relationships (ages 12 through 16).

Responds reciprocally in interpersonal relationships (ages 13 through 16).

Appreciates laws as necessary for the maintenance of order while questioning those that are unjust (ages 14 through 16).

Understands and resolves ambiguity in peer-group values (ages 14 through 18).

Understands and acts in accordance with situationally appropriate social customs (ages 14 through 18).

Is open to the opinions and actions of others.

Is assertive in interpersonal relationships.

Copes successfully with peer pressure.

Selects appropriately from one's repertoire of interpersonal skills as situations and groups change (ages 15 through 17).

Recognizes the feelings and motives behind interpersonal actions.

Conducts oneself in social group situations with poise and confidence.

Appreciates the problems and uniquenesses of one's parents.

Understands to some degree the problems and difficulties of others.

Responds to the feelings of others and is able to express one's own feelings.

Develops support from peer relationships (ages 16 through 18).

Initiates and nurtures mutually satisfying sexual relationships (ages 17 through 20).

Appreciates one's similarity to others (peers) rather than feeling one is an outsider.

[NOTE: In the following items age ranges become much less normative than is the case for childhood and adolescence. The systematic study of adult development and aging is a much newer branch of the behavioral sciences than the life periods that precede it. The literature is therefore much less specific about when certain life-skills are acquired.]

In adulthood, the individual:

Relates to others with appropriate openness (young adulthood).

Manages intimacy with close friends (young adulthood).

Uses one's peer group for support while still maintaining one's individual autonomy (young adulthood).

Chooses relationships that are based on more than physical attractiveness (young adulthood).

Maintains continuous satisfying relationships with family members (young adulthood).

Is able to commit to a long-term relationship with a partner (young adulthood).

Forms close relationships based on interdependence (young adulthood).

Gets along with both superiors and peers on the job (young adulthood).

Communicates one's wants and needs effectively (young adulthood).

Identifies and forms relationships with potential mentors (young adulthood).

Utilizes interpersonal skills to expand the circle of one's relationships (young adulthood).

Is able to listen so well to another that one's response reflects the original statement in both content and affect (young adulthood).

Tolerates and respects those of different backgrounds, habits, values, and appearance (young adulthood).

Behaves in a marriage relationship so as to balance giving and getting (young adulthood).

Utilizes one's personal freedom to make judgments and decisions that are harmonious with the public good (young adulthood).

Assumes responsibility as a community member (young adulthood).

Manages conflicts on the job and at home (young adulthood).

Is able to give and take (young adulthood).

Is able to engage in a mentoring relationship (young adulthood).

Is able to establish and enjoy relationships within social groups (young adulthood).

Undertakes adult civic and social responsibilities (young adulthood).

Maintains intimacy with partner during child-rearing years (young adulthood).

Relates effectively with one's aging parents (young adulthood).

Contributes to the welfare of others (young adulthood).

Relates empathetically and effectively to one's children (if any) at all developmental stages (early middle age).

Recognizes and respects the individual rights, personal worth, and uniqueness of others (early middle age).

Copes effectively with the possible dependence of one's aging parents (early middle age).

Draws on one's reservoir of experiences in understanding broad social issues and community concerns (middle age).

Is able to be at peace with others (middle age).

PROBLEM-SOLVING/
DECISION-MAKING SKILLS

The items in this appendix are taken from the national Delphi study that identified life-skills descriptors for childhood, adolescence, and adulthood, and grouped these descriptors into generic categories. The list is not exhaustive, but it is comprehensive in its coverage. The descriptors below were judged by panels of experts who then assigned them to the categories. Where possible, normative age ranges are attached to the descriptors that indicate the approximate time in a person's life when the skill is usually acquired.

Problem-Solving/Decision-Making Skills

Definition: Skills necessary for information seeking; information assessment and analysis; problem identification, solution, implementation, and evaluation; goal setting; systematic planning and forecasting; time management; critical thinking; conflict resolution; and so forth.

Descriptor

In childhood, the individual:

> Is able to develop and carry out a complex intention.
> Employs fantasy and role playing regarding future vocational aspirations.

Chooses activities suited to interests.

Expands cognitive and sensory understanding by exploring the immediate environment (ages 2 through 4).

Makes perceptual judgments involving one variable (ages 2 through 7).

Utilizes intuition in making judgments (ages 4 through 7).

Utilizes objective data in making judgments (ages 4 through 7).

Anticipates possible consequences of actions through personal reflection (ages 4 through 10).

Understands and relates tasks to goal achievement (ages 5 through 7).

Formulates future plans on a limited basis (ages 5 through 9).

Is able to be goal-directed (ages 5 through 9).

Sticks with tasks to completion (ages 6 through 7).

Makes choices that take personal abilities into account (ages 6 through 10).

Understands age-appropriate cognitive tasks (ages 7 through 8).

Evaluates one's actions and those of others by the perceived intentions, not just by the consequences (ages 7 through 11).

Follows directions in situations involving multiple tasks (ages 7 through 11).

Is able to read for pleasure.

Chooses and participates in activities that are fun.

Tries new methods of problem solving (ages 8 through 9).

Utilizes logical thinking in investigations (ages 8 through 10).

Understands cause and effect relationships (ages 8 through 10).

Is able to work independently on a task (ages 9 through 10).

Is able to reverse cognitive operations (ages 9 through 10).

Uses cognitive and perceptual processes in problem solving (ages 9 through 10).

In adolescence, the individual:

Makes logical deductions in problem solving (ages 9 through 13).

Can manipulate and apply abstract ideas in problem solving (ages 9 through 13).

Analyzes and applies multiple reference systems to problem-solving tasks (ages 11 through 12).

Learns and uses an effective approach to decision making.

Maintains balance between awareness of one's own opinions and those of others in making decisions (ages 11 through 14).

Uses role models to learn about occupations (ages 11 through 17).

Identifies and defines personal problems and goals (ages 14 through 18).

Develops personal talents and considers implications for life planning (ages 14 through 18).

Takes directions and follows through on tasks.

Gathers reliable information about occupations (ages 14 through 18).

Is able to compare and analyze patterns of thought (ages 14 through 18).

Is able to analyze multiple variables in problem solving (ages 14 through 18).

Systematically explores a broad range of potential occupational choices (ages 14 through 18).

Distinguishes between supported opinions and those without support (ages 14 through 18).

Is able to do critical task analysis as an initial step in problem solving (ages 15 through 16).

Narrows one's range of potential occupational choices after having engaged in thorough exploration (ages 16 through 18).

Makes and implements informed educational decisions (ages 16 through 19).

Demonstrates personal values as the basis for making decisions.

Is able to dispute irrational beliefs or ideas.

Generates alternative problem solutions based on pertinent information (ages 17 through 19).

Is flexible in decision making (ages 17 through 19).

Anticipates consequences of actions and decisions affecting occupational choice (ages 17 through 19).

Utilizes experiences in trial, simulated, and part-time work in analyzing tentative occupational choices (ages 17 through 19).

Makes appropriate educational and occupational plans and decisions at critical points in one's career (ages 18 and over).

Makes tentative plans and action steps toward implementing occupational choices (ages 18 and over).

Plans and implements occupational choice (ages 18 and over).

[NOTE: In the following items age ranges become much less normative than is the case for childhood and adolescence. The systematic study of adult development and aging is a much newer branch of the behavioral sciences than the life periods that precede it. The literature is therefore much less specific about when certain life-skills are acquired.]

In adulthood, the individual:

Makes personally appropriate educational and occupational decisions (young adulthood).

Applies information-seeking skills to a job search (young adulthood).

Is able to manage one's finances (young adulthood).

Is able to be confident in one's decisions (young adulthood).

Balances mutual needs and plans long-term goals with one's partner (young adulthood).

Establishes one's own home with constructive parental support (young adulthood).

Establishes one's own home without financial dependence on parents (young adulthood).

Is able to envision one's future (young adulthood).

Assesses evidence with detachment and objectivity (young adulthood).

Is able to think clearly and solve problems, even in a crisis (young adulthood).

Sees multiple perspectives about issues of theoretical and practical importance (young adulthood).

Understands how emotions influence decisions and actions (young adulthood).

Resolves conflicts, makes decisions, and encounters new situations through effective problem-solving strategies (young adulthood).

Is able to think creatively (young adulthood).

Decides and acts based on one's best judgment (young adulthood).

Sets personal goals and plans for their implementation (young adulthood).

Decides how one wants to be involved with children (young adulthood).

Makes choices that lead to a satisfying lifestyle (young adulthood).

Assesses and analyzes one's commitments on an ongoing basis and orders one's priorities and goals accordingly (early middle age).

Realistically assesses one's future career prospects while valuing one's career accomplishments (early middle age).

Maintains satisfactory performance in one's occupation (early middle age).

Sets goals and applies personally chosen performance standards to their achievement (early middle age).

Balances security and risk-taking in occupational decisions, taking one's personal goals and family commitments into account (early middle age).

Analyzes one's relationship with one's partner on an ongoing basis and plans responsibly in light of that analysis (early middle age).

Incorporates a realistic awareness of one's aging into decision making (early middle age).

Maintains one's sense of occupational competence in the face of competition from younger workers (middle age).

Values one's achievements while realistically planning for achieving one's remaining goals (late middle age).

Plans for retirement alternatives (late middle age).

PHYSICAL FITNESS/HEALTH MAINTENANCE SKILLS

The items in this appendix are taken from the national Delphi study that identified life-skills descriptors for childhood, adolescence, and adulthood, and grouped these descriptors into generic categories. The list is not exhaustive, but it is comprehensive in its coverage. The descriptors below were judged by panels of experts who then assigned them to the categories. Where possible, normative age ranges are attached to the descriptors that indicate the approximate time in a person's life when the skill is usually acquired.

Physical Fitness/Health Maintenance Skills

Definition: Skills necessary for motor development and coordination, nutritional maintenance, weight control, physical fitness, athletic participation, physiological aspects of sexuality, stress management, leisure activity selection, and so forth.

Descriptor

In childhood, the individual:

Demonstrates muscle control and coordination (ages 2 through 4).
Acquires self-help skills requiring muscular coordination (ages 2 through 4).

Learns to set reasonable and safe limits on physical activities (ages 6 through 8).

Understands the nature of physical maturation (ages 8 through 9).

Performs fine motor skills with greater consistency (ages 8 through 10).

Can relate the function of sexual organs to one's understanding of reproduction (ages 9 through 10).

Can maintain a high level of energy and stamina.

In adolescence, the individual:

Understands what is normal and natural about sexual arousal and expression.

Participates in competitive, cooperative, and/or individual sports.

Can understand and decide how to control one's rapidly changing body in positive ways.

Understands how body and emotions combine to affect human behavior.

Understands menstruation as a normal physical phenomenon (ages 11 through 13).

Accepts as normal various physiological changes associated with puberty (ages 12 through 13).

Copes with occasionally undesirable side effects of physical maturation (ages 13 through 15).

Copes positively with increased sexual arousal and activity (ages 13 through 15).

Understands masturbation as normal sexual activity (ages 14 through 16).

Applies principles of good grooming and personal hygiene in daily living (ages 14 through 16).

Incorporates avocational and recreational interests into one's lifestyle (ages 15 through 19).

[NOTE: In the following items age ranges become much less normative than is the case for childhood and adolescence. The systematic study of adult development and aging is a much newer branch of the behavioral sciences than the life periods that precede it. The literature is therefore much less specific about when certain life-skills are acquired.]

In adulthood, the individual:

Selects and enjoys satisfying leisure-time activities (young adulthood).

Promotes physical fitness through appropriate regular exercise and dietary habits (young adulthood).

Incorporates appropriate health and fitness activities into one's lifestyle (young adulthood).

Conceptualizes one's health in terms of wellness rather than simply the absence of illness (middle age).

Maintains positive body image as physical changes occur (middle age).

Copes with age-related physical decline and illness (late middle age).

IDENTITY DEVELOPMENT/ PURPOSE IN LIFE SKILLS

The items in this appendix are taken from the national Delphi study that identified life-skills descriptors for childhood, adolescence, and adulthood, and grouped these descriptors into generic categories. The list is not exhaustive, but it is comprehensive in its coverage. The descriptors below were judged by panels of experts who then assigned them to the categories. Where possible, normative age ranges are attached to the descriptors that indicate the approximate time in a person's life when the skill is usually acquired.

Identity Development/Purpose in Life Skills

Definition: Skills and awareness necessary for ongoing development of personal identity and emotional awareness, including self-monitoring, maintenance of self-esteem, manipulating and accommodating to one's environment, clarifying values, sex-role development, developing meaning of life, establishing moral/value dimensions of sexuality, and so forth.

Descriptor

In childhood, the individual:

Identifies with parent or parental surrogate (ages 2 through 4).

Describes emotional, social, mental, and personal characteristics in self and others (ages 2 through 4).

Expresses appropriately the emotions of anger, fear, happiness, and sadness (ages 2 through 7).

Forms gender identity.

Stabilizes gender identity.

Identifies with same-sex peers.

Focuses on development of special talents (ages 3 through 5).

Achieves balance between dependence and independence as a result of maturation (ages 3 through 6).

Carries out age-appropriate family responsibilities (ages 3 through 6).

Understands that one's perspective is often different from that of others (ages 3 through 6).

Performs age-appropriate tasks for oneself (ages 3 through 7).

Understands one's place within one's immediate environment (ages 4 through 6).

Obeys rules in the absence of authority (ages 4 through 6).

Uses self-control, willpower, and cooperation (ages 5 through 7).

Accepts moral responsibility for one's actions (ages 5 through 9).

Takes responsibility for appropriate household chores (ages 6 through 9).

Assumes responsibility for one's actions (ages 6 through 9).

Understands that individual differences are normal and acceptable (ages 8 through 10).

Understands and applies age-appropriate concepts of right and wrong (ages 8 through 10).

Understands differences between child and adult roles (ages 8 through 10).

Understands the differences between absolute and relative standards and values (ages 8 through 10).

Utilizes a variety of coping strategies to express anger (ages 8 through 10).

Deals with ambiguity in unfamiliar situations (ages 8 through 11).

Utilizes intrinsic motivation to avoid punishment.

Faces problems with confidence in one's ability to solve them.

Achieves reasonable, age-appropriate control over emotions (ages 9 through 13).

Has a sense of humor.

Accepts limitations in sports.

Accepts limitations in academics.

Accepts limitations in physical stature.

Is content when alone.

Can overcome the need for immediate gratification.

Identifies with humanity in general, not just parents or peers.

Acts according to humanistic, cooperative, and altruistic values.

Is able to express personal ownership of one's emotions.

Can differentiate losing from failing.

In adolescence, the individual:

Understands and accepts the development of secondary sex characteristics (ages 10 through 11).

Accepts uncertainty without being threatened by it (ages 11 through 13).

Is able to analyze one's thoughts and feelings (ages 11 through 13).

Is able to identify the role of personal feelings in one's values (ages 12 through 15).

Incorporates feelings about one's maturing body with other elements of one's emerging self-image (ages 13 through 15).

Is able to develop a clearer and more realistic self-identity (ages 13 through 15).

Examines and reformulates one's values and beliefs on an ongoing basis (ages 14 through 16).

Deals with one's emerging needs for independence through constructive ways (ages 14 through 16).

Appreciates one's own development and that of one's peers as representative of a broad range of individual differences (ages 14 through 18).

Appreciates the uniqueness of one's identity and expresses it with confidence (ages 14 through 18).

Develops and utilizes a set of personal standards as guides to action (ages 14 through 18).

Synthesizes current developmental processes into a positive self-image (ages 14 through 18).

Expresses one's emotions appropriately (ages 14 through 18).

Acts responsibly in decisions, actions, and relationships (ages 14 through 18).

Incorporates one's life experiences and resources into an independent lifestyle (ages 14 through 18).

Achieves an appropriate balance between dependence and independence (ages 15 through 16).

Utilizes introspection in understanding oneself (ages 15 through 17).

Incorporates a variety of learnings about oneself into one's self-image (ages 15 through 18).

Follows rules through reason and conscious choice rather than through blind adherence.

Examines and utilizes one's value system in resolving personal moral issues (ages 16 through 18).

Is able to analyze sex roles and to assess their applicability to oneself (ages 16 through 19).

Applies one's concept of personal identity in decision making and interpersonal relationships (ages 17 through 19).

Demonstrates positive work attitudes.

Deals with uncertainty in relations with authority.

Understands the significant meaning of a real love relationship and the part sex plays in this.

Understands the difference between physical sexual attraction and real emotional love and/or friendship.

Formulates and reformulates identity and values, taking peer values into account, without being governed by them.

Can laugh at oneself and develop a sense of humor.

Accepts responsibility for one's actions.

Is able to conceive of oneself in a special occupational role.

Understands the place of work, homemaking, leisure, and other roles in self-realization.

[NOTE: In the following items age ranges become much less normative than is the case for childhood and adolescence. The systematic study of adult development and aging is a much newer branch of the behavioral sciences than the life periods that precede it. The literature is therefore much less specific about when certain life-skills are adopted.]

In adulthood, the individual:

Examines and resolves differences between personal beliefs and social norms (young adulthood).

Defines one's identity in terms of personal ideals and values (young adulthood).

Fully participates in intimate sexual relationships (young adulthood).

Identifies values implicit in particular occupations (young adulthood).

Deals effectively with frustration and failure (young adulthood).

Expresses anger in a constructive way (young adulthood).

Maintains excitement and enthusiasm for living (young adulthood).

Manages one's emotions in constructive ways (young adulthood).

Experiences and encourages mutuality in sexual relationships (young adulthood).

Tolerates ambiguous circumstances (young adulthood).

Acts with independence and an awareness of likely outcomes (young adulthood).

Creates a coherent set of personal values (young adulthood).

Expresses one's emotions appropriately (young adulthood).

Integrates one's values and goals into an independent lifestyle (young adulthood).

Learns selectively from models, not just mentors (young adulthood).

Adjusts to change and loss (e.g., moving away, death) in close relationships (early middle age).

Is aware of self and creates personal meaning through one's own efforts (early middle age).

Understands the meaning of dependence, independence, and interdependence, and how to strike a balance among the three (early middle age).

Views objectively the aspirations one has for one's children (early middle age).

Assesses objectively one's strengths and weaknesses for various life roles (early middle age).

Synthesizes elements of personal values and societal norms into a consistent personal morality (early middle age).

Takes risks and seeks to grow in new ways (early middle age).

Can affirm oneself (early middle age).

Understands how one's values are affected by external influence (early middle age).

Achieves a sense of personal identity through translating one's commitments into actions (early middle age).

Copes effectively with grief at the death of one's parents (early middle age).

Maintains an integrated and positive sense of self as one moves through the life span (middle age).

Acts consistently with personally chosen moral values (middle age).

Maintains one's sense of occupational competence in the face of competition from younger workers (middle age).

Realizes that all life is change and that few choices are final (middle age).

Incorporates one's experiences, values, and goals into a personally relevant philosophy of life (middle age).

Is comfortable with one's physical and mental capacities independent of age (middle age).

Adjusts to changes in family role responsibilities (middle age).

Accepts and copes with irreversible effects of aging (late middle age).

Maintains one's identity and self-esteem as occupational involvement changes (late middle age).

Finds purposeful and satisfying activities in all stages of life (late middle age).

Appreciates, copes with, and uses times of solitude (late middle age).

Balances mental, physical, and emotional resources in maintaining effective functioning (later maturity).

Balances the need to maintain independence with the reality of one's resources, asking for help when necessary (later maturity).

Copes effectively with grief at the death of loved ones (later maturity).

Accepts changing commitments as one grows older (later maturity).

Faces death with composure (later maturity).

INDEX

INDEX